Happiness and the Law

Happiness and the Law

JOHN BRONSTEEN,
CHRISTOPHER BUCCAFUSCO,
JONATHAN S. MASUR

THE UNIVERSITY OF CHICAGO PRESS   CHICAGO AND LONDON

JOHN BRONSTEEN is professor at the Loyola University Chicago School of Law. CHRISTO-PHER BUCCAFUSCO is associate professor at the Illinois Institute of Technology's Chicago-Kent School of Law, where he is also codirector of the Center for Empirical Studies of Intellectual Property. JONATHAN S. MASUR is professor and deputy dean at the University of Chicago Law School.

The University of Chicago Press, Chicago 60637
The University of Chicago Press, Ltd., London
© 2015 by The University of Chicago
All rights reserved. Published 2015.
Printed in the United States of America
24 23 22 21 20 19 18 17 16 15   1 2 3 4 5

ISBN-13: 978-0-226-07549-5 (cloth)
ISBN-13: 978-0-226-19566-7 (e-book)
DOI: 10.7208/chicago/9780226195667.001.0001

Library of Congress Cataloging-in-Publication Data

Bronsteen, John, author.
    Happiness and the law / John Bronsteen, Christopher Buccafusco, Jonathan S. Masur.
        pages   cm
    Includes bibliographical references and index.
    ISBN 978-0-226-07549-5 (hardcover : alk. paper)—ISBN 978-0-226-19566-7 (e-book)
1. Happiness.   2. Well-being.   3. Sociological jurisprudence.   I. Buccafusco,
Christopher, author.   II. Masur, Jonathan S., author.   III. Title.
    K380.B765   2015
    340'.115—dc23

                                                                        2014014663

♾ This paper meets the requirements of ANSI/NISO Z39.48-1992 (Permanence of Paper).

FOR MEGAN AND LILY
—J.B.
FOR MY PARENTS
—C.B.
FOR SEEBANY AND KIRAN
—J.M.

Contents

Acknowledgments   ix

Introduction: What Happiness Has to Do with the Law   1

PART I.   **Analyzing Laws' Effects on Well-Being**   7

CHAPTER 1.   Measuring Happiness   9

CHAPTER 2.   Well-Being Analysis   27

CHAPTER 3.   Well-Being Analysis vs. Cost-Benefit Analysis   59

PART II.   **Viewing Two Core Areas of the Law through the Lens of Hedonics**   93

CHAPTER 4.   Happiness and Punishment   95

CHAPTER 5.   Adaptation, Affective Forecasting, and Civil Litigation   118

PART III.   **Well-Being**   133

CHAPTER 6.   Some Problems with Preference Theories and Objective Theories   135

CHAPTER 7.   A Hedonic Theory of Well-Being   154

CHAPTER 8.   Addressing Objections to the Hedonic Theory   164

Conclusion: The Future of Happiness and the Law   183

Notes   187

Bibliography   261

Index   283

Acknowledgments

We would like to thank the many people who have helped us write this book. All the chapters have benefited from the many probing comments and questions we have received during presentations at a number of law schools and at conferences such as the annual meetings of the American Law & Economics Association and the Law & Society Association, among others. We are deeply grateful for the many colleagues who have taken the time to engage with our work and forced us to continually refine and improve our ideas. In particular, we would like to thank the following people who read and commented on parts of this manuscript: Matt Adler, Amitai Aviram, Adam Badawi, Susan Bandes, Stephanos Bibas, Kenworthey Bilz, Frederic Bloom, Josh Bowers, Andrew Coan, Adam Cox, David DePianto, Sharon Dolovitch, David Driesen, Lee Fennell, Brian Galle, Brandon Garrett, Chris Guthrie, Bernard Harcourt, Brooks Holland, Peter Huang, Aziz Huq, Doug Husak, Dan Kahan, Adam Kolber, Russell Korobkin, Alison LaCroix, Brian Leiter, Daryl Levinson, Saul Levmore, Dan Markel, Richard McAdams, Greg Mitchell, Michael Moore, Jennifer Nou, Martha Nussbaum, Eric Posner, Richard Posner, Lisa Robinson, Arden Rowell, Adam Samaha, Dave Schwartz, Larry Solum, Stephanie Stern, Lior Strahilevitz, David Strauss, Jeannie Suk, Tom Ulen, David Weisbach, and an anonymous reviewer.

With respect to the chapters about well-being analysis and cost-benefit analysis, the participants in the 2013 annual symposium of the *Duke Law Journal* provided invaluable assistance. With respect to the chapters about philosophy, we were aided greatly by comments from and discussions with Matthew Adler, Eric Brown, Agnes Callard, Ben Callard, Richard Chappell, Roger Crisp, Fred Feldman, Dan Haybron,

Brian Leiter, Martha Nussbaum, Josh Sheptow, Larry Solum, and Eric Wiland.

Portions of this book draw and expand on previously published articles: John Bronsteen, Christopher Buccafusco & Jonathan S. Masur, *Well-Being Analysis vs. Cost-Benefit Analysis*, 62 DUKE L.J. 1603 (2013); John Bronsteen, Christopher Buccafusco & Jonathan S. Masur, *Retribution and the Experience of Punishment*, 98 CAL. L. REV. 1463 (2010); *Welfare as Happiness*, 98 GEO. L.J. 1583 (2010); John Bronsteen, Christopher Buccafusco & Jonathan S. Masur, *Happiness and Punishment*, 76 U. CHI. L. REV. 1037 (2009); and John Bronsteen, Christopher Buccafusco & Jonathan S. Masur, *Hedonic Adaptation and the Settlement of Civil Lawsuits*, 108 COLUM. L. REV. 1516 (2008). We appreciate the editorial contributions of the students at the *Columbia Law Review, University of Chicago Law Review, California Law Review, Georgetown Law Journal*, and *Duke Law Journal*.

Seemingly innumerable research assistants, library staff members, and administrative assistants at our institutions have contributed greatly to this project over the past half decade, and we are deeply grateful for their efforts. In particular, we would like to thank Joe Bingham, Fred LeBaron, Carl Newman, Kathleen Rubenstein, and Anthony Sexton for their excellent research assistance, and Andrew Dawson for editing the proofs of this manuscript. Jonathan Masur also thanks the David and Celia Hilliard Fund for research support.

We would also like to thank the members of the University of Chicago Press who made this book possible. In particular, David Pervin and John Tryneski believed in it when it most needed someone to do so.

Introduction: What Happiness Has to Do with the Law

Suppose you're crossing the street with your spouse, when a car hurtles through the intersection and crashes into both of you. You each survive but are injured permanently: your spouse ends up with chronic migraine headaches, and you lose one of your arms.

You both sue the driver, and a jury awards you $1,000,000 and your spouse $10,000, because losing an arm is much worse than migraine headaches. Or is it? You realize soon that life with one arm is better than you'd thought it would be, whereas your spouse realizes that chronic migraines are worse than expected. You get used to your injury and adapt substantially to it. When doing many daily activities like watching television, you never even think about your new limitation. By contrast, your spouse can't adapt because the headaches are random, intermittent, and can never be fully ignored. Did the jury get it wrong?

Now consider something else entirely. Suppose Jack talks Jill into robbing a bank with him. Jack enters with a gun, while Jill waits in the getaway car. They get caught and go to prison for 10 years and 5 years, respectively. The point of these different prison sentences is, of course, to make the punishments fit the crimes: years 6 through 10, when Jill has been released but Jack stays behind bars, are supposed to be a lot worse for Jack than for Jill. Jill has paid her debt, whereas Jack must keep paying his. But Jill's punishment doesn't really end at year 5. When she is released, she finds it hard to get and keep a job, much less a desirable one. Her family and friends have distanced themselves from her, and developing new relationships doesn't come easily. Because of her difficulty keeping employment, she is poor, which brings its own set of hardships.

And her former prison conditions and current poverty may have caused her to contract a disease that shortens, or at least worsens, her life. These problems prove difficult to ignore.

To be sure, Jill has advantages over Jack during this second 5-year period. She can go where she wants, and he can't. Still, in many ways the difference between their sentences is smaller than it appears: Jill's second 5-year period shares many of the negative features of prison that Jack faces during that same period. And in fact, Jack's time in prison will be far better during those second five years than during the first five. He will adapt to many aspects of prison conditions, learning to cope with them and developing a routine that makes his life there more bearable than he expected. Jill might still be better off than Jack, but the difference is considerably smaller than anyone—Jack, Jill, the public, the sentencing judge, or the drafters of the sentencing guidelines—thought it would be. Are we punishing Jack's and Jill's different crimes appropriately?

Let's take one more example. Suppose the government wants to use some of its tax dollars to start a new program. One proposal is to help people who live in rental apartments become able to afford houses in the suburbs. Another proposal is to start a public health initiative, akin to the anti-smoking initiatives of years past, to encourage people to get enough sleep. The sleep proposal is laughed out of the room, and the home-buying subsidy is quickly adopted. But the results are unfortunate. Those who buy homes in the suburbs find themselves driving in traffic every day when they commute to their jobs in the city. They are miserable during these drives, which turn out to be among the worst parts of their daily lives. And because the drives occur twice each day, the new living arrangements end up substantially decreasing their well-being. Meanwhile, the benefits of home ownership turn out to be illusory: the owners adapt to their new houses just as they had adapted to their old apartments, and things like the increased space add little to their enjoyment of life. The government program, albeit well-intentioned, actually worsens the lives of those it aimed to help (not to mention its effects on the environment from the additional commuting).

By contrast, getting enough sleep might improve Americans' quality of life dramatically. When people get enough sleep, they live longer and are healthier and more productive. They also feel better and enjoy their lives more, and they contribute more to others' enjoyment of life. More Americans die each year from drowsy driving than from drunk driving, and spectacular disasters such as the *Exxon Valdez* oil spill and the *Challenger* space shuttle explosion resulted from errors caused in part by sleep deprivation. Yet home ownership remains a focus of American life, whereas the value of sleep is not even a blip on the nation's radar screen. If anything, these days sleep is sometimes associated with laziness, and getting too little of it is practically worn as a badge of honor. Do we have our priorities straight?

*   *   *

Happiness and the law—the two concepts seem to have little to do with one another. To many people, they may seem diametrically opposed. In this book, we argue that a proper understanding of the law and legal policy requires an understanding of human happiness.

People write laws to make it easier to live together. Laws stop us from hurting one another, and when someone gets hurt anyway, laws compensate the victim and punish the offender. In those ways and others, laws are meant to improve the quality of life.

Everything the law does is bound up with how people live. For example, if money helps people live better, then the law might bestow money as compensation and confiscate money as punishment. If one possible law would increase people's enjoyment of life, and another would decrease that enjoyment, then the former may well be a better law than the latter.

So if you want to understand the law, you need to understand people. That's why, for the past century, legal scholars have been studying human behavior. They study economics, sociology, and other social sciences that explore what people do and why they do it. The facts about behavior are then applied to law, so that law can be adjusted to affect life more positively.

Sometimes a new discovery in social science reveals things about human life that weren't known before. When that happens, it may show that the law hasn't been interacting with people's lives in the way that was assumed. Well-intentioned laws and policies that seemed to make sense suddenly may need to be reconsidered. Foundational ideas about the legal system may be called into question.

One of the most important things there is to know about human life is what makes people happy. And it is here that social science has had perhaps its greatest breakthrough in the past two decades. Psychologists have developed ways to learn what makes people happy and unhappy, and some of their findings are startling. In particular, it turns out that people shrug off and adapt to certain seemingly major life changes (both positive and negative) and go on living as if nothing happened. Other things, which may seem trivial by comparison, can make people much better or worse off for their entire lives. Moreover, people seem incapable of predicting which is which: they guess incorrectly about what will make them happy, and they constantly make decisions on the basis of those mistakes. Partly for these reasons, the effect of money on happiness (above a surprisingly modest level of income) is far smaller than is widely believed. And yet people keep striving for it, sacrificing time that could be spent engaged in leisure activities, or with friends and family, or even asleep.

This fact is a shock to the system for understanding law. Much legal scholarship uses economics as its primary means of gauging how law interacts with life, and economics is based on the assumption that people act rationally. In recent years, some economists and many law professors have come to grips with certain limitations on rationality. For example, they have accepted that people cannot act in their own interests if they lack relevant information. And they have recognized that people's minds are not like computers that can process all information accurately and dispassionately. Instead, people's minds automatically take shortcuts, and those shortcuts introduce mistakes. We place too much emphasis on things we have heard recently, and on things that seem shocking or memorable. We assume that the way things turned out reveals the probability that they would turn out that way. We assign disproportionate value to things we own, and we make economically unwise choices because of our aversion to financial loss.

A robust literature has emerged to catalog these cognitive limitations and, in some cases, suggest ways to overcome them. The book *Nudge* by Richard Thaler and Cass Sunstein suggests some approaches that can turn these limitations into advantages. It is precisely this sort of contribution that is needed. Ignoring the behavioral insights, and pursuing purely economic solutions to the problems of law and policy, cannot succeed because law and policy work well only if they are based on accurate understandings of people. Nor is it sufficient to note the behavioral truths and stop there. Those truths must be applied in ways that make the law better and improve the understanding of how law interacts with life.

The study of happiness is the next step in the evolution from traditional economic analysis of the law to a behavioral approach to law. This new approach starts by adding a point similar to the ones that form the list of cognitive limitations: that people lack information about themselves and thus frequently make mistakes even if they possess all other relevant information. But the contribution of happiness studies goes far beyond that point. It offers a new way of understanding the quality of life and a chance for the first time to learn, and quantify, what makes people feel good and bad. In turn, this can tell us what we most want to know: how law affects people's lives, and how it can do so in a better way. For the first time, human beings have credible data about the positivity of our experience of life—arguably the most basic and important thing we could know about ourselves. The sooner we incorporate this new knowledge into our laws, the better our laws will be.

This book is devoted to that project. It explains the new way of studying happiness and the new information yielded by that study. Then it asks how the law would be understood differently if the law took that information seriously.

In the first chapter, we explain how hedonic psychology measures human happiness. We show the reasons that social scientists have come to rely on these new forms of measurement and to trust the findings that emerge from them. We then discuss the principal findings themselves: that people adapt to some things but not to others, that people err in predicting what will make them happy, and that money affects most people's happiness less than is assumed. We then answer some of the most common questions about and objections to the use of happiness research in law.

In chapter 2, we show how the happiness data can be used to assess most laws and policies. All laws have benefits for some people, but they also impose costs on other people. Using well-being data, we can analyze how a law or policy will affect how positively or negatively people experience their lives. For example, if a regulation would improve health but raise the price of goods, then happiness data can tell us how much happier people will be made by improved health, and how much less happy they will be made by higher prices. The goal is to help policymakers commensurate and compare the good and bad consequences of a law, providing a new way of evaluating laws that improves upon current methods. We call our approach "well-being analysis," or WBA. In chapter 3, we compare WBA to the tool currently used for policy assessment, cost-benefit analysis (CBA).

We then look at two major areas of the law and ask how they might be affected by the new data on happiness. We begin with criminal punishment in chapter 4. There we explain that virtually all major theories of punishment (including those that fall within retributive, utilitarian, and mixed categories) rely on the point that punishment imposes negative experience on offenders. By showing that this experience is felt differently than the legal system has assumed, the findings of hedonic psychology indicate a need to rethink the current understandings of imprisonment and monetary fines.

We move on to civil lawsuits in chapter 5. The vast majority of such lawsuits settle, and we consider how individuals' ability to adapt to injuries may affect their behavior in settlement negotiations. As with punishment, the canonical models for understanding settlement require recalibration in light of the hedonic data.

In the final part of the book, we explain our view of what happiness is and of its central place in human life. In our view, happiness means feeling good on a moment-by-moment basis, and it is such good feeling that constitutes the quality of life. In chapter 6, we discuss the main alternatives to our view of well-being and the problems we see in those alternatives. In chapter 7, we explain our view in some detail. In chapter 8, we discuss prominent objections to our view.

The book concludes by looking forward and charting a course for future happiness research.

PART I

Analyzing Laws' Effects on Well-Being

planner

The law should improve people's quality of life. For it to do that, law-makers need a way to measure the effect of proposed laws on well-being. In the chapters that follow, we explain how the data from hedonic psychology can be used to improve policymaking in this way. Neither these data nor our methodology is a panacea. Our proposal is not addressed to many of the grand questions of political theory or of policy-making, such as how to balance the overall quality of human life against other considerations, such as fairness or concern for nonhuman animals, among other things. We offer only a new way to measure how law affects human well-being.

This project, of course, does not encompass everything that matters in policymaking. But it does represent an attempt to overcome some of the fundamental limitations of recent policy analysis. For the past thirty years, the primary driver of policy analysis has been the attempt to quantify well-being using cost-benefit analysis. If our proposal, well-being analysis, improves upon the way well-being is quantified, then it constitutes a step forward in the way society makes law.

CHAPTER ONE

Measuring Happiness

What is it like to be injured on a job site and lose a limb? What is it like to be unemployed for a period of time, or to be imprisoned? What is it like to live with poor air quality, or to be prevented from engaging in free expression? Being able to answer these questions accurately is essential to the proper functioning of a legal system. If the law fails to do so, it will struggle to provide adequate compensation for injuries, to punish people for their crimes, and to protect people from harm. Moreover, if the tools a legal system uses to provide answers to these questions are unreliable and inconsistent, similar cases may not be treated similarly. Yet despite the centrality of these questions to the law, there have been surprisingly few attempts to answer them in a rigorous and systematic way for use in legal analysis. This shortcoming can probably be blamed on limited data and problematic assumptions. It was simply too difficult to know, in a way that could be tested meaningfully by the best tools of social science, what losing a limb or being sent to prison is like.

That is no longer the case. The rapidly emerging field of hedonic psychology is now supplying valid and reliable data that can help lawmakers and legal scholars answer these (and many more) important questions. It is now possible to estimate fairly accurately how the experience of losing a limb or being imprisoned is going to make most people feel. How? Simply by asking people who are undergoing those experiences. Relying on people's self-reports of their subjective well-being (SWB), researchers in a number of fields have developed sophisticated and scientifically validated methods for measuring the effects of many circumstances on people's happiness. Importantly, their discoveries are often highly counterintuitive. For example, research has shown that human beings have an astonishing ability to hedonically adapt to changes in their life circumstances. Many seemingly momentous changes will exert surprisingly little long-term hedonic effect on our lives. Yet, also counterintuitively, some seemingly minor changes may have extended effects on our happiness.

This relates to the second important discovery from hedonic psychology. People are often not very good at predicting what will make them happy. Certainly people accurately predict that hitting a hole-in-one will feel better than being hit by a truck, but people often make systematic errors in their estimates of the magnitude and duration of changes in their lives. Often these "affective forecasting errors" occur because people neglect the effects of hedonic adaptation, causing them to overestimate how happy or unhappy many changes will make them feel.

In this chapter we introduce this research in hedonic psychology. We begin by discussing the techniques used to gather happiness data, and then we report on some of hedonic psychology's major findings, those that will be useful again and again throughout the book. Finally, we briefly address some of the most common questions and concerns about using happiness data to inform legal analysis.

The Data of Hedonic Psychology

How can we learn what makes people feel good or bad? The primary way is simply to ask them how they feel at various moments during their day and during their life. Happiness is thus principally studied via self-reports: psychologists learn how people feel by recording what they say about their feelings. Then psychologists try to replicate the results by repeating the studies, and they also compare people's self-reports to other indicia of happiness such as others' reports and neurological and other physiological indicators. These efforts have been highly successful in validating the self-reports, which is why the field of happiness research has received so much attention in recent years.

Social scientists have been attracted to the idea of measuring human welfare directly for a long time, but until recently they have had difficulty securing valid and reliable data.[1] Over the last fifteen years or so, new social science techniques have emerged that enable researchers to study subjective well-being from a variety of different perspectives with

a number of different tools.[2] These techniques allow the more or less direct measurement of people's happiness levels, overcoming the problem
that had initially driven economists to seek monetary proxies for welfare. Importantly, they enable the measurement of what Daniel Kahneman has termed "experienced utility" (how good people feel) in contrast to the "decision utility" that is typically studied in the tradition of
law and economics.[3] "Decision utility" measures only whether people
get what they want, on the assumption that getting it will make them
better off. But because that assumption has been shown to be flawed,[4]
Kahneman and others have turned toward measuring directly the quality of people's experience of life. This section will briefly discuss a few of
the most promising techniques for collecting such experiential data and
their relative strengths and weaknesses.

Experience sampling methods

The best way to figure out how an experience makes a person feel is to
ask her about it while she is experiencing it. The "gold standard" of such
measures is the experience sampling method (ESM), which uses handheld
computers and smartphones to survey people about their experiences.[5]
Subjects are beeped randomly throughout the day and asked to record
what they are doing and how they feel about it. The data that emerge
from such studies provide a detailed picture of how people spend their
time and how their experiences affect them. The data can also be combined with socio-economic and demographic data via regression analyses for even greater insight (e.g., do the unemployed spend more time in
leisure activities than the employed, and do they enjoy them as much?).

   Unlike some of the other measures of well-being discussed below,
ESM studies do not require people to engage in difficult cognitive processes like remembering and aggregating experiences over large chunks
of time. Those processes can cause errors in data collection that ESM
seeks to avoid. ESM studies can, however, be expensive and difficult to
run, so researchers have sought other methods that produce most of the
advantages of ESM but at a lower price. One such technique is the day
reconstruction method (DRM) pioneered by Daniel Kahneman and his
colleagues. DRM uses daily diary entries about each day's experiences
to reconstruct an account of subjects' emotional lives. DRM studies correlate strongly with ESM studies and can be run at lower cost.[6] Similarly,

the Princeton Affect and Time Survey (PATS) asks subjects to report and evaluate their experiences from the previous day.[7] It can be distributed via telephone and incorporated into other survey devices, enabling it to reach a larger population.[8]

Life satisfaction surveys

The oldest method of measuring SWB is the life satisfaction survey. These surveys ask individuals to respond to a question such as, "All things considered, how satisfied with your life are you these days?"[9] Respondents answer on a scale that ranges from "not very happy" to "very happy." Life satisfaction surveys have been included in the U.S. General Social Survey since the 1970s; as a result, we now have substantial quantities of longitudinal data on thousands of individuals. The principal value in such surveys is the ability to correlate SWB data with a variety of other facts about people's lives. Using multivariate regression analyses that control for different circumstances, researchers are able to estimate the strength of the correlations between SWB and factors such as income, divorce, unemployment, disability, and the death of family members.[10] For example, on average, the death of a parent will yield the loss of 0.25 life satisfaction points on a scale of 1 to 7 for a period of time, while the death of a spouse will typically yield the loss of 0.89 points.[11]

Life satisfaction surveys are relatively inexpensive to administer and can be easily included in a variety of larger survey instruments. Accordingly, they are most valuable as sources of large-scale data about many subjects and of longitudinal data about changes in SWB over time. In longitudinal studies, subjects are tracked over long periods of time so that changes in their well-being can be followed. This is especially valuable in assessing the causal effects of life events (such as marriage, disability, or unemployment) on SWB, because the same individual can be surveyed both before and after the event, eliminating the need to make comparisons between people who might be different in a number of important but unmeasured ways.[12] Life satisfaction surveys are less helpful, however, for assessing particularly granular changes in circumstances. More importantly, they rely on global judgments about how people's lives are going, rather than those individuals' moment-by-moment hedonic experiences. Because hedonic experiences are often poorly remembered and aggregated, such judgments can be biased because of a person's momentary mood or the order in which questions are posed, among other errors.[13]

The quality of the data

The ability to generate data is not the same as the ability to actually measure the thing sought to be measured. Nor is it the ability to measure it well. Data are only useful if they are reliable and valid. Although hedonic psychology is a relatively young science, it is already producing data that are trustworthy.

Reliability is an indication of the consistency of a measurement instrument.[14] For example, a scale that reported very similar numbers every time the same weight was placed on it would be judged highly reliable. In the context of well-being measures, reliability can be assessed by examining correlations between tests and retests of the same question at separate times, as well as correlations between different questions that ask about similar concepts.[15] Meta-analyses of different well-being tools have found high levels of reliability for both life satisfaction and experience sampling methods.[16] This is especially true of more advanced multi-item measures.[17]

The fact that a measure reliably provides consistent data does not mean that it is measuring what you want it to measure.[18] The ability to *actually measure* the thing sought to be measured is called validity.[19] Although a full review of the validity of well-being measures is unnecessary here,[20] it is worth noting a number of findings that support the conclusion that a person's well-being can be validly measured by the tools discussed above.

One way of thinking about the validity of happiness measures is to ask how well they are associated with other indicators of well-being. If happiness data are measuring a valid concept, then they should be correlated both with other subjective well-being data and with other, objective well-being indicators. The happiness data score well on both of these fronts. First, despite the rather different techniques used to collect data, the various measures of well-being tend to correlate with one another.[21] Overall life satisfaction is correlated both with the amount of positive and negative affect (emotion) that a person feels[22] and with her satisfaction with the domains of her life (e.g., family, work, friends).[23] As most theories of well-being would predict, the happier a person feels on a moment-by-moment basis, the happier she judges her life to be. In addition, if a person is not happy with areas of his life that we might believe are important to him, then he is not likely to be as happy overall as someone who is satisfied with those areas.

Not only are subjective reports of well-being correlated with one another, but they are also correlated with external, objective measures of well-being. People who report themselves to be happy are rated as happy by third-party informant reports,[24] they smile more,[25] and their neurological activity is consistent with feelings of pleasure.[26] People who rate themselves low on happiness scales are also much more likely to commit suicide than moderately or very happy people.[27] Finally, positive affect is correlated with extraversion and inversely correlated with neuroticism, as most personality theories would predict, but subjective well-being is also clearly different from those traits.[28]

Another way of thinking about the validity of well-being data involves analyzing their responsiveness to events in people's lives. If these data showed no difference between the ways people feel on the day of their marriage and the day of their spouse's death, we would have strong reason to doubt that they are telling us anything about human happiness. The subjective well-being data upon which we rely score well here, too. Well-being measures tend to be fairly stable over time for a given individual and exhibit high test-retest reliability.[29] This is consistent both with our intuitive sense that people tend to have happy or unhappy dispositions that do not change significantly and with psychological theories of stable personalities. But despite their overall stability,[30] subjective well-being data are also sensitive to changes in life circumstances: people who experience apparently positive or negative events do indeed report higher or lower levels of well-being—at least for a time, before they adapt.[31] As we would predict, the death of a spouse represents a significant blow to someone's self-reported happiness.[32]

In addition to accurately measuring valence (good vs. bad), we would expect valid happiness measures to be sensitive to the degree to which an event is good or bad. And again, despite some counterintuitive findings, well-being scales can detect the relative magnitude of life events. For example, people who are more seriously injured predictably report lower happiness ratings than do people who are less seriously injured.[33] And, as mentioned above, the death of a spouse tends to have a stronger negative effect on happiness than the death of a parent. These findings suggest that people are capable of consistently reporting how experiences make them feel, and that their emotional responses generally exhibit credible and predictable patterns following specific events.

Depending on the situation, legal scholars might draw on each of the data sources mentioned in the preceding pages to address different kinds of issues. In some cases, longitudinal studies of overall well-being may provide the best data available for tracking people after events with potentially long-term effects.[34] These studies have been used, for example, by researchers to understand the hedonic impact of no-fault divorce laws on women in different states.[35] In other circumstances, the availability of ESM studies will enable more fine-grained analyses of laws' effects on people's lives.

Hedonic Psychology's Key Findings

Using the techniques discussed above, researchers have been able to study the kinds of things that make people happy, the intensity and duration of people's affective responses, and their ability to predict what will make them happy. Although some of their findings are relatively unsurprising, many are highly counterintuitive.

Hedonic adaptation

Without question, the most surprising findings from hedonic psychology have to do with humans' ability to adapt rapidly to changes in their lives. Both positive changes, like increases in salary, and negative changes, like physical disabilities, often tend not to substantially alter how happy we are in the long term. Accordingly, it has been said that we are on a "happiness treadmill" or that we all have "happiness set points" to which we return after each new experience. In some situations, this will be the case, but in other cases, events can exert long-lasting effects on our SWB. It is not always easy, however, to guess when adaptation will occur and when it won't. In this section, we review some of the areas where adaptation and its limits have been most thoroughly studied.

Some of the earliest uses of hedonic data looked at the effects of income on well-being. For years, the chief economic indicators of national and individual well-being were monetary. Both countries and people were thought to be better off the more money they had to spend. For nations, well-being could be scored according to gross domestic product, and for individuals, wealth and income were believed to be the best proxies for welfare. Of course, economists understood that money was subject to diminishing marginal utility (i.e., each additional dollar is worth less than the one before it), but generally they believed that the more money someone had the better off she was.

Over the last few decades, data from hedonic psychology have fundamentally challenged this assumption. In some of the earliest work in the area, Richard Easterlin showed that although national wealth increased substantially in many countries in the second half of the twentieth century, average national well-being did not.[36] And on the individual level, Philip Brickman presented data showing that lottery winners were not substantially happier than normal subjects.[37] While these initial studies have been challenged since,[38] their general findings remain sound: money is, at best, a weak proxy for well-being.

This is not to say that having more money does not make people happy. In fact, below a certain threshold that is near the poverty line in the United States, income and SWB are positively and strongly correlated. At this level of wealth, additional money can be used to purchase necessities like food and clothing, to cover medical costs, and to generally reduce the uncertainty that living in poverty naturally causes. Once a person's wealth begins to exceed the poverty line, however, the relationship between more income and well-being flattens out considerably. While some studies using life satisfaction measures of well-being find a modest (logarithmic) positive correlation between income and SWB above the poverty line,[39] recent studies of positive and negative affect report no additional increase in well-being above $75,000 per year in income.[40]

How could the economic accounts of income and well-being have been so wrong? Much of the answer has to do with hedonic adaptation.[41] Money, of course, is not valuable in its own right. It has value only to the extent that people use it to buy things that make them happy. As we will describe below, however, people often don't do a good job predicting what will make them happy. Thus, when they spend their raises and bonuses on larger houses, fancier cars, and bigger televisions, they do not realize how quickly they will adapt to these new purchases. As surprising as this may sound to some, watching TV on a 52-inch screen does not create much more happiness than watching on a 47-inch screen. Perhaps the most shocking finding to come from hedonic studies is the discovery that people often hedonically adapt to severe physical disabilities. The effects of hedonic adaptation to disability were first described in a canonical study on lottery winners and individuals with paraplegia or quadriplegia.[42] As noted above, the lottery winners were not significantly happier than control subjects. More surprisingly, the accident victims were not as unhappy as had been expected, and reported their happiness above the midpoint of the scale, indicating that they considered themselves happy.[43] These data suggested that people experience life as if on a "hedonic treadmill" such that good and bad events cause brief changes in well-being with rapid returns to an established set point.[44] Although specific aspects of the treadmill theory have been challenged,[45] a wealth of recent research has confirmed its general finding for other disabilities. For example, studies have found that children and adolescents with limb deficiencies exhibit remarkably good psychosocial adjustment.[46] People with spinal cord injuries report levels of well-being similar to those of healthy controls,[47] as do burn victims,[48] patients with colostomies,[49] and those undergoing dialysis for treatment of kidney disorders.[50] As the authors of this last study note, "Although [hemodialysis patients] report their health as being much worse than that of healthy controls, they do not appear to be much, if at all, less happy than people who do not have kidney disease or any other serious health condition."[51]

The aforementioned studies all applied a cross-sectional methodology that compared the reported well-being of disabled people with that of people who were not disabled. In a compelling and more recent study by economists Andrew Oswald and Nattavudh Powdthavee, the authors track changes in subjective well-being longitudinally by comparing happiness ratings of individuals before their disability with assessments reported yearly following the disability.[52] Since 1996, the British Household Panel Survey has reported information on respondents' psychological well-being and whether and to what extent they suffer from a disability.[53] In these surveys, respondents rated their own level of happiness on a scale of 1 to 7, with larger numbers indicating greater life satisfaction. Oswald and Powdthavee analyzed the responses from people who originally reported no disability but who subsequently became disabled during the course of the survey. They divided these people into those who were moderately disabled ("disabled but able to do day-to-day activities including housework, climbing stairs, dressing oneself, and walking for at least 10 min[utes]") and those who were seriously disabled ("unable to do at least one of the above day-to-day activities").[54]

Oswald and Powdthavee's study produced noteworthy results. The group of people for whom there were five consecutive years of well-being data and who became disabled reported an average well-being score of 4.8 out of 7.0 for the two years preceding disability, an abrupt fall to 3.7 at the onset of disability, and then a subsequent rebound to 4.1 in the next two years despite the fact that the disabilities themselves had not changed.[55] Separating the moderately and severely disabled groups, the authors found approximately 50 percent adaptation to moderate disability and 30 percent adaptation to severe disability in a two-year span.[56] Thus, there is substantial evidence that hedonic adaption to disability is significant, if incomplete.[57]

One reason that they did not find higher levels of adaptation may be due to their inability to distinguish between disabilities that people can readily adapt to and those that are, in effect, "unadaptable." A number of studies have found that people have difficulty adapting to particular categories of negative events. Low-level, chronic stimuli like noise, dull pain, and headaches have substantial long-term effects on happiness, as do diseases associated with progressive deterioration.[58] One study, for example, found that instead of adapting to noise problems, some college students actually became sensitized to them, experiencing higher levels of annoyance as time went on.[59] In addition, chronic or progressive disorders such as rheumatoid arthritis and multiple sclerosis appear to be resistant to adaptation in part because of the deteriorating nature of the stimuli associated with such diseases.[60] It is also worth pointing out that even where hedonic adaptation occurs, it is neither inevitable nor invariable. Although adaptation effects may be seen in the aggregate, individuals experience a range of responses to adaptable disabilities.[61]

As with money and disability, the effects of other life circumstances on long-term happiness are not always straightforward and predictable. Family relationships and unemployment exhibit interesting patterns of adaptation and resistance to adaptation. Spending time with one's family and friends (although not necessarily one's children) rates among the happiest things that people do. And strong family relationships are an important predictor of overall well-being.[62] A recent study by the psychologist Richard Lucas, however, suggests that people adapt fairly rapidly to the pleasures of getting married.[63] People experience a honeymoon bump and then return to their previous level of well-being. Losses of family relationships can have stronger impacts on well-being, though. A person who gets divorced or whose spouse dies often experiences a long-lasting diminution in SWB from which he or she may not recover.

The data on the hedonic effects of unemployment are particularly striking and unusual. Unemployment is one condition about which there exists substantial hedonic data, both moment-by-moment (DRM) and life satisfaction data. Interestingly, however, the life satisfaction and moment-by-moment data differ. Life satisfaction studies conclude that unemployment has a significant, long-term effect on well-being.[64] People experience substantial diminutions in SWB while unemployed, and, notably, they continue to experience reduced happiness even after finding a new job. On the other hand, a study of moment-by-moment affect found that the unemployed actually had *greater* well-being than people who held jobs.[65] Though this result may seem suspect, it was supported by very particularized findings. The unemployed enjoyed any given activity less than similarly situated employed individuals. That is, they enjoyed themselves less while socializing, or playing a sport, or reading, or even doing housework.[66] However, they were able to spend much more time in comparatively enjoyable pursuits, such as socializing or playing a sport, because they did not have to work.[67] The employed naturally spent much of their days at work, which is a relatively unpleasant activity for most people, according to the hedonic data.[68] The ability to spend more time engaged in pleasurable activities more than balanced out the decreased enjoyment of each individual activity.

The psychological and physiological processes underlying hedonic adaptation are not fully understood, but scientists have developed several related theories about its causes. The earliest explanation for adaptation was the idea that people have happiness set points that are based, to a considerable extent, on genetic factors. A person's level of happiness, according to this idea, is like other personality characteristics that tend not to change significantly over the course of her life. Research on twins has partially corroborated this idea, finding that between 40 and 80 percent of our happiness may be genetically determined.[69]

Yet long-lasting changes to well-being do occur, so it was important to have a theory that took into account when adaptation was likely to occur and when it wasn't. Most recently, psychologists and economists have focused on the role *attention* plays in moderating the effects of negative events. Drawing an analogy between the psychological response to negative events and the body's response to disease, Daniel Gilbert and his colleagues have suggested that people possess a "psychological immune system" that dampens the hedonic effect of disability.[70] Defense mechanisms such as "rationalization, dissonance reduction, . . . [and] positive illusions" diminish the intensity of the emotional response to disability by directing attention away from the disability and toward new skills and new sources of pleasure.[71] Initially, the changes brought about by new circumstances are the sole focus of our cognitive and emotional attention, but over time, these changes fade into the background to become part of our "normal" selves. People come to understand themselves as rich people (if they have won the lottery) or widows, and they focus less and less on the changes that brought them to that state.

This helps to explain why some things, like chronic headaches, ringing in the ears, or divorce might lead to enduring changes in SWB. Unlike the loss of a limb, chronic headaches don't involve a change in state; they are unpredictable and a constant annoyance. Once someone has lost a limb, she has always lost a limb, but someone suffering from migraines is intermittently and unpredictably going to feel the pain they cause. She cannot let the pain slip into the background. Somewhat differently, getting divorced or becoming unemployed may cause long-term diminutions in well-being because each tends to weaken the psychological immune system. The increased self-esteem brought by family relationships and success at work can buoy a person's well-being through the normal ups and downs of life. But once those support mechanisms have been taken away, the rest of life's troubles will tend to be felt more strongly and to last longer.

Affective forecasting errors and misremembering

Although people are capable of hedonically adapting to a variety of positive and negative life events, recent social scientific research suggests that they consistently fail to anticipate such adaptation. Over the past decade, psychologists and economists have begun to study "affective forecasting"—people's ability to judge how future experiences will make them feel.[72] Most people, it turns out, do a surprisingly poor job of predicting the intensity and the duration of future feelings.[73] This inability is particularly important in situations concerning disability and adaptation where it likely affects decisions about treatment.

When asked to predict how they will feel on the occurrence of some future hedonic event—eating a bowl of ice cream every day for a week, having their favorite candidate win an election, being denied tenure, or suffering an injury—people are able to estimate whether that event will make them feel good or bad ("valence") and which emotions they will feel. They are not very good, however, at predicting how strongly they will feel ("intensity") or how long the feeling will last ("duration").[74] For both positive and negative events, people predict that they will feel more strongly than they actually do, and they predict that the feeling will last longer than it actually does. Accordingly, a growing number of studies have shown that, in the case of physical disabilities, healthy people regularly predict that disabled people will experience greater unhappiness for a longer period of time than they actually do.[75]

The most compelling explanation for the mispredictions associated with affective forecasting suggests that people suffer from a "focusing illusion"[76] (also called "focalism"[77]) that causes them to pay too much attention to the narrow aspects of life that will be affected by a change while ignoring the much broader ways in which life will remain the same.[78] As Timothy Wilson and his colleagues note, "People think about the focal event in a vacuum without reminding themselves that their lives will not occur in a vacuum but will be filled with many other events."[79] For example, when people are asked to think about the effect paraplegia would have on their lives, they tend to focus on the limitations it would create rather than, say, their unaltered ability to enjoy a glass of wine or a conversation with friends.[80] By directing their attention to the changes wrought by disability, healthy people underestimate how happy they will remain. Focalism thus accounts for a substantial amount of their mispredictions about affective intensity.

Faulty predictions about the *duration* of feelings associated with negative events are often caused by a failure to anticipate how rapidly the psychological immune system enables people to adapt to unpleasant emotions. Some researchers have referred to this failure to predict adaptation as "immune neglect."[81] When asked to predict how long they are likely to feel bad following a negative event, subjects ignore the "set of dynamic psychological processes . . . that produce a change in the relationship between what happens and how one feels."[82] The underestimation of hedonic adaptation "is probably the most commonly observed error in research on hedonic prediction."[83] When making predictions about future changes, people tend to focus principally on the early stages of those changes, when hedonic reactions are most intense. Adaptation, as noted above, takes time, but the mental simulations people use to predict later emotional states are tightly condensed. *Ex ante* predictions thus tend to overvalue the intensely emotional change and undervalue the long period of recovery and adaptation.

Perhaps the most significant research on focusing illusions and immune neglect is the increasing body of evidence indicating that healthy people fail to predict the limited impact of disabilities on their quality of life (QoL).[84] One early study showed that, on a scale of 0 (conditions as bad as death) to 1 (perfect health), the general public estimates that the quality of life for patients receiving home dialysis for life is 0.39, while dialysis patients report their QoL as 0.56.[85] Similarly, patients with colostomies rate their quality of life at 0.92, while patients without colostomies predict that QoL with a colostomy would be 0.80.[86] Part of the problem with affective forecasting is that when people are asked to make these predictions, they evaluate the various outcomes as changes rather than states. David Schkade and Daniel Kahneman write, "[I]f people judge what it is like to *be* a paraplegic by imagining what it is like to *become* a paraplegic, they will exaggerate the long-term impact of this tragic event on life satisfaction."[87]

Not only do people often fail to accurately predict what will make them happy, but they also do a poor job of remembering the affective quality of past experiences. For example, Kahneman has shown that people tend to evaluate the quality of an experience not by thinking about the aggregate quality of the moments of the experience but by averaging their feelings from the time when the experience was at its most extreme and when it ended. This leads to people preferring a longer painful experience that ends with a period of mild unpleasantness to a shorter painful experience that doesn't end as mildly.[88] Other studies show that people overestimate the hedonic effects of things they have already experienced. Gilbert and Wilson's studies indicate that people make forecasting errors about things like being dumped or having one's favorite team lose even though people had experienced these things before. And, more strikingly, former colostomy patients were willing to sacrifice substantially more of their future life to have avoided the colostomy than current colostomy patients were.[89] The most plausible interpretation of this finding is that the former patients simply misremember the experience and overrate its badness compared to those who are currently experiencing it.

Of course, we are not making the claim that people are always unable to remember what has made them happy in the past and to predict what will make them happy in the future. When people have made decisions many times and when those decisions have produced relatively immediate feedback about their success, people may choose well. For example, we suspect that most people make good choices in terms of their own happiness when deciding whether to eat a bagel or a muffin for breakfast. They will have made this decision many times before, and they quickly learn whether they made the right choice. If you hate muffins, you don't have to eat too many of them to realize it. Many decisions in life will share these characteristics, and we expect that people will make good decisions in those situations. Many other decisions, including ones that are often relevant to the law, will be made only once or rarely, and they may have hedonic effects that are experienced substantially after the decision has been made. For example, choosing which 401(k) plan to invest in is a decision that we will rarely make and about which we will not receive rapid feedback.[90] In such circumstances, people will have a much more difficult time remembering and predicting what makes them happy.

Addressing Some Concerns about Happiness and Legal Analysis

Over the years that we have been writing about the implications of hedonic psychology for the law, we have received a number of questions from other scholars. We are grateful for the attention they have paid to our work, and we want to address a few of the questions and concerns that they often express. Most of those concerns will be addressed in detail within the body of this book, but here at the outset, we would just like to mention very briefly our basic skeletal responses to some of the simplest and most fundamental questions.

1. "Happiness is different for every individual, so it cannot be studied in ways that are broadly applicable."
   It is certainly true that people differ in the activities they enjoy. Some like snorkeling, whereas others dislike it, and the same can be said for shopping or perhaps for virtually any other endeavor. In addition, the studies that we discuss often report substantial interpersonal differences in reactions to events, so while some people may adapt rapidly to a disability, others may not.

   In many respects, however, patterns in the data on happiness reveal that people's similarities tend to outweigh their differences. Various forms of health problems affect happiness in predictable ways across large numbers of people, as do increases or decreases in wealth. Moreover, laws are generally made on the basis of such similarities because they apply to all of society. Accordingly, legal systems typically paint with a broad brush.

2. "It would be Orwellian for law to be concerned with people's happiness."

It is understandable that people view happiness as deeply personal, and that they might recoil at the idea of law's taking account of what goes on in their minds and bodies. But law does so, unavoidably, by its very nature. Law limits and affects people's behavior, both for their own benefit and for the benefit of others. In a democracy, the people themselves make laws for their own benefit. And the only way for law to benefit people is if it is made with an understanding of what makes people better off. Such an understanding comes from the study of how people experience life. Other disciplines like economics and sociology have been used to direct law, and there is no difference in the legitimacy of using psychology on grounds that it is too intimate or personal.[91]

3. "Quality of life comprises more than just happiness."

This major claim is pressed by many economists and philosophers, and it is the entire subject of part III of this book. As a brief preview here, we note that there is no dispute that happiness is at least one important element of the quality of life. Economists care about people's self-interested preferences—what people want for themselves—and strong empirical evidence supports the commonsense notion that at least one thing people want for themselves is to be happy. And philosophers who contend that well-being is best conceived not as happiness alone, but rather as the satisfaction of objective criteria, rely on criteria that tend very strongly in many cases to make people happy. Thus, at a minimum, happiness is one important component of well-being. It follows that hedonic psychology has much to add to the understanding of law, because it reveals law's effect on that aspect of the quality of human life. We believe that happiness constitutes all of well-being, but the connection between happiness and the law does not depend on the truth of that belief.

4. "Quality of life is not the only goal of law or policy."

It could be argued that, in the broadest sense, the ultimate goal of virtually any major human endeavor is to make the world a better place. Law is one such endeavor, but improving the world need not be conceived solely in terms of increasing the quality of human life. For example, the law can be thought of as procuring justice or protecting civil rights. Similarly, the way in which the quality of life is distributed among people may also matter, as may other things such as the quality of the lives of non-human animals. Even considerations wholly independent of anyone's well-being could conceivably be goals of the law.

We do not dispute any of this. We argue only that human welfare is at least one value that is highly relevant to the law, and that happiness is at least one major component of human welfare. (We believe it is the only component, but none of our points about law or policy depend on that belief.) To whatever extent well-being matters, hedonic psychology has much of use to say.

5. "Emotions vary along dimensions other than positivity or negativity."
There is no doubt that people experience a range of emotions that is not fully described by the words *happiness* and *sadness*. Eating a chocolate chip cookie does not feel identical to listening to "Ode to Joy," even if those two acts happen to make a particular individual equally happy. This fact poses no problem for our project. We would never claim that hedonic psychology reveals everything about human experience. Instead, we claim only that it reveals one thing—the level of positivity or negativity of that experience. That one thing is important to anyone who cares about being happy, as the vast majority of people do.

This claim about emotions could, though, be put into a stronger form that would if true pose a threat to our approach. Specifically, it could be argued that emotions vary solely along dimensions other than positivity. The claim would be that there is no such thing as feeling good or bad, better or worse, but rather that emotions can be described only in other qualitative terms.[92] We think, however, that such a view is at odds with both ordinary experience and physiological evidence. "Feeling good" is an experience that people recognize and understand, as is feeling bad.[93] And people are readily able to express different levels of the experience: some things feel slightly good or bad, whereas others feel very good or bad. This claim is supported by the empirical work of Kahneman, who has identified positivity (or negativity) as a common thread running through emotions that vary in other ways.[94] On this view, which we find persuasive, positivity is one but not the only dimension along which feelings can be similar or different.[95]

We would also like to mention that although we focus only on the positive/negative dimension, that focus in no way disparages the importance of the others. Indeed, at times in this book we discuss the more specific emotions that are recorded in hedonic studies. For example, our chapter on punishment goes into detail in explaining the specific feelings that prisoners experience and the ways that these feelings do and do not adapt to being in prison and to having been in prison in the past. Indeed, even our core claims about the experiential nature of welfare are broadly consistent with the multidimensionality of emotions. Like those scholars who focus on the broad spec-

trum of emotions people feel, we value subjective experience over preferences or objective-list factors. Positive-negative valence is one way to convert
subjective experience into a measure of welfare, but someone who conceives
welfare as multi-dimensional (rather than uni-dimensional) subjective experience would still benefit from the arguments we make throughout the book
in favor of subjective experience per se.

*   *   *

Although it is only a few decades old, hedonic psychology is already providing exciting, valuable, and reliable data that have significant implications for the law. As institutions and governments continue to recognize the value of hedonic data, the kinds of questions that can be asked
and answered will continue to grow. It is essential that the appropriate
resources be invested in accumulating more robust hedonic data. As we
explore in the following chapters, however, hedonic psychology can already make important contributions to a number of legal areas.

CHAPTER TWO

Well-Being Analysis

Virtually every law makes people's lives better in some ways but worse in others. For example, a clean-air law could make people healthier, but it could also force them to pay more money for the products they buy.[1] Every proposed law thus raises the question: Would its benefits outweigh its costs?[2]

To answer that question, there needs to be a way of comparing seemingly incommensurable things like health and buying power. One way to make that comparison is to ask how much money people are willing to pay for benefits like improved health (or how much money they are willing to accept for harms like increased risks to their health). Suppose, for example, it could be determined that people are willing to pay $100 more per year in return for the health benefits of cleaner air. Those benefits could then be compared, by this first approach, to increased consumer costs.

This approach is called cost-benefit analysis (CBA), and it has long been the dominant method of systematic analysis for evaluating government policy.[3] Every economically significant regulation from executive branch agencies must, by law, be evaluated via CBA[4] (or in some cases via cost-effectiveness analysis[5]). This has been the case since 1981, when President Reagan mandated it by executive order.[6] That order has been reaffirmed by every president since, including Presidents Clinton[7] and Obama.[8]

Despite CBA's prominence, however, it has been criticized harshly from the moment it was first required by executive order[9] to the present day,[10] and countless times in between.[11] More often than not, the criticisms are scathing.[12] Indeed, even CBA's most prominent defenders have

written entire books and major articles prompted by their own acknowledgments of CBA's flaws.[13]

Along these lines, an important if subsidiary contribution of this part
of the book is to combine our own criticisms of CBA with those of others to make the case that CBA suffers from limitations inherent in its
methodology.[14] The only method ever used to compare the pluses and
minuses of laws—the method that has been mandated for the past three
decades—is fundamentally flawed.

Yet it survives. A primary reason for its survival is voiced often: the
view that no comparably rigorous, quantitative, and workable alternative
exists for commensurating a law's positive and negative consequences.[15]
Although any law will both help people and hurt them, an important
element of deciding whether to enact it will typically be to weigh the
good against the bad. Asking how much people are willing to pay for
the good, and thereby converting all consequences into dollar figures, is
viewed by many as the best option for rigorously attempting to commensurate the effects of a law.[16]

In this chapter, we propose an alternative method for comparing the
positive and negative consequences of a law. This method, which we label "well-being analysis" (WBA), would analyze directly the effect of
costs and benefits on people's quality of life. For example, clean-air laws
would be assessed by comparing how much more people would enjoy
their lives if they became healthier with how much less they would enjoy
their lives if their buying power were reduced.[17] This is the most natural
and direct way to put seemingly incommensurable things on the same
scale. And it yields the specific answer that is needed: whether a law will
make people's actual experience of life better or worse on the whole.

Until now, this sort of direct assessment has been assumed to be impossible. But it has been made feasible by the emergence of hedonic psychology. As we explained in chapter 1, hedonics is the study of how people experience their lives, and in particular the measurement of how
much any factor improves or worsens that experience. Originally, some
critics questioned whether hedonic studies could credibly measure the
quality of people's experiences. But over the past fifteen years, these
critics have been quieted by the success of such studies in producing rep-
licable results that pass social science's rigorous tests of validity.[18]

Accordingly, there have been widespread calls for the findings of hedonic psychology to be used to inform government policy. The United
Nations General Assembly recently passed a resolution urging countries

"to pursue the elaboration of additional measures that better capture the importance of the pursuit of happiness and well-being . . . with a view to guiding their public policies."[19] This view has also been endorsed by Great Britain's prime minister David Cameron,[20] France's then-president Nicolas Sarkozy,[21] three widely divergent winners of the Nobel Prize in Economics,[22] and a recent president of Harvard University.[23]

To make this a reality, however, a methodology must be created for using the data from hedonic psychology to evaluate prospective laws.[24] We lay out such a methodology in this chapter, and we show how it can be used to analyze the same regulations currently assessed by CBA. We then explain in chapter 3 the way that WBA would overcome many of CBA's limitations.

Policymaking and social science are not like mathematics, and thus any legal or political tool will have imperfections. WBA is no exception, as we readily acknowledge. However, WBA cures many of the largest problems of CBA. It is capable of immediate implementation, and even in its infancy may be able to produce analyses more accurate than the ones CBA now produces after three decades of refinement.[25] We demonstrate this point by using WBA to reengineer an actual CBA that was used to assess a clean-water regulation.

In the first section of this chapter, we explain what WBA is and discuss the methodological choices it involves. In the second section, we give an example of how it would work in practice by contrasting an actual CBA with a prototype of a WBA for the same regulation. In the third and final section, we respond to some potential objections.

Well-Being Analysis

How do elected officials and regulators decide which policies to enact? They are surely influenced by political considerations,[26] and they may also have ideological commitments. But at least in some cases, they simply want to make good policy. And even when politics or ideology constrains a choice, a range of acceptable options typically remains.[27] Accordingly, regulators and elected officials and their staffs devote substantial time to identifying which policies are worth undertaking.[28]

Before they even begin, they must define what makes a policy worthwhile. A metaphysically correct definition of worth, if such a thing exists, may be beyond humanity's current grasp. However, there is widespread agreement that improving the quality of human life is at least an important component. Because virtually everyone deems it desirable to make people's lives better, at least when all else is equal, that has become the primary focus of policy analysis.[29] What it means to make someone's life better is, in turn, a potentially difficult question.

In chapter 6, we argue that a person's quality of life—or, as it is more commonly labeled in economics, "welfare" or "well-being"[30]—is simply the sum of the positive and negative feelings she experiences throughout her lifetime. As just discussed, this view differs from the view held by some philosophers and many economists that welfare is preference-satisfaction—that is, getting what one wants—and from the view held by other philosophers and economists that welfare is the attainment of certain objective qualities or capabilities. Importantly, however, the different conceptions of welfare overlap in practice far more than they diverge.[31] The question, then, is not what it means to make life better, but rather how to decide which policy would do so.

Cost-benefit analysis and welfare

It is often difficult to know whether a regulation improves the quality of life. Although a regulation could theoretically create some benefit at no cost, we know only of cases where the benefits of a regulation to one group of people come at the expense of costs borne by either the same or another group of people.[32] Policymakers thus need a tool that can tell them whether a proposed law or regulation would improve the overall quality of human life. That is, would the policy help those who benefit more than it would hurt those who are harmed (including cases in which those are the same people)?[33]

Suppose a regulation would reduce the amount of chemical pollution emitted into the waterways and thereby reduce the number of people who die of cancer from the chemical. In so doing, however, it would increase the cost of manufacturing some product, forcing the millions of consumers who purchase it to pay more per person for the product. Whether the benefit of reducing cancer rates is greater than the cost of increasing the prices that consumers must pay depends, in part, on the respective effects of health and consumer purchases on human welfare.

CBA provides a method for comparing such seemingly incommensurable values. Its solution is to convert all costs and benefits into a uniform metric, monetary value, by figuring out how much money people would be willing to pay for the benefits that regulations can provide. Via this method, an agency can monetize the value of health and compare it to the monetary value of consuming goods.

Imagine that the clean-water regulation would save ten lives per year,[34] but it would also drive up manufacturing costs substantially. Each of the 1 million consumers who purchase the affected good would have to pay $50 more per year to acquire that product. CBA asks whether it is worth spending $50 million ($50/person × 1 million people) to save ten lives. To answer this question, CBA must place a price on the lives being saved.

To find out the price people would be willing to pay for any type of regulatory benefit, such as avoiding the loss of life from cancer, CBA has two methods available. The first is "revealed preferences," and the second is "stated preferences," the latter of which is most commonly determined by contingent valuation surveys that ask people how much they would be willing to pay for a benefit.[35] Revealed preferences are available when people have been faced with an opportunity to choose between some regulatory benefit or some amount of money in their actual lives, such that CBA can simply observe which option they chose. Their decision is said to reveal whether they prefer, for example, having more money or reducing their risk of death. Identifying that preference enables regulators to place a value on something like increased water quality, because it shows how much money people are willing to spend in order to minimize or eliminate a risk to their life. When they are available, revealed preferences are typically preferred to stated preferences, although this is not an absolute: a high-quality stated-preference study may be chosen over a lower-quality revealed-preference study.

When analyzing actual regulations with trade-offs like those of the clean-water regulation mentioned above, economists performing CBA would typically use the revealed-preference method.[36] They would look for a real-life situation in which people have chosen between having more money and avoiding a low-probability risk of death. Such a situation is said to arise when people choose their jobs, because one thing that differentiates jobs is the degree of mortality risk they entail. Being a firefighter, for example, is more dangerous than being an accountant. CBA's idea is as follows. First, it uses statistical analysis to try to identify two jobs that are the same in every way except two: Job A is riskier than Job B, and to compensate for that risk, Job A pays more than Job B. People who choose Job A rather than Job B are said to have willingly accepted a somewhat higher risk of death (one that is low-probability in absolute terms, but still higher than the risk in other jobs) in return for the benefit of higher wages. The amount of extra money that they make is the revealed market value of risk avoidance. If a job with a 1-in-10,000 annual risk of death pays $600 more annually than an otherwise comparable job with no risk (the hypothetical no-risk job is used here for simplicity of explication), then the value of avoiding such a risk is pegged at $600. Accordingly, society would collectively be willing to spend $6 million ($600 multiplied by 10,000) for each life saved.[37] Indeed, this is close to the actual number that economists employing CBA have produced.[38] A regulation that will save ten lives is thus deemed to increase overall well-being if and only if it costs consumers a collective total of $60 million or less.

If no revealed preference were available, then CBA would call for the use of a contingent valuation study. This would entail giving people surveys that ask how much money they would be willing to spend in return for avoiding a 1-in-10,000 risk of death. These surveys have also been used, for example, to learn people's willingness to pay for things like preserving the lives of endangered species.[39]

The core advantage of WBA over CBA

CBA is based on this idea: how much money you are willing to pay for a thing shows how much the thing increases your welfare. But that is not true. When someone buys a thing in the hope of improving her welfare, she has made a prediction—a guess—about how the thing will affect her. That prediction may well be wrong, and indeed it usually is. Daniel Gilbert's pioneering work has demonstrated that people are not good at predicting how their choices will affect how they feel in the future.[40]

By contrast, people are good at reporting how they feel right now. In-the-moment self-reports pass the same tests of reliability and validity that are failed by affective predictions. This should not be surprising: guessing how you will feel in the future is of course more error-prone than saying how you feel now. And the reasons for this are apparent: "[The mind's] simulations are deficient because they are based on a small number of memories, they omit large numbers of features, they do not sustain themselves over time, and they lack context. *Compared to sensory perceptions, mental simulations are mere cardboard cut-outs of reality.*"[41]

Thus, a decision tool will be better at approximating welfare if it is based on self-assessments of how people feel in the moment than if it is based on predictions of how people will feel in the future.[42] This is the central insight behind WBA and its primary advantage over CBA.[43]

WBA: The basic framework

Defenders of CBA have long argued that, despite its flaws, cost-benefit analysis is the best available means for determining the welfare effects of a project or regulation.[44] That may no longer be the case. We propose here an alternative method for analyzing regulatory policy: well-being analysis. WBA shares the basic framework of CBA, that of comparing costs and benefits, but it differs in the data and analytical tools it employs to make such comparisons.

Instead of monetizing the effects of regulation, WBA "hedonizes" them. That is, it measures how much a regulation raises or lowers people's enjoyment of life. For example, if a regulation would result in improved health but higher prices of products, then WBA would compare how much more people enjoy their lives when they are made healthier with how much less they enjoy their lives when their buying power decreases. WBA employs individuals' self-assessments in order to determine their level of subjective well-being (SWB), or "happiness." Recently, psychologists and economists have developed increasingly sophisticated surveying and statistical methods that enable the collection and analysis of well-being data on a large scale.[45] WBA uses these data to evaluate the welfare consequences of regulations by comparing the well-being gains and losses of affected parties. In theory, such measures could perhaps be purely neurological—taken by a machine that reports how good someone feels at all times. But unless and until that sort of technology is created, psychologists must rely instead on individuals' personal assessments of how their lives are going for them at a particular moment in time. Fortunately, these self-assessments can be taken in ways that yield highly credible results—results that have been replicated and that correlate with physiological and neurological data as well as with third-party assessments—as we explained in chapter I.

WBA then relies on the same basic cost-benefit-weighing principle that undergirds CBA: all else equal, regulations whose benefits exceed their costs are valuable because they enhance overall welfare. The main difference between the two techniques involves the way in which costs and benefits are calculated and compared. Instead of converting regulatory effects into monetary values, WBA converts them into well-being units (WBUs). WBUs are intended to be subjective, hedonic, cardinal, and interpersonally comparable units that indicate the degree of a person's happiness for a given period of time. They are, in some respects, similar to the quality-adjusted life years (QALYs) that are increasingly popular in health economics.[46]

WBA maps a person's well-being onto a scale that would ideally run from −10 to 10, in which 10 indicates perfect happiness (subjectively defined), −10 indicates perfect misery, and 0 indicates neutrality or the absence of experience. This type of scale would allow individuals to register experiences that are worse than non-experience (undergoing a root canal, for instance) and would simplify the comparison between experience and non-experience. Most of the well-being data that have been collected to date have been measured on a scale from 0 to 10.[47] Accordingly, in the WBA that we conduct below, we utilize a scale running from 0 to 10. As the science of WBA evolves, we would envision transitioning to the preferred −10 to 10 scale.[48]

Each decile of the scale is equivalent and indicates a 10 percent change in the person's well-being.[49] Moreover, we treat the scale as identical across individuals,[50] although, of course, the kinds of things that affect different individuals' well-being may not be. One WBU is equivalent to 1.0 on the scale for a period of one year. Thus, if a person lives to the age of 100 and has a well-being score of 7.0 for each year, that person has experienced 700 WBUs (7.0 WBU/year × 100 years). If an event such as illness causes a person's well-being to drop from 7.0 to 5.5 for a period of ten years, that person loses 15 WBUs (1.5 WBU/year × 10 years).

This type of scale has significant benefits for any type of decision analysis, particularly regulatory analysis, because it enables the direct comparison of the hedonic impact of proposed policy changes. Imagine, for example, that the Occupational Safety and Health Administration (OSHA) is contemplating a simple regulation of workplace safety that will prevent 100 workers from suffering hearing loss and chronic ringing in the ears. Implementing such a measure, however, will increase the costs of production and force factories to fire 300 workers in the affected industry.

CBA would attempt to calculate the value of the regulation by monetizing the costs and benefits it generates. With respect to the costs, CBA would in theory be able to estimate the lost wages of the 300 unemployed people—though in practice CBA typically ignores the costs of unemployment, and in any event those costs are not captured accurately by monetary values alone. Calculating the benefits is even harder for CBA: it is not easy to establish a market price for hearing loss and chronic ringing in the ears. We discuss the many possible shortcomings of CBA's attempts to do so in the next chapter. Accordingly, CBA may substantially and systematically misstate the benefits of the regulation.

Unlike CBA, WBA would attempt to quantify the cost of unemployment. But rather than looking solely to the workers' lost wages, it would calculate the hedonic cost of being unemployed. Some data suggest that unemployment has a significant effect on well-being.[51] Thus, the welfare costs of unemployment may be much greater than CBA predicts. On the other side of the ledger, WBA is well positioned to hedonize the benefits of the regulation. Studies of people who have suffered from hearing loss and ringing in the ears provide fairly accurate information on the hedonic loss associated with those disorders (and thus the benefits of avoiding such an injury).[52] Again, the results are likely to be different from those determined by CBA. Studies show that individuals who experience such ailments often suffer substantial hedonic losses and have great difficulty adapting.[53] This result is contrary to the predictions of healthy people, who may underestimate how harmful such pain will be and how difficult they will find it to adapt.[54] Accordingly, the welfare benefits of the regulation may be understated by CBA if contingent-valuation or revealed-preference surveys rely on mispredictions about well-being.

As this example suggests, the effect of using WBA instead of CBA will often be uncertain. In some cases, WBA will point in the direction of more stringent regulation than CBA would suggest. For many regulations, the chief benefits will involve extending human lives, and the major costs will come in the form of higher consumer prices. In the context of WBA, loss of life constitutes an enormous hedonic cost, whereas many studies indicate that money has a relatively small effect on well-being.[55] When money is traded off against life, therefore, WBA is likely to favor health and safety regulations more than does CBA. In other cases, WBA may favor less stringent regulation than CBA would support. The point is not that WBA will necessarily point in a pro- or anti-regulatory direction in the majority of cases. The point is that we believe WBA will yield more accurate results, as we will explain in this chapter and the next one.

Before we proceed further, we have two final thoughts. First, it is important to note that when we say that well-being is how good people feel in the moment, we do not mean that future moments are excluded from the calculus. Policymakers always rely on predictions about how regulations will affect people: CBA uses these predictions to gauge well-being by aggregating people's willingness-to-pay for benefits, whereas WBA uses the same predictions to gauge well-being by aggregating people's subjective well-being (happiness). Future happiness is not calculated by people's predictions of how they will feel, but rather by current reports of how other people felt while experiencing the condition that the policy would bring about.[56] Thus, WBA would attempt to estimate the total future costs and benefits of any regulation, just as CBA would. The differences lie in the types of data that each method would use, and the ways in which those data are analyzed. This is the topic we address in chapter 3.

Lastly, we note that like CBA, WBA is a tool for analyzing the welfare effects of policies and not a panacea meant to be the last word on what should be done. Policy analysis often proceeds by analyzing welfare effects and then weighing those effects against whatever other considerations are deemed relevant by regulators, legislators, and the citizenry they serve,[57] including fairness, justice, and human dignity.[58] Our contribution is to try to improve upon the first step of the process—the step in which welfare effects are measured. This would influence policy, but it in no way implies that we think the first step is the only step. Like proponents of CBA, we acknowledge the role that other considerations may play.[59]

Well-Being Analysis: An Example

How feasible is well-being analysis, and how would it differ from cost-benefit analysis in practice? To answer those questions, in this section of the chapter we take an actual cost-benefit analysis conducted as part of an Environmental Protection Agency (EPA) regulation and recalculate the costs and benefits of the regulation using WBA.

This exercise actually stacks the deck overwhelmingly in favor of CBA and against WBA. The actual CBA used here was the product of decades of opportunities to refine CBA, and countless millions of dollars spent on studying these phenomena and performing these analyses.[60] By contrast, the following example constitutes the first WBA that has ever been conducted. There has never been any systematic collection of well-being data related to the regulation we analyze here.

For that reason, our analysis falls far short of the level of accuracy that could be achieved were WBA to be adopted in practice. Nonetheless, and strikingly, the WBA sketch we provide yields results that are likely more credible assessments of the policy's well-being effects than are those of the cost-benefit analysis that the EPA itself conducted. This demonstrates the inherent advantages of WBA, the ease with which it could be implemented, and its potential for truly impressive results were it conducted with the resources currently available to CBA.

EPA regulation of pulp and paper production: A cost-benefit analysis

The regulation we examine was promulgated by the EPA under the Clean Water Act in 1998 to curb toxic effluents from pulp and paper mills.[61] Prior to 1998, pulp, paper, and paperboard mills used a number of chlorine-based chemicals in the normal manufacturing process. Dioxin and furan, two carcinogens, are among the by-products that result from producing paper and paperboard with these chlorine-based chemicals. Pulp and paper mills then released those chemicals into the waterways in quantities great enough to sicken and kill fish and cause a number of diseases, including cancer, in people who ate the fish.

The EPA considered three regulatory options. "Option A" required the mills to substitute chlorine dioxide for elemental chlorine in the production process, which reduces but does not eliminate the discharge of dioxin and furan.[62] "Option B" was a stricter rule, combining the Option A limits and a requirement that the mills eliminate lignin (a material in wood pulp), along with several other restrictions on the manufacturing process.[63] Option B would have resulted in even lower emissions of dioxin and furan than Option A. Finally, "Option TCF" ("totally chlorine free") required that pulp and paper mills eliminate all chlorine from the production process, thereby also eliminating the discharge of furan and dioxin.[64]

The EPA estimated that this regulation would produce several different types of benefits. First, there would be fewer cancer deaths among recreational and subsistence anglers who eat fish that have swum near pulp and paper mills.[65] The EPA refused to specify a single monetary value of life, instead announcing that each life saved was worth between $2.5 and $9 million.[66] However, it is worth noting that these figures refer only to the value of the lives lost. The EPA did not possess and did not employ data on the cost of being stricken with cancer, above and apart from eventual mortality.[67] Second, reducing the quantity of dioxin released into fisheries would reduce the number of "fish consumption advisories," during which fishing must cease, and thus increase the number of days that fishing could take place.[68] Third and finally, pulp and paper mills produce sludge, which must be disposed of. Reducing the amount of dioxin and furan in the sludge would allow the mills to dispose of the sludge via cheaper means.[69]

At the same time, the regulation also imposed significant costs. Mills were forced to switch from chlorine-based chemicals to more expensive alternatives, and to treat their effluents before the effluents were released into the waterways.[70] Table 2.1 lists the annual costs and benefits, as calculated by the EPA, of all three options the agency considered in its regulation of pulp and paper. Each cost is shown by a negative number, whereas each benefit is shown by a positive number.

According to the EPA's numbers, the benefits of preventing several cancer deaths are dwarfed by the costs of forcing firms to produce pulp and paper using safer chemicals. Can this be right? Is the cost really so great that it dramatically outweighs the deaths? To find out, we think it is important to learn how much money affects people's quality of life. Only then can one know how much people would be harmed by the costs of pollution control. This is, of course, exactly what WBA is designed to do, as we will show in a moment. But first, we digress to make a couple of other points about this CBA.

As table 2.1 makes clear, none of the options is cost-benefit justified according to standard CBA methodologies. The EPA selected Option A,

TABLE 2.1. **Annual costs and benefits, EPA pulp and paper regulation (in millions of 1995 dollars)**

	Option A	Option B	Option TCF
Total compliance costs	−262.8	−324.0	−1081.9
Benefits of cheaper sludge disposal	12	12	12
Benefits of eliminating fishing advisories	10.8	10.8	10.8
Monetized benefits of lives saved	11.7	12.2	13.6
Median net benefits	−228.3	−289.0	−1045.5

Note: This table was assembled using data found in EPA, Economic Analysis for Pulp and Paper Production, at 5–25 tbl.5–16, 5–28 tbl.5–18, 8–12 tbl.8–6, 8–23, 8–25, 8–46, 8–23, 8–26 tbl.8–12.

which appears to do the least harm, yet even under that option the costs exceed the benefits by more than $228 million per year.[71] By choosing Option A instead of no regulation, the EPA showed that tools like CBA and WBA are guides that will not always be followed. But by choosing Option A over Options B and TCF, the EPA showed how much these tools can still influence policy choices.

In addition to the calculations in table 2.1, and importantly for our analysis, the EPA calculated that the regulation would lead to the loss of a significant number of jobs. The increased regulatory costs would drive up pulp and paper prices, reducing consumer demand for pulp and paper products.[72] This reduction in demand would force mills to lay off workers.[73] As pulp and paper production declines, suppliers and affiliated industries would also suffer and be forced to lay off workers. However, the EPA did not include these lost jobs in its cost-benefit analysis. We suspect that this stemmed from a belief, which continues to hold sway throughout the regulatory state, that workers will soon find alternative employment, and the net costs of unemployment will be zero.[74] This assumption is almost certainly false, and one of us has separately criticized the EPA and other regulatory agencies for refusing to include the costs of unemployment in their cost-benefit analyses.[75]

We calculate, in table 2.2, a revised cost-benefit analysis that includes unemployment costs. (The welfare costs of unemployment will also figure prominently in the WBA that follows.) Following earlier work by one of us, we estimate an annual employment cost of $3,300.[76] For ease of use, we list the compliance costs from table 2.1 separately but com-

TABLE 2.2. **Annual costs and benefits, EPA pulp and paper regulation, including unemployment costs (in millions of 1995 dollars)**

	Option A	Option B	Option TCF
Compliance costs	−262.8	−324.0	−1081.9
Median total benefits	34.5	35	36.4
Median net benefits excluding unemployment costs	−228.3	−289	−1045.5
Jobs lost from plant closures	400	900	7100
Total jobs lost	3094	5711	N/A
Estimated annual unemployment costs	−10.2	−18.8	N/A
Median net benefits including unemployment costs	−238.5	−307.8	N/A

Note: This table was assembled using data found in EPA, Economic Analysis for Pulp and Paper Production, at 5–25 tbl.5–16, 5–28 tbl.5–18, 6–15 tbl.6–4, 6–34 tbl.6–14, 6–44 tbl.6–19.

bine the median figures for the three types of benefits (cheaper sludge disposal, elimination of fishing advisories, and lives saved) in one row, which we label "Median total benefits." It is worth noting that the EPA did not estimate the total unemployment that would result under Option TCF, though it did estimate the number of jobs that would be eliminated under that option as a result of pulp and paper mill closures alone. Based on those numbers, which we provide below, the job loss from Option TCF would have likely been far greater than the job loss from the other options.

What should be immediately evident from table 2.2 is that regulatory-compliance costs—principally the costs of shifting to nonchlorinated chemicals—dominate even this revised cost-benefit analysis. Even for Option A, the least costly regulatory option, these compliance costs are nearly ten times greater than the total estimated benefits and more than twenty times greater than the costs related to unemployment. It is not atypical for compliance costs to dominate the cost side of the ledger in cost-benefit analysis. Still, for these costs to outweigh both unemployment and life-saving so easily is at least worthy of scrutiny. These are remarkable claims, and they shed light on the (possibly distorting) effects of monetizing costs and benefits. The question is whether they capture the true welfare effects of the regulation. That is the question we seek to address in the next section.

The EPA's cost-benefit analysis as a well-being analysis

We now proceed to reengineer the EPA's cost-benefit analysis as a well-being analysis. To do so, we convert the costs and benefits of the regulation into well-being units. Wherever possible, we make this conversion directly. That is, we translate the benefits of reduced cancer deaths directly to WBUs, rather than adopting the EPA's pricing of those lives and then converting the dollars into WBUs.[77] All calculations are based on a well-being scale that runs from 0.0 to 10.0, because the relevant studies of subjective well-being used that range of numbers. What follows is a summary of the conversion of each of the costs and benefits involved.

COMPLIANCE COSTS, SLUDGE DISPOSAL, AND FEWER FISHING ADVISORIES.   Compliance costs and the benefits of cheaper sludge disposal are both entirely monetary. Ideally we would measure the welfare value of fewer fishing advisories by estimating the hedonic value of fishing and multiplying it by the additional hours that anglers would be able to spend engaged in that activity, in addition to the hedonic value of being able to eat the fish that are caught. However, to our knowledge hedonic data on fishing do not yet exist. Accordingly, we use the EPA's monetary esti-mate of this benefit. We sum these three quantities to determine the net monetary cost of the regulation.

The next question is how to translate that monetary cost into well-being units (WBUs). These expenditures will have an effect on well-being only to the extent that they are paid for and felt by individuals. Some of the benefits will accrue to the anglers who are able to fish with fewer interruptions. Compliance costs and sludge-related benefits will affect some combination of consumers of pulp and paper and sharehold-ers in pulp and paper companies. (The exact division depends on the ex-tent to which pulp and paper firms are able to pass their costs along to consumers.)

It is impossible to know precisely how many households will share these costs, though nearly every household consumes paper to some de-gree. For the purposes of this analysis we assume—conservatively, for reasons that have little effect on the analysis[78]—that the monetary costs and benefits will be equally borne by 1 million Americans. Each individ-ual will bear several hundred dollars in net monetary costs, depending on the regulatory option. We also assume that everyone affected earns the median household income, which in 1998 was $38,885.[79]

What effect will these monetary costs have on welfare? Studies have found that life satisfaction increases logarithmically with income. We use the results of one of the largest and most recent of these studies, which found that an approximately threefold increase in income was as-sociated with a 0.11 increase in well-being units (WBUs).[80] (Similarly, a two-thirds decrease was associated with a 0.11 decrease in WBUs.[81]) That is, an individual whose income increased from $100,000 per year to $272,000 per year would gain 0.11 WBUs per year. If that same indi-vidual's income decreased from $100,000 to $36,700, then she would lose 0.11 WBUs. The total gain or loss is given by the following formula:

(1) Welfare loss due to income decline = 0.11 WBU ×
      (ln (new income) − ln (old income))

In table 2.3, we apply this formula to the income loss caused by the net costs of the EPA's regulation.

CANCER CASES AVOIDED. The EPA provided a range of estimates for the number of cases of cancer that will be avoided under each regulatory option. In the interest of simplicity, we base our calculations on the median number. There are limited available data on the welfare loss that an individual experiences when she is sick with cancer, but one study calculated the welfare loss from "stomach/liver/kidneys or digestive problems," which we believe is the closest analogue.[82] That welfare loss is 0.238 WBUs per year while the person is sick.[83] We assume that the typical individual who dies from cancer caused by dioxin and furan effluents is sick with cancer for two years and then dies thirty years before she normally would.[84] This is obviously a rough assumption, but it is no rougher than the EPA's assumption that all lives are equivalently valuable and have a median value of $5.75 million.[85] The average American has a life satisfaction of 7.4 (again, on a scale of 0.0 to 10.0).[86] When an individual dies, she loses all the welfare that she would otherwise have experienced throughout the remaining years of her life.[87] Thus, we calculate the welfare benefit from avoiding one fatal case of cancer with the following equation:

(2)   Welfare benefit from avoided fatal cancer =
$$(2 \times 0.238 \text{ WBU}) + (30 \times 7.4 \text{ WBU}) = 222.48 \text{ WBUs}$$

UNEMPLOYMENT. Unemployment is one condition about which substantial hedonic data exist. Studies indicate that unemployment has a significant impact on well-being.[88] Unemployed individuals suffer a loss of 0.83 WBUs per year during the time that they remain unemployed.[89] Even after finding new employment, these same individuals lose an average of 0.34 WBUs per year during the next seven years after they begin working again.[90]

For the purposes of this WBA, we assume that the average person who becomes unemployed as a result of this regulation is out of work for six months. This corresponds roughly to the average duration of unemployment in the United States in the years 2011 and 2012.[91] Each unemployed individual thus loses 0.83 × 0.5 = 0.415 WBUs during the period of unemployment. In addition, she loses 0.34 WBUs per year for the seven years following reemployment, for a total of 0.34 × 7.0 = 2.38 WBUs.

The EPA's CBA presents only yearly costs and benefits, not total costs and benefits. The agency annualized all costs over a thirty-year period.[92]

However, the agency calculated total (as opposed to yearly) unemployment. Accordingly, we divide the hedonic costs of being unemployed by 30 to obtain the yearly costs, similarly annualized over a thirty-year period. The hedonic effect of the unemployment caused by the EPA's pulp and paper regulation is given by the following equation:

(3)   Welfare cost of unemployment per job lost =
          $[(-0.83 \times 0.5) - (0.34 \times 7.0)] / 30 \approx -0.093$ WBUs

We are now prepared to aggregate the welfare effects of the various costs and benefits. Table 2.3 presents the WBA of the EPA's regulation.

This WBA diverges from the EPA's CBA in two particularly notable respects. First, Option A now appears welfare justified: it will increase overall well-being in the net. Option B is still not welfare justified, but it appears less egregiously harmful than it did through the lens of cost-benefit analysis. The EPA may well have been correct to choose Option A (rather than not regulating at all), contrary to what the CBA indicated.

Second, and perhaps more importantly, the monetary costs of the regulation, which dominated the CBA, are nearly irrelevant here. Instead, the benefits of saving lives and the costs of unemployment produce the dominant welfare effects. This may appear surprising to scholars steeped in cost-benefit analysis, but it is entirely consistent with reams of evidence demonstrating that changes in wealth and income have extremely small impacts on individual well-being.[93]

TABLE 2.3. **Well-being analysis of EPA's pulp and paper regulation**

	Option A	Option B	Option TCF
Net monetary costs (millions of 1995 dollars)	−240.0	−301.2	−1059.1
Welfare effects of net monetary costs (WBUs)	−0.00068	−0.00086	−0.00304
Median cases of cancer avoided	1.57	1.62	1.79
Welfare effects of avoided cancer cases (WBUs)	349.29	360.42	398.24
Total jobs lost	3094	5711	N/A
Welfare effects of unemployment (WBUs)	−287.74	−531.12	N/A
Total welfare effect (WBUs)	61.55	−170.70	N/A

Note: This table was assembled using data found in National Emission Standards for Hazardous Air Pollutants, at 18,588, 18,591; and EPA, Economic Analysis for Pulp and Paper Production, at 6–34 tbl.6–14, 8–45.

In the actual CBA for this regulation, compliance costs were deemed twenty-five times more important than cancer deaths. In the WBA for this regulation, cancer deaths are deemed vastly more important than compliance costs. The only thing other than life-saving that this WBA weights heavily is unemployment, because of the evidence that losing one's job worsens one's life so much.

This is not to say that policymakers should begin ignoring the effects of their regulations on wealth. As we explain in chapter 3, regulations that increase welfare at the expense of vast amounts of wealth might eventually become self-defeating and eliminate future opportunities for welfare gains. This is why we would not rule out preserving CBA as a complement to WBA. But the WBA we perform here indicates the distortions introduced by CBA's focus on wealth and monetization. Regulations that do not appear cost-benefit justified might in fact be found to greatly enhance welfare once welfare is measured more directly.

Of course, we present here only a back-of-the-envelope sketch of a WBA. Our conclusion that the EPA's pulp and paper regulation was welfare enhancing is necessarily tentative and dependent on our assumptions, which may be incorrect. But this exercise should demonstrate the feasibility of WBA as a workable decision tool. It is possible to conduct a full-scale WBA of a major regulation using only the scattered data currently available. With sustained effort and attention on the part of the regulatory state, WBA could revolutionize the accuracy with which prospective laws are evaluated.

Methodological and Theoretical Issues in Well-Being Analysis

The introduction of a new decision-making procedure such as WBA is likely to raise many questions and objections. We will try to anticipate and answer some of those in the sections that follow.

As we do so, it is essential to bear in mind the distinction between (*a*) whether WBA is better than the other methods of evaluating laws and policies and (*b*) whether WBA is a perfect measure of net welfare. With respect to the latter, WBA falls far short. But so do all other ways of evaluating policies, because human life is chaotically complicated and thus evades attempts to analyze it with anything like complete accuracy and precision. For one thing, no one can predict the future, and perfect policy evaluation depends upon such prediction. And for another thing, no one can measure the complexity of the welfare of millions of people (whether by CBA, WBA, intuition, non-numerical deliberation, or any other means) with perfection or anything close to perfection. Yet policy choices must be made. If a society reacts to such uncertainty by enacting no laws or policies at all, or by choosing laws and policies randomly, then it will be far worse off than if it tries by some means to gauge which laws and policies will increase welfare more than others. The question whether to use WBA thus does not turn on how WBA compares to perfection, but instead on how WBA compares to alternative ways of deciding which laws and policies to enact. Chapter 3 is devoted to the latter question. There, we compare WBA to CBA, since CBA is the only alternative for the comprehensive analysis of laws' well-being effects that is taken seriously in policy circles (and in many, though not all, scholarly circles).[94]

The case we hope to make is that even with its shortcomings, WBA improves on the alternatives that have been devised. It goes without saying that this represents only a step along the path toward understanding the likely effects of a law on the quality of human life. Many people believe that CBA, despite its limitations, constitutes a step forward from the impressionistic approach that came before it. In our view, WBA is similarly a step forward from CBA. Someday, an entirely new approach may improve upon WBA, and in the meantime WBA will certainly benefit from refinements and changes that critics suggest. We view this chapter as the beginning of the conversation.[95]

Well-being data and welfare

In chapter 1, we described how happiness data are collected and why such data are considered to be valid and reliable. Fifteen years ago, there was skepticism about whether self-reports of happiness could be trusted. If someone said she was happy, how could one know whether it was true? But since then, many tests have been done both to replicate happiness studies and also to show the correlation between self-reports and other indicia of happiness, such as others' reports and physiological indicators. We refer readers to our discussion of the quality of the data in chapter 1. At this point, so much evidence supports the basic credibility of happiness studies that critics have shifted their focus to somewhat subtler points.

But before we delve into those subtler points, it is worth saying something more about the core trustworthiness of the happiness studies relative to alternative proxies for well-being. Happiness may seem to be, at least in some deep sense, an unobservable phenomenon. Even if Jane says she is happy, and those closest to her say she is happy, and she is smiling broadly, and her dopamine levels are high, perhaps no one can *know* for sure that she is happy. Where does that leave policymakers? One option is to do what we propose here: use the best indicia of happiness to make educated guesses about what makes people happy. Psychologists have greatly refined their techniques for studying happiness and have tested those techniques in the ways that are standard in social science. The happiness surveys have passed the tests because of their replicability and their correlation with other indicators. This does not mean that they perfectly capture people's true happiness, but it does provide reasons to believe that they are a closer approximation to that truth than is any alternative available. What Jane says about how happy she is reveals much more about her well-being than does, say, her level of wealth. That matters because prioritizing other means of assessing the welfare effects of laws—as cost-benefit analysis does—yields results far more removed from actual welfare than does relying on the happiness studies. We spell this out in more detail when we compare CBA to WBA in the next chapter. The fundamental issue in determining the value of happiness data to policymaking is not absolute value about ultimate choices—that is, whether happiness data are an ideal measure of all the things that might matter to a decision-maker. Instead, the fundamental issue is *relative value* about welfare effects: do happiness data do a better job than the available alternatives of capturing the welfare effects of legal policies?

We now turn to the set of foundational, yet somewhat subtler, objections to and concerns about the happiness studies that are currently voiced by some critics. The first, and most important, is that well-being data lack interpersonal cardinality because different individuals may interpret the scales differently.[96] For example, a 5.0 on one person's scale may not be the same as a 5.0 on another person's scale. If people interpret the hedonic scales differently, it becomes impossible to know whether one person's reported change from an SWB of 5.0 to 6.0 is equivalent to another person's reported change from 5.0 to 6.0.

Before addressing how much of a problem this may be for WBA, it is essential to note that it is more of a problem for CBA. Whereas a reported 5.0 *might* reflect a different level of well-being for one person than it does for another, a particular sum of money will *definitely* affect one person's well-being differently from another's. Most obviously, $1,000 might mean everything to a homeless person and nothing to Bill Gates. Because of the diminishing marginal value of money, two individuals with differing levels of personal wealth can obtain vastly different amounts of welfare from the same gain (or loss) of income.[97] Adjusting CBA in accordance with variations in marginal values of money is quite technically complex, and the proper solution is frequently unclear or highly context dependent.[98] And the problems for CBA do not end there. Even two equivalently wealthy individuals may have vastly divergent welfare functions: additional wealth might benefit one far more than the other. Individuals' welfare functions are unobservable;[99] economists know (or assume) that marginal values of money are positive and diminish with increasing wealth, but they can be sure of little else.[100] Economists typically respond to this problem by simply ignoring it[101] or assuming that its effects wash out across large populations[102]—and the latter is precisely the same way of addressing the problem that we envision for WBA. It is thus hard to imagine that interpersonal comparisons will present greater difficulty for WBA than they do for classical CBA.

For WBA, differential use of the scale should be a problem only when that differential use is related to the populations being compared. For instance, imagine an agency using WBA to evaluate a project that will reduce traffic and commuting times on a highway. To determine the hedonic cost of commuting in traffic, the agency would compare the well-being of people while they are commuting with the well-being of people who are not commuting. Unless people who commute in traffic *systematically* use the hedonic scale differently from people who do not, different uses of the scale will simply show up as random noise. Variations among individuals in how they rate their own happiness—what they mean when they rate themselves a 5 or a 6, for instance—are likely to be random, not biased.[103] This randomness should wash out across large numbers of people.[104] In many of the situations most relevant to WBA, this seems very likely to be the case.[105]

A second possible obstacle for WBA lies in the ambiguities involved in aggregating interpersonal welfare states. For instance, if Person A's welfare decreases from 6.0 to 5.0, and the welfare of Persons B through Z increases from 6.0 to 6.1, it is difficult to know whether this net gain of 1.5 WBUs[106] actually indicates that overall welfare has increased, decreased, or remained constant.[107]

This objection has two components. The first is simply a repetition of the interpersonal comparison problem discussed above: it is impossible to know whether a hedonic improvement for Person B from 6.0 to 6.1 is of equivalent magnitude to a hedonic regression for Person A from 6.0 to 5.9. As we said above, the same problem exists in a more acute form for CBA, and WBA would deal with it by relying on the same assumption that CBA uses—namely, that such issues will wash out across large populations, since there is no reason to think they will be systemically biased in one direction. The second component is the argument that when a project leaves some people better off and others worse off, a weak welfarist[108] cannot conclude that it is worth pursuing merely because overall welfare has increased. This claim is certainly correct, but it is again identical to the problems faced by CBA or any other wealth-based decision procedure. The simple fact that a project will result in Person A receiving $100 and Person B losing $50 is not sufficient reason to undertake the project, because that fact might be outweighed by distributional issues— for instance, how much wealth do A and B have, and are there other reasons to favor one over the other?—and other considerations beyond aggregate welfare.[109] This is merely another way of stating that there is no independent moral significance to Kaldor-Hicks efficiency. A Kaldor-Hicks efficient outcome is one in which the parties that benefit from a project "could fully compensate those who stand to lose from it and still be better off."[110] The fact that Kaldor-Hicks efficiency is not morally decisive is by now a well-accepted conclusion among even CBA's most sophisticated defenders.[111]

Another important objection to WBA focuses on hedonic compensations for prior events—when someone is compensated during Time Period 2 for a decrease in welfare that occurred during Time Period 1. Imagine that an individual has been injured in a car accident, causing her average well-being to fall from 6.0 to 5.0 for a period of one year (after which time it returns to 6.0).[112] Imagine that there were two potential methods of compensating her for her injury: Plan A would raise her well-being from 6.0 to 7.0 for one year, and Plan B would raise her well-being from 6.0 to 6.5 for two years. A critic might argue that it is unclear whether these plans would compensate her equally and whether either of them would compensate her appropriately.

Upon examination it becomes evident that this objection again reduces to a combination of the two arguments we have just addressed. The issue of whether a decline from 6.0 to 5.0 is of equivalent magnitude to an improvement from 6.0 to 7.0 (or twice that of an improvement from 6.0 to 6.5) is merely an intrapersonal variant of the quandary regarding interpersonal comparisons and the shape of hedonic curves. We have already dealt with this question and shown that it is, if anything, more easily handled than the parallel problems surrounding CBA. On the other hand, the intertemporal problem—whether a gain in Time Period 2 effectively counterbalances a loss in Time Period 1—is simply an intrapersonal variant of a broader question of interpersonal aggregation. That is, if a project increases overall welfare, is that a sufficient condition for it to be worth pursuing, even if it decreases the welfare for some individuals? This is a difficult moral question, and one that we do not attempt to answer here. There may be many instances in which a project is welfare increasing but, for distributional reasons, should not be undertaken. WBA is not meant as an answer to distributional concerns—either involving the distribution of welfare between different individuals or the distribution of welfare between time periods for the same individual—though of course it could be used to provide information relevant to those concerns.

Collection and manipulation of well-being data

Theoretical problems with well-being data aside, it is also possible that individuals or groups would seek to manipulate well-being data in order to accomplish various policy objectives. After all, it is nearly costless for an individual to answer untruthfully in response to a well-being survey. An individual who hoped to affect future policy decisions could shade her responses in order to make similar policy choices appear more or less beneficial. For instance, suppose that social conservatives in the state of Washington, where same-sex marriage became legal in December 2012,[113] wished to prevent it from being legalized in other states as well. They might begin registering extremely low levels of subjective well-being in the wake of the legalization in order to make it appear to policymakers as if the law has harmed overall well-being in the state.

This is a serious concern, but there are a number of potential policy correctives. First, policymakers would ideally be collecting well-being data on an ongoing (longitudinal) basis in order to facilitate analysis of policy changes. This means that an individual in Washington would complete the same well-being survey after the legalization of same-sex marriage that she completed before same-sex marriage was ever placed on the agenda. This would reduce the salience of any given policy issue to survey respondents.

In addition, respondents would not know what policy their responses would be used to analyze. Policymakers might use a given set of responses to gauge the effects of same-sex marriage, or they might use them to estimate the effects of a park being built across the street or the installation of a new light-rail line. An individual who reported artificially low (or high) well-being in an effort to hamper (or promote) one type of project or regulation might well end up influencing another instead.

Policymakers could also employ the same types of algorithms that online reputation regimes (such as Zagat or eBay) use to detect deliberately malicious feedback.[114] These algorithms typically screen for outliers—reports that are highly inconsistent with the vast majority of other feedback on the same firm or individual.[115] Here, policymakers could conceivably use algorithms that screen out data that are inconsistent with an individual's other self-reports with no discernible basis for the inconsistency. In some cases this might mean throwing out useful information, but such screening algorithms have nevertheless proven to enhance accuracy in other contexts.[116] More generally, online reputation regimes have remained fairly reliable despite the strong incentives of particular individuals and firms to spread misinformation.[117] It is unlikely that well-being surveys will fare worse.

Moreover, CBA is hardly immune from this type of problem. An individual who responds to a contingent valuation survey has no incentive to provide an accurate response.[118] Thus, for instance, the same social conservative might offer an artificially high answer when asked how much she would be willing to pay to keep same-sex marriage illegal. Similarly, an environmentally conscious individual might provide an artificially high answer when asked how much she would pay for cleaner skies. Sophisticated social scientists have attempted to devise correctives to this issue, but it is impossible to eliminate the problem entirely.[119]

These types of problems are, if anything, more significant for contingent valuation surveys than they are for well-being surveys. The reason is that a contingent valuation survey necessarily highlights and makes salient the policy choice in question—the individual is asked how much she would pay for some policy outcome—which makes it easier for an individual to provide a deliberately misleading answer. The question at issue is not obscured, as it is within well-being surveys. We will discuss contingent valuation surveys in much greater detail in the next chapter. For the moment it suffices to note that the types of highly charged political issues that might cause individuals to manipulate well-being surveys would also cause them to manipulate contingent valuation surveys, probably to greater effect.

Finally, we would like to acknowledge a different concern about WBA's data. Some critics may worry that collecting and analyzing the data necessary for WBA will be difficult. The extent to which this is true depends, like so much else, on the baseline for comparison. There is already a treasure-trove of longitudinal data on life satisfaction that has been collected over the decades in the United States, Great Britain, and Germany.[120] Much of what would need to be analyzed is already captured, to one degree or another, in that data. In addition, new approaches to collecting moment-by-moment data using smartphone apps have expanded the horizons of happiness analysis yet further.[121] Nonetheless, the ideal of comparing a population with one relevant feature to an otherwise identical population without that specific feature—or of comparing the same population before and after having that feature but without any other changes—is unreachable in practice. Again, the merits of WBA, as of other decision-making tools, lie not in their absolute value but in their relative value. All one can do is ask whether WBA offers a better mechanism for measuring human welfare than CBA or any other alternative. And because CBA faces the same problems of statistical analysis as does WBA, while having a far more tenuous link to welfare, we think that WBA is the better tool.

Governmental objectives and WBA morality

That governments are capable of measuring and aggregating subjective well-being does not answer the question of precisely what governments should seek to achieve, and, in particular, what role distributional consequences should play. It is well beyond the scope of this book to conduct a thoroughgoing analysis of these questions or to reach conclusions, and we will not attempt such steps here. Rather, our objective is to give a few examples of criteria that could form the basis for WBA-based government policy. We take no position on how a government should balance these competing concerns, with the exception of one instance that we believe gives rise to a clear normative conclusion.

AGGREGATE WELFARE.   One conceivable objective of government is to maximize the aggregate welfare of its citizens.[122] A government might thus pursue projects that increase the total WBUs of all individuals, aggregated across the entire span of their lives. We take no position on the importance of aggregate welfare in comparison to other measures or goals, with one limited exception: a project that increases the subjective well-being of one or more individuals while leaving the welfare of the other individuals unchanged is normatively desirable with respect to welfare. That is to say, WBA satisfies the Pareto principle.[123] Within the normative framework of welfarism, there can be no objection to a project that will make some people better off without harming others. There may of course be non-welfare reasons for opposing such a project, but WBA (like CBA) is merely a tool for measuring welfare.

It is worth noting that this conclusion does not hold for conventional CBA. A project that makes some people wealthier without altering the wealth of the remaining people might nonetheless make those unaffected worse off. Inflation effects could diminish their purchasing power and reduce the value of their money, or their diminished status in comparison to their fellow citizens could make them unhappy and reduce their welfare.[124] These complications arise because wealth is only a weak proxy for welfare. In contrast, if a person's subjective well-being remains unchanged, that person's welfare has not decreased. Formally, this particular claim—unlike virtually any of our other claims—does depend on our philosophical argument that well-being equates with happiness. But, practically, it does not depend on that argument but only on the far less controversial point that happiness is a closer proxy for well-being than is money.

Conventional CBA is designed to measure changes in aggregate welfare—really, aggregate wealth. Accordingly, we used aggregate happiness as the analytic criterion of choice when we re-engineered the EPA's CBA as a WBA. That is why we described a regulation as "well-being justified" or "welfare justified" if it increased the overall welfare of the population. But as we explain in the following paragraphs, policymakers need not look to aggregate welfare alone.

PER CAPITA WELFARE.   Another conceivable objective of government is to maximize the per capita welfare of its citizens, even at the expense of aggregate welfare.[125] Thus, a government might conceivably favor a project that would produce a population of 1,000 people, each with 6 WBUs, instead of a population of 1,550 people, each with 4 WBUs. (A program such as state-funded counseling for parents who are planning to start families might have this type of effect.)

INTERPERSONAL DISTRIBUTION.   Another conceivable objective of government is to reduce the interpersonal disparities of welfare among its citizens, even if that comes at the expense of aggregate welfare.[126] Thus, a government might conceivably favor a project that would result in a population of 1,000 people, each with 5 WBUs, instead of a population of 550 people with 6 WBUs and 450 people with 4 WBUs. (A progressive income tax might have this type of effect.)

INTRAPERSONAL DISTRIBUTION.   Another conceivable objective of government is to reduce the amount its citizens' welfare changes over time, even at the expense of aggregate welfare. Individuals might prefer stable levels of happiness, just as economists suggest that individuals rationally favor stable levels of consumption.[127] Thus, a government might conceivably favor a project that would ensure an individual 5 WBUs of welfare for the entire duration of her life, instead of that individual spending the first half of her life at 6 WBUs and the second half of her life at 4.2 WBUs. (Social Security and Medicare might have this type of effect.)

We are at pains to reiterate that we take no position on which, if any, of these objectives are normatively legitimate aims of government. We mean only to give some examples of the types of objectives that a government, guided by a WBA-based decision procedure, might choose to pursue. Regardless of which goal or set of goals a government elects, WBA will prove to be a useful analytical tool.

Objections to the nature of our project

Beyond objections to the data or the methodology, many readers may have global concerns about the nature of WBA itself. We expect such criticisms to come from widely divergent camps—in particular, from both CBA's strongest adherents and staunchest critics. We will try to address both sets of concerns, starting with those of CBA's defenders.

Many economists may have trouble getting past the initial premise of WBA, which is that people do not spend their money in ways that do much to increase their happiness (unless their incomes are toward the low end of the spectrum). For an economist, this may seem inexplicable and unacceptable. Yet it is supported by a great deal of evidence from hedonic psychology, and the conclusion also receives empirical support from an even deeper ocean of studies about people's cognitive limitations and weaknesses at predicting things (including, but certainly not limited to, what will make them happy). Contrary to economic dogma, we find the data not only definitive but also intuitive: it is unsurprising to us that the average person who makes $1 million per year is only slightly happier, if at all happier, than the average person who makes $75,000 per year.[128]

At the other end of the spectrum, CBA's staunchest critics may accuse us of claiming that incommensurable things can be commensurated and of overvaluing numerical analysis of things that would be better considered qualitatively. We now turn to addressing these concerns.

A society needs to make choices about what laws and policies to enact. When it does this, one major thing (though not necessarily the only one) that it typically wants to know is which choice would most improve the lives of its citizens. In a huge, complicated, and technologically sophisticated society like the United States today, that sort of thing is often impossible to know with any certainty. For example, should regulators set the level of permissible particulate matter emissions at x parts per million or at $2x$ parts per million? These decisions need to be made and will be made, but there is gross uncertainty about how they will affect people's lives, and which choices will be better than others.

What is a society to do in the face of such uncertainty? One option is to choose randomly, but we know of no one who advocates that. Another option is to eschew any sort of numerical analysis and try to get a general sense of which choice would be better. But in our view, there are good reasons to be skeptical of such an approach. First, it is hard to know how much better x parts per million of particulate matter is than $2x$ parts per million, or even whether that distinction will make any difference to anyone's life. Even to make a non-numerical choice, one has to know what is at stake: the possible health- and life-threatening consequences, and on the other hand the costs to businesses and consumers. Already, considering such factors brings in a tremendous amount of conjecture and uncertainty—just the things that critics may rightly emphasize that WBA cannot avoid. Our point here is that no other approach can avoid those problems either.

Once one starts to think about the costs and the benefits, is one better off learning some relevant data about those consequences, or closing one's eyes to such data? It seems fairly clear to us that one should consider data that help one know something rather than nothing about the effects of health and money on happiness, not to mention data that might tell one something rather than nothing about the likelihood of health effects from changes in particulate matter emissions.

Armed with such data, should the regulator now make the decision without putting numbers on the competing considerations, or would numbers be useful? Unquestionably, the data cannot tell us everything we might want to know about a given policy. But that is also true of nonnumerical attempts to assign value, and behavioral economics scholarship has revealed the mistakes people are prone to make in such attempts. True, WBA is not a way of resolving every issue or making every decision, but it is something that can help regulators make decisions. We do not propose that the outcomes of a WBA be automatically accepted and enacted as law whenever the benefits of a proposal outweigh its costs. Other factors, including the value of democratic decision-making, are vitally important to these decisions as well. We do think, however, that the data generated by WBA can be crucially important for thinking about the kinds of decisions the government often faces.

We also want to point out that when people make decisions without using numbers, *in effect they are often still assigning numerical values* to the good and bad consequences of the policies under consideration. They just aren't *articulating* those numerical values to themselves, much less to the public. CBA has been criticized for concealing its decision-making apparatus under a false veneer of rigor, but at least CBA's apparatus can be inspected, critiqued, and refined—as can WBA's. When people make decisions "qualitatively," their de facto use of hidden numbers rather than explicit ones prevents anyone from inspecting, critiquing, or refining the decision-making because the key part of it remains opaque. To a degree, this is inevitable: even WBA is meant to be used only as a guide, so the ultimate decision will still be based on reasons that might not be fully transparent. But increasing the degree to which the process can be inspected, and increasing the use of data to inform decision-making, improve the likelihood that welfare-enhancing decisions will generally be made and that citizens will understand the reasons behind those decisions. The point of WBA is not that it reveals exactly how happy people will be with x parts per million as opposed to $2x$, but rather that it perhaps increases the chance of a welfare-increasing policy decision from something like 60 percent to something like 70 percent. That might not sound too exciting, but over the course of time, it could change many lives for the better.

Having just made such an extravagant suggestion, now is a good time for us to acknowledge the limitations of our proposal. Critics of numerical analysis rightly point out that it can sometimes lend itself to misuse by offering a false veneer of precision. We are acutely aware, as we have said repeatedly, of the large inherent imprecision in any tool designed to measure human well-being. WBA is certainly no exception. All we will say on this score is that we think it unfair to criticize WBA (or CBA) on the ground that numbers *look* precise, so when doing something imprecise, it is better not to use them. On the contrary, the goal is to measure welfare as accurately as possible, even if the best that can be done is still quite inaccurate. If numerical tools measure welfare more accurately, then they should be used—accompanied by the strong caveat that they undoubtedly contain inaccuracy and divergence from true welfare, like any other tools of this kind in social science.

Moreover, we think that qualitative approaches capture less well than numerical ones the non-binary nature of many policy choices. Suppose there is a range of options for limiting pollution, such that the more restrictive an option, the greater the health benefits but the higher the monetary costs, and vice versa. In the book *Priceless*, perhaps the canonical tome advocating for qualitative analysis, we do not see how such a range would be grappled with.[129] The closest thing to an answer seems to be an example where a choice is presented as binary: "A holistic approach to the arsenic problem, for example, encourages us to ask whether it is worth the price of one or two bottles of water per person per year to ensure that everyone has tap water with the lowest possible level of arsenic. . . . For regulations to protect fish from power plants, the holistic approach makes us think about our willingness to pay a penny a day to avoid an underwater massacre."[130] It is not clear how this would work, however, in cases where the choices are not binary. Choosing the "lowest possible" level of arsenic in tap water might be desirable, but in many cases some balance must be struck between safeguarding environmental values and permitting economic activity, where both extremes will be unpalatable and there will be countless different ways of making the trade-off in between the extremes. What then? In our view, choosing how to make such trade-offs involves placing a value on both things (economic concerns and environmental protection), and we prefer making those valuations explicit. Numbers show the spectrum of options, rather than arbitrarily cutting off parts of the spectrum—as is likely to happen if a choice is described without numbers in the form that the above quotation from *Priceless* describes.

Relatedly, critics of quantification may oppose the idea underlying both CBA and WBA that human well-being should be treated separately from moral considerations. This is an interesting idea, and we have only a few limited things to say about it. First, we of course believe that WBA should never be substituted for moral judgment. We mean what we say when we label it a tool for assessing aggregate welfare and nothing more. Aggregate welfare is no small thing, but it also isn't the only thing, and WBA's results need to be scrutinized for divergence from other values that people may want to incorporate into their ultimate decisions. Second, we tend to think it can be beneficial to divide the question of what to do so as to better analyze one major part before factoring in the others. This is not meant as some form of trickery to illegitimately accentuate the value assigned to aggregate welfare,[131] but rather a way to try to make the process more manageable and accurate (within the limits imposed by the messiness of the thing being measured). Finally, if nothing else, we have followed the approach currently being used—that is, separating out aggregate welfare for analysis independent of other considerations. Whatever the merits or demerits of that approach, if WBA improves on CBA then it will get policymakers closer to the truth than they are currently. If that is the least we can claim, it is enough to justify WBA.

Some people believe that CBA is merely a cover for a political agenda— typically a pro-business, anti-regulatory, politically conservative one. Perhaps these people will see the same thing in WBA. But nothing could be further from the truth. WBA grew out of our research into the implications of hedonic psychology for law, and that research in turn grew out of the growing consensus that hedonic psychology was making important breakthroughs in how to understand human life. Thus WBA was a natural consequence of this way of looking at behavioral science, and ultimately of well-being itself. It was certainly not created to advance any sort of political agenda. Nor do we know what results it would have. On the one hand, would it decrease regulation by focusing on adaptation to negative life events? Or would it increase regulation by weighing death heavily and monetary costs lightly? We do not know, and we consider that a virtue.

There are certainly scholars in the field of regulatory analysis who seem to be motivated by political concerns, for better or worse. Some, but not all, advocates of CBA likely fall into this group; as do some, but not all, critics of CBA. Those advocating qualitative approaches often seem to want there to be more environmental regulation, and to suggest modes of analysis designed to reach that result. And certain proponents of CBA seem to want the opposite. We do not say this to criticize either group. Perhaps one or the other is correct with respect to what the outcomes should be, and perhaps the procedure should be designed with the correct outcomes in mind. For our part, though, we can say only that we have no idea whether it would be better to have more or less regulation, and that we are not striving for either result. We aim to create a more accurate way to measure welfare—nothing more, nothing less.

The final point we would like to address is the claim that WBA is unimportant because it concerns only welfare. If WBA offers no way to resolve conflicts between welfare and other values, the claim would go, then WBA does nothing significant to guide or improve upon policy analysis. The problem with this criticism, though, is that it conflates doing nothing with failing to do everything. The ultimate goal is to figure out what should be done, and one valuable piece of information toward that end is understanding a prospective policy's effects on aggregate well-being. Sometimes it will be a total solution: the policy that increases well-being the most will be deemed the best policy. At other times the value of overall well-being will be weighed against other values, which will be judged to trump it or to modify the extent to which it is pursued. In all cases, though, policymakers will benefit from having a clearer picture of the welfare effects of a policy than they would have had without WBA. And because overall quality of life matters a lot, providing that clearer picture makes a big difference.

CHAPTER THREE

Well-Being Analysis vs. Cost-Benefit Analysis

Although well-being analysis offers an exciting opportunity for evaluating and reevaluating policies and legislation, it is far from perfect. Well-being analysis (WBA) has the same limitations as does any attempt to describe the chaotic complications of life in a way that allows for decision analysis. But decisions must be made. And given the limitations of human knowledge, predictive capacity, and ability to account for complexity, the question is not how WBA measures up to perfection but rather how it measures up to the alternatives. The relevant alternative is cost-benefit analysis (CBA). Not only is CBA the lone decision procedure that has been used for the past thirty years, but it is also the only one that comprehensively attempts to answer the sorts of detailed questions posed by regulatory law. If WBA improves upon CBA, then it becomes the best available option for evaluating prospective laws.

This chapter addresses the major problems with CBA that undermine its reliability and validity, and suggests how WBA solves these problems. The first section of the chapter concentrates on the shortcomings of CBA's use of stated and revealed preferences as proxies for well-being, the second section focuses on limitations in the way that CBA defines the value of life, and the last section discusses issues associated with discounting the value of future money. At each step, we explain the ways in which WBA would overcome CBA's shortcomings and provide a more accurate accounting of a prospective policy's effects on the quality of life.

Willingness to Pay and Well-Being

We begin with what is perhaps the most central point of comparison: CBA's need to monetize costs and benefits and WBA's corresponding efforts to hedonize them. To translate costs and benefits into dollars, cost-benefit analysis relies on measures of how much individuals are willing to pay to acquire benefits or avoid harms.[1] These "willingness-to-pay" (WTP) measures are determined in two types of ways. In some cases, economists attempt to measure individual valuations through studies of revealed preferences—studies that demonstrate how much individuals are implicitly willing to pay to gain some benefit, or are willing to accept to bear some harm.[2] For instance, some studies center on the wage premium for workers who take dangerous jobs: they examine how much more a firm must pay a worker to accept a job that carries some type of risk, thus revealing the price a worker would pay to avoid that risk.[3] Sometimes, however, CBA must place prices on costs or benefits that are not traded in a robust marketplace, such as clean air.[4] In these cases, in which revealed preferences are unavailable, economists often rely on surveys that ask respondents hypothetically how much they would be willing to pay to procure a particular benefit or eliminate a particular harm. These surveys are known as stated-preference (in contrast to *revealed*-preference) or contingent valuation studies.[5]

Both revealed-preference studies and contingent valuation studies are fraught with difficulties and error. These difficulties have led to challenging theoretical and methodological disputes among CBA's proponents, and they are widely cited as undermining the validity and reliability of CBA. Nevertheless, CBA continues to rely on them because it is believed that there is no viable alternative. Yet WBA, if conducted properly, could in fact ameliorate or even eliminate many of the difficulties endemic to WTP measures. The sections that follow describe some of the most important sources of error involved in the measurement of WTP and explain how WBA could constitute an improvement or supplement to the status quo.

Revealed preferences

CBA's preferred method for quantifying costs and benefits is to examine what actual consumers of a good (such as workplace safety or clean air) are willing to pay to acquire that good.[6] These revealed-preference studies are particularly common in the context of workplace hazards: there are many studies of the wage premiums paid to workers who take dangerous jobs.[7] Indeed, CBA prices lives primarily by using wage premiums—the amount by which the wages of dangerous jobs exceed those of jobs that are safe but otherwise comparable.[8] If, for example, a job with an annual death risk of 2 in 10,000 paid $100 more per year than a comparable job with an annual risk of death of 1 in 10,000, that would imply that workers had priced their lives at $1 million (10,000 × $100). According to this approach, high wage premiums reveal that people value their lives a lot, because they need to be paid a lot in order to incur the risk of death. Low wage premiums mean the opposite.

The value of a life is central to CBA in part because so many regulations involve trading off some good (such as consumer costs) against a risk of death from injury or disease.[9] Accordingly, accurate calculations of the value of life are absolutely essential to CBA.[10] In addition, in theory revealed-preference studies could be used to price other goods, such as clean air or a new road or park, by looking at those goods' effect on housing prices.

Yet these revealed-preference studies have many potential sources of error. The error sources fall loosely into three categories: informational and computational problems, wealth effects, and affective forecasting difficulties. The first two could conceivably be overcome with significant effort and expense; the third is likely insuperable. WBA, by contrast, offers a solution to many of the most difficult of these problems.

Consider first the informational and computational problems inherent in revealed-preference studies. Economists favor revealed-preference studies because they focus on individuals' actual economic decisions.[11] However, that means that these studies must rely on individuals to make accurate and informed decisions regarding their own welfare. Errors in individual decision-making will lead to errors in the measurement of costs and benefits. The problems with this approach are particularly acute in the context of wage-premium studies, and they are manifold.

First, wage-premium studies assume that people are able to assimilate a 1-in-10,000 risk of death so as to decide whether they prefer avoiding that risk or earning extra money. But empirical evidence contradicts that assumption.[12] In study after study,[13] "survey respondents display[]" an utter inability to modulate their willingness to pay for increases in safety according to how much those safety increases actually would diminish the probability of harm."[14] People's minds are not designed to differentiate between exceedingly small risks and infinitesimally small risks, and when asked to do so rationally, they frequently fail.[15] As a result, small differences in pay between certain risky jobs and certain safe jobs cannot be attributed to a rational demand by workers to be compensated appropriately for the risk.

Second, most wage-premium studies are based on the assumption that workers know the actual mortality risk (1 in 10,000, for example) of their job relative to that of other jobs.[16] There is no reason to believe that this is so, and if it is not, then the studies' validity breaks down; one cannot rationally demand a specific amount of extra money in return for a specific amount of risk if one does not know what the amount of risk is.

Third, even if people could assimilate these low-probability numbers and knew the actual mortality risk of their jobs, they might act on such knowledge in ways other than demanding slightly more money for those jobs. For example, they might choose to incur the cost of being more careful on the job rather than incur the cost of taking a safer job that they enjoy less. Such a choice would fulfill CBA's dubious assumption of economic rationality while still rendering grossly inaccurate the life-value numbers arising from CBA.

Fourth, it may be that 1-in-10,000 risks of death are simply too fine-grained for regression analysis to detect. There are countless differences between one job and another. Even a careful CBA study that identifies a few dozen of those differences has necessarily left out scores of smaller ones. The small risk to life, if it is traded off at all by workers, could be traded off against these smaller differences rather than the larger ones that are visible to econometricians. Indeed, CBA's wage premiums seem to fluctuate for reasons independent of risk to life. For example, when unions in the trucking industry lost some of their capacity to influence management, drivers' wages failed to keep pace with those of comparable jobs in other industries.[17] Developments like that one, which had nothing to do with workers' tolerance for risk, resulted in CBA's use of lower wage-premium numbers (and thus lower values for life).[18] In theory, one might say that a perfect CBA would isolate the value of risk by accounting for union power and everything else like it that can affect wages. But this has not happened in practice, and it might be impossible even in theory. No two jobs are truly equivalent in every relevant feature except their risk to life. And even if there were two such jobs, they could not remain equivalent over time, because their wages would be affected in different ways by economic developments independent of risk.

In light of these problems, it should not be surprising that wage-premium studies have produced widely variant values of life. Studies using similar methodologies have set the value of a statistical life as low as $100,000 and as high as $76 million.[19] Such large variation in the results of the studies casts doubt on their reliability and validity and suggests that random noise or unmeasured variables, rather than rational risk trade-offs, account for the numbers.

WBA, by contrast, sidesteps nearly all these problems. WBA does not require that individuals understand the risk of death in the workplace, nor must they be able to accurately grasp what it means to face a 1-in-10,000 risk. Under WBA, an individual is required only to report how happy or satisfied she is right now—a far simpler cognitive task. There is no need to assume that individuals make perfectly rational choices under conditions of perfect information. The value of an individual life can be measured simply by aggregating the positive and negative moments in that life, as reported by the individual.

WBA also eliminates some of the need to perform complicated regression analysis in order to compare similarly situated jobs or marketplace goods. Here, WBA's advantage lies in the ability to capitalize on longitudinal studies. Suppose that an agency is attempting to value the cost of a case of emphysema (in terms of pain, suffering, and diminution in the quality of life) to analyze a regulation that would protect workers from contracting emphysema in the workplace. CBA would examine the wages paid to workers in industries in which emphysema is a workplace hazard, and then, using regression analysis, would attempt to isolate the wage premium that is attributable directly to the risk of emphysema. This is an extremely difficult endeavor, as we explained. WBA, on the other hand, would simply look at the well-being of a given individual *before* and *after* she contracted emphysema. The post-emphysema loss in well-being represents the hedonic cost of the disease, a cost that the agency can then weigh against other hedonic costs and benefits. Economists have already made use of large sets of social-survey data to conduct exactly these types of studies.[20]

We hasten to add that this approach will not eliminate the need for regression analysis entirely. Other circumstances in the individual's life may have changed during the same time period. For instance, her disease may have forced her to take a different job, reducing her wages. WBA will have to account for these changes as well, using regression analysis, but the problem will be much simpler. Because the study will involve the same individuals at multiple different times, it will not be necessary to control for nearly so many variables. That CBA cannot similarly utilize longitudinal studies, and must instead rely on how much money a (potentially uninformed) individual would pay or accept at a given instant, is just one of its methodological shortcomings.

Next, consider the effect of wealth on revealed preferences. It has long been understood that the value an individual places on a risk or a benefit will necessarily be affected by that individual's wealth.[21] A millionaire might think nothing of paying $10,000 to breathe slightly cleaner air, but someone who must support a family on $25,000 per year will be much more hesitant to make the same trade-off. Similarly, wealthy people rarely take high-risk jobs because the wage premium is worth less to them and is insufficient to compensate them for the risk. The reason is not that the benefit or risk involved is greater for the wealthier person (though there may be slight differences). Rather, "wealth effects" are driven by the fact that the *money* is worth less to the wealthy person.[22] Because CBA involves translating harms and benefits into dollars, these wealth effects will undermine cost-benefit calculations.

Wealth effects play a large and undeniable role in wage-premium studies, yet CBA cannot fully account for these effects. The fact that rich and poor people (who presumably care equally, or at least comparably, about staying alive) would be willing to pay vastly different amounts to avoid a 1-in-10,000 risk of death illustrates the inadequacy of this metric for valuing lives. WBA circumvents these issues entirely by valuing lives based on individuals' own assessments of their well-being.

Yet the problem of wealth effects for revealed-preference studies and CBA is even more general. To demonstrate this, let us abstract away from wage studies to more general methods for using revealed preferences. In theory, an agency employing CBA could use housing prices or other data that reflect the benefits and costs of living under various conditions in order to put a value on those conditions.[23] Imagine, for instance, that an agency is attempting to put a dollar figure on the cost of having a nearby factory that emits noxious fumes. The agency could compare housing prices in locations with clean air and locations with noxious fumes and use multivariate regression to isolate the effect of the noxious fumes on those prices. This represents a particularly advanced method for revealing preferences in that the method can encompass circumstances in which individuals are not directly exchanging money for a good.

Now imagine a government project—a waste storage facility, for instance—that will create noxious fumes, resulting in a uniform decrease in well-being of everyone within range of those fumes, but will have overall positive effects more generally. This project can be located in a rich area with 500 very wealthy people or a poor area with 1,000 people. Imagine that the agency is able to determine that the 500 wealthy people would be willing to pay $50,000 each to avoid having the waste storage facility placed in their neighborhood, whereas the poorer people would be willing to pay $10,000 each.

If the agency that is deciding where to site the project can tax and transfer as part of the project, then the efficient solution is clear. The government would locate the project in the poor area, and make a compensating transfer from the wealthy to the poor. The wealthy people would prefer to pay $50,000 per person to avoid having the project located in their neighborhood, and that would be enough money to compensate the poorer people such that they would prefer to accept both the money and the facility over receiving neither. (This still would not necessarily mean that CBA would reach the right overall conclusion. Only if the poor people were right in believing that such a transfer would make them happier on balance would WBA agree with CBA in recommending that the agency pursue that course.)

Suppose, however, that the agency cannot implement the transfer. If the agency is using CBA based on actual WTP statistics from the two areas, it could find that the 500 wealthy people are willing to pay more to avoid the noxious fumes (500 × $50,000 = $25 million) than the 1,000 poor people (1,000 × $10,000 = $10 million), purely because of wealth effects. It thus might end up locating the project in the poor area rather than the wealthy area. But doing so will actually lead to a greater reduction in welfare than locating the project in the wealthy area, simply because there are more people who will be affected by the project in the poorer neighborhood.

By contrast, a decision-maker employing WBA would pick up on the actual welfare effects of these two options. The decision-maker would realize that the welfare loss will be greater if the project is located in the poor area than if it is located in the wealthy area, because it will affect twice the number of people in the poor area. It will site the project in the wealthy area. If (counterfactually) people's WTP accurately reflected what was best for them, then the best solution would be to put the waste facility in the poor neighborhood and then tax the members of the wealthy neighborhood and transfer their money to compensate those in the poor neighborhood. But because agencies cannot tax and transfer, an agency can choose only the "second-best" solution of putting the facility in the wealthy neighborhood, or else the "third-best" solution of putting it in the poor one. Using WBA will lead to the second-best solution, whereas using CBA will lead to the third-best.[24] To be sure, political realities may constrain an agency's actions, but that is a separate issue. Agencies should choose the analytical mechanism that identifies the best policy outcome they can achieve within their powers, and WBA does this better than CBA.

Any time a government agency must decide between two projects—or two locations for the same project—one of which will affect wealthy people and the other of which will affect poor people, it risks being led astray by wealth effects. It may be led to believe that the "wealthy" project will have a greater effect on welfare than the "poor" project, simply because of the impact of wealth on WTP. When the agency cannot tax and transfer—and nearly all agencies lack that authority—it will err and select the wrong project. WBA, on the other hand, would not be confused by wealth effects. WBA does not require that costs and benefits be translated into dollars, and so the wealth of the affected population cannot confound the analysis.

CBA could conceivably address the wealth-welfare disconnect by applying distributional weights to costs and benefits. For instance, CBA might value a dollar of costs or benefits more if it is experienced by a poor person and less if it is experienced by a rich one. The greater an individual's wealth, the less a dollar of cost or benefit experienced by that person would affect the CBA.[25] The main problem with this approach is that it is difficult or impossible to determine what those distributive weights should be; an individual's marginal utility of money is essentially unknowable.[26] This may be part of the reason that CBA has never adopted distributional weights of this type. And in any event, applying distributive weights would merely reduce, not eliminate, this particular advantage of WBA over CBA because even adjusted WTP would remain a weaker proxy for welfare than the more direct happiness measures.

Some of the problems with CBA that we have discussed in this section—wealth effects and informational and computational difficulties—could conceivably be cured via enormous expenditures on data collection and the use of extremely delicate and sophisticated statistical methods.[27] No practitioner of CBA has come close to implementing these types of solutions, though they remain theoretically possible.

However, revealed-preference studies suffer in addition from an incurable flaw, one that WBA does not share. The flaw—as Cass Sunstein has explained[28]—is that they rely on affective forecasting: an individual's prediction about how she will feel about an event or a condition before it happens. This is an activity that individuals often struggle greatly with. Imagine a government project that improves air quality in a particular location. Suppose that an agency wishes to place a monetary value on this cleaner air using housing prices in a revealed-preferences study. The theory behind using housing prices to measure the value of this project is that individuals will pay more to live in the locality once air quality has been improved. In theory, then, home prices in the affected area will depend on how much both current homeowners[29] and prospective purchasers value the improved air quality.[30] Inevitably, these valuations require comparisons between what it is like to live in areas with better and worse air quality. Thus, the current homeowner must remember what the air was like before the improvement and estimate her welfare loss from returning to such a state, and the prospective homeowner must estimate how valuable the improved air will be to her in the future.

A wealth of psychological research has shown that both of these exercises are fraught with error. Humans are notoriously bad at affective forecasting.[31] And they have surprising difficulty even *remembering* how they felt about an event or condition long after it has passed.[32] Although people usually do a good job of anticipating the valence of life events— that is, whether they will be good or bad—they tend to make systematic errors about both the magnitude and the duration of their affective responses to those events.[33] If individuals make significant errors when valuing something, then CBA will similarly make significant errors when it adopts and incorporates those valuations.

WBA, by contrast, will require asking people only about their *current* well-being. The governmental agency can then compare the current well-being of a population that is receiving the benefits of a similar regulation with the well-being of that population (or a similar reference population) before the regulation was implemented to determine its impact. These findings can then be applied to similar situations in other locations. No prospective or retrospective judgments are necessary.

Revealed-preference studies in conjunction with wages and workplace conditions have precisely the same problem. Imagine a job that comes with some undesirable working condition, such as an increased risk of contracting emphysema because of airborne chemicals in the workplace. A typical wage study would compare the salary accompanying this job to the salary accompanying a comparable job that lacked the risk of emphysema.[34]

This approach, like the housing study described above, relies on the predictions of employees regarding conditions with which they have no experience.[35] The hypothetical employee, asked to choose between the safer and riskier workplaces, would have to anticipate what it would be like for her to contract emphysema and then put a price on the risk of that occurring. This is a significant cognitive hurdle. This employee presumably does not already have emphysema, and she may not even know anyone who has ever contracted emphysema. How, then, could she possibly forecast what it will be like? The result is that agencies often exclude such risks from CBAs, treating them as if they did not exist.[36] Studies used to determine the value of a statistical life fare little better; how can an individual reliably estimate the value of her own life or what it would be like to lose it?[37]

WBA simply avoids all these difficulties. Under WBA, researchers would ask people with and without emphysema to report on their current levels of well-being.[38] No prospective forecasts or retrospective judgments are necessary; the individual need report only her current feelings. Researchers would then compare the well-being of people with emphysema to people without. The differential is the hedonic cost of emphysema, which could then be plugged directly into a WBA. Because they eliminate any possibility of affective forecasting (or memory) errors, these contemporaneous self-assessments are likely to be far more accurate than the guesses about the future and past that revealed-preference studies demand. WBA thus offers significant advantages over revealed-preference studies.

Contingent valuations

Revealed-preference studies are widely considered the best methodology for pricing costs and benefits.[39] However, economists cannot rely entirely on revealed-preference studies because not all costs and benefits involve goods that are traded in markets. Absent a market that can be used to set the price for a good, CBA must turn to contingent valuation studies: survey-based hypothetical questions regarding hypothetical payments for hypothetical projects.[40] For example, imagine that the government is considering mandating the installation of improved automobile exhaust systems. The primary effect of these systems would be to reduce the amount of pollutants emitted by cars, leading to less smog (and clearer skies) across the country.

The economic costs of the exhaust systems might be easy to measure, but how can an agency determine the value of cleaner skies? Individuals do not have opportunities to buy and sell units of clean sky for amounts of money. Indeed, government regulation exists in part because these sorts of transactions are sufficiently difficult that they do not occur.[41] An agency might attempt to use a sophisticated housing-price study, as described in the previous section, but those types of studies are extremely difficult to implement and have never found widespread use in CBA.[42] With no markets to scrutinize, and with no opportunity to determine WTP by examining revealed preferences, agencies are forced instead to employ contingent valuation surveys. These surveys simply ask people how much they would be willing to pay to receive a benefit (such as cleaner skies) or to avoid a harm, with little additional guidance.

To their credit, contingent valuation surveys avoid many of the informational and computational problems that plague revealed-preference studies. Respondents need not know the risk presented because it is stated in the contingent valuation survey. There is no possibility that they will respond to the risk other than by demanding more money, because the surveys do not allow for such actions. And by asking directly how much a respondent would pay to avoid a risk or obtain a benefit, contingent valuation surveys eliminate the need for difficult regression analysis.

Yet despite these advantages, contingent valuation surveys are nonetheless riddled with serious, perhaps decisive, flaws.[43] Not surprisingly, the problems with contingent valuation surveys center on the fact that they necessarily involve hypothetical questions. Subjects are asked to speculate about how much they would be willing to pay without actually having to pay anything, which renders their speculation less trustworthy.[44] Subjects are rarely subject to any true budget constraint: they can state freely that they would be willing to pay $1 million for cleaner skies without worrying about the other projects that would go unfunded as a result of such expenditures.[45] And if a researcher wishes to impose a budget constraint, it is difficult to choose one that is not arbitrary. Subjects are asked frequently about topics they may know little or nothing about—for instance, how much they would pay to avoid persistent construction noise that they have never before experienced.[46] This implicates all the insurmountable problems related to affective forecasting that we described in the preceding section. When real money and real experiences are not at stake, individual statements about WTP are simply unreliable. Economists have long understood this point.[47] But CBA cannot avoid such hypothetical surveys because market transactions do not exist for all potential costs and benefits.

These weaknesses in contingent valuation surveys have predictably resulted in prices that are all over the map. To take just one example: contingent valuation surveys have set the value of a statistical life anywhere from $40,000 to $13 million.[48]

Other tests of the validity of contingent valuation surveys have produced results that similarly fail to inspire confidence. For instance, WTP should be proportional to the size of the benefit conferred or the risk reduced. That is, if people are willing to pay $1,000 to eliminate a 1-in-1,000 mortality risk, they should be willing to pay $5,000 to eliminate a 5-in-1,000 risk.[49] Yet numerous studies have shown that this is not the case; individual WTP does not scale proportionately with the size of the risk reduction.[50] For instance, in one study respondents were willing to pay only 1.6 times as much to reduce a 5-in-1,000 risk as they were to reduce a 1-in-1,000 risk.[51] Many contingent valuation studies do not even include this type of validity test. In one recent meta-analysis of forty contingent valuation studies, only 50 percent of them incorporated a test for validity.[52] Of those that did include such a test, only 15 percent of the studies "passed" the test, in the sense that WTP was "nearly proportional to the risk reduction."[53] It is hard to put much faith in policy made on the basis of studies such as these.

One of the principal strengths of WBA is that it need not rely on such hypothetical inquiries. Instead, WBA compares individuals' contemporaneous levels of happiness before and after an actual project is completed and then uses that information to make projections regarding future projects. The surveyed individuals need not speculate as to how much money they would pay, and they are not subject to all the biases and distortions that asking hypothetical questions regarding money might generate. Rather, they are simply asked to state their current level of well-being—a question that has been demonstrated to produce reliable and valid answers.[54] For instance, to estimate the value of clean skies, an agency would collect data on well-being in a location with clean skies and a location with smog-filled skies—or, better yet, in the same location before and after it initiates some project that will lead to cleaner skies. By comparing well-being figures with and without clean skies, economists could measure the welfare benefits of reducing smog. These benefits could then be compared with the economic costs.

Of course, in some cases it may be difficult to isolate the hedonic effects of clean skies amid all the other confounding variables. For instance, the same jurisdiction that has cleaner skies might also have lower unemployment rates, which could itself generate greater well-being. One way to combat this problem would be for WBA to rely on regression analysis—which triggers one of the problems with CBA we described in the previous section.[55] Even when this is necessary, it presents a hurdle (surmountable with adequate data and analysis) that is less severe than the combination of hurdles facing CBA. Moreover, regression analysis will not always be necessary. Agencies will often be able to employ intrapersonal data—essentially, longitudinal studies—to circumvent many of the problems with multivariate regression we described above. For instance, suppose that an agency wished to evaluate the benefits of a project that would reduce commute times by upgrading public-transit systems. Rather than relying on erratic contingent valuation surveys—or trying to isolate how much people are willing to pay for shorter commutes by analyzing housing prices or wages via regression—WBA could simply determine the well-being of individuals as they are in the process of commuting. It could then compare that number to those individuals' well-being when they are engaged in some leisure activity—whatever they might have more time for if their commutes were shortened. The difference between those two figures, aggregated over the total reduction in commuting times, is the welfare gain from such a project. The results that WBA will generate are likely to be more reliable than those that contingent valuation surveys (or revealed-preference studies) are currently producing.[56]

Because they involve asking individuals how much they would pay for a benefit (or to avoid a cost), contingent valuation surveys will suffer from all the same wealth effects that plague revealed-preference studies. Respondents will necessarily filter their responses through the lens of their own finances: a wealthy person might think nothing of paying $10,000 for cleaner skies, whereas a poorer individual would be highly unlikely to suggest such a price. Of course, these prices are decoupled to some degree from individual wealth because contingent valuation surveys do not actually require respondents to pay anything. But this is a disadvantage, not an advantage. Instead of values that are distorted somewhat by wealth, contingent valuation surveys produce values that are distorted significantly by their hypothetical nature.

Using *average* WTP values would solve some of CBA's problems with wealth effects, though it would leave untouched CBA's other problems relative to WBA, such as affective forecasting errors. And using average WTP also has other limitations. First, the population of people affected by some potential government action may not be "average." For instance, imagine a project that would produce cleaner skies over Los Angeles. CBA would run into significant problems if it attempted to gauge the value of this project by surveying a representative sample of all Americans or even of all Californians regarding their WTP for improved air quality. Many of the surveyed individuals would live in areas that already have clean air, and would thus value a project to improve air quality less than a typical Angeleno. Consequently, a survey that sampled all Americans or all Californians would understate the benefits of cleaner skies in Los Angeles in particular.

Second, average WTP values provide no information as to *where* a potential project should be sited when there are multiple possibilities that might affect different populations of people. More generally, they are not useful in deciding between similar projects that affect different populations. The only workable approach in such a situation is to evaluate the actual effect of the project on the different groups, a task that cannot be accomplished using average WTP values.

As we described in the previous section, WBA avoids the problems caused by wealth effects because it does not require translating costs and benefits into dollars. By relying directly on self-evaluations of well-being, WBA simply sidesteps the biases and errors that are introduced when individuals are asked to price nonmonetary goods. To be certain, WBA requires aggregating interpersonal welfare states, and there is no guarantee that each individual is reporting her welfare identically on any given scale. Yet there is no reason to believe that these self-reports will be systematically biased in any given direction, and differences should wash out over large sample sizes, as we explained in the previous chapter. The same cannot be said for wealth effects and CBA, because differences in wealth *are* systematically biased to yield differences in WTP that have nothing to do with differences in welfare.

Willingness-to-pay measures and WBA: A summary

What all this means is that CBA will have great difficulties in pricing costs and benefits via either revealed-preference or contingent-valuation studies. This is significant because the pricing of nonmonetary goods is essential—even central—to CBA. Many government regulations and projects will produce some nonmonetary benefits and costs, and in many cases the nonmonetary benefits (reducing risks to life, in particular) form the entire basis for the regulation. Accordingly, the difficulties inherent in converting costs and benefits to dollars that we describe here will necessarily limit the accuracy and usefulness of CBA as a welfarist decision procedure.

WBA, by contrast, has no such problem. Instead of trying to isolate the amount of money that some individual might demand in return for accepting a low-probability risk to her life, or might hypothetically be willing to pay for some uncertain benefit, WBA simply adds up the positive experiences of life that individuals stand to lose or gain under a given project. For instance, to evaluate a regulation that reduces the risk of death from some workplace safety hazard, WBA would aggregate the positive experiences that would be lost if an individual were to die early[57] and then multiply that total by the odds of early death. After multiplying the resulting number by the number of people affected by a proposed regulation, regulators would then compare it with whatever diminution in positivity may be associated with enacting the regulation (due to increased consumer costs or some other factor).

To be sure, WBA's process is imperfect in practice. It relies on self-reports as proxies for well-being, because science cannot provide a perfect hedonimeter.[58] That proxy is better than CBA's analogous proxy of WTP, but it is still not the same as well-being itself. Moreover, WBA relies on estimates of likely outcomes, and it provides only a window into expected human well-being without resolving how to weigh that against other potential values. But relying on estimated outcomes is as much a feature of CBA or anything else as it is of WBA: no one can predict the future with certainty. Similarly, CBA like WBA is merely a gauge of human welfare that does not resolve or factor in welfare-unrelated considerations. The only problem specific to WBA is its reliance on self-reports as proxies, but that imperfection is outweighed by the analogous one of CBA, which uses proxies such as the wage premium that are far more removed from actual well-being.

Wealth and welfare

Before we proceed, we must pause to consider an entirely separate line of argument that defenders of CBA might offer. The argument is that WBA is fundamentally misguided *precisely because* it attempts to measure welfare directly, rather than wealth. In so doing, WBA will naturally capture distributional effects: movements of money from wealthier individuals to poorer individuals will increase welfare and be judged favorably by WBA, whereas CBA would view them as neutral. In the preceding pages we have treated this as an advantage of WBA. After all, if the goal is to improve welfare, it makes sense to measure welfare: as Cass Sunstein has said, "There is no plausible argument that WTP [willingness to pay] is important in itself. If policymakers should attend to it, it is because of its connection to welfare."[59] But defenders of CBA might instead cast WBA's focus on welfare as a disadvantage. This argument has several related strands, which we describe and address in turn.

We begin with the most fundamental and conceptual critique. Some defenders of CBA might argue that it should not be concerned with welfare at all, only with wealth and efficiency.[60] CBA, by using monetary values, will lead to a maximization of aggregate wealth, which in turn will maximize individuals' ability to purchase and use goods and services (that is, their consumption). Many economists believe that welfare increases linearly with consumption.[61] If this is the case, then maximizing consumption would maximize welfare as well. If there are distributional concerns that implicate welfare, those can be addressed subsequently through the tax system. Economists generally believe that it is more efficient to allocate resources via taxes and transfers than through regulations and new policy proposals.[62] Accordingly, agencies should concentrate on maximizing aggregate consumption, and welfare and distributional concerns should be left to the tax system. If agencies were to switch to a welfarist decision procedure such as WBA, they would be measuring the wrong quantity.

Another way of describing this critique of WBA would be to say that CBA will lead to outcomes that are Kaldor-Hicks efficient, while WBA may not.[63] A Kaldor-Hicks efficient outcome is one in which the parties that benefit from a project "could fully compensate those who stand to lose from it and still be better off."[64] Or, put another way, a project is Kaldor-Hicks efficient if it is possible to make a transfer of wealth that would leave all parties better off than before the project was implemented.[65] For instance, in the toxic waste example we used above, the government could locate the waste dump in the poorer area, and then, using the tax system, transfer $25,000 from each of the rich individuals to the poorer individuals, leaving each better off than before the project was begun.

We believe that this critique is incorrect for a number of reasons. First of all, there are strong reasons to believe that CBA will not lead to decisions that maximize the value of consumption or are Kaldor-Hicks optimal. The reason is that the prices CBA must rely on are likely to be highly inaccurate, in the sense that they deviate from what individuals would actually be willing to pay or accept under conditions of better information.

For instance, imagine that a workplace safety regulation could save ten lives at a cost of $100 million. If the value of a statistical life (VSL), based on wage-risk studies, is $7 million, then the regulation will not be cost-benefit justified, and the agency will not promulgate it. But what if that VSL is far too low because of individuals' affective forecasting errors? If the true VSL—what individuals would be willing to pay if they could accurately anticipate their own future welfare—were much higher, then the agency's failure to promulgate the regulation will decrease welfare. This is entirely apart from whether any compensating transfer takes place. Conversely, imagine a workplace safety regulation that will prevent ten workers from each losing a finger but cost $3 million. If workers have indicated a willingness to pay $500,000 to avoid losing a statistical finger, then CBA would favor promulgating this regulation. But what if that figure is far too high, because workers are failing to anticipate their own adaptation? (Or far too low, because the workers fail to anticipate how little the extra money will impact their happiness?) Workers acting under full information, including knowledge of their own adaptation, might be willing to pay only $100,000 to save a statistical finger. If that is the case, then this regulation will similarly decrease welfare, again irrespective of whether any compensating transfer takes place.

The entire premise of our argument for WBA is that these types of individual forecasting and prediction errors are commonplace and systematic, not merely random or occasional. Over the past decade, hedonic psychology has provided abundant evidence in support of this point. If we are correct, then CBA will lead to welfare-diminishing results regardless of whether the tax system is properly distributing wealth. CBA will not even lead to proper determinations of efficiency when the prices it relies on are distorted.

In addition, the argument that CBA is justified because it leads to Kaldor-Hicks efficient outcomes rests upon a tenuous assumption: that the tax system actually will be used to transfer wealth appropriately. Absent such a transfer, a project that is Kaldor-Hicks efficient could well lead to a decrease in welfare, as the toxic waste dump example above demonstrates. This is why even some of CBA's most sophisticated defenders have acknowledged that "Kaldor-Hicks efficiency has zero moral relevance."[66] It is of course difficult to speculate as to whether these welfare-enhancing compensating transfers will occur in a meaningful fraction of cases, and little reliable data exists. But there is every reason to believe that they will be rare, not least of all because they involve redistributions from politically powerful groups and individuals (the wealthy) to groups and individuals with much less political power (the poor).[67]

All this is to say that WBA really involves two separate improvements over CBA. The first is that it uses hedonic studies, rather than WTP or contingent valuation studies, to measure the true value of goods and lives more accurately than CBA can. The second is that it measures changes in welfare, rather than in efficiency or wealth, by assessing costs and benefits in well-being units (WBUs) rather than dollars. We believe that agencies that rely more heavily on WBA and less heavily on CBA will produce greater welfare gains over time. We are skeptical that the tax system will succeed in making the transfers necessary to turn efficiency gains into welfare gains. Of course, it is possible that we are wrong, and the tax system will be highly effective at making welfare-enhancing transfers. But even if we are wrong (and we doubt that we are), the use of hedonic studies instead of WTP and contingent valuation studies still constitutes a marked improvement over CBA. Agencies and policymakers should continue to employ hedonic studies—in effect, performing WBA—even if they later translate the results back into dollars in the pursuit of efficiency.

A second, more practical criticism within this line of argument might be that if agencies can generate aggregate well-being gains by redistributing wealth, they will spend all their time redistributing wealth to the exclusion of other projects and regulations that could lead to greater overall improvements in welfare. For example, the EPA might spend all its energy transferring wealth from rich to poor, rather than regulating hazardous chemicals. Yet this is just a criticism of agenda-setting. Agencies do not have open-ended mandates to act in the public interest; they have authority over specific regulatory domains and types of activities. Congress and the president could simply order the EPA to engage in well-being-justified environmental regulation, or to ignore distributional consequences, and then separately promulgate a welfare-enhancing tax code if they believed that to be appropriate. This is, of course, essentially the current governmental division of labor. There is no reason to believe that WBA would be an open invitation for agencies to disregard their regulatory missions.

Finally, CBA's defenders might offer an even more limited variation on the themes of these arguments. Although CBA will occasionally support projects that diminish welfare, WBA could equally favor projects that diminish wealth. To take the simplest possible example, a project that causes a wealthy individual to lose $1,100 and a poor individual to gain $1,000 would pass a WBA test (because it would increase welfare), just as it would fail a CBA test. Over time, defenders of CBA might say, single-minded use of WBA would lead to a diminution in national (or worldwide) wealth, with long-term negative consequences. For instance, a welfare-enhancing but wealth-diminishing project might be so expensive that the government would later be unable to implement an additional (superior) welfare-enhancing project, leading to the loss of future welfare gains.[68]

This argument is correct so far as it goes, though it hardly offers a reason to prefer CBA to WBA. A methodology that can lead directly to welfare-diminishing results (CBA) is not uniformly preferable to one that might conceivably lead indirectly to welfare-diminishing results at some point in the indefinite future (WBA). Nevertheless, it is because of the strength of this argument that we see potential value in CBA as a complement to WBA. Although we have argued that WBA could replace CBA in the current role that CBA plays, it does not necessarily follow that CBA should be left with no role at all.[69]

A full specification of how an agency might decide among competing projects when CBA and WBA disagree, as they often will, is beyond the scope of this project. But we can offer a brief sketch. It would be a mistake for an agency to promulgate a regulation that fails a WBA test even if it passes a CBA test, for that regulation will likely decrease welfare.[70] On the other hand, a regulation that barely passes a WBA test and drastically fails a CBA test may be undesirable as well. For regulations that pass WBA but fail CBA, agencies should scrutinize the ratio of net WBUs gained to net dollars lost. When that ratio is very low—small welfare gains at the expense of significant decreases in wealth—the agency generally should not promulgate the regulation on welfarist grounds, because of the possible indirect harm to welfare of wasting dollars that could more efficiently increase welfare by being spent otherwise either now or later. One potential way in which agencies could determine which ratios are too low might be to examine these ratios across large numbers of regulations, past and present, to determine how a given regulation compares with historical precedent.

Needless to say, when WBA and CBA conflict we favor placing greater weight on WBA for the many reasons set forth in this chapter. But we are not unmindful of the valuable role that CBA could play as a complement to WBA.

WBA and the Value of Lives

When a regulation would save lives, the value of those lives must be assessed so that the value of saving them can be compared with the costs necessary to do so.[71] In the first section of this chapter, we discussed the basic mechanisms by which CBA determines the value of a life. We now explore the many subtleties that those mechanisms ignore and the ways in which WBA accounts for those subtleties.

For CBA, every death is typically counted as equivalent to every other death; and although many within the CBA community have suggested ways to address this problem, some of their most important suggestions have rarely been implemented and would constitute only partial solutions anyway.[72] As CBA is currently conducted, a slow, painful death can be equated with a quick death in one's sleep. The deaths caused by a terrorist attack can be equated with those that occur in skiing accidents. And the death of a twelve-year-old is typically deemed to diminish overall welfare no more than the death of a ninety-year-old.[73] Moreover, CBA often counts all lives equivalently—*not* on supportable moral grounds but on insupportable welfarist grounds—such that a life with a debilitating but nonfatal disease is said to have as much welfare as a life with perfect health. The problem with all these equivalencies is that such differences affect overall welfare, and CBA's stated purpose (like that of WBA) is to measure overall welfare. Because WBA accounts for the actual effects on welfare of different types of life-saving regulations, it measures the benefit side of the ledger more accurately than does CBA.

To be sure, CBA has means at its disposal of trying to address these problems, and it actually employs some of them. For example, it can ask people how much money they would pay to avoid certain sorts of risk to life rather than other sorts of risk to life. But that approach has the core limitation shared by everything based on WTP: it focuses on people's unreliable predictions of how certain risks would affect them, rather than on direct measurements of how those risks do affect them. WBA solves this problem, as we discuss below.

In the section "CBA's Attempted Improvements" below, we discuss CBA's capacity to address the problem of equating all lives notwithstanding their differences in length and quality. First, though, we turn to the issue of equating types of death.

Not all types of death are equivalent

When policymakers consider whether a proposed health and safety regulation is worth its cost, the standard cost-benefit approach is to consider how many lives are actually likely to be saved.[74] This approach, which differentiates among risks only in the quantitative terms of their likelihood and magnitude, is widely favored by proponents of CBA.[75] Indeed, those proponents treat this approach as a strength precisely because it elevates true dangerousness over public misperceptions thereof.

Critics of CBA, however, have attacked this approach by pointing out the degree to which it is at odds with people's actual views of risk and actual preferences toward regulation.[76] For example, a CBA analysis by Robert Hahn in 1996 indicated that the number of lives likely to be saved by increased airline security was far too low to justify the expense.[77] Of course, this analysis did not foresee the attacks of September 11, 2001; but the more interesting issue surrounds what the analysis would have concluded if it had foreseen those attacks. As Frank Ackerman and Lisa Heinzerling note, the number of people (about 3,000) who died on September 11 is dwarfed by the number who die from many other causes that are potential subjects of regulation.[78] Hahn's study itself suggests that "side impact standards for automobiles and cabin fire protection in aircraft," which are "two-hundred times more cost-effective" than pro-

posals for safeguarding airplanes from terrorism, may well have been favored by CBA under any circumstances.[79] For critics, this demonstrates
CBA's inadequacy.[80]

It seems very likely that most Americans would prefer to have
thwarted the 9/11 attacks even if doing so had required public expenditures that could have saved lives more efficiently if directed elsewhere.
Such a preference would accord with other findings about the way people
perceive risk.[81] Rather than focusing only on the likelihood and magnitude of harm, they also consider the nature of the risk.[82] "When a hazard
is unfamiliar, uncontrollable, involuntary, inequitable, dangerous to future generations, irreversible, man-made, and/or catastrophic, ordinary
people are likely to view it as risky,"[83] whereas "a hazard that is familiar,
controllable, voluntary, equitable, dangerous only to the present generation, reversible, natural, and/or diffusely harmful is unlikely to generate
much concern in the populace."[84] These views raise important questions
about how to regulate public health and safety. Many regulatory matters
such as those involving nuclear power and toxic waste would be resolved
one way via CBA and a very different way via the views of the public.[85]

What WBA adds to the picture is a way of counting the crucial fact
that people's *feelings* about risk—not just the statistical probability of the
risk—affect their well-being.[86] Although the fact that a risk is "dreaded"
does not make that risk any likelier, "[p]rolonged exposure to dreaded
risks frequently leads to deep and widespread anxiety, depression, and
distrust."[87] In cataloging these effects, one scholar has noted the anger,
confusion, and fear produced by the risks,[88] as well as their harmful effects on couples[89] and children.[90] Another scholar has written at length
about the "trauma" imposed by dreaded risks.[91] Yet another scholar focuses on the breakdown of trust that those risks tend to cause.[92]

Anxiety, depression, and distrust can diminish well-being substantially, and these tangible effects on people clearly must be counted by
any tool that aims to measure well-being. Indeed, even Hahn's CBA
study that argued against airplane antiterrorism measures acknowledged the possibility that people might "benefit psychologically" from
such measures.[93] That study further acknowledged, "It may be that people are willing to pay large sums to feel safer," but it concluded that "absent concrete research supporting this assertion, the money would be far
better spent" elsewhere.[94]

WBA supplies such concrete research. In contrast to studies like
Hahn's, WBA can be used to forecast the effects of regulation on peo-

ple's well-being. By using hedonic data from communities that have been subjected to the relevant risks, WBA captures the harms that CBA has been so extensively criticized for missing. The reason that people's qualitative judgments of risks matter is that those judgments themselves influence, sometimes profoundly, people's experience of life. Such influence is the thing that WBA exists to measure.

It is essential to note that WBA does not ignore the actual likelihood and magnitude of harm on which CBA focuses. Actual deaths, of course, eliminate well-being and are thus profoundly weighted in any WBA calculus. This is especially significant because the harshest critics of CBA, in pushing for a more democratic approach to risk assessment, can be insufficiently sensitive to quantitative measures. Hazards that are "familiar," "equitable," and "natural"[95] still ought to be taken very seriously if they are likely to kill many people. So WBA provides an appropriate mediating measure between the critics' focus on psychological triggers of risk and the lament of CBA's practitioners that the public is simply irrational.

CBA also chooses not to differentiate between quick deaths and slow, painful ones,[96] and this weakness of CBA reveals one of WBA's strengths. The primary reason that people hope to avoid painful deaths is, simply and obviously, that people dislike pain because it decreases their well-being. If we hold constant the time at which a person will die,[97] and contrast two different sets of "circumstances preceding death"[98] — one in which the person is in pain and miserable, and the other in which the person is pain-free and relatively happy—several things become clear: (1) the person is better off in the pain-free scenario, (2) the primary reason for this is that she feels better in the pain-free scenario, (3) the amount by which she is better off is the amount by which she feels better, multiplied by the amount of time during which she feels better, and (4) the better a tool of analysis takes account of these facts, the better it captures the likely effects of a policy on human well-being. WBA is designed precisely to account for these considerations. CBA ignores them in practice, and even in theory it could address such concerns only via proxies that are less reliable and less direct than those of WBA.

In addition, CBA counts death as a cost to the person who died,[99] but not as a cost to others who may be affected by that person's death. We mimicked that practice in our model WBA in the previous chapter, but in actual policymaking this is a mistake that should be corrected. WBA is well positioned to do so, because hedonic data already exist about the effect of people's deaths on those close to them.[100] By contrast, CBA would have to add this element by asking people how much money they would be willing to pay to avoid losing a loved one (or to avoid a risk to that person's life). Such an approach implicates all the problems with CBA we discuss throughout this chapter, such as wealth effects, theoretical questions, and people's difficulty in thinking about infinitesimally small numbers, among others. But the largest problem, as may always be the case with CBA, is that it requires people to guess the effect of something on their life in the future. How much welfare do people lose when their loved ones die? Instead of relying on what people predict the effect will be, along with their capacity to convert that effect into dollar figures, it is better to rely on measures of how such deaths actually affect people's happiness, as measured by their in-the-moment self-reports of happiness at various stages of time after the deaths. Hedonic studies measure precisely that.[101]

CBA's attempted improvements

When considering whether or not to regulate a risk to human health, CBA quantifies the value of that risk primarily by determining the number of lives likely to be saved by regulation and multiplying it by the statistical value of a human life. The value of a statistical life (VSL) is computed using the various methods described in the first section of this chapter. Accordingly, its reliability suffers from the methodological limits discussed above. In addition, CBA's use of statistical lives also has conceptual faults. When determining an average value for lives saved, VSL treats the lives saved by regulation indiscriminately. In doing so, VSL ignores essential data regarding both the length and the quality of the lives protected. Accordingly, a CBA that used VSL would underestimate the value of a regulation that prolonged life or improved the quality of life without "saving" it.[102]

Over the past several decades, scholars and policymakers have developed new tools to overcome VSL's limitations. This section discusses two such tools—"value of statistical life years" (VSLYs) and "quality-adjusted life years" (QALYs). The movement toward VSLYs and QALYs represents an acknowledgment of the limitations of traditional CBA methods. The inadequacy of equating all lives saved with one another is the impetus for moving beyond VSL. But VSLYs and QALYs are merely way stations on the road from CBA to WBA. They are efforts to bend

CBA to be more sensitive to the nuances it has been ignoring. But no such tweaks can solve the problem as comprehensively as can WBA.

When standard CBA is applied to regulations that seek to protect human health and welfare, policymakers calculate the benefits side of the equation by predicting the number of lives likely to be saved by the proposed regulation.[103] To compare the number of lives saved to the costs of the regulation (for example, in higher prices, unemployment, etc.), the value of those lives must be monetized. Thus, each life saved must be assigned a specific monetary value. CBA derives this value—known as VSL—by reference to the various techniques discussed in the first section of this chapter: revealed-preference and contingent-valuation studies.[104]

As we noted in the first section of this chapter, the techniques used to derive VSL have considerable methodological limitations. Perhaps more importantly, however, the conceptual relationship between VSL and the welfare-maximizing goals of regulation is deeply strained.[105] By focusing solely on lives saved, CBA's use of VSL entirely ignores data that are relevant to judging the value of regulation. For VSL, the length of the life saved is immaterial.[106] By ignoring longevity, CBA risks creating highly counterintuitive results. Imagine, for example, that the government has a finite supply of a vaccine for a deadly disease that has recently broken out, and it can provide that vaccine either to 100 children or 101 hospice patients. Under CBA, using the VSL approach, the government should prefer to give the drug to the hospice patients, because doing so would potentially save one additional life. We doubt, however, that anyone would suggest that giving the vaccine to the hospice patients increases overall welfare. After all, the benefit from the drug will likely prolong the lives of the hospice patients for only a few weeks, whereas the children might be expected to live for decades.

In response to these kinds of problems, scholars have suggested that regulators consider instead the number of "life-years" at issue.[107] Rather than relying simply on statistical lives, researchers should calculate the value of a statistical life year (VSLY), which involves dividing the VSL by the average life expectancy of the subjects of the studies.[108] VSLY has an estimated value of approximately $180,000.[109] Looking again at the vaccine example from the perspective of VSLY, the answer is obvious and intuitive: 100 children × 50 life-years per child × $180,000 = $90 million; 101 hospice patients × 0.1 life-years per patient × $180,000 = $1.8 million. By considering the number of life years saved by a regulation, the VSLY method offers a closer proxy for the actual welfare value at stake.[110]

Nonetheless, the VSLY approach has been criticized both for its lack of empirical support and for the potential outcomes that it generates.[111] These concerns are based on the claim that VSLY inappropriately undervalues the lives of older people. Empirically, in surveys of willingness to pay to avoid risk, there is mixed evidence about whether older people actually value risk less than younger people, as VSLY would suggest.[112] Although some studies show that willingness to pay to avoid risk declines with age, as one might expect, some show no difference, and others show the inverse.[113] According to Richard Revesz and Michael Livermore, the failure to observe a decrease in WTP should not be surprising in light of the typically higher wealth of older people and the greater scarcity of the limited years they have remaining.[114] In situations in which the data appear to diverge from the theory, however, it is just as possible that the data are misleading as that the theory is incorrect. There are a number of plausible explanations for the finding that older people are sometimes willing to pay more to avoid risk than younger people, and many of these explanations do not undermine the idea that saving more life-years saves more welfare. For example, as Revesz and Livermore note, older people typically have greater wealth than younger people do, and wealth is strongly correlated with increased WTP.[115] If the greater WTP on the part of older people is based on wealth, it should be treated as a confounding factor rather than evidence of welfare. Additionally, "older people have less to do with their money" and fewer other options for spending it, as saving is not a strong priority.[116] Further, when valuing goods and risks in contingent valuation studies, people often demonstrate significant "scope neglect." For instance, they are often willing to pay the same amount to save one thousand, ten thousand, or one hundred thousand birds from some type of hazard.[117] Plausibly, then, when forty-year-olds and seventy-year-olds are asked to value losing "the rest of your life" they may treat these different time periods similarly.

Opponents of VSLY also contend that it exacts a "senior death discount"[118] because it treats the lives of older people as less valuable than those of younger people. But we think this conflates welfare and separate moral considerations. Both CBA and WBA are concerned with welfare alone. In welfare terms, it is better to extend a person's life by ten years than to extend it by one year; and it follows that it is better (in welfare terms) to extend one person's life by ten years than to extend another person's life by one year. If moral considerations rule out choosing between people like that, then neither CBA nor WBA can be used. But if the question is what increases welfare, as it always is when CBA or WBA is involved, then we think there is no doubt that length of life should be factored in. Moreover, as Cass Sunstein has suggested, people placed behind a "veil of ignorance" would overwhelmingly favor regulations that save more life-years.[119] To the extent that one is trying to maximize welfare, it is better to save thirty-year-olds than eighty-year-olds.

We consider the VSLY approach to be a substantial improvement over the VSL technique traditionally favored by CBA. But although VSLY directs attention to welfare-relevant data overlooked by VSL, the life-years approach itself ignores a meaningful component of the value of risk regulation: the *quality* of the years saved. As with the VSL approach, this has the potential to create counterintuitive results. For example, the life-years approach would be indifferent between (1) a program that extended the lives of 100 people for ten years with those years spent in poor health, and (2) a program that extended the lives of 100 people for ten years with those years spent in excellent health. Despite people's capacity to adapt hedonically to certain types of poor health, there is almost certainly a greater welfare gain in the second program because poor health will almost always be associated with meaningful hedonic penalties.

To remedy this shortcoming, some scholars have recommended adopting quality-adjusted life years (QALYs) in CBA.[120] The QALY was initially developed in the related context of cost-effectiveness analysis (CEA) to provide data on the efficient use of scarce resources in medical decision-making.[121] Unlike the VSL- and VSLY-approaches, QALYs were not initially designed with respect to standard welfare theory,[122] but some commentators[123]—including courts[124] and agencies[125]—see value in the use of QALYs in CBA. As yet, however, QALY analysis faces a number of methodological hurdles before it can be successfully incorporated into CBA.[126]

QALY analysis requires researchers to determine the relative values of living in different health states. The goal is to arrange various health states along a quantitative, cardinal dimension in which 1.0 is equivalent to perfect health and 0 is death.[127] The quality-adjusted value of a health state is then multiplied by the number of life-years spent in that state to determine the QALY.[128] Thus, if a treatment option will extend a person's life by ten years but in less than full health (say, 0.7), it generates 7 QALYs. Such a treatment would be preferred over a treatment that extended a person's life by twelve years at worse health (say, 0.4 = 4.8 QALYs) or one that extended the person's life five years in full health (5 QALYs).

To generate values for the necessary quality adjustments, researchers rely on three principal survey techniques. In rating scale studies such as the EuroQOL 5-item scale, subjects are asked to compare health states that differ in a variety of dimensions, such as pain, mobility, and self-care.[129] In time trade-off studies, subjects are asked to choose between being in a state of poor health for a set period of time and being in full health for a shorter period.[130] In "standard gamble" studies, subjects choose between ill health for a period of time or a treatment that has a chance of restoring them to full health, and a chance of death.[131] Researchers then use the subjects' responses to calculate the relative value of, say, walking with a cane and being confined to a wheelchair.

The first difficulty with adopting QALY analysis as part of traditional CBA is determining how to monetize QALYs. When QALYs are used in CEA in health-care decision-making, no effort is made to quantify the value of a QALY. Instead, different programs may be compared to one another or a program may be compared to an arbitrary threshold.[132] This resistance to quantifying the value of health and life has likely played a role in making QALYs attractive to health-care professionals,[133] but it has done so at the cost of failing to provide a clear decision rule.[134] To provide such a rule, scholars have attempted to calculate a constant WTP-per-QALY figure that can be plugged into CBA. As yet, however, no clear number has been developed.[135] This difficulty may arise for some of the same reasons that calculating the value of a life-year is a problem, as we discussed above throughout this chapter.[136]

More problematic, however, is the method that researchers use to elicit QALY values. Just as contingent valuation studies suffer from having people attach monetary values to things like health and the environment that are difficult to think about and monetize, QALY studies often require healthy individuals to make value judgments about health states that they have never experienced. To be valuable in welfare analysis, QALYs should reflect how people feel *in* various states of health. Instead, when healthy people are asked about states of poor health, they will tend to provide answers about how they feel *about* those health states.[137] A rich empirical literature demonstrates individuals' inability to accurately assess the value of health states they have not experienced.[138] Healthy people regularly overestimate both the magnitude and the duration of the hedonic impact of many negative health states, including cancer, dialysis treatment, paralysis, and colostomy.[139] When asked to think about these negative health states, healthy people suffer from several cognitive and affective biases that hinder their judgment: they neglect the role of hedonic adaptation, they concentrate primarily on the transition from good to poor health, and their attention is focused on the health domain to the exclusion of other domains.[140] Thus, in time trade-off and standard gamble studies, healthy people are willing to give up significantly more remaining life than are current patients.[141] This results in biased QALY scores that overestimate the welfare losses from many health states.[142]

Although asking current or former patients to respond to these studies might help, it is unlikely to resolve all measurement issues. Time trade-off and standard gamble studies, like contingent-valuation and revealed-preference studies, rely on what Daniel Kahneman has called *decision utility*: subjects make judgments about the value of past or future states of the world. In addition to the prediction problems listed above, such studies also suffer from cognitive biases associated with recollection of past states. For example, colonoscopy patients have been shown to prefer longer, more painful procedures to shorter, less painful ones when the former ended with a period of diminished but still significant pain.[143] It is also possible that current and former patients who are adapting or have adapted to their conditions may neglect the pre-adaptation period during which their condition was causing substantial welfare losses.[144]

Our proposal to replace CBA with WBA is based on the ability of WBA to overcome CBA's limitations in measuring the value of life. WBA incorporates the valuable corrections offered by VSLYs and QALYs while avoiding their shortcomings. As we explained, CBA's preferred tool, VSL, provides a weak proxy for welfare because it neglects data about both the longevity and the quality of life. The VSLY and QALY approaches go some distance toward solving this problem, but they run into problems of their own.

The WBUs that we propose can be thought of as QALYs derived from experienced utility rather than decision utility. By using elicitation techniques that more or less directly measure subjective well-being, WBA can generate a more accurate measure of both the quantity and the quality of the value of life. Ecological-momentary assessment, day-reconstruction method, and life-satisfaction surveys provide data on the

lived experiences of people in a wide variety of states. Accordingly, they
can measure the value of a broader spectrum of experiences, including
not just health risk but also the impact on well-being of social, professional, and environmental factors. WBA is also more attuned to the importance of emotional well-being, including positive emotions, which are
almost entirely ignored by CBA.[145]

In addition to providing a more nuanced and accurate picture of the
quality of life, the techniques used by WBA avoid a number of the methodological problems faced by various versions of CBA. The cognitive biases that hinder contingent-valuation, revealed-preferences, and QALY
studies are substantially muted in WBA. Respondents are asked to answer only simple questions rating their current level of happiness. Such
questions do not require them to value nonmarket goods, make complex health trade-offs, or predict or remember different experiences. As
such, they are less susceptible to wealth effects, demand effects, framing effects, and affective forecasting errors. Unlike traditional CBA and
QALY analysis, which require people to make incredibly difficult judgments about the monetary or health value of things they have never experienced, WBA directly tracks people's experiences and the emotions
those experiences create.

Finally, because WBA does not attempt to translate experiences into
money, it avoids difficult problems associated with monetizing QALYs.
In WBA, the costs and benefits of proposed policies are hedonized, and
their impact on people's well-being is weighed. To the extent that a policy increases or decreases wealth, the effects of the changes in wealth
on welfare will be measured directly.[146] Moreover, in WBA the welfare
value of a year at a certain level of well-being is less likely to be altered
for welfare-irrelevant reasons by the effects of age or wealth than it is
with VSLs, VSLYs, and QALYs.

Discounting in CBA and WBA

One of the most intractable problems within CBA involves the choice
of a discount rate.[147] CBA is based on monetary values, and the value
of money is not constant across time.[148] A dollar is not worth the same
amount in 2014 as it was in 2004, much less in 1914. It is better to have
one dollar today than one dollar one year from today. In addition, governmental projects and regulations do not always produce benefits in

the same years as they generate costs.[149] For instance, a regulation that banned emphysema-causing chemicals in the workplace might create immediate costs—firms that used those chemicals would have to eliminate them immediately and find safer (and presumably more expensive) alternatives. But the benefits would arrive only several years later, because emphysema is a slow-onset disease that typically takes years to develop.[150] CBA would thus measure the costs of such a regulation in 2014 dollars, and the benefits in (for instance) 2024 dollars, which are less valuable. To make a true apples-to-apples comparison, the agency would then be forced to discount the 2021 benefits to present value—effectively determining what those 2024 benefits are worth in 2024 terms.

The mathematics behind such discounting is easy. What is difficult is determining the proper discount rate to use. That is, how much less is a benefit in 2014 worth than a benefit in 2013? Ten percent less? Seven percent? Five or three percent? The answer can have a significant impact on regulatory decisions. For instance, consider the question of how aggressively the United States should regulate to reduce greenhouse gas emissions. In 2009, the Obama administration convened a multiagency working group to determine how much harm was being done to the world economy by global warming on account of greenhouse gas emissions.[151] The working group calculated the cost to the world, for each ton of carbon dioxide emitted, in U.S. dollars.[152] Many of the harms from global warming will only occur 50 or even 100 years from now, and so it was necessary to discount those harms to present-day dollars. However, as is often the case, the agency could not settle on a single discount rate. Instead, it reported the cost of carbon emissions at three different discount rates: 2.5 percent, 3 percent, and 5 percent. The results are reported in table 3.1.

As is evident from table 3.1, the choice of discount rate has a tremendous effect on the estimate of harm. Halving the discount rate, from 5 percent to 2.5 percent, more than *septuples* the cost of each ton of carbon dioxide. This is because a cost or benefit that occurs in the distant future must be discounted heavily when translating it into 2014 dollars—

TABLE 3.1. **Worldwide cost of emitting one ton of carbon dioxide in 2011 at various discount rates**

Discount rate	5%	3%	2.5%
Cost	$4.90	$21.90	$35.70

Source: Masur & Posner, *Climate Regulation*, at 1580.

the value of the cost decreases 5 percent or 2.5 percent *per year*. Over several decades, small differences in the discount rate compound into substantial differences in overall costs. Accordingly, it is no exaggeration to say that the choice between a 2.5 percent discount rate and a 5 percent discount rate could determine whether the United States regulates greenhouse gas emissions fairly stringently or not at all.[153]

Why is it difficult for agencies and other decision-makers to select a discount rate? The reason is that there is no agreement about precisely why discounting is necessary; and even when there is agreement on the reasons for it, there is no agreement on what discount rate would be proper given the rationale behind discounting.

The predominant reason that future costs and benefits must be discounted is the "time value of money"—the fact that one dollar is not worth the same amount at every point in time. This is partly because of inflation: one dollar buys fewer goods and services in 2014 than it bought in 1914.[154] It is also because money can earn interest if it is saved, rather than spent. For instance, imagine a regulation that would require an expenditure of $10,000 in 2014 and yield $15,000 of benefits in 2024. Is this regulation worth enacting? One approach is to consider how much $15,000 is worth in 2024, compared with $10,000 in 2014. This would involve calculating the rate of inflation and determining which sum of money has more purchasing power in the given year. If this approach is correct, then the discount rate should be the long-term rate of inflation, which is approximately 2.4 percent.[155] Another approach is to ask how much the original $10,000 would be worth in 2024 if it were invested, instead of being spent on complying with the regulation.[156] If this approach is correct, then the discount rate should be the typical long-term rate of return on an investment of that size.[157] There is a great deal of disagreement regarding what that rate of return is, but most estimates place it at 7 percent.[158]

Thus, even when the discount rate is based purely on the time value of money, different approaches to calculating that value can produce widely divergent results. Many administrative agencies avoid this issue by refusing to decide between these approaches: they do CBA with both of them. For instance, the Office of Management and Budget recommends that agencies perform CBAs using both 3 percent and 7 percent discount rates.[159] Most agencies follow this advice, including the Occupational Safety and Health Administration and the EPA.[160] Yet the choice among those discount rates is often determinative of whether a regulation produces more benefits than costs.[161] Consider the emphysema example from the previous paragraph. At a 3 percent discount rate, the regulation would provide approximately $11,160 in benefits, discounted to their 2014 value.[162] But at a 7 percent discount rate, the regulation provides only $7,625 in benefits—far below the $10,000 in costs.[163]

CBA has no way to avoid these difficulties, but WBA does. Unlike money, well-being is time invariant. Five WBUs in 2024 are worth just as much in welfare terms as 5 WBUs in 2014. Indeed, the entire reason that the value of money varies over time is that the amount of well-being it can be used to purchase varies over time. Thus, there is no need to discount in order to accommodate the time-value of well-being. Many of the difficulties with discounting that force the EPA to report results at two different discount rates, and the interagency climate change working group to do so at three different rates, are simply irrelevant to WBA.

That is not to say that WBA will necessarily be able to avoid discounting entirely. We noted above that there is no agreement on precisely why (or whether) discounting should occur. In the preceding paragraphs, we described a leading theory: inflation and the possibility of investment interest alter the value of money over time. However, there are other candidate theories that are not so easily dealt with by WBA. For instance, it might be that individuals simply have pure time preferences for immediate gratification over later benefits.[164] Someone might prefer having 6 WBUs today and 5 WBUs tomorrow to the reverse. This could be driven by the fear that the individual will die before she is able to enjoy the more distant rewards, or it could simply be human impatience.[165] Alternatively, there might be some separate moral reason to privilege present welfare over future welfare (for example, a duty to one's own generation), or conceivably the reverse (a duty to future generations).[166]

We take no position on whether discounting is appropriate for any of these reasons, though we note that the case for doing so has hardly been conclusively established.[167] If discounting is appropriate, then WBA will have to include discounting as well. But for CBA, this discounting would be *above and beyond* any discounting that might be necessary as a result of inflation and interest rates. CBA would have two sets of problems to sort through. WBA simplifies the issue at least by half. And when it comes to such a thorny and yet potentially decisive problem as what discount rate to select, that constitutes progress.

*   *   *

For decades, cost-benefit analysis has been the primary tool by which policymakers analyze prospective laws and administrative regulations. Hundreds of millions of lives have been affected profoundly by the answers that CBA generates. All along, critics from within and without have pointed to the fact that CBA relies primarily on mechanisms—such as contingent valuation surveys (how much would you pay to avoid a risk of getting emphysema?) and wage premiums (how much more do dangerous jobs pay than safe ones?)—that have been demonstrated to yield unreliable and invalid data. But CBA persists because no rival account has emerged to replace it.

We offer well-being analysis as an alternative. WBA aims to measure how people actually experience their lives: what makes them happy and unhappy, and what they enjoy and dislike. Instead of introducing the distortions created by using money as a proxy for people's quality of life, WBA analyzes that quality directly. Psychological studies of hedonic well-being have yielded data that pass the same canonical tests of social science that CBA's studies fail. Those hedonic studies, which form the backbone of WBA, provide the same capability for numerical comparison of policy choices as does CBA. The difference is that WBA's answers avoid many of the pitfalls that plague CBA.

Although WBA is not meant to give a complete answer to the ultimate question of what policies should be chosen,[168] we think it improves upon CBA in playing a key role in the decision-making process: the role of assessing policies' effects on the quality of human life. That need not be the only consideration in making policy,[169] but it is at minimum an important one.

Scholars, regulators, and even heads of state have known for years of CBA's weaknesses. But they have felt compelled nonetheless to accept CBA on the ground that an attempt at rigorous comparison is preferable to the absence of any comparison at all. WBA offers a viable alternative. The question is not whether WBA is perfect—no tool of social policy is—but rather whether it constitutes an improvement on the status quo. We think the answer is yes.

PART II

Viewing Two Core Areas of the Law through the Lens of Hedonics

In part 1 of this book, we laid out a road map for applying hedonic data to policy and regulation. Well-being analysis (WBA) was the product of that attempt. But not all of law is made via regulation, and although certain areas of law incorporate explicit or implicit cost-benefit tests (such as Learned Hand's formula for tort negligence) there are many areas of law that do not.

We nonetheless believe that the insights of hedonic psychology can shed light on a broad spectrum of law, and that those insights may indeed offer reasons to rethink some of the most basic assumptions underlying our legal system. In that spirit, part 2 of this book considers the implications of some of the most important hedonic findings, including adaptation and the failure to predict it, for two core areas of the law—criminal law and tort law. It is beyond the scope of this book, one of the first to apply hedonics to law, to cover every major area of American law in great detail. Nonetheless, we hope that the discussions that follow will usefully illuminate the analytic value of examining law through a hedonic lens.

CHAPTER FOUR

Happiness and Punishment

If Alan murders Beth, then he might be imprisoned for thirty years. If instead Alan shoots at Beth and misses, then perhaps his sentence would be twenty years. If Alan does neither of those things but instead robs Beth on the street, then his sentence might be ten years. And if Alan instead burglarizes Beth's house, his sentence might be five years.

Why should Alan go to prison at all for committing those crimes? Perhaps imprisoning Alan will deter other people from doing what Alan did. The different sentence lengths might be part of this deterrence: if both robbery and murder received life imprisonment, then a robber would have no incentive not to murder the person he is robbing.

Alternatively, perhaps the reason for imprisoning Alan is simply that it would be wrong for him to get away with his misdeeds.[1] If so, then the different sentence lengths might reflect different levels of misdeed and appropriate retribution: Alan deserves to be punished more for murder than for robbery.

In either case, the punishment will not serve its purpose unless it is something that people dislike.[2] Suppose Alan were "punished" not by prison but by a series of pleasant massages and sumptuous meals. Such "punishments" would not deter others from doing what Alan did because people *enjoy* massages and tasty food: their happiness is increased by those things rather than decreased by them. Nor would the retribution that Alan deserves for his misdeeds be accomplished by such "punishments": indeed, they would make matters worse by rewarding him for those misdeeds.

Punishment isn't really punishment unless it does something to the criminal that people generally dislike—something that reduces their happiness. And although happiness reduction may not be the only goal of punishment, it is essential for both deterrence and retribution. For that reason, understanding punishment requires understanding (un)happiness. We need to know how punishment actually affects criminals: does it make them less happy, to what degree, and for how long?

At the heart of criminal law is the need to make the punishment fit the crime. At a minimum, punishments for much less serious crimes are supposed to be substantially milder than punishments for much more serious crimes. To know whether the system is working as it's supposed to, one must learn whether current punishments actually impose the variations in severity that they are assumed to impose. In this chapter, we show how hedonic data can reveal the answers.

In the examples above, as in real life, Alan goes to prison for more years if he commits a more serious crime than if he commits a less serious crime. Everyone assumes that this makes sense because it must be worse to go to prison for a longer time than for a shorter time. But how much worse is it actually? Happiness studies provide direct evidence for answering that question.

Before continuing, we would like to stress something about the project of applying hedonic studies to punishment—and more broadly about focusing on the fact that punishment imposes negative experience. Such a focus certainly does not embody an inhumane view of punishment. By saying that punishment involves imposing negativity, and that its goals cannot be achieved otherwise, we neither endorse such imposition nor argue for more of it. Indeed, hedonic studies are valuable in this context in part because they help guard against excessive impositions of negative experience and because they make people aware of and thus (it is hoped) sensitive to the suffering that offenders undergo, both during and after their incarcerations. To say that punishment need not be sensitive to the hedonic studies is to say that it need not concern itself with what the state is doing to these offenders and how that affects their well-being. Decreasing well-being through punishment may be justified, but to do so without concern for how much it is decreased would be callous.

Our aim in this chapter is to use recent psychological findings to describe more accurately the effects of punishment. In the first section, we analyze the findings and the studies that give rise to them. In the second section, we show how the findings are relevant to the utilitarian approach to punishment. And in the third section, we show how they are relevant to retributive and mixed approaches to punishment. In the last section, we offer some thoughts about the implications of these points for the criminal justice system.

The Hedonic Consequences of Punishment

This section explores the evidence from hedonic psychology on the two principal forms of punishment used in the United States: monetary fines and imprisonment.[3] Recent social scientific studies support the notion that criminals adapt to these punishments in a way that reduces the hedonic difference between a larger fine and a smaller one, as well as the difference between a longer prison term and a shorter one. Yet while offenders are likely to adapt to paying fines and spending time in prison, other research has shown that incarceration substantially affects former inmates for many years following prison. People who have spent any time in prison are significantly more likely to experience chronic, stress-related health impairments, unemployment, and the breakdown of psychologically vital social ties. These post-prison consequences of incarceration are likely to generate substantial and long-lasting hedonic penalties for ex-inmates regardless of the lengths of their sentences.

Adaptation to economic loss

Perhaps hedonic psychology's only finding more important—and more counterintuitive—than adaptation to disability is its consistent evidence of the limited hedonic impact of changes in income. Since the economist Richard Easterlin first proposed his "paradox" about the lack of correlation between income and happiness,[4] numerous studies have supported the idea that, except below the level of subsistence, increased income produces only very modest gains in subjective well-being.[5] A variety of explanations for this phenomenon have emerged, ranging from constantly rising aspiration levels[6] to altered social comparisons,[7] but the message is clear: money can't buy happiness. This point is not undercut by recent scholarship indicating a correlation between money and life satisfaction at all income levels.[8] That scholarship demonstrates that even though the correlation between money and satisfaction is persistent, it is extremely weak: once an individual's income reaches even a modest level, vast changes in wealth are required to alter her life satisfaction by even a very small amount.

But can losing money make you less happy? There is less research on the hedonic impact of economic losses, but what does exist suggests that people adapt to losses much as they do gains.[9] Ed Diener and his colleagues tracked people who lost at least half a standard deviation of their annual income in a longitudinal study over a period of nine years.[10] These people were no less happy than those whose incomes increased or remained the same during the period. In another study, subjects who lost a \$3 gamble had returned very close to pregamble happiness levels in only ten minutes.[11] Although these amounts and time periods are very small, the authors extrapolate to more substantial sums.

As we will explore later, studies such as these may have implications for the imposition of monetary penalties on criminal offenders. This is not to say that all losses of money are equivalent. First, if a fine is imposed on a criminal below the poverty line or if the size of a fine decreases the criminal's income below the poverty line (where income and happiness are more strongly correlated) the hedonic effect of the fine may be greater. Certainly, a fine that bankrupts a previously wealthy criminal can be expected to produce a significant hedonic penalty (although perhaps still less than might typically be assumed). Additionally, criminals may react differently to fines than workers do to reductions in income. But near-complete adaptation in the latter context likely implies at least meaningful adaptation in the former. Although criminal fines will likely cause immediate decreases in offenders' well-being, their effects will probably be smaller and of shorter duration than one might expect by failing to anticipate adaptation.

Adaptation to imprisonment

Monetary fines are regularly used as punishment in the United States, but imprisonment serves as the "linchpin" of the nation's response to crime,[12] and understanding its effects on offenders is essential. Social scientific interest in prisoners' responses to incarceration began in the 1950s following Donald Clemmer's theory of "prisonization," which predicted the steady deterioration in prisoners' physical and psychological health over the course of a sentence.[13] More recently, however, these findings have been challenged by evidence that prisoners rapidly adapt to incarceration.[14] Consistent with evidence of adaptation in other domains, incarceration appears to result in substantial psychological distress on initial imprisonment, followed by gains in well-being as the prison term progresses.[15]

An early cross-sectional study compared inmates who had served one year of a long-term sentence with those who had served about a decade of such a sentence.[16] The recently incarcerated offenders exhibited significantly higher levels of self-reported anxiety, depression, and psychosomatic illnesses than the longer-serving inmates.[17] According to the authors,

> These results suggest that the early period of incarceration is particularly stressful for long-term offenders as they make the transition from the outside world to institutional life. No evidence supports the notion of psychological deterioration over time. Instead, with more time served, long termers appear to develop strategies for coping with prison.[18]

Cross-sectional studies can suffer from intergroup comparison problems, but the evidence for adaptation to prison has been bolstered by longitudinal studies tracking inmates across prison terms.[19] One such study surveyed a group of prisoners regularly over seven years. As in the cross-sectional studies, the researchers found that prisoners interviewed in their first month of incarceration showed alarmingly high levels of negative affect associated with depression and anxiety.[20] Within a few months, however, the prisoners' self-reported mental health had improved substantially, with reports of depression and anxiety falling by nearly one-third.[21] A year later, reports of negative affect fell further but were still higher than in a random sample of released inmates.[22] Interviews conducted six years later revealed additional decreases in negative affect and improvements of positive affect such that, on at least one scale, prisoners' reports fell within the normal range.[23]

From these studies a pattern of hedonic response to imprisonment emerges. Initial entry into the prison environment triggers significant psychological distress and low levels of well-being. Within weeks, however, inmates develop coping mechanisms that enable them to adjust to their situations and improve their well-being.[24] After this initial period of substantial adjustment, offenders' well-being appears to improve more moderately throughout the remainder of their terms.[25] Thus, the "pains of imprisonment"[26] are felt immediately, with diminishing hedonic penalties over the remainder of the sentence.

The long-term effects of prison on well-being

Whereas being in prison may be less uniformly harmful than expected because some of its features lend themselves to adaptation, *having been in prison* for any length of time may be more harmful than expected because some highly negative features of post-prison life resist adaptation. Researchers have discovered that any amount of incarceration creates a significantly higher likelihood that ex-inmates will suffer a variety of health-related, economic, and social harms with substantial negative hedonic consequences. These harms are also particularly difficult for individuals to adapt to.

Until very recently, it was widely believed that incarceration produced no direct, causal effects on ex-inmates' health, employment, and family lives.[27] Any correlation between imprisonment and poor health or job prospects was thought to be the result of selection effects; that is, the people who ended up in prison disproportionately came from groups with poor health and limited employment opportunities to begin with.[28] In the past few years, however, researchers have begun using longitudinal surveys to track offenders in the years before and after imprisonment in order to isolate the effects of imprisonment itself.[29]

Using data from the National Longitudinal Survey of Youth, Michael Massoglia has found that an ex-inmate is much more likely than the average person to report health problems associated with stress and communicable diseases.[30] Former inmates are more than twice as likely to report hepatitis C infections, HIV/AIDS, tuberculosis, and urinary tract infections.[31] Moreover, they report substantially higher levels of chronic headaches, sleeping problems, dizziness, and heart problems.[32] Considering the high incidence of prison sexual violence[33] and the many stressors associated with post-prison life,[34] these results should not be surprising. What is surprising, however, is evidence from Massoglia and others that the incidence and severity of these health problems are almost entirely unrelated to sentence length.[35] Incarceration for any length of time greater than twelve months exposes offenders to the full complement of negative postincarceration health outcomes. After twelve months, the marginal health effect of additional time in prison is negligible.[36]

Studies examining ex-inmates' employment prospects report similar findings.[37] Felony imprisonment results in social stigma, the erosion of job skills, and disqualification from stable government and union jobs.[38] Accordingly, former prisoners experience lower wages, slower wage growth, and, importantly, greater unemployment. According to Bruce Western, the average annual number of weeks ex-inmates worked dropped from thirty-five before imprisonment to twenty-three after,[39] and they tended to have much shorter job tenure.[40] Additionally, imprisonment was related to poor employment continuity for many years after release. After release, offenders are typically shunted into secondary labor markets with little job security, little opportunity for advancement, and miniscule earnings.[41]

Recent research also reveals that ex-inmates are more likely to experience substantial disruptions in their post-incarceration family and social lives.[42] Being in prison makes communication with family and friends difficult and cohabitation with spouses and children challenging.[43] Moreover, imprisonment likely hinders community integration, trust, and intimacy.[44] Accordingly, men who have spent time in prison are less likely to get married than similar men who have not, and they are more than twice as likely to get divorced as their never-incarcerated peers.[45]

As bad as these health, employment, and social consequences of imprisonment seem, there might be little reason to be concerned about them in light of human beings' uncanny ability to adapt hedonically. But as mentioned above, certain experiences appear to cause severe and long-lasting diminutions in well-being and resist adaptation. The hedonic effects of imprisonment—chronic and deteriorating illness, unemployment, and the loss of family and social ties—are all significant, and all have been found to be particularly resistant to adaptation.

The health problems to which imprisonment exposes inmates, including chronic headaches, hepatitis C infections, HIV/AIDS, and tuberculosis, significantly and consistently diminish self-reported quality of life in sufferers, even with treatment. Studies have found that people who become unemployed end up with lower baseline levels of happiness, and these decreases last even after they find new jobs.[46] Additionally, longer terms of unemployment result in more intense well-being penalties.[47]

Imprisonment's impact on ex-inmates' family and social lives could have especially severe consequences for well-being due to its multiple effects. First, the increased incidence of divorce will have direct effects on well-being, because adaptation to divorce is often slow and incomplete.[48] Additionally, strong social and family ties have been shown to encourage adaptation,[49] and the disruptions inflicted by incarceration could be deleterious to a prisoner's ability to adapt to other negative events.[50] Finally, a variety of learned behaviors that enable inmates to cope with the experience of incarceration—including mistrust, blunted emotions, and lack of planning—are likely to prove maladaptive "on the outside."[51] The ways in which people learn to deal with the physical and psychological trauma of imprisonment will prevent people from successfully returning to society.

We depict these effects in figure 4.1.

As figure 4.1 indicates, incarceration takes an immediate hedonic toll on the prisoner. After a few weeks or months, however, these significant initial effects on reported happiness may decrease as the prisoner adapts. By the end of the prison term, the prisoner is certainly not as well-off as he was before being incarcerated, but his situation has likely improved markedly from those first few weeks or months behind bars. The ex-inmate, no longer subject to many of the deprivations associated with being in prison, becomes happier still upon being released. But the lingering negative effects of imprisonment will likely prevent him from reaching the levels of well-being he enjoyed before his incarceration. Alone or in tandem, the ongoing negative health, employment, and social effects of having been imprisoned have severe consequences for life-long happiness.

Of course, the unadaptable negative features of post-prison life tend also to be features of prison life. Our point, though, is that life in prison is characterized not only by those problems but also by other problems

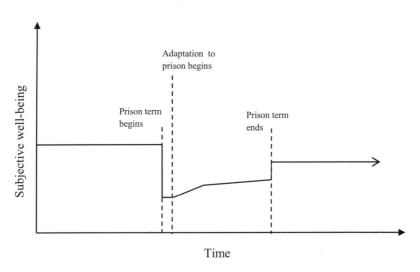

FIGURE 4.1. The prisoner's well-being over time.

that do admit of adaptation, as figure 4.1 indicates. We do not mean to downplay how bad it is to be in prison or to suggest that life after prison is no better than life in prison. Rather, the point is that that different time periods during a prison term are associated with different levels of negative experience felt by a criminal, and that the level of negative experience (due to the imprisonment) that is felt after release from prison is nonzero and probably substantial.

If the modern research in hedonic psychology is correct, it has significant implications for the theory and practice of punishment. Our criminal justice system tailors punishments to fit crimes by adjusting the size of fines and the length of prison sentences. If those adjustments do not affect the magnitude of the negative experience of punishment in a linear fashion, then the state would need to adjust its approach to sentencing in order to create the levels of imposed negative experience it intends. To be sure, the state has at its disposal ways to make a sentence more or less punitive and thereby perhaps to address some of these concerns. For example, the state has ways to make prison more or less tolerable, and there are also variously desirable forms of parole and community-service programs. Perhaps some criminal justice officers already use these tools to make punishments more fine-grained than they would otherwise be. That said, the criminal justice system still relies to a great degree on the size of fines and the duration of imprisonments to differentiate between one punishment and another. Our point is simply that this basic reliance may well not be producing the level of differentiation that it is probably assumed to produce.

The next two sections of this chapter elaborate the points above.

Adaptation and Asymmetry in Utilitarian Calculations of Punishment

At the start of this chapter, we wrote about Alan, who spends thirty years in prison for murdering Beth but only five years if he instead burglarizes her house. Perhaps Alan is punished to deter others from murdering or burglarizing. And perhaps Alan is punished less for burglary so that he has a reason not to murder Beth in the course of the burglary. Or perhaps Alan simply should not be harmed more than is necessary to deter others, and five years suffices to deter would-be burglars.

This sort of thinking comes from utilitarian punishment theory. Utilitarians want to increase the total sum of happiness, and although punishment harms criminals, it deters crime and thereby helps would-be victims. So utilitarians need to know the extent to which punishment decreases criminals' happiness. This is essential to the calculus, and of course it is precisely the information provided by the hedonic studies.

Utilitarians also need to know how punishment deters crime. Punishment deters crime because people believe it will decrease their happiness. But people mispredict how things will affect their happiness, so a punishment might deter more or less than its actual effects warrant. For a utilitarian, the best punishment is one that people *believe* to be worse than it is. This deters crime and saves would-be victims while minimizing the harm imposed on criminals. This is precisely how adaptation works: it makes punishments less harmful than people predict. And people continue to mispredict the harm even after experiencing the punishment. For utilitarians, this is good news.

Unfortunately, there is also bad news. When someone gets out of prison, he is much less happy than he was before he entered, and his happiness will never rebound fully. This makes him more likely to commit future crimes: getting caught will harm him less because he is already miserable. Suppose Jim believes that prison will reduce his happiness to a level of 4 out of 10. That prospect seems a lot scarier if he is currently at a level of 9 than if he is currently at a level of 6. The worse his life is, the more crime becomes worth the risk of getting caught.

In these ways, the hedonic data inform the utilitarian calculus and are of use to scholars and policymakers who focus on how punishment affects overall happiness.

Deterrence at reduced cost

If the state tortured people to death for committing even the smallest crimes, then there would be far less crime. Is that a good idea? Obviously not, even on utilitarian grounds: a utilitarian must weigh the positives of deterrence against the negatives of harming those who still commit crimes and are tortured as a result.

The goal of utilitarianism, in the words of its founder, Jeremy Bentham, is "to augment the total happiness of the community; and therefore, in the first place to exclude, as far as may be, every thing that tends to subtract from that happiness."[52] Utilitarians thus primarily want to achieve deterrence—to set punishment at a high enough level to dissuade potential offenders from committing crimes.[53] Other goals, such as rehabilitating criminals and incapacitating them from committing future crimes, are also utilitarian. But we will focus on deterrence because most utilitarians today identify it as their chief concern.[54]

Deterrence can be achieved by stiff punishments, but only at a cost.[55] Part of that cost is the public expense of detecting, trying, and imprisoning a criminal;[56] and part of it comes from removing individuals from the workforce and transferring them to comparatively unproductive confinement.[57] For present purposes, however, the most important component of these costs is the pain inflicted on the criminal. For a strict utilitarian, the criminal's welfare is part of the overall calculus: the utilitarian goal is to increase the overall welfare of society, and the criminal, despite his deviance from societal norms, remains a part of that society.[58] Therefore, one of punishment's costs, on a utilitarian calculus, is the amount by which it decreases the criminal's well-being.

Accordingly, increasing deterrence would seem to require increasing the harm to criminals, because that is what creates the deterrence. The greater the deterrent effect desired, the greater the necessary punishment. But as punishment (and consequently deterrence) increases, so too does the social price (i.e., the harm to the criminal) paid to purchase that deterrence. Utilitarian legislators who draft sentencing codes and utilitarian judges who impose sentences are thus forced to come to some sort of accommodation between the twin goals of achieving deterrence and avoiding too great a decrease in the criminal's well-being, and much of the struggle in setting appropriate levels of punishment revolves around this difficult question of balancing.[59]

This explains in part why no state should impose terrible penalties—including the death penalty—for very small crimes. There would certainly be far less crime. But a utilitarian must weigh the good of deterrence against the bad of harming those who still commit crimes and are tortured as a result. (Later in this chapter, we will discuss other reasons why such a scheme would be catastrophically bad.)

Utilitarian theorists have assumed that the deterrent "punch" of punishment was equal to the pain that punishment inflicted on an offender, and that therefore the deterrent effect could not be uncoupled from its cost.[60] Yet new evidence of hedonic adaptation casts doubt on this assumption.

As we discussed in the first section of this chapter, happiness data strongly suggest that people adapt over time to criminal punishment.

That is, a criminal's felt experience of punishment will likely become less negative over time: both the prisoner and the recipient of a fine will be happier one year after the punishment is imposed than one day after, even if the prisoner remains behind bars and irrespective of whether the fined criminal has recovered any of the lost funds.

Crucially, however, would-be criminals are unlikely to foresee this adaptation, even if they are repeat offenders who have been punished before.[61] So potential criminals will be just as deterred as they would be if they could not adapt, because they will not foresee the adaptation.[62] This lets punishment achieve its goal at lower cost.[63]

Is it really true, though, that criminals will not learn from their past experiences? Having once experienced punishment (and the attendant adaptation), won't the criminal understand that the initial shock of prison or a large fine will soon dissipate? Perhaps not, as we explained earlier.[64] People, as a general rule, do not remember their adaptive responses to negative stimuli.[65] They report their experiences to others as having been worse than they really were, and they do not draw on their experiences to make more accurate predictions the next time. Because they misreport their experience, the broader community does not learn of it. The consequence is that affective forecasting errors are remarkably consistent over time: having overestimated the harshness of prison or a fine once, people are likely to do so again, and to a similar degree.

Suppose, though, that recidivist criminals *are* able to anticipate their own adaptation, as a result of their past experiences with imprisonment. That could create a disconnect between policymakers' and criminals' respective assessments of the deterrent effect of punishment: criminals would learn from their experience, but policymakers would not because they never had the experience. Unless policymakers learned from the hedonic data, they would choose punishments that deter less than they expect because criminals, unlike them, would be factoring in adaptation. Thus adaptation affects the utilitarian calculus whether or not criminals foresee it. The effects differ depending on that variable, but either way they influence the way punishment works.

Life after prison

The previous section addressed how criminals adapt to fines or imprisonment. But the hedonic impact of prison does not end when the prisoner is released. A convicted felon feels the lingering after-effects of imprisonment in nearly every area of his life, from legal to social to economic. In many cases, these ongoing effects of imprisonment are hard to adapt to. Consequently, prison decreases happiness beyond the time an offender spends in prison itself.

The social and economic effects of having served time in prison can be extremely serious. As we outlined in the first section of this chapter, prisoners often witness the breakups of their marriages and relationships while in prison and have greater difficulty forming other relationships (including friendships) upon their release. They experience greater rates of unemployment. Ex-prisoners also suffer from more debilitating health problems and far higher rates of incurable diseases than the general population.[66] And as we described above, unlike the loss of money, these types of afflictions have severe long-term hedonic effects and are very difficult to adapt to. Measured by happiness, life after prison may resemble life *in* prison more than it resembles life *before* prison.

The negativity of post-prison life has two effects on the utilitarian calculus. First, it makes punishment more costly, because reducing criminals' happiness is a cost for utilitarians. Any cost-benefit analysis of punishment that terminates when the criminal is released from prison understates the negative effects that begin or endure after the prison term has finished.[67] And these negative effects do not accrue only to the former prisoner. Individual unemployment and social dislocation hurt others, too. The former prisoner often must be supported by state aid, cannot adequately support his family, and is more likely to commit further crimes.[68] These are, unquestionably, costs that a utilitarian calculus will want to include.

Second, post-prison harm may affect deterrence in several ways. One is that would-be criminals might factor that harm into their choices about crime, thereby increasing deterrence. Perhaps judges and legislators have been taking this into account all along, but there are indications that they have not. Although federal and state laws have occasionally acknowledged the difficulties of reintegrating criminals into society,[69] these efforts have been scattered and limited,[70] and the public record is otherwise devoid of indications that politicians are concerned about the lingering effects of prison on convicted criminals.[71] Moreover, no sentencing code directs judges to take account of the post hoc effects of the punishments they are considering.[72] Even if judges wished to account for the post-prison costs of imprisonment, they might thus be barred from doing so.

For potential offenders, the picture may not be quite so clear. Some scholars believe criminals discount the future so strongly that even increasing prison terms beyond ten or twenty years provides little additional deterrence.[73] On the other hand, at least one study has demonstrated that punitive measures that affect only life *after* prison—in this case, laws that force convicted sex offenders to notify local residents when they are released from prison[74]—have demonstrable effects on deterrence.[75] For at least one population of potential criminals, then, the post-prison effects of incarceration play a meaningful role in the decision of whether to commit a crime.

If would-be criminals take post-prison harm into account but judges do not, then judges would be systematically underestimating the deterrent effect of prison sentences. Judges thus may be overpunishing: they think, for instance, that a three-year sentence will be too short because they neglect the post-prison harm that potential criminals are factoring in. Legislators may be making the same mistake.

On the other hand, post-prison harm may *decrease* deterrence by reducing the baseline happiness of released inmates. When they contemplate whether to commit further crimes, they must weigh the hedonic consequences of prison against their devalued post-conviction lives, not their happier pre-prison lives. If potential offenders have less to lose by being sent to prison, then they will be more likely to select crime over law-abiding behavior. This, too, should be included in the utilitarian calculus. Utilitarian scholars may want to investigate whether the deterrent advantage of post-prison harm (i.e., that potential criminals will foresee it and be deterred by it) is larger or smaller than the deterrent disadvantage of that harm (i.e., that it reduces the baseline happiness of released inmates and thus gives them less to lose if they get caught while attempting to recidivate).

Finally, post-prison harms combine with adaptation to prison to reduce the disparity between different punishments. Suppose Alan commits murder, and Barbara commits burglary. They go to prison on the same day, and both of them see their happiness initially plummet but then soon rise as they adapt. After five years, Barbara gets out of prison, but Alan stays in. Barbara's life after prison is not as good as one might think, because she suffers from unadaptable post-prison harms. And Alan's continued life in prison is not as bad as one might think, because he has adapted to his circumstances. Even if Alan's life is still worse than

Barbara's, it may not be nearly as much worse as is commonly assumed. How do we know what is commonly assumed? Varying the length of a prison sentence is the primary way the penal system differentiates between punishments for major crimes like murder and burglary.[76] The penal system surely would not rely so heavily on this mechanism—to the exclusion of others—if the policymakers in charge of the system did not believe that the length of the prison sentence made a large difference.

This perceived difference between prison sentences of various lengths is essential to the criminal justice system. Among other reasons, the criminal justice system needs to punish murder far more than burglary if it is to achieve marginal deterrence.[77] For instance, if burglary, armed robbery, and murder were all punishable by life in prison, potential burglars might elect to commit the more serious crime of armed robbery instead, calculating that they have little to lose; similarly, burglars who were in danger of being apprehended might not hesitate to commit murder in order to escape. If potential offenders consider the post-prison effects of punishment when they decide whether to commit crimes (a plausible assumption), then the variation in deterrence among different punishments begins to erode. A one-year sentence is far more than half as severe as a two-year sentence, because a substantial part of the negativity associated with those punishments—the post-prison harm—will be equal for the two sentences. As punishments begin to appear more uniform to the potential criminal, the law's ability to achieve marginal deterrence begins to break down.

Although many scholars believe that criminals have extremely high discount rates—valuing the present far more than the future—economists remain divided as to why this is, and no fully satisfying explanation has yet emerged. The hedonic data suggest the possibility that some behavior previously explained through high discount rates may in fact be attributable to other causes. For example, offenders may be responding rationally to the front-loading of punishment in prison sentences, understanding that much of the hedonic cost of being imprisoned will accrue whether they are forced to serve two years or ten. (This would, however, apply only to first-time criminals; recidivists, having been imprisoned once, already will have been afflicted with most of the negative effects of having served time.) This idea is, of course, highly tentative, but it raises questions about prior assumptions regarding the level of information possessed by first-time offenders.

Of course, it is not news that convicted criminals face reduced opportunities—particularly economic ones—after release from prison and are more likely to opt for criminal activity as a result.[78] But the way this affects the goals of punishment and the sentencing calculus have not been sufficiently analyzed. The hedonic data can shed new light on this crucial issue.

Retributive and Mixed Theories

At the start of this chapter, we noted that deterrence is one, but not the only, possible goal of punishment. Another possible goal is simply to insure that criminals do not get away with their misdeeds, and this goal is based on the idea that criminals deserve punishment or that it would be wrong not to punish them. For some people, this retributive principle is the entire justification of punishment; whereas for others, it is a supplement to or a limitation on the pursuit of objectives like deterrence.[79]

Like deterrence-based theories, retributive theories rely on the fact that to "punish" means to impose something that people typically dislike. As we noted at the chapter's outset, someone who believes it morally wrong to let a murderer go unpunished will not be satisfied if the murderer's "punishment" is something pleasant and enjoyable like a massage. Nor would that satisfy someone who values punishment on the ground that punishment expresses societal condemnation. In order to fulfill whatever values that non-utilitarian theorists attribute to punishment, punishment must make criminals less happy.

Indeed, this is what all punishments do. Criminals have been punished for thousands of years, in every nation and culture, and virtually every such punishment has been something that decreases happiness. This, of course, is no mere coincidence. Any plausible theory of sanctions depends on this feature of punishment. Therefore, the hedonic data about punishment are as relevant to retributive and expressive theories as they are to deterrence. This section considers several leading theories from the non-utilitarian family and evaluates the extent to which those theories are affected by the behavioral insights about punishment detailed in the first section of this chapter.

Simple retributivism

A retributivist is "one who believes that the justification for punishing a criminal is simply that the criminal deserves to be punished."[80] The amount of punishment imposed must correspond to the offender's desert: "[R]etributivists at some point have to answer the 'how much' and 'what type' questions for punishments of specific offences and they are committed to the principle that punishment should be graded in proportion to desert."[81] In short, offenders must be punished; they must be punished only because they deserve it; and the amount of punishment must correspond to the wrongness of their acts.[82]

On this view, Alan deserves more punishment if he murders Beth than if he burgles her because murder is a more serious crime. Suppose Alan would spend thirty years in prison for the murder, and only five years in prison for the burglary. Does that difference between sentences reflect the different amounts of punishment Alan deserves for murder and for burglary? That depends on how much punishment those sentences entail, which in turn is linked very closely (if not entirely) to how much they each decrease happiness.[83] Suppose five years in prison decreased happiness *more* than thirty years in prison. Then the two respective punishments would clearly be unacceptable on retributive grounds because the burglar would be punished more than the murderer. And even if the thirty-year sentence decreased happiness more than the five-year sentence, but not much more, that too would presumably be a retributive failure. The two sentences are supposed to capture the difference in how much punishment each criminal deserves, and the difference is supposed to be large.

We are not insisting on an unrealistic level of detail in how much punishment is deserved. All we are saying is that the hedonic data are valuable whether one focuses on deterrence or retribution. Either way, when policymakers choose sentences, they can achieve their desired ends better the more accurately they understand how punishments are actually experienced.

Perhaps some judges and sentencing commission members already understand the hedonic data, although we see no evidence of this. At a minimum, many others may well be unaware of it or have yet to take it into consideration when crafting punishments. This matters: if a fine of $1,000 is thought to inflict a certain amount of harm, but it actually inflicts only half that harm because of hedonic adaptation, then such a fine does not achieve its retributive objective.[84] Understanding the effects of adaptation is valuable in crafting punishments on retributive grounds, not just utilitarian grounds.

Limiting retributivism

Both retributivism and utilitarianism have a profound influence on actual penal policy in the United States, and a prominent mixed theory of punishment reflects that reality. In this theory, known as "limiting retributivism"—which has been "adopted by most state guidelines systems"[85]—retributive considerations set upper and lower bounds on punishment,[86] but within those bounds the sentence is determined by utilitarian aims.[87] After thé bounds have been set by the offender's desert (measured principally by the severity of the crime), the specific punishment is chosen "not only [by reference to] traditional crime-control purposes such as deterrence, incapacitation, and rehabilitation, but also a concept known as parsimony—a preference for the least severe alternative that will achieve the purposes of the sentence."[88] Among other things, parsimony reflects the acknowledgment that punishment is expensive. If less punishment can achieve the desired end, then society gains monetarily by eschewing a more severe alternative (in particular, a longer prison sentence).

At first blush, it might seem that the effects of adaptation are somewhat less problematic for limiting retributivism than for pure retributivism. The mixed theory does not, after all, require that each offender receive the precise amount of punishment that corresponds to his level of desert. But hedonic data are relevant to both parts of the mixed theory (setting the bounds and fixing a specific punishment within them) for the same reasons that they are relevant, in turn, to both pure retributivism and pure utilitarianism.

Suppose Alan robs Beth. The state decrees that it would be wrong for Alan to receive less than one year in prison or more than three years in prison. Between those two extremes, practical considerations like deterrence will determine Alan's sentence. This is how limiting retributivism works. And every step of it will benefit from data that help reveal how punishment actually affects criminals. Consider the lower bound: one year in prison. The state chose that as the lower bound based on assumptions about what it's like to be locked up for a year. If those assumptions can be rendered more accurate by using hedonic studies to inform them, then the state can do better at choosing the punishments that best achieve its desired ends. For example, understanding that one year in prison will impose severe, unadaptable harms for the rest of Alan's life may well be relevant to whether it is the smallest punishment that he could deserve.[89]

The same sorts of considerations apply to the upper bound, and to the utilitarian choice between the bounds (as described in the second section of this chapter). For example, adaptation makes it easier for limiting retributivism to achieve one of its principal goals: parsimony. Because would-be offenders may overlook their own abilities to adapt, less punishment is needed to achieve the deterrent aim, thereby saving money and avoiding unnecessary (on this account) suffering. Just as adaptation affects the analysis of utilitarian theories of punishment, it affects the analysis of utilitarian elements within mixed theories.

Expressive theories

Some scholars believe that the state punishes criminals primarily for the sake of expressing or communicating condemnation.[90] As Dan Kahan wrote, "Punishment is *not* just a way to make offenders suffer; it is a special social convention that signifies moral condemnation."[91] Are hedonic data relevant to punishment on this account?

We believe the answer is yes. If Alan robs Beth, the state could simply *tell* Alan that his act is unacceptable. This would express and communicate condemnation. But instead the state supplements that statement with a punishment such as imprisonment, a monetary fine, or something else that people dislike. Why? For an expressivist, the answer is that punishment conveys the seriousness of the state's message.

We contend that punishment serves this expressive purpose precisely because it is unpleasant. The seriousness of the state's condemnatory message would not be conveyed by a massage, a sumptuous meal, or a Hawaiian vacation. It is conveyed instead by punishment because punishment reduces happiness.

To be sure, prison conveys condemnation even if a particular inmate enjoys it. Our point is that the *typical* experience of punishment must be negative in order for punishment to express or communicate condemnation. Moreover, the typical experience of a larger punishment must be worse than that of a smaller one in order for the intended relative messages of the two punishments to be conveyed. For the same reason, the typical experience of a punishment for murder must be *far* more negative than the typical experience of a punishment for burglary.

Hedonic data reveal the typical experience of punishment, providing highly useful information to expressivist scholars and policymakers. Admittedly, the message sent by punishment may depend on people's perceptions of the negative experience imposed rather than on the experience itself. But surely expressivists would not want the penal system to be grounded in a mistake. Reality, not just perception, matters. For example, torturing prisoners would not become acceptable if the public mistakenly believed the prisoners were enduring no pain.

It is thus unsurprising that retributivists widely share the view that imposing negative experience is the thing that expresses condemnation.[92] On the expressive view, then, both the theory and the practice of punishment are aided by hedonic data.

Counting post-prison effects

As we conclude our discussion of the various types of retributive theory, it is worth making a point applicable to virtually all of them. The harm that prison imposes *after* inmates have been released should, in many cases, be treated as part of the total retributivist punishment that the offender experiences. We have made this argument at length elsewhere,[93] and we summarize it here. When the state selects a punishment, it has many methods available to it.[94] The choice it makes may "determin[e] whether a duty to punish has been discharged or perhaps even violated."[95] When an individual is sentenced to prison, it is at minimum reasonably foreseeable to many of the state actors involved—prosecutors, judges, prison wardens, and even legislators—that the individual will suffer the panoply of harmful post-prison effects we have described.[96] This means that prison is a proximate cause of these post-prison harms, and that by electing to sentence the individual to prison, state actors are at minimum negligent in causing these effects. (We say "at minimum" because some state actors may well affirmatively know that former prisoners will suffer this set of post-prison effects.) Given the state's role in causing these negative post-prison effects and state actors' negligence (at least) in allowing them to occur, it is reasonable to treat the post-prison effects as part of the punishment the state is inflicting on the criminal.

For example, prison forces an offender to spend time out of the workforce, which decreases his earning potential when he returns.[97] His skills in the profession fade, and he is unable to keep up with new developments, making him less attractive than other potential employees. Although he may feel these effects only after he is released from prison, the manner of his punishment was a proximate cause of his loss of job skills, and state officials could at least have foreseen what would occur. We contend simply that these post-prison effects should be taken into account when assessing the severity of prison as a punishment.

And the effects of prison go far beyond lost earning power. As we described above, prisoners show a surprising ability to emotionally adapt such that each month or year in prison is generally less bad than the one before it. We noted, however, that this adaptation comes at a price upon release. The coping mechanisms that prisoners rely on to adapt to their conditions—distrusting others, keeping to themselves, emotional hostility when threatened—prove maladaptive on the outside when they return to normal life.[98] Surely it is fair to hold the state responsible for this irony of incarceration, because it created the prison conditions that caused the harmful emotional response.[99] If the psychological deprivations created by the prison environment result in ex-prisoners who are objectively less attractive employees, spouses, and friends, then the state cannot disclaim responsibility for the hardships they experience upon release by pointing to decisions made by others not to employ, marry, or befriend them. This situation is different from one in which ex-prisoners are less attractive as employees, spouses, and friends because of *the nature of their offense.* In such a case, these harms are not a consequence of punishment.

Given the research that we cite above, the psychological hardships experienced by former inmates are foreseeable, proximate effects of the nature of their punishment. In many instances, former inmates' unemployment and social isolation arise directly and predictably from the prison environment. Again, because the state selects from a spectrum of possible punishments, the state bears responsibility for its selection. It must account for the proximately caused harms that its choices impose on prisoners. If criminals continue to suffer in the years following their release from prison, then this physical and emotional pain adds to the severity of their sentences.[100] Failing to account for this additional suffering can lead to severe disproportionality in sentencing regimes.

What Should Be Done?

The purpose of this chapter is to describe certain effects of punishment and to note issues that they raise. It is not to provide solutions for those issues. We will simply offer a few tentative observations about the challenges that emerge from the hedonic data. Perhaps the most interesting inference to be drawn from the data is that altering the size of monetary fines and the duration of prison sentences may not alter the amount of harm imposed on criminals as much as it might seem to. If that is the case, then the penal system is not differentiating between punishments as much as it aims to. This is a concern for both retributive and utilitarian approaches to punishment, as explained above.

There are two ways to address that concern. One is to help prisoners reintegrate into society after their release and to otherwise try to improve their post-prison lives. Because post-prison harm does not vary by length of sentence (except for sentences shorter than one year), such harm is a major element that causes different sentences to impose similar unhappiness. In part, this solution could be accomplished by lessening the physical and psychological trauma of prison so that inmates do not have to engage in maladaptive coping mechanisms. Additionally, aspects of prison life that increase the spread of diseases, including overcrowding, poor health care, and rape, should be eliminated to diminish the post-imprisonment burden that ex-inmates face.

The other way to address the concern is much harder. It involves finding punishments that, unlike prison and fines, are likely to be hard to adapt to. There are certainly unadaptable conditions, but imposing them would strike many people (including us) as cruel. For example, the serious mental health effects of lengthy solitary confinement may be resistant to adaptation,[101] as is significant sleep deprivation. Subjecting prisoners to long periods of unpleasant noise could also be unadaptable. We emphatically do *not* support using any of these punishments. Instead, we mean to point out that they would combat the problem of adaptation—namely, that adaptation tends to decrease the range of different levels of imposed harm.

Focusing on adaptation thus helps reveal how people trade off the value of proportionality against the value of avoiding inhumane punishments. Even if the Constitution did not forbid cruel punishments, many people might not want to subject prisoners to unadaptable conditions like solitary confinement. Others might accept that in return for improving the proportionality of punishments.

Such choices venture far beyond our project in this book. We mean merely to highlight them and to note that the hedonic data are of great value in understanding how punishment works and in fashioning punishments to achieve whatever aims are sought.

*   *   *

Society punishes criminals by imposing negative experiences on them. Whatever goals the state seeks thereby to achieve, be they retributive or utilitarian, depend upon imposing negative experience in proportion to the severity of the crimes committed. To do so, the state should use the best evidence available for gauging the typical level of negativity associated with punishments such as fines and incarcerations. This includes foreseeable negative outcomes caused by these punishments, including the harm that lingers after inmates complete their time behind bars. Judges and legislators can thus benefit from the data on happiness when deciding how, and how much, to punish.

CHAPTER FIVE

Adaptation, Affective Forecasting, and Civil Litigation

Imagine that you are riding your bike one afternoon when the driver of a car parked in front of you suddenly opens her door right in your path. Unable to react in time, you crash into the door and are severely injured. Your injuries are so severe that you will be a paraplegic for the rest of your life. While you are in the hospital recovering, you will be able to initiate a lawsuit against the driver of the car to compensate you for your injuries, including your medical expenses, your lost wages, and your pain and suffering. In the course of the litigation, the driver (or her insurance company) might offer to settle the case with you for some amount of money. In order to determine whether to accept the settlement offer, you will naturally tend to consider the amount of money that will compensate you for the effects of your injuries on your life. This will further require you to make a prediction about the magnitude and duration of those effects in order to accurately assess the cost of your injuries.

If you are like most people, you will predict that the catastrophic nature of your injuries will result in intense and long-lasting unhappiness. But, again, if you are like most people, you will be wrong. As we explained in chapter 1, research in hedonic psychology has shown that people have a surprising ability to emotionally adapt to all kinds of life events. Among the most important and robust findings is the discovery that many positive and negative life experiences—including significant events such as winning the lottery, being denied tenure, and becoming disabled—have smaller long-term effects on well-being than people expect.[1] Immediately after experiencing these and other events, people initially show substantial changes in reported happiness, but in the weeks, months, and years that follow, they undergo a process of hedonic adaptation that moves them at least part-way in the direction of their pre-event level of well-being. This adaptation occurs, in part, because people tend to shift their attention away from the novel consequences of the event and back toward the mundane features of daily life. Interestingly, however, while individuals are able to adapt to many changes within a couple of years, other changes, it seems, tend to resist such adaptation—particularly injuries that cause constant or worsening pain.

As we also explained in chapter 1, although people often experience hedonic adaptation to major life events, researchers have found that people fail to recognize and remember adaptation's effects.[2] This failure then leads to an inability to predict the hedonic impact of future experiences. An overwhelming body of evidence now shows that when people are asked to predict how future changes are likely to affect their well-being, they make significant errors in their estimations of both the intensity of the change and its duration. Thus, healthy people tend to predict that becoming disabled will have a more substantial impact on their well-being and that the impact will last longer than it actually does. In effect, they neglect to account for the strength and speed of hedonic adaptation.

In this chapter, we apply this research on hedonic adaptation to the settlement of civil lawsuits—that is, situations in which the plaintiff and defendant agree to a compensatory dollar amount rather than going to trial. This is a particularly important subject, since so many lawsuits end in settlement. Specifically, we examine the likely effects of adaptation on a plaintiff seeking the recovery of pain and suffering in a personal injury suit. We suggest that such a plaintiff, when making her initial settlement demands shortly after her injury, will tend to overestimate both the severity and the duration of her injury. Her attention will be drawn toward the novel and painful features of the injury, and she will fail to recognize the extent to which hedonic adaptation will enable her to cope with her new circumstances. During the many months that she will have to wait before trial, she will begin to experience the effects of hedonic adaptation, lifting her perception of her own well-being, and, we suggest, making her more willing to settle for a lower sum.

This point is purely descriptive, *not* normative. We believe that adaptation may prompt certain plaintiffs to settle their lawsuits for less money than they would have if adaptation did not occur. Some may view this as a good thing, and others may view it as a bad thing. We take neither side in that dispute. Our point is simply that, for better or worse, it may well occur.

The first section of this chapter sets out the principal law and economics model of civil settlement as well as recent challenges to the model drawn from psychological research. In the second section, we apply the findings of hedonic psychology to the settlement of personal injury lawsuits, and in the last section, we offer a series of empirically testable predictions about such lawsuits and reflect on potential implications and objections.

The Factors That Drive Cases toward Settlement

Fewer than 2 percent of federal civil lawsuits go to trial,[3] but any case that does presents a puzzle: trials create costs that can be avoided if the parties agree to settle. Plaintiffs and defendants alike stand to gain from such a deal, so why would they ever choose to forgo it in favor of a trial?

If money is what motivates people, then settlement could be derailed only by things like hard-bargaining strategies or differences in the information possessed by the plaintiff and the defendant. But in recent years, scholars have turned their focus toward the possibility that people are motivated by things in addition to money alone. Other goals—principally, a desire for an outcome perceived as fair—influence a plaintiff's decision whether to settle. As a result, that decision may well be affected in turn by a plaintiff's changing perception over time of the sum that constitutes fair compensation.

This section surveys the development of the literature on settlement, describing the analytical framework we aim to augment via insights from the psychological literature on happiness.

The rational actor model of settlement decision-making

Since Charles Dickens wrote about *Jarndyce and Jarndyce* more than 150 years ago,[4] many others have bemoaned that litigating a civil case all the way through trial takes a long time.[5] Today, the median interval in federal court between filing and trial adjudication is about two years.[6] That period of time encompasses the filing of preliminary motions, the taking of discovery, the filing and adjudication of summary judgment motions, and finally the jury trial itself. Yet even that figure does not include the time that elapses after an injury has occurred and before filing, while the harmed party decides whether to pursue a legal remedy. When that decision is made and a lawyer is found, the lawyer must investigate whether the issue merits litigation.

Few cases continue through all the phases of litigation. A lawsuit can settle at any time from filing through adjudication, or it can be terminated by a grant of a motion to dismiss or a motion for summary judgment. The point is simply that when a case does not settle early, the steps it must take to wend its way through the litigation process to judgment take considerable time.

Along the way, lawyers will typically continue to engage in settlement negotiations with little or no involvement from the clients, who are not professional negotiators and whose involvement might therefore run contrary to their own interests. Even if these negotiations have not borne fruit by the time the pretrial litigation is nearing completion, a party still has much to gain by settling before trial. The expense of trial itself can be considerable or even, in some cases, vast. Much is to be saved, therefore, by avoiding trial even if the parties have failed to avoid the costs of pretrial litigation.

A settlement is possible, of course, only if the largest amount of money that a defendant is willing to pay exceeds the smallest amount of money that a plaintiff is willing to accept. In the early 1970s, William Landes and Richard Posner began to analyze settlement through the lens of law and economics.[7] Landes and Posner developed the core insight that the cost of litigating a case opens up a zone of bargaining within which the result for each party will be better than that party's expected outcome from litigating to trial. Specifically, a litigant will calculate the value (or cost, for a defendant) of a lawsuit by multiplying the expected damages by the probability of winning, then subtracting the cost of litigation.[8] If the litigants each come to a similar assessment of the value of the case, then they will settle, because doing so saves them the cost of litigation.

It is the introduction of litigation-related transaction costs that makes all the difference. For example, suppose a plaintiff sues for $100,000 in damages and has a 50 percent chance of winning on the merits at trial. Assume that litigating the case to adjudication would cost the plaintiff and defendant each $10,000. That would make the expected value of the litigation $40,000 for the plaintiff [($100,000 × 0.50) – $10,000 = $40,000]. Assuming that the defendant also expects the damages payment to equal

$100,000, the expected cost to it will be $60,000 [($100,000 × 0.50) + $10,000 = $60,000]. Any settlement between $40,000 and $60,000 would be better for both parties than a trial. The bargaining zone would thus be $40,000 to $60,000, and one would expect a settlement somewhere within that zone.

Importantly, the wider the bargaining zone, the higher the probability of settlement.[9] Parties are more likely to reach agreement if they have a greater degree of bargaining space—space in which both sides will benefit—with which to work. In addition, this model implies that settlement becomes more likely as the plaintiff's claim shrinks relative to the transaction costs of litigation.[10] As this occurs, this available bargaining zone comes to occupy a greater proportion of the valuation space within which the two parties will be negotiating.

Fairness and other behavioral concerns in settlement decision-making

The classic economic model is based on the assumption that litigants act rationally to try to maximize their wealth. As we mentioned in the introduction to this chapter, there are strong reasons to believe that plaintiffs' changing perceptions of how much they have been injured may affect the amount of money they demand in settlement. Under the classic economic model of settlement bargaining, this would be impossible. A wealth-maximizing plaintiff would never accept less money to settle based solely on a change in her own perception of her injury. If she believes the court has not changed how it values her injury,[11] then her settlement decisions will remain unchanged even if *she* now values her injury at a lower amount. But this is true only if her lone goal is to maximize her wealth. Essential for our argument, then, is recent evidence that litigants pursue goals other than wealth maximization—in particular, that they are more likely to accept a settlement offer if they perceive it as fair.[12] This evidence corroborates the emphasis that scholars have long placed on fairness or justice in civil procedure.[13]

Over the past several decades, new social science research has thoroughly rejected the notion that people care only about maximizing their own personal wealth. This research, much of which emerges from the field of behavioral game theory, indicates that most people also care deeply about fairness, to the extent that they are willing to give up monetary gains to preserve or achieve fair distributions of wealth. In dozens of studies, people are placed in strategic interactions with one another where they have to figure out whether and how to cooperate, how to split monetary payouts, and how to share resources.

One of the most famous games, and the one most relevant to our work, is the "ultimatum game."[14] In these games, the Proposer must divide a pot of money (say, $10) between himself and the Responder. If the Responder accepts the distribution, both subjects keep the money, but if the Responder rejects the distribution, both subjects get nothing. If people care only about optimal monetary outcomes for themselves, then Responders should accept any distribution of the money greater than $0; something is better than nothing, after all. Additionally, since Proposers should expect that Responders will be rational and accept any distribution, they should offer the least amount of money they are allowed (e.g., $1). This is not, however, what happens. Across populations and cultures, Responders regularly reject distributions of the pot that give them less than a 30 percent share, and Proposers, predicting this will be the case, often split the pot fifty-fifty.[15] The most plausible explanation for these results is that subjects care about fairness; they believe that unequal distributions are unfair; and they expect to experience more unhappiness from receiving an unfair distribution than they would if they received no money at all.[16] Importantly, results of these studies hold even when the amount of money at stake is equivalent to three months of income.[17]

In the legal setting, Russell Korobkin and Chris Guthrie have conducted experiments regarding settlement that support the view that people are often motivated by more than just selfishly maximizing their monetary gains.[18] In one such experiment, subjects were asked to decide whether to accept a settlement offer in a hypothetical personal injury case. All subjects were told that they had been hurt in a car accident through no fault of their own and that they were suing an insurance company. If they won at trial, they would receive $28,000, whereas if they lost, they would receive $10,000 (the amount undisputed by the insurer). Their lawyer told them that the result of a trial could go either way and that the defendant offered to settle for $21,000.

There were two groups of subjects. Those in Group A were told that they had owned a car worth $14,000 that was destroyed in the accident, and those in Group B were told the same thing except that their car had been worth $28,000. Members of Group B were far less likely to accept the settlement offer than were members of Group A.[19]

This experiment is particularly revealing. The odds of winning at trial, the damages sought, and the settlement offer were held constant for both groups. According to the assumptions of the rational actor model, both groups should have viewed the offer similarly. But the groups diverged. One characterization of these results is that the subject plaintiffs cared about values other than maximizing wealth—in particular, that they cared about achieving a result they viewed as fair compensation for their loss.[20]

Even if one rejects this fairness-based characterization, there is an alternative explanation that equally supports the point we will make about how hedonic adaptation affects settlement. Daniel Kahneman and Amos Tversky have famously demonstrated that when people face the prospect of a gain, they are risk averse; whereas when they face the prospect of a loss, they are risk seeking.[21] A settlement is a fixed gain for a plaintiff or loss for a defendant, whereas a trial holds out the prospect of a larger but uncertain gain or loss.[22] Applying this theory to the topic of settlement, Jeffrey Rachlinski has used experiments to illustrate that plaintiffs can be expected generally to be irrationally risk averse, whereas defendants can be expected generally to be irrationally risk seeking.[23] Simply put, plaintiffs are willing to settle for less money because they do not want to take the chance of getting nothing.

Both the fairness-based view (supported by the Korobkin and Guthrie experiment) and the risk-aversion view (supported by the Rachlinski experiment) suggest the following conclusion: *plaintiffs compare settlement offers to the amount they have been harmed and are more likely to accept offers exceeding that amount.*

Such a conclusion has important implications in light of hedonic adaptation to injury or adversity, as we will explain. As a result of such adaptation, a plaintiff's assessment of how severely she has been harmed will often change over time. This change, in turn, can be expected to affect the range of offers that she will be willing to accept in order to settle.

Putting it all together

Among the points that appear in the literature surveyed in this section, one simple idea stands out in importance. All commentators agree that the less money a plaintiff is willing to accept in order to settle, the more likely settlement will be. Contrary to some early assumptions, there is now evidence that plaintiffs' lowest acceptable sum is determined in part by reference to the amount they feel would fairly compensate them for the harm they have suffered.

If a plaintiff's perception of what would constitute fair compensation were to decrease as time passed, then that passage of time would accordingly increase the likelihood of settlement. To be sure, many factors could influence a plaintiff's demand, and her current experience of the injury is only one of them. But holding constant all such other factors, a typical plaintiff would be more willing to settle if, over time, she came to view a smaller amount as representing a fair payment for her injury.

Hedonic Adaptation and Increased Likelihood of Settlement

Consider the class of injuries that involves ongoing disabilities or losses of function, but not continuous pain—in other words, those to which humans tend to adapt hedonically. Where these types of injuries give rise to lawsuits for personal injury, hedonic adaptation will likely instigate a greater number of settlements than standard models would predict. The explanation rests with the psychological healing that the injury victim will undergo during the period before trial. During the first few months that follow a severe injury—a period of time that includes the filing of litigation and the initial pretrial procedures—the plaintiff is likely to suffer from a focusing illusion. With her attention focused on her injury, the plaintiff will overestimate its impact on her future happiness: she will anticipate that the injury will prevent her from achieving the same enjoyment of life that she experienced before being hurt.

During the nearly two years that it takes a typical civil case to reach trial, however, the plaintiff is likely to adapt hedonically to her injury—even if that injury is permanent—and will report levels of happiness closer to her pre-injury levels than she had anticipated. This adaptation will decrease the amount of money that the plaintiff believes will fairly compensate her for her injury. Immediately after a serious injury, a plaintiff is likely to feel that only a sizable amount of money will adequately compensate her for the loss of function she has suffered. Two years later, after the plaintiff has had the opportunity to hedonically adapt, and the injury seems less debilitating, what the plaintiff perceives as appropriate compensation will decline.[24]

This effect will drive down a tort plaintiff's settlement price over the course of litigation. Consider, for instance, a plaintiff who loses a limb in a traffic accident through no fault of her own. Imagine that in the months that follow the injury, when the lawsuit is initially filed, the plaintiff views her injury as highly incapacitating and believes (a rough estimate, of course) that she will need $300,000 to make herself whole. Over the course of the two years between filing and trial, the plaintiff adapts to her injury and comes to believe that only $150,000 is necessary to fairly compensate her for the harm she has suffered.[25] Even though the expected jury award has not changed, the plaintiff may view a lower settlement amount as acceptable given the reduced value she assigns to her injury. As the plaintiff's settlement price declines commensurate with the hedonic adaptation that humans typically experience, the chance of settlement increases.

Extensions and Objections

The foregoing sections set forth our case for why adaptation may increase the likelihood of settlement. In the sections that follow, we outline a number of ways in which that hypothesis could be tested empirically, and we confront several of the most significant potential objections.

Testable predictions

One of the strengths of our approach is that it generates testable hypotheses regarding settlement rates for particular types of civil cases. Consider two hypothetical personal injury lawsuits, one in which the plaintiff has lost some mobility in an auto accident, and one in which the plaintiff—as the result of a botched medical procedure—now suffers from recurring migraine headaches.[26] These two cases, if brought in the same jurisdiction, will involve the same pretrial procedures: discovery, mediation, motions to dismiss and for summary judgment, and so forth. Suppose that whatever differences there may be between the plaintiff and defendant in one of the two cases—for example, they may have different information, or different beliefs about the likely outcome of the litigation or about the damages the jury will award—will be the same as the differences between the plaintiff and the defendant in the other case. Imagine further that the two cases have approximately the same expected value when litigated before a jury: for example, in both cases the plaintiff has a

50 percent chance of victory and will recover $100,000 if she wins. Based on these considerations alone, the auto accident plaintiff and the medical malpractice plaintiff should be equally likely to settle.

The lone difference between these cases, as conceived here, is that the auto injury plaintiff will likely be able to adapt to his injury while the medical malpractice plaintiff will not. The loss of mobility is a paradigm case for hedonic adaptation; studies have shown that even people who lose the power to walk recapture a significant percentage of their lost pre-injury happiness.[27] By contrast, recurrent conditions such as headaches and ringing in the ears present among the worst cases for adaptation. Assume for the sake of argument that our two hypothetical plaintiffs suffered the same amount when they were first injured. By the time that months or years of pretrial procedure have run their course, the medical malpractice plaintiff may well still perceive herself as suffering to a degree that the auto accident plaintiff does not. If so, then the auto accident plaintiff may be willing to settle for a value that the medical malpractice plaintiff would still consider inadequate. Our theory thus generates three predictions:

1. During the time between filing and trial, settlement demands from plaintiffs with adaptable injuries will decrease in value more than settlement demands from plaintiffs with nonadaptable injuries.

2. Consequently, personal injury cases involving adaptable injuries will settle at higher rates than personal injury cases involving nonadaptable injuries, *all else being equal*.

3. Independent of the effects of monetary costs and informational advantages, hedonic adaptation will cause settlement rates for adaptable personal injuries to increase as the time between filing and trial increases.

This last hypothesis needs some explanation. Lengthy litigation procedures can make settlement more likely for reasons other than lengthening the time for hedonic adaptation. First, those procedures may be expensive for the litigants. This makes settlement more attractive, because settlement is a way to avoid paying those costs. Second, litigation procedures frequently (though not always) give the litigants more information about the likely outcome of the case. This information tends to narrow the gap between the plaintiff's and defendant's respective opinions of the likely outcome, and that narrowing makes settlement more likely.[28] Consider, then, a set of accelerated pretrial procedures that provide the same informational gains to the parties as standard litigation practices and generate the same level of costs. (An accelerated litigation calendar—for instance, the Eastern District of Virginia's famous "rocket docket"[29]—would possess this feature.) We predict that cases litigated on such an accelerated schedule will settle at a lower rate than cases litigated at a more deliberate speed, when adaptable injuries are involved.

Empirical tests of these hypotheses are beyond the scope of this book. Nonetheless, the necessary data, particularly concerning hypotheses 2 and 3, may be obtainable. Empirical analysis of hedonic adaptation has matured into a vigorous science; we hope that empirical research into adaptation's effects on the civil justice process will soon follow suit.

Principal objections

The picture we have painted could raise many different concerns. First, we have said nothing about lawyers. When a plaintiff decides whether to settle, does she merely do what her lawyer—who is unaffected by adaptation—tells her to do? In recent years, much has been made of the growth of an attorney-centered litigation model, in which the attorney—the sophisticated repeat player—drives the litigation and makes most of the important decisions.[30] Certainly, if the plaintiff exerts no control over a lawsuit, her adaptation is irrelevant.[31] But that is a caricature of the attorney-client relationship. More likely, each of the two people will have some input into the most important litigation choices, particularly the question of when and whether to settle.[32] To the extent that plaintiffs play a role in the decision, adaptation will make settlement more likely.

Moreover, 95 percent of personal injury plaintiffs are represented by attorneys working on a contingent fee basis.[33] Contingent fee attorneys will tend to prefer early settlement over protracted litigation because they bear all the costs and risks of protracted court battles.[34] Thus it is the rare contingent fee attorney who will stand in the way of an adapted plaintiff's desire to settle. Far more frequently, cases do not settle because an unsatisfied client preferred to continue to trial. Adaptation will limit this effect.

Second, delays and time lags in litigation are often caused by hard bargaining and acrimony between the parties. As much as the adaptation that follows from delay might increase the rate of settlement, the rancor that accompanies it might act in the opposite direction. We wish to stress that we make no claim about how common settlement will ultimately be in protracted cases or speedy ones, and no claim about which type of case will settle more often. We mean only to say that *holding constant all other effects of delay*, delay will make settlement more likely by enabling hedonic adaptation in cases that involve adaptable injuries. As we note above, lengthy cases may generate greater information or drive up costs, making settlement more likely; these effects are separate from the point we are making, just as is the acrimonious nature of long cases. When litigation is delayed by factors that do not otherwise affect settlement and are beyond the parties' control—a court's docket schedule, for instance—the effects of adaptation should be most evident.

Third, what if defendants began to understand the processes of hedonic adaptation and refused to begin settlement negotiations until later in the case, after the plaintiffs had an opportunity to adapt? It is entirely possible that the result would be to curb the rate of early settlement, simply because early settlements cannot happen if defendants refuse to settle early. We make no claims to the contrary. But the reason defendants would refuse to settle early is to give plaintiffs time to adapt, so plaintiffs will later be willing to settle for less than they would have settled for at the early stage. If this happens, it will still be consistent with our predictions: plaintiffs' settlement prices will diminish as time passes, and settlement will ultimately become more likely as litigation drags on.[35]

Fourth, there is the possibility that settlement negotiations themselves might inhibit adaptation by forcing the plaintiff to think about her injury rather than shift her focus to other things. But that seems unlikely to us because typical settlement negotiations do not involve the type of discussions that are most likely to undermine adaptation. The beginning of a lawsuit might focus on the extent of a plaintiff's injury, as might a trial at the end. But in between, settlement offers and negotiations often involve dollar figures and little else. By the time the parties reach the negotiating table, the attorneys will have latched onto approximate case valuations and acceptable settlement ranges, and reaching agreement on a particular number will be the sole priority.

Importantly, plaintiffs are most often bystanders to these negotiations. Any conversation between the plaintiff and her lawyer will almost certainly concern only whether the plaintiff wishes to accept a proffered settlement offer or hold out for more money. These communications do not usually involve rehashing the facts of the case or reexamining the plaintiff's injuries. To the extent that this sort of hard bargaining takes place, it will occur almost entirely between the attorneys. Later-period settlement negotiations thus will not remind the plaintiff of her condition in the same way that a full trial on the merits—complete with extensive testimony by the plaintiff—might. As such, they are unlikely to force the plaintiff to focus much on her injuries. In personal injury cases, the attorney may function as an emotional screen that facilitates hedonic adaptation and thereby increases the likelihood of settlement.[36]

Lastly, one could object that our view reverses cause and effect: whereas we say that a plaintiff settles because she has gotten happier, perhaps she has instead gotten happier because she settles. On this view, tort victims are increasingly happy over time not because their psychological immune systems have successfully adapted them to their injuries, but because insurance payments and tort settlements have kicked in and restored them to their prior level of happiness. For an economist, this recovery of happiness indicates that insurance and tort settlements are achieving the proper effect, genuinely functioning as "make whole" remedies for accident victims.

Yet the data do not appear to support this view. If cash payments via insurance or tort lawsuits were driving hedonic improvements, then personal income should serve as the best indicator for when hedonic adaptation would occur. If this were the case, researchers should find no evidence of adaptation after controlling for income. However, studies of people with moderate and severe disabilities produce evidence of hedonic adaptation even after controlling for household income.[37] The conclusion we draw from these studies is that although wealth may aid the process of hedonic adaptation, the normal functioning of the psychological immune system alone is enough to drive adaptation and thus increase settlement.

*   *   *

When one person files a lawsuit against another, it will typically be resolved by a settlement. Understanding settlements is thus essential to understanding lawsuits, so settlement behavior has been studied extensively. The data on happiness may improve these studies.

There is evidence that one factor in settlement behavior is the amount a plaintiff perceives she has been harmed. The happiness data suggest that in many cases this perceived amount is likely to decrease over time as plaintiffs adapt to their injuries. One would then expect such plaintiffs, as time passes, to settle for less money than they would have settled for if they had not adapted. Understanding adaptation may thus improve the accuracy of models of settlement behavior.

We take no position on whether it is good or bad that plaintiffs adapt and settle for less money. Our point is merely that they may be expected to do so.

PART III
Well-Being

This book explains how the data on happiness can be used to inform people's understanding of law and public policy. That project is useful as long as happiness is *one* thing of value, which virtually everyone agrees it is.[1] Happiness need not be the only thing of value, or even the only component of the quality of life. Still, the importance of happiness is hardly undermined by such a concession. Daniel Haybron calls happiness "merely-one-of-the-most-important-things-in-the-world."[2] Like justice and other values, happiness need not be the only important thing in order to matter a lot.[3]

Because happiness is uncontroversially one thing that contributes to human welfare, nothing in the previous chapters depends at all on hotly contested philosophical claims about happiness. In that respect, this final part of the book—in which we discuss such philosophical claims— may be considered superfluous.

Yet we have included it because the topic it addresses has been a focus of scholars for thousands of years and remains at the center of both thought and policy today. Of all possible values, improving human life is perhaps the most widely agreed upon. So it is natural to ask, What does it mean to improve someone's life? The following chapters address that question, which is commonly phrased as, What is "well-being"—or, equivalently, "welfare," "utility," "quality of life," or "self-interest"? All these terms are intended as labels for the concept of what it means for a person's life to go well for her.

We believe that well-being is simply happiness, and by happiness we mean the sum of positive and negative affective states. Thus, we believe that a person's well-being or quality of life is how good or bad she feels during the aggregated moments of her life. This was Jeremy Bentham's view, though unlike us, Bentham also believed that happiness (and thus well-being) was the only value of any kind.

Developments in social science and philosophy often influence one another. Bentham's view of well-being was overtaken by a rival approach when early-twentieth-century economists argued that happiness is unobservable, and thus that policymakers should focus instead on people's choices. That argument carried the day, and the economists' favored approach to well-being—preference satisfaction—replaced happiness as the leading philosophical theory of well-being. Later in the twentieth century, Amartya Sen and others challenged the traditional economic approach for being insufficiently attentive to the needs of people in developing nations, who lacked objective indicators of well-being even if their preferences had adapted to their circumstances. Out of that concern sprang not only new approaches to economics and public policy, but also a philosophical turn toward "objective" theories of well-being as alternatives to both happiness and preference-satisfaction.

Now, social science research has created reliable proxies for subjective happiness, and policymakers have started to return their focus to it, so it makes sense that the hedonic theory of well-being would receive renewed consideration. We think it deserves such consideration, so we devote the following chapters to that claim.

We begin by considering the theories of well-being that currently predominate: preference theories and objective theories. In chapter 6, we explain the problems we see in those theories and thus the need for an alternative. In chapter 7, we lay out our favored alternative, the hedonic or happiness theory. In chapter 8, we address the most prominent objections to our view.

CHAPTER SIX

Some Problems with Preference Theories and Objective Theories

If policymakers want to improve people's lives, what exactly is it they want to do: what is "quality of life" or "well-being"? We think the answer is happiness, by which we mean net affect. The better someone feels throughout the aggregated moments of her life, the more well-being she has. We will defend this view in chapters 7 and 8.

Our view is one of the various theories of well-being, which are often said to fall into three major categories.[1] Currently, the most prominent category comprises theories that conceive of well-being as preference satisfaction, or getting what you want. The second category involves theories that conceive of well-being as objective features like health, friendship, and liberty. Finally, the third category, which includes our view (as described in chapter 7), contains the theories that conceive of well-being as happiness.

This chapter is devoted to explaining the dominant category, preference theories, and its primary current rival, objective theories. We discuss the problems we see in those accounts, beginning with the category that focuses on preferences.

What Is a Theory of Well-Being?

We begin by considering, albeit very briefly, the nature of the question at issue, the sort of answer there could be to that question, and how competing answers might be tested.

Scholars have long tried to understand what "quality of life" means because improving the quality of human life is one thing that people tend to value. The basic concept is typically described as what it means for someone's life to go well for her.[2] This concept receives varying labels, such as "well-being," "welfare," and "self-interest"—labels we use interchangeably in this book. The crucial question is what this concept entails: what is well-being?

To answer the question, one must rely on people's intuitions. Consider this statement: All else being equal, Jack is better off if he spends the next hour playing his favorite game than if he spends it undergoing excruciating torture. Most people would probably agree with the statement, but how could it be verified or falsified? It may well not be provable in any sort of purely empirical or logical way.[3] Instead, it is based on common intuitions about what it means for Jack to be "better off." So people's intuitions play a major role in explaining what well-being is.

However, if a theory of well-being were judged solely by how well it tracks people's intuitions, then the best approach would be the absence of a theory—the view that well-being is whatever people's intuitions say it is in any situation. Few scholars hold that view, because one person's intuitions will sometimes conflict with another person's intuitions. To resolve such conflicts, one needs a theory—a principle that gives intuitive answers in most situations and that seems to capture what people think well-being is about. If a theory does well on those dimensions, then people may be willing to change or discard their intuitions in the cases where their intuitions do not accord with the theory.

From these basics, two important points follow. First, a theory must provide answers. Is Jim better off if he doubles his salary by working twice as much? Is Jane better off if she becomes famous but falls out of touch with her friends? Is Sam better off if he extends his life an extra year by making healthy choices that sacrifice some of his enjoyment of life? Is Beth better off if her novel becomes popular after her death? *Answering questions like these is the reason for having a theory of well-being.* A theory must give answers, or at least it must explain what additional information one needs to know in order to find the answers, and how that information will reveal the answers. What it means to be a "theory" is to provide a *principle that yields answers.* Relying instead on intuition to supply the answers is the opposite of having a theory. To be sure, a theory's quality can be tested in part by comparing its answers to people's intuitions about what the answers should be. But if intuition supplies the answers in the first place, then there is no theory.

John Rawls makes this point forcefully in the context of theories of justice: it is "an essential and not a minor part of a conception [i.e., a theory] of justice" to "reduce the direct appeal to our considered judgments [i.e., our intuitions after reflection]."[4] If a theory or conception fails to do this and instead asks people to rely on their intuitions to find answers, then it "is, one might say, but half a conception."[5] To the extent that people must rely on intuitions merely to understand what a theory's answers are, Rawls declared, "the means of rational discussion have come to an end."[6]

Second, it is impossible for a theory to give answers that everyone finds initially intuitive in every situation. Judged by that standard, any theory would fail, precisely due to the reason that theories are sought in the first place: people have conflicting intuitions. Instead, a good theory should accord with people's intuitions in the mass of cases, and where it diverges, there should be a plausible explanation for why it diverges. A theory that is good in this way may be able to persuade people to rethink their intuitions in the rare cases of divergence because the theory seems otherwise to have such power in explaining intuitions and in giving persuasive reasons for them.

If these points seem abstract in isolation, we hope they are clearer as applied to the theories discussed below in this chapter. We now turn to explaining the two main alternatives to our own theory of well-being.[7] Many readers will have reservations, including strong ones, about the theory we endorse in chapter 7. But no matter how deep one's suspicion runs, one cannot properly assess our theory without comparing it to the alternatives. If one cannot find an alternative theory that seems more appealing than ours, then it may be worth rethinking whether one's reservations about our theory are truly decisive. No theory can satisfy every concern, and the question is not whether a theory can do so but rather how it fares in relation to other theories and in relation to the absence of a theory.

Preference Theories

Preference-satisfaction theories conceive of well-being as getting what you want.[8] We think this approach has two main problems: some wants are not self-interested, and getting what you want does not always turn out best for you. We turn now to a discussion of these two issues.

Which preferences increase well-being?

Suppose Jill believes she has sinned and wants to suffer for her wrong-doing.[9] Moreover, suppose that her desire to suffer does not derive from hoping to relieve her guilt and make her feel better, but from precisely the opposite motive: she wants to feel worse because she believes it is morally or religiously right for such a fate to befall her. Jill does not view the suffering as improving her well-being; indeed, she wants to suffer because she is convinced that suffering will decrease her well-being. But preference theories equate well-being with getting what one wants, so if Jill gets the suffering she wants, will it increase her well-being? Matthew Adler says that "surely" it will not,[10] and we think most people would join us in agreeing with him. If one's intuitions depart from Adler's and ours—that is, if one believes the suffering would actually improve Jill's well-being—then we may adjust the example to replace generic suffering with years of excruciating torture resulting in death. At some point, we think, it becomes very difficult to sustain the claim that *anything* Jill wants for any reason will automatically benefit her if she gets it. The upshot is essential: *well-being cannot be getting what you want*, because it is conceptually possible to want to decrease one's own well-being.

Should that example seem too odd, one can find countless others in which a person wants something that would decrease her own well-being. Suppose Ada prefers to marry Bill because she has promised to do so, even though she now realizes she will be miserable with him.[11] Ada understands that if she breaks her promise, she will be much happier on the whole because the advantage of avoiding Bill will vastly outweigh the disadvantage of feeling guilty about doing so. But she still prefers to keep her promise, because she believes so firmly in the moral importance of promise-keeping. We share Ada's view that her well-being is not improved by spending the rest of her life with a man who makes her miserable. Why would her well-being be improved by that? Although she prefers that outcome, she prefers it for a reason that has nothing to do with what is best for her.

More generally, the concept of self-sacrifice is familiar to virtually everyone. The nature of that concept is for someone to want an outcome even though that outcome makes her worse off. People want things for all sorts of reasons. They want some things for their own benefit, they want other things for the benefit of others, and they want still other things for the sake of moral or religious beliefs they hold. When one wants something for a reason other than one's own well-being, getting that thing may well not increase one's well-being. Indeed, the concept of self-sacrifice would be nonsensical otherwise.

It might seem hard to believe that something so basic could reveal a critical flaw in the dominant theory of well-being, but we think it does so. Preference theories seem to have only two options available for dealing with this problem. The first would be to bite the bullet by claiming that Jill and Ada are actually better off suffering than not suffering and that it is both conceptually and practically impossible ever to prefer to decrease or sacrifice one's own well-being for the sake of other goals or values. If anyone has made that claim, we are unaware of it. Since such a claim seems insupportable on its face, that leaves the second option: to design a theory of well-being that includes only preferences for one's own well-being. But such a theory—"well-being is preferences for well-being"—is hardly more meaningful than the statement that "well-being is well-being."[12] Many scholars have pointed out this problem with preference theories,[13] but an answer has not been forthcoming.

Some of the most famous preference theories, such as those advanced by John Rawls[14] and John Harsanyi,[15] offer no suggestion at all for overcoming the problem of non-self-interested preferences. Others offer suggestions that are clearly inadequate. For example, Derek Parfit famously imagined (without endorsing) a "Success Theory" in which well-being is conceived as "all of our preferences about our own lives."[16] Similarly, Mark Overvold has suggested including only preferences wherein "the agent is an essential constituent."[17] Also similarly, a preference theory could include only preferences for things that affect the "body or mind" of the person in question.[18] All these solutions fail for the same reason: at most, they assure only that getting what you want will *affect* your well-being—not that it will *improve* your well-being. Jill's preference for reducing her own well-being is a preference about her own life (and one in which Jill is an essential constituent whose body and mind are affected), as is Ada's preference for marrying a man she detests. Those preferences would count according to the Success Theory and its variants, but they should not count because satisfying them does not improve well-being. Thus, such theories fail to solve the problem.

Could it be that a solution will someday be forthcoming? Will a smart preference theorist eventually find a way to explain, without circularity, how to define the subset of preferences that yield well-being? We think that even if this could be done, the contribution would have little or nothing to do with preferences. At bottom, the point of a theory of well-being is to explain the nature of what it means for someone to benefit from something. Preferences—getting what one wants—are not the answer, because one can want things other than to benefit oneself. The answer requires finding the *feature* that makes certain preferences benefit someone, and looking for that feature lands you back at square one in looking for what well-being is in the first place. Preferences get you nowhere.[19]

Mistakes

Suppose Dave wants to be famous, but he would be much happier living in obscurity. Is Dave better off if he gets his wish and is miserable, or if he doesn't get it and is happy? We think most people will agree that he is better off happy. Getting what you want can make you worse off, which is a problem for preference theories.

The standard answer is to count only "fully informed" preferences, but that term, like the term "preference theories" itself, is an importantly misleading label. Suppose Jill could peer into the future and see each different possible state of the world, comprehending every detail about all of them. Her well-being might then be said to depend on the extent to which the actual state of the world approximates the state she would most prefer. Jill's perfect understanding of every possible future world would include (among countless other things) perfect information about Jill's own happiness—how Jill would feel in each different possible state. If a theory conceives Jill's well-being as the satisfaction of such perfectly idealized preferences, it might solve the problem of mistakes—but at a major cost. Even if we leave aside the conceptual troubles with superhuman idealization,[20] such a theory is hopelessly opaque. It is useless for providing answers and for resolving intuition conflicts—the primary values of having a theory—because one can never know what Jill would prefer under the hypothesized conditions. People who ponder the nature of well-being are not superhuman and thus cannot know what Jill needs to know in order to decide what is best for her under this theory. This makes it impossible to test the theory by comparing its answers to people's intuitions[21] because the theory's dictates will never be accessible.[22]

Because the superhuman preference theory yields no answers for any real or hypothetical cases,[23] it sheds little light on the nature of well-being. And because it cannot be tested against intuitions, its merits cannot be evaluated. In our opinion, these limitations disqualify the theory.

And without the superhuman version, preferentism returns to facing the problem of mistakes. That problem too may be decisive because—as virtually every preference theorist implicitly acknowledges by requiring informed preferences—getting what one wants does not always make one better off.

Objective Theories

During the past three decades, a group of alternatives to preference theories has become prominent in philosophy, economics, and law. These theories are typically grouped under labels like "objective,"[24] though they can and often do contain elements such as preferences or happiness that are frequently deemed subjective. What characterizes these theories is that they contain other elements either in addition to or instead of preferences and happiness.

Within this group, two prominent sub-categories stand out: list theories and eudaimonist theories.[25] We will discuss each in turn.

List theories

A list theory deems well-being to be some combination of things such as "life," "bodily health," "bodily integrity," "senses, imagination, and thought," "emotions," "practical reason," "affiliation," "[relationship with] other species," "play," and "control over one's environment."[26] To discuss such theories, we begin with examples involving three of the most basic and oft-cited list items: health, loving relationships, and money. The examples are not meant to disprove particular list theories, but merely to help illustrate our view that list items increase well-being only if they increase happiness. After the examples, we make our substantive case against list theories.

Good health almost always increases happiness, but if it failed to do so in some rare case, then would it still increase well-being? Suppose Jack has a toxin in his system that he *doesn't know* about. It will kill him at age seventy,[27] but until then it has no effect that he's aware of: it is harming his body, but it is doing so in ways that won't affect his felt experience of life (and thus his happiness) in any way whatsoever until he dies at age seventy. Everything Jack does, and everything he feels, is identical with or without the toxin until age seventy. Now suppose Jack dies at age sixty-five in a car accident. Did he have less well-being because of the toxin than he would have had without it? We think not. Even something as crucial as health improves well-being only insofar as it improves happiness.[28]

The same goes for loving relationships, another oft-cited constituent of well-being. Loving relationships, like health, improve happiness in almost all cases. But what if they didn't do so in some rare case: would well-being attach to the relationships or to the happiness? Suppose Jill is a loner to the core. Being around people makes her feel great anxiety. She is frequently told that she is warped or that there is something wrong with her, so she tries hard to cultivate an appreciation for human interaction—but to no avail. Consider two possible life paths for Jill. In one of them, she forces herself to endure social interaction. She makes friends and even has a family, and she is loved by many people. But she is absolutely miserable. Throughout every moment that she is with these people who love her, she feels stress and wishes she were alone. But she endures it because that is what is expected of her. Alternatively, imagine that Jill moves out to a remote location and lives a life by herself, without any loving relationships. And she savors every minute of it. She feels relaxed and free, and she relishes her life of solitude. In which life does Jill have more well-being? We think it is clear that she is better off alone than with others. Like health, loving relationships improve well-being because (and only because) they make people happy.

This is even clearer with money or success. Suppose Ben chases those things and achieves them: he works very hard at a job he hates, and he is miserable but wealthy and powerful. Is his life better or worse for him than if he had failed to achieve wealth and success and had instead ended up in a much lower-paying job that he thoroughly enjoyed? We think that money and success improve people's lives only insofar as they make people happy. A list theorist might respond to these examples by saying that well-being is some combination of happiness and other factors. Happiness itself could be a list item. If so, however, the theorist would have to explain how happiness gets traded off against the other items.

Presumably, list theories would hold that a person who has more of one list item has greater welfare than she would have if she had less of that item, assuming she had the same amount of the other items. But, of course, this is rarely the situation. Gaining more of one may entail having less of another. How are such things to be ordered when they conflict? Does Jane have more welfare if she has (a) slightly above-average play and slightly below-average control over her environment, or if she has (b) slightly above-average control over her environment and slightly below-average play? The possible trade-offs and combinations among the list items are virtually limitless.[29] Thus, the theory will not provide any answers about well-being unless it offers some way to weigh its components. As Rawls wrote, "[t]he assignment of weights is an essential and not a minor part of a conception."[30]

Accordingly, it might be inappropriate to think of list theories as theories at all. We are not the first to question whether objective lists should be considered theories of well-being.[31] For example, T. M. Scanlon argues that "a theory would go beyond this list by doing such things as . . . provid[ing] a standard for making more exact comparisons of well-being—for deciding when, on balance, a person's well-being has been increased or decreased and by how much."[32] What prevents list theories from meeting the standard that Rawls and Scanlon describe is not just that they offer no way to resolve conflicts between different list items. It is also that those theories offer no way to resolve conflicts *within* list items. Consider the item "health." Does Jack have better health if he has chronic back pain but full use of both arms, or if he is pain-free but has use of only one arm? The happiness theory says that the effect of such things on well-being depends on how they make Jack feel, but the list theory has no way to decide even their relative effects on Jack's health, let alone the role of health in his well-being.

To give answers, a list theory needs some method of weighing the items on the same scale—perhaps a formula or algorithm. Some welfare objectivists recoil at this suggestion. Bernard Gert has said that "there is no argument" in favor of preferring a formula to a list,[33] and Martha Nussbaum has praised "[t]he rejection of general algorithms" in ethical inquiry.[34] Simon Keller has championed the rejection of a formula in a particularly straightforward way,[35] and we think it will be clearest to draw contrasts between our view and the argument he makes. Keller gives the example of physical fitness, one component of which is strength and another component of which is the ability to run far. He says that "[i]f I can run a mile farther than you and you can lift ten pounds more than me," then "I am fitter in one way and you are fitter in another," and neither of us is fitter overall.[36] However, for Keller this does not mean "that there is no such measure as physical fitness on the whole. . . . You may be able to lift greater weights than can many of the world's best marathon runners, but still, those runners are fitter, on the whole, than you."[37]

We think that Keller's argument may well have a lot in common with the way that many objectivists—including both list theorists and many eudaimonists, a group we will discuss in the following section—believe normative argument should go. Their idea is that practical reason will decide matters about well-being. To learn whether Jack has better health if he has only one arm or if he has chronic back pain, one will simply engage in reasoning of the kind Keller used with respect to fitness. And this is how all conflicts among list items will be resolved. Some scholars argue that this is how people resolve issues in real life: they think about them and figure them out on the ground.

We confess that we find it difficult to appreciate the merits of this view. Consider fitness. For us, the only two possibilities are (a) that there is no single concept of fitness (and instead that there are separate, incommensurable concepts such as strength and ability to run far), or (b) that there is some formula for commensurating things like strength and running ability to yield a concept of fitness. We believe, as every welfare theorist either assumes or argues, that the first possibility is not the case for the concept of welfare. Let us suppose it is not the case for fitness either, for the sake of analyzing Keller's claim: suppose Keller is right that a great marathon runner is fitter than a normal person who can lift slightly more weight than the runner. What that must mean is that "fitness" refers to a concept that involves some metric for weighing things like running ability against things like strength. It might not be obvious what that metric is, so cases that are close do not always yield answers that are easily discerned through intuition. To discover the metric, one would have to probe people's intuitions via examples and thought experiments. For example, people might intuit that if A can lift 200 more pounds than B, but B can run only 5 feet farther than A, then A is fitter. To figure out people's intuitional fitness trade-off between strength and distance, one might simply alter the quantities until equal fitness was intuited. That process might ultimately yield a theory of what fitness refers to. To say that there is a concept of fitness is to say that the different components of that concept can be commensurated via some method of comparison. Admittedly, unearthing the precise nature of the metric might be difficult, but whether the metric is perfectly discoverable is a different question from whether it exists. If Keller is right that the term "fitness" refers to a real, unified concept, then the existence of the method of comparison follows logically from that fact. Moreover, although discovering the exact metric may be difficult, making substantial progress toward that end seems very realistic.

A theory is, as Rawls said, an attempt to overcome intuition conflicts. Keller's view is that in many cases no attempt should be made. Other objectivists might say that the attempt can be made by practical reason, but we are not sure we understand what that entails. One thing it could entail is searching for a principle that commensurates different things and explains a mass of intuitions. (This is the way Rawls conceives a theory, but not the approach objectivists seem to favor.) Another thing it could entail is simply thinking harder about the concept in question. Surely we have not expressed this second option well, but that is because we cannot understand what that option is supposed to be. The only way we see to resolve intuition conflicts is to look for some kind of principle, and the only way we see to use different list items to yield answers about welfare is to commensurate them with weights or a metric for comparison. If one denies this while still using intuitions (or practical reason) to reach conclusions—like Keller's conclusion that marathon runners are fitter than slightly stronger non-runners—then one has necessarily though unwittingly relied on the existence of such a metric. The precise nature of the metric may be unknown, but it must be operating in the background for such comparisons to be made. The comparison *is* a commensuration, and a commensuration is a formula-style weighing, whether or not the formula is known or acknowledged.

In any event, a list theory is vulnerable to the criticism we made above about restricted preference theories: it is opaque. List theories require people to use their intuitions to find answers in virtually all real and hypothetical cases, so the theories cannot be tested against intuitions and cannot resolve conflicts among intuitions.[38]

Finally, we would like to press a more basic point against list theories that may well apply to all objective theories. Consider the essence of what makes a theory "objective": in objective theories, the feature that makes something increase your well-being is primarily a feature of *it* rather than of *you*. Suppose your last act in life is to take a walk. In one scenario you enjoy it, whereas in another scenario you don't, but everything else in the two scenarios remains the same. Subjective theories locate the well-being value of the walk in *you*: the walk increases your well-being if you enjoy it or prefer it. Objective theories, by contrast, locate the well-being value of the walk not in you but in the walk itself: a walk increases your well-being if *it* has objective value. This is a problem for objective theories because they have trouble making sense of the intuitive point that, in the example as given, the walk increases your well-being if you enjoy it and decreases your well-being if you dislike it, even though the walk itself is identical in both cases. What changes is only the positivity or negativity of how the walk—the objective thing—is subjectively experienced. And that change makes all the difference precisely because subjective experience, rather than objective value, best captures the nature of well-being.

Consider the original question: what is well-being? That question is defined as what makes your life go well *for you*. The leading scholars of well-being—including preferentists, objectivists, and hedonists—uniformly phrase the inquiry in those terms:

> Griffin: "The notion we are after is not the notion of value in general, but the narrower notion of a life's being valuable solely to the person who lives it."[39]

> Sumner: "Welfare assessments concern what we may call the prudential value of a life, namely how well it is going *for the individual whose life it is*"[40] (emphasis in original).

> Haybron: Well-being "concerns what *benefits* a person, is in her *interest*, is *good for* her, or makes her life *go well for* her"[41] (emphasis in original).

> Arneson: Well-being is "not the morally best life, but the life that is best for me."[42]

> Scanlon: Well-being "is not itself a moral notion. It represents what an individual has reason to want for him- or herself, leaving aside concern for others and any moral restraints or obligations."[43]

> Velleman: Well-being is "how well [a life] goes for the person living it."[44]

> Raz: Well-being "is the concept of a life which is good for the person whose life it is."[45]

Thus, whereas objective value concerns what is good, well-being concerns what is good *for you*.[46] An objective theory of well-being therefore faces a difficult challenge: it must somehow find a way to connect what is best objectively with what is best for you.[47] For the "list" variety of objective theories, the only way to do so seems to be via brute possession: something is good objectively, and it becomes good for you merely because you possess it.[48] But as Wayne Sumner has pointed out, this approach reverses cause and effect.[49] In the example above, taking a walk is good for you *because* you enjoy it. You do not enjoy it because it is good for you. Indeed, the feature that makes the walk improve your well-being is precisely your enjoyment of it—*not* anything about the walk itself that exists independently of that enjoyment. The nature of objective value is inherently at odds with the nature of well-being.

Eudaimonistic theories

List theories are not the only theories of well-being that are often labeled "objective." Another group of theories tends to locate value not in list items but rather in things such as nature-fulfillment. Suppose Bob has a choice: he can devote substantial time either to philosophizing or to watching TV. If he chooses philosophizing, he will be great at it, but he will feel nervous and strained most of the time. If he instead chooses TV-watching, he will feel relaxed and happy most of the time. On the whole, he would enjoy TV-watching much more. Which choice would give Bob greater well-being?[50] We think the answer is TV-watching, and we expect most readers to share our intuition. Certainly, some readers will not like the idea of a person's choosing to watch TV instead of doing something more active, productive, and challenging. But we believe that such feelings reflect those readers' judgments about either the objective value of the respective activities or else the subjective value *they* place on them, rather than judgments about what is best *for Bob*. Those who are averse to "loafing," or judgmental of it, sometimes don't want to accept that a loafer can be made happier thereby. But the question so stipulates. Of course, one could argue—contra our view—that well-being is not just about happiness but also about something else. But if that something else is objective value,[51] then one must confront the point we made near the end of the previous section that such value does not satisfy the "for you" requirement inherent in well-being.

These sorts of questions relate to a major category of objective theories of well-being that may be labeled "eudaimonistic" theories. *Eudaimonia* is an ancient Greek word frequently translated as "happiness" but perhaps better translated as "well-being."[52] Eudaimonistic theories include theories espoused by ancient Greek philosophers—in particular, but not exclusively, the theory advanced by Aristotle—as well as theories of modern scholars whose views lean heavily on the ancients' ideas. It is very difficult to pin down precisely what any one of these theories has to say about well-being,[53] let alone to identify a common thread unifying them all. Still, there are certain features that are widely associated with such theories. One is nature-fulfillment—the claim that well-being consists in living "a 'fully' or 'truly' human life."[54] Nature-fulfillment, in turn, is frequently associated with two other things: perfecting human capacities and being morally virtuous.[55] Yet, despite focusing on these things, eudaimonists do not neglect pleasure. They often say that a person has well-being if she acts virtuously (in terms of morality and/or perfection of capacities) *and* feels enjoyment in doing so.[56] Thus, a typical theory might emphasize both the pleasure and the good acts that bring it about: "faring well and doing well."[57] Some of the scholars whose work is often included in this category are Philippa Foot,[58] Rosalind Hursthouse,[59] and Richard Kraut.[60]

There seem to be two different ways of understanding eudaimonistic theories. One is that they make a descriptive empirical claim: people will be happier (in terms of feeling good) if they act virtuously. If that is the claim, then it is consistent with the hedonic theory of well-being. If a eudaimonist is merely prescribing the most effective way to achieve happiness, then she is not disagreeing with the hedonic theory. Moreover, if eudaimonists believe that happiness and virtue go together all (or almost all) of the time, then perhaps those scholars should lead the charge for using happiness studies as guides to public policy.

Thus, for a eudaimonistic theory to be a rival of the happiness theory, it must be more than merely descriptive. It must claim not just that virtue will lead to happiness but rather that faring well and doing well—not happiness alone—constitute well-being. If this is the claim, then what does that claim entail? What does it mean to conceive of well-being as doing good activities and feeling good thereby? The only assumption we can make confidently is that a eudaimonistic theory would hold that if (*a*) Kate devotes her time to philosophy *and* feels good as a result, then she has more well being than if (*b*) Kate instead devotes her time to watching TV (or memorizing the dictionary)[61] *and* does not feel good as a result. Happiness plus good activities yields more well-being than does the lack of happiness plus the lack of good activities. If this is all that eudaimonistic theories have to say, then a couple of points are worth noting. One is that these theories still would not diverge from the happiness theory. In the only cases on which they take a position, they yield answers identical to those of our view. In addition, they are not really theories at all because they cover so few of the cases that might arise. Rather, they are claims about specific, uncontroversial cases.

If a eudaimonistic theory aspires to more than this, it must explain what well-being entails when good activities and pleasure diverge. Life provides no shortage of such examples to consider.[62] This section began with one of them: Bob, who enjoys loafing more than philosophizing. Other examples, focusing on moral virtue rather than perfecting capacities, are equally common. Suppose Abe makes a serious blunder at work and deserves to be fired, but his boss mistakenly blames the error on someone else. Abe can either come clean and be fired, or else keep quiet and retain his job. If he comes clean, then his conscience will be clear, but that benefit to him will be vastly outweighed—in terms of his lifetime happiness—by the harm to him of unemployment. Conversely, if he stays quiet, he will feel guilt; but his guilty feelings will dissipate over time, and he will be much happier on the whole than if he'd taken the high road and lost his job. Even if the morally right thing for Abe to do is to turn himself in, Abe himself would benefit from keeping quiet. Similarly, suppose Beth cheats on her husband. If she tells him what she has done, then he will leave her, which will dramatically reduce her happiness. So she conceals her infidelity, recognizing correctly that whatever guilt she feels about concealing it will easily be trumped in terms of her lifetime happiness by the negative consequences of admitting it. Her silence does not seem virtuous (and if this is in doubt, we can change the example to imagine that she keeps many important indiscretions from her husband that he would want to know about and would benefit from knowing about), but it does seem to increase her well-being. Finally, suppose Carl needs an organ transplant and commits various dishonest acts to have his name placed higher on the list. As a result, he receives the transplant when he needs it. He thereby avoids pain and early death in favor of a long, pain-free life, but at the expense of those whose names he leapfrogged. Carl feels some guilt, but those feelings are dwarfed by his feelings of joy and relief at being alive. His act was not virtuous, but it increased his well-being.

We do not know what eudaimonistic theories would say about these examples, or about any of the countless cases pitting happiness against moral and perfectionist virtue that arise every day in people's lives. To the extent that those theories do not yield answers, they are not rivals of the happiness theory, because a theory by its nature must yield answers.

Without doing so, it can neither resolve intuition conflicts nor be tested by the process of weighing intuitions known commonly in philosophy as "reflective equilibrium"—the standard way of testing a theory's quality. To the extent that eudaimonistic theories would say that well-being accords with happiness rather than virtue, they equate with the happiness theory. So the only thing that would preserve eudaimonistic theories as rivals of the happiness theory is for them to hold that well-being connects with virtue instead of happiness in at least a substantial number of cases where virtue and happiness conflict. If that is their favored approach, then they must also explain whether well-being always follows virtue in cases where virtue conflicts with happiness; and if not, then what differentiates the cases where virtue "wins" from the cases where happiness does. If intuition alone is relied on to make that differentiation among cases, then eudaimonistic theories face the problem of opacity that we discussed above in the context of both preference theories and objective list theories.[63] And in the cases where virtue rather than happiness is what leads to well-being, eudaimonistic theories are insufficiently attentive to the fact that well-being concerns what is good for the individual rather than what is good objectively. We pressed this point in the previous section in the context of discussing list theories.

Moreover, our views about the disconnect between virtue and well-being represent the norm rather than the exception and accord well with common usage and understandings of the terms. As Wayne Sumner writes,

> Indeed, the conclusion of Aristotle's argument, the equation of welfare and virtue, has always seemed too good to be true. We simply have too many examples, from our day as from his, of villains and miscreants who seem (as Bernard Williams puts it) "by any ethological standard of the bright eye and the gleaming coat" to be faring very well indeed. With any luck there is a strong tendency for virtue and interest to coincide, but we push our luck if we ask for more than that. Certainly they do not coincide conceptually, nor are they analytically linked in the tight way that Aristotle would have us believe.[64]

Daniel Haybron makes the identical point,[65] amid a piercing and wide-ranging attack on Aristotelian theories of well-being to which we refer interested readers.[66] Eudaimonists must rely on the claim that well-being connects with virtue, but that claim runs up against the way those concepts are widely understood. Consider how thoroughly self-interest and morality seem to diverge in everyday thought and speech. The word "selfless" usually expresses great moral admiration. The word "selfish" is perhaps the single most common term used to judge a person as morally wanting. If the eudaimonists were right, then it would be hard to make sense of these facts, because doing the virtuous thing would also be doing what is best for oneself. Indeed, prioritizing others' well-being over one's own is typically thought to be the very epitome of virtue, but it is nonsensical on the eudaimonist view because that view equates acting virtuously with increasing one's own well-being. If the eudaimonists were correct, everyone who uses the terms "selfless" and "selfish" in the belief that morality can diverge from self-interest would be deluded. According to the eudaimonist view, one cannot succeed at benefiting oneself by unethically prioritizing one's own interests over others' interests, and one cannot harm oneself by ethically prioritizing others' interests over one's own interests. We believe—as did Sumner, Williams, and many others—that such an outlook grates powerfully against people's widespread understandings and experiences of life.

Aristotelian philosophy, and literature about objective goods such as capabilities,[67] may well be able to reveal much that is valuable about life. They are "miscast" as theories of well-being,[68] but that does not at all call into question their overall value. It is regrettable that they have been "dragooned into service as accounts of well-being,"[69] instead of being considered in their proper role as broader claims about what it means for a life to be good not just for the person living it but more broadly, including in moral and perfectionist terms.

*   *   *

From the discussion of preference and objective theories, one thing that emerges is how hard it is for a theory to yield testable answers to questions about well-being. How can one know which of Jill's preferences are about Jill's life, or what Jill's fully informed preferences would be, or whether Jill's health or loving relationships contribute more to her well-being, or whether Jill's behavior is virtuous or characteristically human? Those questions rely on intuitions for answers, but they are no more likely to avoid intuition conflicts in the mass of cases than is the original question of how much well-being Jill has.

The reason those theories face this problem is that they rely on multiple components and/or vague and inaccessible principles. To solve the problem, one needs a theory that is simpler and is based on a concrete, accessible principle. Ideally, the principle will provide a way to commensurate all things that affect well-being. It should yield answers in every case and thus be testable against people's intuitions. Then it should pass that test by according with standard intuitions in the mass of cases. And in the cases where it does not accord with intuitions, there should be plausible explanations for its divergence.

The hedonic theory fits this bill. It says that well-being is equivalent to net affect, which means that every case can be assessed by how good or bad a person feels. A person's well-being is her sum of overall lifetime happiness. Those who disagree must explain how something can make a person better off even when it reduces that sum of her happiness. As the preceding discussion shows, this isn't easy: people's intuitions strongly support equating happiness and well-being. For an alternative theory to be even remotely plausible on its face, it must align very closely with the happiness theory.

This idea is no secret. Susan Wolf, a leading eudaimonist about well-being, cites happiness as the primary reason for people to "care about living a meaningful life"—that is, a life involving the good activities Wolf thinks are essential to well-being. "Nine times out of ten, perhaps ninety-nine times out of a hundred, a meaningful life will be happier than a meaningless one."[70] And Matthew Adler, a leading preferentist, acknowledges that his theory might yield results identical to those of the happiness theory: "To be sure, the account I propose is consistent with the proposition that . . . mental states are, as a matter of contingent fact, the sole source of well-being."[71]

But the reverse is not true. Recall the examples in which happiness diverges starkly from seemingly core aspects of well-being such as health, loving relationships, and money or success (which are not only typical items on objective lists, but also typical preferences and typical components or sources of eudaimonia). In those examples, it is intuitive that well-being tracks happiness rather than those other things. The happiness theory does not depend for its plausibility on the connection between well-being and anything other than happiness. By contrast, every non-happiness theory does depend for its plausibility on the connection between well-being and something other than what those theories emphasize—and that something is happiness.

In chapter 8, we will address some famous examples that purport to show the disconnection between happiness and well-being. We will argue that those examples are problematic because they make it hard to believe that the supposedly worse-off person is actually just as happy as the supposedly better-off alternative. Whatever one thinks of our claims, it is important to note that our argumentative strategy is unavailable for proponents of alternative theories in dealing with the examples we have given above. Our examples do not make it hard to believe that Jack's toxin worsens his health, that Jill the loner has few loving relationships, that Ben has little money, or that Bob watches TV and thereby does something that eudaimonists consider worse for him than philosophy. Happiness theorists need not rely on examples that obscure whether other things are in fact sacrificed, because those other things are not particularly important for well-being unless they yield happiness. By contrast, non-happiness theorists *do* need to rely on examples that obscure whether happiness is sacrificed because happiness is intuitively essential for well-being.

CHAPTER SEVEN

A Hedonic Theory of Well-Being

This part of the book is concerned with the question of what it means for someone's life to go well for her. What is well-being or quality of life? In this chapter, we explain our view that well-being is happiness—the aggregated moments of how good and bad someone feels throughout her life.[1] As we described in chapter 1, feeling good is measured by proxies that seem valid on their face and generally accord with one another. These proxies include self-reports, others' reports, dopamine levels, and smiling, among other things. To some degree, one may still have to use intuitions in certain cases to decide whether someone feels good; but the intuition conflicts about that are likely to be far less frequent and intractable than the intuition conflicts about the initial question of someone's well-being. None of the other leading theories of well-being come close to achieving the same success on this essential ground.

We believe that happiness captures people's intuitions about well-being in the mass of cases. When we picture someone with well-being, we picture her feeling good. We think that things like money or achievement contribute to well-being only because, and insofar as, they make people happy. Even health and longevity contribute to well-being via happiness: pain and discomfort are bad for people because they make people feel bad, and living longer is good for people because and insofar as people tend to enjoy life.[2]

Perhaps because of these strengths, the happiness theory has enjoyed somewhat of a renaissance in recent years. Two important recent books about well-being have prioritized some form of hedonic measure over preferences or objective values as the primary component of welfare.[3] And the authors of these books, Wayne Sumner and Fred Feldman, are far from alone. The hedonic theory has been defended in varying forms and degrees not just by Sumner and Feldman but also by Roger Crisp,[4] Joseph Mendola,[5] Adam Kolber,[6] Richard Layard,[7] Torbjörn Tännsjö,[8] and Elinor Mason.[9] These recent voices add to the chorus of scholars, many of whom utilitarian, who were hedonists (in one form or another) all along.[10]

We will now try to explain some basic features of the happiness theory we favor.

Happiness and the Subjective Experience of Life

A person experiences life wholly through a set of physical and psychological processes in her body. All feelings and thoughts arise from these processes.[11] Psychologists refer to the most basic of these feelings as "core affect."[12] Core affect is the irreducibly simple state of feeling good or bad at a given moment.[13] It is related to the fundamental evolutionary concerns of approach and avoidance,[14] and it can be conceived of as spanning a continuous spectrum from happiness to unhappiness or from pleasure to displeasure.[15]

Core affect is a mental representation of a person's physical and psychological states, but it is not necessarily "about" anything.[16] Core affect is pervasive and constantly felt even when a person is not thinking about it.[17] It is the valenced affective component of our moods. Like body temperature, it is always there even though it isn't always or often thought about.[18] In addition, core affect is the underlying feeling that undergirds the huge variety of more complex human emotions. People experience many different emotions that they characterize as good or bad. For example, both *gratitude* and *pride* are positive emotions. They inherently share a similar substrate of positive core affect. Their difference resides, in part, in the objects toward which that positive affect is directed or felt—with *gratitude* toward another person and with *pride* toward oneself.[19] It is the fundamental component of core affect in both emotions, rather than the cognitive elements that differ between them, that concerns us for the purposes of determining a person's well-being. In this book, we use the term "happiness" to refer to this commensurability among varying feelings based on their underlying degree of core affect.[20]

There is a wealth of scientific evidence from various disciplines, including psychology, behavioral economics, neuroscience, and linguistics, that supports the existence of a common good-bad dimension of affect underlying individuals' experiences.[21] For example, all known human languages contain the expressions "I feel good" and "I feel bad," and the notions of good and bad feeling are "universal and semantically primitive."[22] The same is not true for the words "emotion," "fear," and "anger."[23] Additionally, pleasure and displeasure have been shown to be essential to many aspects of behavior and decision-making, including sex, eating, aggression, and drug abuse, as well as higher-order cognitive effects.[24] In his canonical chapter "Objective Happiness," Daniel Kahneman describes eighteen different empirical studies supporting the idea that "each moment [is] uniquely characterized by a value on the Good-Bad dimension."[25] In one experiment, for example, "the prior presentation of any positively evaluated word (such as *water*) was found to facilitate selectively the rapid pronunciation of any other positively evaluated word (such as *Friday*)."[26] Other experiments showed that "differences in the activation of the anterior regions of the left and right cortices are correlated with the quality of experience. Starting in infancy . . . , a predominance of left-sided anterior activation is associated with positive states, whereas a predominance of right-sided activation indicates a negative affect."[27] In fact, "[a]t a still more basic level, there are discussions of specific neural pathways that deal with the computation of overall reward value . . . and specific neurotransmitters that appear to be involved in the control of approach/avoidance tendencies."[28] Kahneman concludes that "[a]ll these lines of evidence, from the introspective to the biochemical, point to the existence of a . . . continuous Good/Bad commentary."[29]

As a person progresses through life, her experiences are associated with affective states, some of which will be positive, while others will be negative, neutral, or a combination of positive and negative. Some of these experiences will also entail cognitions, such as beliefs and thoughts, which will themselves produce affective states. Our theory conceives of a person's welfare during any moment (of any duration) of her life as the sum of the positive and negative affect that she feels during the moment. Ralph's welfare while cooking dinner for his family is determined by the positive feelings that he had while cooking minus the negative feelings he had. Ralph's welfare over the course of his life is determined in the same way. Our account of well-being as moment-by-moment net affect owes much to Kahneman's work on "objective happiness,"[30] and it also evokes the accounts of welfare contained within the utilitarian theories of Jeremy Bentham and Peter Singer.[31]

Different kinds of experiences are capable of affecting the way people feel in a variety of different ways. Touching a hot stove and recoiling in pain is a negative experience, whereas stepping into a warm bath and feeling a sensation of pleasure is a positive one. Between these experiences and the affective states they produce there is little or no cognition or reflection. Higher-order experiences, such as reading a book or thinking about a loved one, also produce cognitive or emotional sensations in a person's brain that the individual registers as positive or negative; either the individual is enjoying the book, or she is not. Although these experiences involve more complicated cognition than do the stove and bath examples, they still generate the same fundamental kind of core affect in the person.

A person's experience of life is the collection of these sorts of experienced moments, and because each moment is positive or negative for the person depending on how she feels during it, these feelings make up the subjective quality of her life. They determine whether someone experiences her own life as positive or negative, and how positively or negatively she experiences it. Thus on our view, what it means for something to be a bad experience for an individual is for it to make the individual feel bad. Negative feelings constitute bad life experiences, and positive feelings constitute good ones. Of course, a negative experience can increase welfare in the long run by decreasing the duration or intensity of other negative experiences in the future (or increasing positive ones in the future).

Obviously, feelings vary along dimensions other than just positivity. We do not believe that two feelings are entirely identical if they are equally positive or negative. The feelings of *anger* and *sadness*, for example, are of course different in many important respects. Instead, we believe merely that two feelings are equally good (or bad) for the person experiencing them if they are equally positive (or negative). On our view, Jane's well-being at any moment is how good or bad she feels during that moment. The measure of welfare for a period of any duration is the aggregate of a person's moment-by-moment experiences of positive and negative feeling.

Feeling vs. Evaluating, and the Choice of the Time Interval

To reiterate, we believe that a person's lifetime well-being is the aggregation of how good and bad she feels during all the moments of her life. For these purposes, a moment refers simply to the shortest time interval in which someone can have a feeling.

Some might argue, however, that certain events should be considered as a whole, rather than as an aggregation of moments.[32] Perhaps relatedly, one could claim that a person's evaluation of an event affects her well-being independently from how she feels about the event moment-by-moment. We reject this approach. We believe that what matters is how people feel in each moment, so judgments or memories are treated the same as any other moments: they count toward well-being insofar as they are themselves felt positively or negatively.[33]

An example will help illustrate these points. Suppose that someone has long hoped to run a marathon. She trains for many months, and finally the day of the race arrives. During the marathon, she feels many moments of pain. But upon completing the race, she feels great satisfaction in her achievement. "That was absolutely worth it," she announces. A critic of our hedonic approach to welfare might say that we cannot make sense of the runner's proclamation that the marathon was "worth it" if we view her happiness only on a moment-by-moment basis. Such a view would not, according to the critic, capture the point that the marathon has increased the runner's well-being insofar as it enabled the runner to complete a project that was important to her.

This criticism contains three separate issues that must be disentangled. The first is whether it would be possible to make sense of the runner's statement from the perspective of our feeling-based account of welfare. The second is whether the runner's own evaluation of the race's effect on her welfare should be given special weight that is not captured by our moment-by-moment approach. The third is whether the marathon should be viewed as an aggregated series of moments or instead as a single project.

Regarding the first question, the runner's statement that the race was "worth it" does not necessarily contradict our conception of welfare. For one thing, it may simply be that the marathoner's feelings during the race involved more positivity than negativity: the pain may have been offset by a deep satisfaction in striving to perform a difficult task of which she was capable. Such striving is often associated with the most intense state of positive affect.[34] But even if the moments spent running the marathon were negative and outweighed (in intensity and duration) the moment of joy at the finish line, the runner might believe that the marathon will increase her long-term well-being by adding to her subsequent aggregated moments of happiness. She may anticipate having proud memories of her accomplishment for the rest of her life (and perhaps even anticipate gaining the confidence from it to achieve success in other endeavors), thereby experiencing many moments of happiness—that is, the moments that occur whenever she thinks of the achievement and feels good about it.

The marathoner's post-race proclamation could be attributable to this expectation. When someone declares a difficult endeavor to have been worthwhile or expresses happiness at having completed one, she often does so because of her anticipation of the long-term benefits that the project's completion will bring. She is happy to have finished because she recognizes that over the coming weeks or months, the fact of having completed the project will pay dividends, dividends that will increase her welfare in the net. This explanation accounts conversely for the fact that, for example, someone who eats a delicious but unhealthful food may immediately regret having done so because he anticipates the future decrease in well-being that might be entailed. He may decide to exercise more to avoid gaining weight, eat more vegetables to counteract the negative nutritional consequences, or forswear other fatty foods for some period of time. His expressed regret—"That wasn't worth it"—is a judgment about predicted long-term subjective well-being, and the marathoner's statement may well be the same thing.[35]

Let us next assume for the sake of argument that neither of the conditions from the previous paragraph hold true. Specifically, the pain of running the marathon exceeds the positive feeling, or sense of "flow,"[36] experienced during the race itself. In addition, no feelings of satisfaction occur after the race:[37] for example, suppose the runner dies immediately upon completion of the race, from an unrelated physical condition that would have killed her at that moment regardless of whether she had run. In that case, running the marathon did not increase her well-being. Upon her death, if we were to look back at her life and evaluate the well-being she had during her life, then we would deem her to have had lower overall well-being than if she had done something on her last day that she would have enjoyed more than running the marathon. Forced to exclude the consideration of future benefit (future moments of happiness attributable to having run the race), most people would, we believe, find it intuitive that the marathon did not in fact increase the runner's well-being.

But suppose the runner herself believes that the race did make her better off. If her statement that it was "worth it" does not refer either to the positive feeling (flow) of running the race or to the anticipated benefit of feeling good while recollecting her accomplishment, then what? The answer is that we do not have to take her word for it. A person's own stated judgment that completing a project increased her well-being does not resolve whether the project in fact increased her well-being. Imagine a survivor of torture who tells himself that he was actually made stronger by the experience and is better for it. There may sometimes be good reasons, in terms of psychological health, for people to persuade themselves that an experience was valuable.[38] But when we, as observers, evaluate whether the person would have been better off not having been tortured, we are not bound by the judgment stated by the person himself. The same goes for the marathoner. Our theory judges a person's well-being by how good *she feels*, so it is subjective in that sense. But our theory, like every other theory we know of, does not judge well-being by deferring to a person's *opinion* about her own well-being.

More broadly, we may ask *why* judgments or evaluations of the quality of an experience would matter independently of feelings.[39] Judgments tend not to determine well-being on any theory, hedonic or otherwise. Suppose Jim believes that his well-being will be increased if the temperature on a planet in another galaxy increases next year (even though he will never learn whether it increased and doesn't spend any time thinking about such matters). Does his belief make it so? We think not, and here there seems to be widespread agreement. People could have any number of puzzling beliefs about their own well-being, but their beliefs about their well-being need not equate with their well-being itself.

To be sure, the judgment may well involve positive feeling: while reflecting on the marathon, the runner feels good about what she has done. That good feeling counts, of course, in our assessment of her well-being. But the good feeling from the reflection counts no more or less than does her negative feeling while running (assuming, by hypothesis, that it was negative). Evaluations are simply moments during one's life, no different in their inherent value or meaning from any other moments of felt experience.

We now move, finally, to the third issue raised by the marathoner example: choosing the relevant time interval for aggregation. Should the marathon be deemed a single project—and thus counted toward the runner's well-being as one block of time that she regards positively—or instead an aggregation of moments that include substantial pain?

The problem with the "project-based" approach is that it excludes, without justification, parts of the person's life that she actually experienced. If she chooses to (or just does) remember the marathon positively, then that counts insofar as her memories themselves become experienced feelings in her life. Those memories or reflections on the marathon are parts of her life while she feels them, no more or less so than the actual running was a part of her life while she felt it. Misremembering the pain affects the experience of recalling the marathon, but it does not retroactively eliminate from life the moments of feeling the pain as those moments happened. Those moments also count because they too were real. To view the marathon as a whole is to exclude a part of life that occurred (and was felt and experienced) and that therefore should not be excised from the record of the person's life.

Feeling Good vs. Positive Attitudes

Ours is not the only happiness-related theory. To take one example of an alternative, Fred Feldman conceives well-being not as feeling good but instead as positive attitudes.[40] We will not go into the details of his theory, but instead focus on one example that he uses to distinguish between feelings and attitudes. The example involves a researcher who suppresses the part of the brain that is responsible for what Feldman calls "cheery feelings" and what we would call "positive feelings."[41] The researcher then spends time playing with his children but "feels decidedly strange" because he "cannot feel any cheery feelings." Feldman claims that the researcher would still be happy because he "takes pleasure" in playing with the children despite not feeling any pleasure. But what does it mean for the researcher to "take pleasure" in playing with his children if he can feel no pleasure while doing it? If he feels pleasure about it after the fact, then that feeling makes him happy after the fact. But Feldman wants to say that he is happy *while* he feels no positive emotion. Feldman cites five scholars who find this claim unsustainable,[42] and we must say that we see it their way rather than his. Various things can affect the way a person feels, including that person's experiences and her thoughts about those experiences. People's thoughts are often connected with some affective quality (that is, their thoughts make them feel a certain way). But it is the feelings caused by the thoughts and experiences that affect welfare, and not the thoughts or experiences themselves. If the researcher is thinking, "I'm playing with my kids, which I like," then that thought would cause him to feel good (absent the hypothesized suppression), as would the experience of playing with his children (again, absent the suppression), and it is the feeling good that people associate with happiness. This is revealed by imagining what the researcher would look and feel like if his happiness were truly suppressed. He would not be smiling. He would not feel good. He would experience no joy or positive emotion, positive sensation, or positive feeling of any kind. In the absence of all those emotional states, it is unclear what "taking pleasure" would entail. In fact, it seems impossible that a person so constituted would even be capable of meaningfully having that thought. We think that if such a person seems happy to Feldman, then Feldman's idea of happiness is at odds with the typical understanding of the term.[43] Thus, we depart from Feldman and believe that positive feelings rather than positive attitudes best capture the concept of well-being.

Weak Welfarism

Economists and utilitarian philosophers occupy such a central place in the literature on well-being that, to avoid confusion, we will close with a brief explanation of the difference between our view and traditional welfarism or utilitarianism. Whereas those theories deem well-being the only thing of value and seek to maximize the overall amount of it, we take a more limited tack. Like the "weak welfarism" of Matthew Adler and Eric Posner,[44] our approach is entirely open to the possibility that things other than overall human welfare could have value. Examples include "moral rights, the fair distribution of welfare, and even moral considerations wholly detached from welfare, such as intrinsic environmental values."[45]

*   *   *

We believe that well-being is simply net affect—the sum of a person's good and bad feelings throughout the moments of her life. We think this simple, straightforward view accords best with people's intuitions about well-being and solves many of the problems associated with other theories. In the next chapter, we address objections to our view.

CHAPTER EIGHT

Addressing Objections to the Hedonic Theory

A mong the many possible objections to the Benthamite happiness theory we favor, two have been pressed most forcefully. The first is that there simply is no such thing as "feeling good" in a sense that applies across different sorts of other mental states, and the second is that people's lives are not going well for them if they are happy but deceived or ignorant. We now address those two criticisms.

The Two Most Common Objections to the Happiness Theory

Feeling good

For us, well-being is net affect—the sum of a person's good and bad feelings. But is there such a thing as feeling good? Many philosophers have expressed doubt.[1] They suggest that different sorts of things—for example, "eating, reading, working, creating, helping"[2]—may be irreducibly different in how they make people feel, with no ingredient in common that could make those feelings more positive or negative. But many other scholars, from across the disciplines of philosophy, psychology, and neuroscience, have disagreed with them and supported the notion that positivity is a feature running across different experiences.[3]

In chapter 7, we discussed at length the considerable empirical support for our position that has emerged across a range of disciplines. James Russell and Daniel Kahneman have separately cataloged dozens of studies that indicate that at the base of each of our experiences is a common dimension of affective valence.[4] Our bodies and minds naturally and unavoidably produce feelings of goodness and badness during all our experiences, whether we consciously realize it or not. This is the case both for "lower-order" experiences like taking a bath or eating a bowl of pasta and for "higher-order" experiences such as watching a play or doing philosophy. It is also the case that the various forms of negative emotion, such as fear and anger, appear to share a fundamentally similar affective "badness" despite the other differences between them.[5] These studies lend strong credence to the belief in a uni-dimensional good-bad affective core.

In addition to the scientific evidence, our theory receives support from general intuitions and behaviors. We believe it is common sense to most people that "feeling good" refers to a real thing: a common element of experience that embodies how people enjoy some things more than others and enables comparisons across activities on that dimension of enjoyment. To us, it does not seem strange—much less impossible—for someone to think like this: "I have a free hour. I could spend it reading (either *People* magazine or *Anna Karenina*) or exercising (either jogging or weight lifting) or talking to a friend (either Jack or Jill). Of all these options, I think I'd most enjoy talking to Jill, so I'm going to do that." This sort of thinking can be, we believe, not just a choice (i.e., a preference) but a choice about what would be most enjoyable. Not every choice is about that, but some choices are, and they require comparing different sorts of activities with regard to what the person would like the most. We think people make these choices all the time and often do not find them difficult.

Indeed, when people are asked how happy they are, they do not say that the question is nonsensical but instead respond to it willingly. Martha Nussbaum denies the significance of this fact, writing, "People are easily bullied . . . , and so they do answer such questions, rather than respond, 'This question is ill-informed.'"[6] But the evidence suggests otherwise. Many people refuse to respond to survey questions about their willingness to pay for non-market goods,[7] and they are bullied no more or less to answer those questions than to answer happiness surveys. Moreover, people are far more likely to answer questions about their happiness or life satisfaction than to answer other questions *on the same survey*.[8] We think this supports the view that people believe feeling good is a real thing that can be assessed across experiences that are otherwise different. Given this evidence, we think the ball is in the court of those who would deny the existence of a thing called "feeling good" that runs across different sorts of experiences.

Before leaving this topic, we will briefly note a different version of the objection: that our Benthamite happiness theory is insufficiently subjective. Sumner presses this point: "An objective account does not become more plausible when pleasure, understood as a homogeneous sensation, comes to be substituted for the more common list of perfectionist goods."[9] Needless to say, we disagree. For one thing, no one subscribes to a theory of welfare that is truly subjective in the sense of letting an individual decide what constitutes her own welfare. Suppose Jane believes that getting what she wants will not increase her well-being.[10] Then even a preference-satisfaction theory does not let Jane decide what is best for her: it dictates, contrary to her view, that getting what she wants *does* increase her well-being. Preference theorists observe something about Jane—what she wants—and dictate that that thing is her well-being. Similarly, our view observes something about Jane—what makes her feel good—and dictates that that thing is her well-being. Some might still say that the preference approach honors Jane's perspective more because it lets her choose what she wants, whereas she can't choose what makes her feel good. But it is not clear how free people really are to choose what they want;[11] nor are they completely unfree to affect what makes them happy. Most importantly, it is far from clear why this difference between preferences and happiness (to the extent it is a difference at all) matters for well-being. Objective theories may have a problem differentiating between what is "the best life" and what is "the best life *for Jane*." But the happiness theory does not seem to have this problem. Happiness, like preferences, is connected inextricably with what makes Jane Jane, and happiness is clearly unconnected with other sorts of methods of valuing Jane's life, such as how much virtue her life embodies.[12]

Confronting the hardest cases

The second major criticism of the happiness theory is that it cannot account for the intuition that one's welfare is diminished by things outside of one's experience or knowledge. This criticism has been advanced via several forceful sorts of examples, and we will now try to deal with the most difficult ones.[13]

We begin with the example that we find most difficult for the hedonic theory to explain. It is far more problematic than the experience machine, which we address later in this chapter.

Jack is very happy in his marriage to Jill, and he fully believes she is faithful to him. In one possible state of affairs, Jill is actually faithful; whereas in an alternative state of affairs, she is cheating on Jack without his knowledge. We are asked to suppose that these two states of affairs are identical but for the cheating, as far as Jack's experience of life is concerned. To wit: Jill treats Jack *identically* whether she is cheating on him or not; everyone else treats Jack identically whether Jill is cheating on Jack or not; Jack never learns that Jill is cheating on him; and Jack's experience of life is never affected by the cheating in any way.[14]

According to critics of the happiness theory, people overwhelmingly believe that Jack is better off if Jill is faithful than if she is cheating. To begin with, we are not even certain that this is the case. We think the happiness theory holds such powerful intuitive appeal that if the question were made truly clear, people's intuitions might not be as overwhelming as many philosophers assume. But suppose we are wrong on that score. What then?

Let us argue backward from another example to this one. Imagine that Jill has always been faithful to Jack, and that one day she embarks on a six-month business trip to Nepal. While she is in Nepal, she has a one-night affair with a man there. By an incredible coincidence, Jack had died back at home in a car crash two hours before Jill's affair. Jill had not known of Jack's death, and Jack never knew about what Jill was going to do. Did Jill's affair decrease Jack's well-being? Some philosophers will argue that it did, even though it occurred after Jack had died. The hedonic theory, by contrast, would hold that it did not. After all, Jack never even knew about the affair, much less experienced a thought or emotion related to it.

We will not litigate that issue here, nor is it necessary for us to do so. The point of the deceived spouse example, like that of the experience machine, is to show that the happiness theory is irredeemably inconsistent with standard intuitions. Although people may disagree about the post-death version, there is certainly no strong consensus (among philosophers or, we assume, anyone else) for rejecting the happiness theory's answer. If anything, we suspect there may well be a strong consensus (among those who are not committed to theories that insist on post-death welfare) that the happiness theory gets it right in this case.

We believe that many readers will find the hedonic theory's answer (that Jack's well-being was unaffected) far more compelling than the alternative—though, again, our point here does not depend on that claim.

Now consider whether it would matter if Jack's death had occurred two hours after Jill's affair instead of two hours before it. The two events were still completely unrelated, and Jack never had any idea of what Jill had done. Did Jill's affair decrease Jack's well-being? Even more so than with the post-death example, many scholars will argue that Jill's affair did indeed decrease Jack's well-being. But this, too, is not a worry for the happiness theory. We believe that many people will intuit not only that there was no welfare effect in the post-death case, but also that the post-death case is not meaningfully distinguishable from the barely pre-death case. Intuition conflicts and fierce normative arguments are likely to come from this barely pre-death example, but once again, that is hardly a significant blow to the happiness theory. The deceived spouse example, together with its cousin the experience machine, is supposed to be *the* refutation of the happiness theory. Even if most people believed that the happiness theory had generated a severely counterintuitive result in this case, that might not suffice as such a refutation. And this example hardly supplies such a counter-intuitive result: the intuitive answer is far from clear, and again we suspect that many people will believe that the hedonic theory is right to suggest that Jack's welfare was unaffected. If one wants to argue that Jill's infidelity in Nepal decreases Jack's welfare, then that requires an argument rather than just an appeal to the obviousness of the intuition. And the argument may be rough sledding. If, for example, it is based on Jack's preferences or on objective considerations, then it will need to address the concerns about those respective approaches that we noted in chapter 6.

We now turn back to the original example. Although we do not presume to know what most people's intuitions would be about any of the three cases—post-death Nepal, pre-death Nepal, and the original example—we think it may well be the case that the original is viewed quite differently from the Nepal variants. If so, why would this be? We would like to suggest a possible explanation. In the Nepal variant, it is obvious that Jack's experience of life is wholly unaffected by Jill's infidelity, whereas this is stipulated but hard to believe in the original example. We think that people's intuitions about the original example may be driven by their failure to honor the example's rules. This would make sense because it is almost impossible to believe that Jill would treat Jack *identically* if she were cheating and if she were faithful. When we try to imagine those two states in the original example, we picture Jill very differently in each of them. In the state where she is faithful, we picture her loving Jack and having no interest in cheating on him. This picture seems like a recipe for a solid, lasting marriage and for great happiness along the way. But when we picture the unfaithful state, we struggle to imagine Jill acting *exactly* the same way toward Jack. How could she possibly do that unless she were some sort of sociopath, or a pathological liar, or at minimum a cold and unfeeling person? We think that for most people, their feelings would show through in one way or another. Either they would feel guilty and let it show, or their cheating would be motivated by dissatisfaction that would show, or there would be some other manifestation of their cheating. If Jill really showed nothing, then it means that Jack is married to someone who seems a lot different from our picture of Jill in the faithful state, and that affects our intuitions about how much happiness Jack is getting out of his marriage (notwithstanding the stipulation to the contrary). And the problem isn't just Jill's identical behavior, but also the fact that she chose differently in the two states at all. Why did she cheat on Jack in one state but not in the other? It is very difficult for us not to infer from that difference that their marriage was less experientially positive in one state than in the other.[15]

Philosophers of ethics sometimes disparage this method of argument. They assert that they are practiced in taking seriously the rules of these hypotheticals, and that of course they have done so here. Their intuitions are not, they say, influenced by the sorts of things that are ruled out.[16] Where does this leave matters? For one thing, we must say that we have doubts about that assertion. There are all sorts of psychological experiments that have been devised to test people's implicit feelings about things, and whether those implicit feelings have changed after deep reflection. We strongly suspect that even the most seasoned philosophers might well be revealed by such tests to have been unable to rule out the things that are deeply unnatural to ignore. Philosophers might claim that no such tests can prove or even suggest such failure, but even if that were true, the upshot would simply be an irreconcilable conflict between their and our intuitions about everyone's capacity to take the rules seriously. We know that we ourselves cannot be relied on to do so, despite serious effort and many years of engaging with these issues.

In any event, one who maintains that Jack's well-being is obviously diminished in the original example would still need to explain why it is less obvious in the Nepal pre-death example. And we acknowledge that such explanations are available. Perhaps one might say that the original example is worse for Jack because he lives years rather than hours after having been cheated on. But this rejoinder seems questionable. We think that many people may well intuit that Jack's well-being was not decreased *at all* by Jill's cheating in the Nepal pre-death example—not just that it was diminished less than in the original example. If so—if there are many people who believe that Jack's welfare was not diminished at all in the Nepal case but was diminished in the original example—then what could account for that difference other than the (completely understandable and likely) failure to take seriously the (stylized and wholly unrealistic and unbelievable) rules of the original example? Holding constant (at one) the number of episodes of infidelity in both examples, the only differences seem to be geographical distance and Jack's imminent death. One could argue that the geographical distance matters—for example, that Jack is harmed more by having Jill cheat on him when she is closer—but this seems like an intuition that should not matter and that therefore might not survive reflection.

Let us be clear: we are not purporting to prove, or even to argue in any sort of systematic way, that Jack's well-being is unaffected by Jill's infidelity in these examples. That is not our burden. The deceived spouse is the single hardest case for the happiness theory, so our goal is simply to show why it does not deserve to have so much importance attached to it. If the example's force may derive from pumping inadmissible intuitions, then a new example is needed that does not do so. Such an example may exist, but we have not seen it. The other two canonical examples that we describe below fail this test more spectacularly than does even the example of the deceived spouse.

We now turn to the next example meant to demonstrate the problems with the happiness theory. In this canonical example, there are two possible states of Jane's life. In one state, Jane lives in poverty in a society that discriminates against her based on her sex. But she has adapted to the poverty and discrimination and feels quite happy despite it.[17] In the other state, Jane lives a life of comfort, activity, and commitment to justice, all in a society that gives her full political and social rights and nourishes her capabilities. But she feels no happier throughout her life than if she had lived in poverty and oppression. Her happiness is equal in both states.

Those who attack the happiness theory claim that Jane obviously has more well-being in the second state (free) than in the first state (oppressed), yet her happiness is equal, so happiness must not equate with well-being. Our response here is the same as the one above (and below): the example gains all its intuitive traction from telling people to disregard something that they cannot in fact disregard. Both common sense and overwhelming evidence indicate that people who are oppressed and in poverty are far, far less happy than are people who are free and economically comfortable.[18] If one intuits that Jane is better off free, then that may well be the source of the intuition.

Again, we expect that many philosophers will simply deny this. They will say that they have carefully considered the hypothetical and held constant Jane's happiness. But we would like to suggest respectfully that their good-faith belief in this may not constitute a strong enough reason to take their word for it. Absent some empirical demonstration of their success, what is needed is a different sort of example that does not pump inadmissible intuitions. It falls to critics of the happiness theory to supply such an example, since they are the ones relying on such examples to disqualify the theory.

As with the deceived spouse, we will explain what happens when we ourselves try to ponder the two states in this example. Because we have been told that Jane's happiness is equal in the two states, and because both common sense and vast evidence deny that this is possible, we try to imagine *how* it could be possible. Certainly, there are ways it could be possible, but those ways defeat the original purpose of the example. Imagine that Jane is equally happy in the two states because in the oppressed state she belongs to a tight-knit social group of friends, extended family, or fellow religious worshippers, whereas in the free state she has few close social ties. If one starts to flesh out the reasons that she might be just as happy in the oppressed state, then one's intuition that her free life is better starts to erode. The more one comes to believe that she is actually equally happy, the more it seems that she has an equally good life.

But such an exercise will of course be rejected by critics, who can argue that this sort of fleshing out involves attributing to oppressed Jane but not to free Jane aspects of life that are valuable in non-happiness terms. The critics' claim would be that people care about social ties not because those ties make them feel good, but because those ties are part of, for example, preferences or human flourishing. Or so the argument would go. It is hard to sort out answers to such challenges because there is such overlap between the things valued by objective-list and nature-fulfillment theories of welfare and the types of things that make people feel good. It can be difficult to know what is driving one's positive assessment of the thing in question.

So what is one to do? The point of the oppression example is to hold constant everything, including Jane's happiness, except for the poverty and oppression. And the problem is that doing so requires one to imagine that the poverty and oppression do not make Jane any less happy than she would otherwise be. To make this leap of imagination, one might try to picture Jane as a highly unusual type of person who is not made happier by freedom or less happy by poverty. Maybe Jane is a Buddhist monk who has spent decades training herself to let go of all desires and attachments. She is wholly unaffected by her poverty and oppression, and wholly unaffected by her alternative freedom and comfort, because she has learned not to let any of those seemingly positive or negative things penetrate her experience of life. In this case, we no longer intuit that Jane is better off in the free state. Both the welfare-related negatives of the oppressed state, and the welfare-related positives of the free state, are simply lost on her. To be sure, others will have the opposite intuition. But we do not think their intuition is the sort of knockdown argument that it would need to be in order to show on its own the wrongness of the happiness theory.

This brings us finally to the example of Robert Nozick's experience machine.[19] An individual (call her "Helen") can choose to enter a machine that would make her think she was experiencing anything she desired; in real life, however, the individual would be floating in a tank and would have electrodes attached to her brain.[20] While inside the machine, Helen would have no idea she was not living in the real world.[21] Could someone sitting motionless with her head attached to electrodes actually have as much welfare as someone whose experiences are real? The answer is yes, once one has laid aside all the intuitions that the example is meant to exclude.

Many scholars have joined us in rejecting the experience machine because of the inadmissible intuitions it pumps.[22] As Richard Layard puts it, the experience machine "is a weak test case, especially because it describes a situation so far from our reality that we have almost become a different animal."[23] Joseph Mendola writes: "The experience machine is unfamiliar gadgetry which invokes our fear of the unfamiliar. It certainly is wildly unrealistic. It involves a troubling irrevocability. And it seems to at least threaten risks of even hedonic harm that the corresponding actual life would not present."[24]

When one pictures the machine life, one might well get a mental image of what Helen looks like to someone who is not on the machine (that is, she looks like someone sitting alone, plugged into electrodes). Or perhaps one suspects that Helen knows she is on the machine and views her experiences there as false or shallow as a result. But life within the world created by the machine would look like ordinary life, complete with social ties, soaring natural beauty, and whatever else Helen derives happiness from. To the extent that negative feelings are necessary to maximize overall happiness,[25] those negative feelings would be present too. Absent would be any pain or suffering (much less early death) that is not necessary for overall happiness.[26] In other words, a life on the machine is a life that would be self-evidently wonderful for the person living it if she were living it in the real world. The question is whether it matters that she is living it on the machine.

When we work hard to picture what a life would be like in the machine, it seems like an awfully good life to us in terms of the welfare of the attached person. Maybe the life is selfish or immoral, but those issues are separate from well-being. Our intuition is that if Helen's life feels identical to Helen both on and off the machine, then her welfare is identical both on and off the machine. A critic will assert the contrary intuition and claim that his view is widely shared. But that claim is not self-evidently true, and even if it were true, it might well be due to the wild and problematic nature of the example—that is, how the example trades on people's inability to truly accept its rules.

Or it might be due to the intuitions pumped by the hypothetical about welfare-unrelated values like morality. Suppose a murderer hooks himself up to the machine. While there, he enjoys killing computer-generated facsimiles of innocent people (which he erroneously believes are real people) but kills no one in the real world. Is the murderer worse off on the machine than in the real world? Many will say yes, but we suspect that typical intuitions may favor the machine more weakly in this case than in the case of a normal person. If we are right, then that supports the notion that people's intuitions about the machine involve not just the subject's well-being but also other considerations. (An objectivist might say it shows instead that well-being is connected with morality. We addressed that idea in chapter 6.)

There are other non-welfare-related reasons for people not to want to attach themselves to the machine. For example, they might not want to forgo the opportunity to use their lives to improve the lives of others, they might not be convinced the machine will actually work, or they might fear that while on the machine they will be vulnerable to harm from those in the real world.[27] But these reasons, while entirely valid, are not about the welfare of the individual on the machine as contrasted with her welfare off the machine while feeling the same things. When one assesses the well-being of someone attached to the machine, one must look behind whatever visceral aversion to the machine one might have and assess both whether that aversion relates to welfare, and also whether it springs from rejecting the rules of the example.

What is the core claim that the machine hypothetical is supposed to bring out? The most plausible claim seems to be that Helen is better off if she is actually loved by those she cares about than if she merely thinks she is loved by them. This would explain why Helen's welfare seems no lower if she spends an hour reading a book on an experience machine than if she spends the hour reading the same book in real life. Once framed this way, it is hard to imagine that this example elicits knockdown intuitions in favor of real life. Consider, too, a loner who avoids all human interaction and spends his life happily in a remote cabin until he dies naturally at age seventy-five. When his life is assessed after it has ended, does one intuit that the loner had more well-being if his life of isolation took place in the real world rather than on the machine? Again, that question does not seem likely to elicit nearly the knockdown level of intuitions that the typical example of the machine is said to elicit. One possible reason for this is that people "vote" against the machine life not because they are focusing on the well-being of the person on the machine but rather because they are focusing on the *other* people who would miss out on interacting with that person. Even if one intuits that the loner is somewhat better off in the real world than on the machine, one's thought process in reaching that conclusion might involve picturing the benefit to animals or the positive effect on the world that the loner could have—or else the idea that the real world *must* somehow feel better to live in and interact with than the machine world—all things that should be kept separate from the question of the loner's welfare.

If the experience machine example elicits powerful intuitions, which may not be the case, then we think it does so by embodying the notion that Helen is worse off (*a*) if she thinks and feels she is loved by real people but actually is not, than if (*b*) she is in fact loved by real people. That means, however, that the machine example essentially reduces to the deceived spouse example discussed above, and it may be dealt with similarly. Let us exclude the machine itself and see how well the example's underlying claim holds up. Suppose Helen has a beloved daughter Amy who lives 10,000 miles away in Nepal. Helen believes that Amy hates her, and this belief causes Helen great sorrow and suffering. Suppose the belief is true, but an hour after Helen dies in the United States, Amy (not knowing about her mother's death) happens to renew her love for Helen. Did that improve Helen's welfare, even though it occurred after Helen's death? We suspect that many people will agree that it did not, and at minimum there is no obvious answer. What if Amy's change of heart happened an hour before Helen's death but was unbeknownst to Helen? Still no decisive intuition. What if it occurred twenty years before Helen's death, but Helen never learned of it and spent those twenty years in sorrow and suffering? We believe that many people will share our intuition that in this tragic case, Helen is no better off than if Amy had continued hating her: what makes the case tragic is that Helen could not benefit from the thing that would have made her so happy. As we said above in the context of the deceived spouse, all these cases are highly disputable. But that is precisely the point. They do not do the work needed to show that the happiness theory is irredeemably inconsistent with standard intuitions. And notice how much force is lost from the experience machine example when its relevant component is retained, but the irrelevant, science-fiction components are discarded.

Finally, we would like to register some skepticism about the weight that has been accorded the experience machine example. Even if it clearly and uncontroversially revealed that the happiness theory leads to a counterintuitive result in this one case—which, as we have argued and as many others have argued as well, is anything but clear and uncontroversial—why would that constitute anything like a refutation of the hedonic theory? The hedonic theory explains what well-being is in any situation, covering countless millions or billions of cases. If it yields intuitive results in the overwhelming majority of those cases (or perhaps even in nearly all of them), and if it otherwise fulfills the requirements of a theory by (for example) resolving intuition conflicts, then its failure to accord with intuitions in *every* case is hardly a disqualifier. One would expect that the best theory of virtually any important ethical concept would not yield intuitive answers in 100 percent of the cases. Instead, if a theory has enough going for it, then its rare conflicts with intuition are best seen as an occasion to reconsider people's standard intuitions in those cases.[28] Moreover, if it takes problematically unrealistic cases to elicit counterintuitive results, then one might question whether this is due to the difficulty of imagining the cases rather than to the flaws of the theory.

Indeed, there seems to be considerable acknowledgment that the hedonic theory does in fact accord powerfully with the mass of people's intuitions and reflective judgments. Consider the following statement, made not by a proponent of the happiness theory but instead by a leading proponent of eudaimonism about well-being: "the association between the concept of a person's welfare and what contributes to his overall happiness is very strong. Defending the claim that something contributes to someone's welfare despite its making no contribution to his long-term happiness is an uphill battle."[29]

Some Lingering Questions about Feeling Good

We know from experience that some features of our view may still not be clear, and that readers will have questions and concerns that have not been addressed above. In particular, many may question whether "feeling good" is important and capacious enough to equate with well-being. We now address this within the context of a few common concerns and objections.

Drugs—part 1

At an academic conference, a law professor once asked us this exact question: "Doesn't your view mean that someone would increase his well-being if he ate a bucket of fried chicken, snorted a bunch of cocaine, and died?" The answer is no, as we describe below. Two other excellent scholars have separately raised the issue of even-keeled fuzziness. Would it increase someone's welfare to spend her life on a dopamine drip (or, alternatively, in a warm bath), feeling perpetually calm and peaceful, as opposed to living a normal life? Because the two concerns raise similar issues, we will treat them both here.

First, with respect to an early but ecstatic death, the hedonic costs of such a behavior would surely outweigh its benefits. Our view is that someone's well-being is her aggregated happiness (how good she feels) over the course of her life. So someone who dies at age forty will lose all the potential happiness that she would have had if she had lived to age eighty. No amount of momentary happiness right before dying at forty could possibly make up for all those years of lost happiness. (This assumes that the remaining years are happy ones overall. They would be for virtually everyone, since almost all people are happier than neutral as a matter of their average affect over long periods of time.)

Moreover, it is not clear that cocaine and fried chicken would indeed induce ecstasy and feelings of the most intense joy. But suppose those things would produce such joy. And suppose someone were about to die anyway. If he chose to spend his last moments doing the thing that made him happiest, then we would say he increased his well-being thereby. Some might contend that it was not the most elegant or noble way to spend his last moments, but that does not mean it wasn't the best use of them for the limited sake of his own welfare.

This distinction matters, because when other scholars mention the example of drugs, it is not inconceivable that at least some of those people may be influenced by the cultural and political climate of opposition to drugs. (This is probably not the case for the person who raised the above question with us, however.) Two points must be made on this score. First, the putative objective badness of something is separate from its effect on well-being. And second, drugs *are* bad for well-being on the happiness account. Drug addicts report exceedingly low levels of happiness.

Similar issues arise with the dopamine drip example. What would increase someone's well-being is not the same as what she would choose.[30] Suppose Jill would not choose to be hooked up to a dopamine drip for the rest of her life, if given the chance. Her choice might implicate concerns other than her own well-being. For example, she might not want to leave in the lurch all the other people—friends, family, and so on—who love her, depend on her, or simply benefit from her presence. And when people intuit that a drug-induced haze would decrease someone's well-being, they may be importing value judgments that should be kept separate from the conceptual question of well-being. Abandoning the rest of humanity to spend one's life seeking drugged-out pleasure may strike many people as abhorrent, so when they report that they do not believe this increases someone's welfare, their report may be clouded by their moral judgment. Admittedly, one could argue this phenomenon shows that moral considerations *should* count as part of welfare. But as we said in chapter 6, that would make it hard to explain people's ordinary understandings of terms like "selfless" (morally good) and "selfish" (morally bad). Moreover, imagine someone who has a terminal disease that causes extreme pain and will kill her in a week. Would people strongly intuit that spending that week in a drug-induced state results in less welfare for that person than experiencing the pain would? If not, then the force of the drug-haze example relies on the long time that an otherwise healthy person would spend in a drug-induced state. And that makes the example less reputable because it pumps welfare-independent intuitions. Also, focusing on the long time horizon clouds people's intuitions about the *hedonic* merits of the drug state. We turn now to that point.

Consider the anti-hedonist assertion that most people would think that being in a long-lasting state of ecstatic pleasure or in a long-lasting state of warm fuzziness would be bad for a person despite her feelings of happiness.[31] This is an interesting theoretical point, but it runs into major problems in a couple of ways. One is that it asks people to imagine something that contradicts human nature in too profound a way. Emotions vary both in their valence (how good or bad they feel) and in their level of excitement or calmness.[32] And just as people adapt to good and bad experiences, they also adapt to changes in degrees of excitement, returning to a more moderate level relatively quickly. Thus, people aren't emotionally constituted to live in states of unending high excitement or unending semi-consciousness. And we suspect that people are unable to accurately assess how it would feel to live in a state so far from typical human experience.

Furthermore, the ecstasy and fuzziness objections are likely pumping incorrect intuitions about welfare because they are conflating the separate issues of valence and intensity. Trying to imagine what it would be like to be in a constant, never-ending state of drug-induced ecstasy is likely to lead one astray in drawing conclusions from the thought experiment. When we ourselves try to imagine a feeling that is "intense, uninterrupted . . . and long-lasting,"[33] it seems terrible because constant ecstasy would actually not be pleasurable but rather overwhelming and horrible—like torture. But this intuition likely has more to do with the level of excitement of the feeling than its valence (that is, how good or bad it feels). People may well find themselves intuiting, consciously or otherwise, that a hypothesized long-lasting state of intense pleasure makes the pleasure seem somehow less pleasurable, or that long-lasting semi-conscious fuzziness will stop creating happiness. But this is because they misunderstand the terms of the hypothetical, which stipulates that the feeling involves only positive affect. Our theory has nothing to do with a feeling's level of excitement (which the word "intensity" might prompt one to imagine), only its valence. And it seems neither undesirable nor unpleasant to spend one's time in long-lasting happiness at moderate or varying levels of excitement. If one still recoils at that state of affairs if it is brought about by drugs, then one may well be importing welfare-independent values or be influenced by the unrealistic nature of the example. Many of our points about the experience machine and other examples are applicable here as well.

This seems like a good place to mention a related example that is often used against proponents of happiness in public policy. People claim that our approach entails support for "putting Prozac in the water supply." Our two responses should be obvious. First, such a policy would deprive people of the freedom to choose whether they want to ingest Prozac, and freedom to choose is a value that may well be important independent of well-being. We never say that happiness is the only value or even the most important one. And second, it is not clear to us whether the ubiquitous administration of Prozac would increase overall happiness.

Finally, the drug questions and examples implicate the problem of changed selves, which we will address in the next section.

Drugs—part 2 (mind alteration)

A famous example used against the happiness theory is that at the end of his life, Sigmund Freud refused palliative drugs because he wanted to keep his mind clear, even though he was in pain.[34] If Freud was better off without the drugs, even though he felt less good, then the happiness theory must be wrong.

To begin with, we are not convinced that Freud was better off without the drugs. Feeling excruciating pain is extremely negative for well-being. If he could have relieved that pain to a significant degree, at the cost of some level of mental acuity, then it might well have been worthwhile to do so in well-being terms. Perhaps Freud himself made a mistake, or perhaps he valued something else above his own well-being.[35] It is also possible, though perhaps less likely, that Freud rightly perceived that the hedonic benefit of staying sharp-minded outweighed the pain-reduction of the drugs.

Not everyone will be persuaded by these rejoinders. For many, it may seem that Freud was indeed prioritizing his own well-being and that he was right that he'd be better off without the drugs. If so, there is another important issue to consider. Things that alter people's minds or person-alities create unique concerns that may be problematic for assessing well-being. Specifically, if Freud takes mind-altering drugs, to what extent is he still Freud? Has he decreased his pain at the cost of losing the person whose pain was decreased? If so, then it may not be right to draw the straightforward inference that well-being is more than happiness, even if one rejects all the points we made in the previous paragraph.

Self-alteration is very complicated.[36] In one sense, no one is the same person from one day to the next because we all undergo changes constantly. In another sense, there is a certain continuity in one person's life all the way from conception to death, despite all the changes that occur along the way. In between these extremes lies some middle ground that may be important for considering examples such as the one of Freud and mind-altering drugs. We do not know how to draw that line, but we would simply like to point out that mind-altering drugs raise this unique type of issue, and therefore it is unclear what can be extrapolated from examples such as the one about Freud.

"A sense of meaning"

Some people are concerned about the finding that children tend not to increase their parents' happiness. More broadly, people sometimes contend that feelings other than positivity—such as "a sense of meaning"—should be counted toward well-being. Beyond the question of children, there are questions like this: if Jack cares for his dying grandfather, then doesn't he gain more well-being than if he had played his favorite video game, even though caring for sick relatives tends to score near the bottom of all activities in happiness data?

Once again, we confront the problem that people may be conflating well-being and other sorts of values. Caring for a dying relative may well be morally better than playing a video game, and it may well improve the well-being of the relative, but those things are separate from whether it improves the well-being of the caregiver. Such behaviors are often lauded precisely because they involve sacrifice. To insist that Jack benefits is to deny that any such sacrifice is involved, which we think misses the most plausible way to describe what is going on in the example. If Jack wants to provide this care, one still must ask why he wants to provide it: is it for his own sake, or is it because he feels a sense of duty?[37] Even if it is for his own sake, that might also be explained in terms of hedonic positivity:

he may worry that he will be forever plagued by guilt (and thus will feel worse on the whole during his lifetime) unless he provides this care.

Regarding children, some might ask how it could be that so many people choose to procreate if children do not make people happier. But there are straightforward explanations for this. To take a few examples, there are powerful biological and cultural pressures (which may be mutually reinforcing), people may have goals other than increasing their own well-being, the unhappiness may come far enough after the decision to obscure the effect, and the peak-end phenomenon may obscure people's predictions of their own well-being even after having had their first child.[38]

Too fleeting?

One last common concern is that feeling good is too fleeting to capture well-being or perhaps even to capture happiness.[39] We believe, however, that this objection focuses too much on *one* feeling and may not fully account for the fact that our view refers to *all* feelings collectively. When Jill eats a peach and enjoys it, some might claim that this gives her only pleasure, and not happiness or well-being. But what does give her happiness or well-being on that view? Perhaps it is said to be more lasting things such as the love of her family. We think that the love of her family affects her—including her happiness and well-being—by affecting her experience of life: she feels loved and enjoys that feeling, and this affects both the moments when she focuses on it and perhaps also the many other moments when she does not. For instance, perhaps love and affection make her more confident and more resilient in the face of negative events. The thing that is more lasting gets cashed out, in our opinion, in the form of many momentary feelings of increased positivity. Eating the peach is less significant not because it is different in kind but merely because it is different in duration (and intensity, if this is the case): it does not provide many moments of happiness itself, nor does it affect many non-peach-eating moments positively.

* * *

We think that happiness—the aggregation of how good one feels in every moment—is the most attractive theory of well-being. We have laid out the primary reasons that we hold this belief, and we hope that readers will at least grant the plausibility of the view. But even if they do not, we reiterate that nothing in the rest of the book depends on it. As long as feeling good is one thing that matters—a point that is uncontroversial—the law will benefit from an improved understanding of how it affects that thing.

Conclusion: The Future of Happiness and the Law

Scholars have known for more than a century that to understand the law one must understand people. And perhaps the most important thing to understand about people is what makes them happy and unhappy. Hedonic psychology reveals many of the answers, and those answers open the door to a more complete and accurate picture of how law interacts with human life.

This book makes two principal contributions to the field of law. First, it introduces well-being analysis (WBA) as a method for assessing law, policy, and regulation. WBA should replace or at least supplement cost-benefit analysis (CBA), which has been used in that role for decades. Via WBA, lawmakers can learn whether proposed policies will increase or decrease overall happiness. Because happiness is a better proxy for quality of life than money, WBA advances the cause of using law to improve people's lives.[1] We call on the regulatory apparatus of government to incorporate WBA into its evaluation of public policies, and in chapter 2 we have provided a blueprint for how it can do so.

Second, this book explores the ways in which two core areas of the law—criminal punishment and tort litigation—can be better understood when viewed through the lens of hedonic psychology. Both of those major areas of law concern the interaction between legal rules and the quality of life, and empirical data about life quality is essential to fully understanding how law is and should be structured in those fields.

The two areas we covered are just the beginning. Everything in law affects the way that people live their lives. And to a significant degree, the ultimate purpose of law is to make people's lives better. It has been forty years since economists started to fully dedicate their methodological tools to overhauling the understanding of law, and all areas of law have since been scrutinized by those tools. But economic tools have limitations that hedonic psychology can help to overcome. Only now, through psychology, can we peer directly into the effect of the law on how good or bad people feel throughout the moments of their lives. Only now can we truly know how law makes life better or worse. Every corner of the law, from wills to admiralty to the First Amendment, is aimed at regulating human life for the sake of its improvement. Thus every corner of the law should be examined via the new hedonic data that can measure directly the effect of law on life.

On that journey, law must walk hand in hand with psychology. Much has been discovered about happiness, but much remains to be learned. The best way to learn it is through moment-by-moment studies of how people feel and what makes people feel good or bad. These studies are expensive in their traditional form, but new approaches to data collection have made them far more practical.[2] The best thing that policymakers could do is to commission the study of moment-by-moment happiness on a large scale. Armed with more data and increased methodological refinement, the hedonic study of law could make unprecedented strides in connecting law with life.

More specifically, a number of areas deserve the immediate attention of scholars and could quickly benefit from empirical data on well-being, adaptation, and affective forecasting. Contracts and civil rights are two such areas. Using the experimental protocols that Daniel Gilbert has applied to his affective forecasting studies, scholars could explore the hedonic effects of contract breaches or denials of due process. They could also measure the extent to which people accurately predict how they will feel in these circumstances.

In addition, it would be hugely valuable to have longitudinal studies that tracked people through and after a variety of civil proceedings, including civil litigation and bankruptcy. Scholars need to know how bankruptcy affects individuals and how long those effects last in order to craft rules that will accomplish the law's goals.

Hedonic studies also have promise for illuminating issues in intellectual property law. Copyright and patent law, in the United States, are fundamentally utilitarian and devoted to improving human welfare. Copyright and patent rights are given out to incentivize creators to develop new works and inventions. As yet, however, there has been only limited empirical study of whether intellectual property laws actually succeed in incentivizing innovation. More important, perhaps, would be data indicating whether and what kind of creativity and innovation have the biggest effects on people's lives. Some innovations, including those that dramatically lengthen people's lives, have obvious benefits to well-being, and other innovations may be evidently worthless. But many creations and discoveries may prove to have unexpected impacts on well-being. Knowing this could help people better understand how to draft intellectual property laws and doctrines.

For a field that is so deeply concerned with improving human lives, the law has been notably lax in its interest in properly understanding the kinds of things that make people happy or sad and how people respond to those things. To a considerable degree, the law's shortcomings in this regard are the result of a lack of reliable data on these kinds of questions. With the emergence of hedonic psychology, the data are no longer lacking. Accordingly, it is time for the hedonic study of law to take its place alongside the other accepted methodologies in legal analysis.

Notes

Chapter One

1. *See* David Colander, *Edgeworth's Hedonimeter and the Quest to Measure Utility*, 21 J. ECON. PERSPECTIVES 215 (2007).

2. For a review of well-being measures, *see* ED DIENER ET AL., WELL-BEING FOR PUBLIC POLICY 46–66 (2009).

3. *See* Daniel Kahneman et al., *Back to Bentham: Explorations of Experienced Utility*, 112 Q.J. ECON. 375, 375 (1997).

4. *See* chapter 3.

5. *See* Kahneman et al., *Back to Bentham*, at 375.

6. *See* Daniel Kahneman et al., *A Survey Method for Characterizing Daily Life Experience: The Day Reconstruction Method*, 306 SCIENCE 1776, 1776 (2004).

7. Alan B. Krueger et al., *National Time Accounting: The Currency of Life*, in MEASURING THE SUBJECTIVE WELL-BEING OF NATIONS 30, 34–36 (Alan B. Krueger ed., 2009).

8. Krueger et al., *National Time Accounting*, at 36.

9. *See* William Pavot & Ed Diener, *Review of the Satisfaction with Life Scale*, 5 PSYCHOL. ASSESSMENT 164 (1993).

10. *See, e.g.*, Richard E. Lucas et al., *Reexamining Adaptation and the Set Point Model of Happiness: Reactions to Changes in Marital Status*, 84 J. PERSONALITY & SOC. PSYCHOL. 527 (2003); Andrew E. Clark et al., *Lags and Leads in Life Satisfaction: A Test of the Baseline Hypothesis*, 118 ECON. J. F222, F231 (2008); Richard A. Lucas, *Time Does Not Heal All Wounds: A Longitudinal Study of Reaction and Adaptation to Divorce*, 16 PSYCHOL. SCI. 945 (2005).

11. Andrew J. Oswald & Nattavudh Powdthavee, *Death, Happiness, and the Calculation of Compensatory Damages*, 37 J. LEGAL STUD. S217, S217 (2008).

12. *See* Lucas, *Reexamining Adaptation*, at 547. Between-subjects comparisons can be a problem if the two groups (e.g., married people and single people)

differ about more than just the comparison issue. Married people are not simply happier because they are married; the people who get married are more likely to have been happy people in the first place than the people who are single. *Id.*

13. *See* Krueger et al., *National Time Accounting.*

14. DAVID L. STREINER & GEOFFREY R. NORMAN, HEALTH MEASUREMENT SCALES: A PRACTICAL GUIDE TO THEIR DEVELOPMENT AND USE (4th ed. 2008).

15. DIENER ET AL., WELL-BEING FOR PUBLIC POLICY, at 71.

16. DIENER ET AL., WELL-BEING FOR PUBLIC POLICY, at 72–73. Test-retest reliability results typically range from $r = 0.55$ to $r = 0.70$. These are fairly high numbers especially given the difficulty of using test-retest calculations on a measure of well-being that is likely to change significantly over time.

17. DIENER ET AL., WELL-BEING FOR PUBLIC POLICY, at 74.

18. For example, a bathroom scale may provide highly reliable data—it may indicate the same weight every time—but those data are probably not a very good measure of your well-being.

19. Samuel Messick, *Validity of Psychological Assessment: Validation of Inferences from Persons' Responses and Performances as Scientific Inquiry into Score Meaning*, 50 AM. PSYCHOLOGIST 741, 741 (1995) ("Validity is an overall evaluative judgment of the degree to which empirical evidence and theoretical rationales support the adequacy and appropriateness of interpretations and actions on the basis of test scores or other models of assessment.").

20. For such a review, see DIENER ET AL., WELL-BEING FOR PUBLIC POLICY, at 74–93.

21. DIENER ET AL., WELL-BEING FOR PUBLIC POLICY, at 70.

22. Michael Eid & Ed Diener, *Global Judgments of Subjective Well-Being: Situational Variability and Long-Term Stability*, 65 SOC. INDICATORS RES. 245 (2004).

23. *See* Ulrich Schimmack, *The Structure of Subjective Well-Being, in* THE SCIENCE OF SUBJECTIVE WELL-BEING 115 (Michael Eid & Randy J. Larsen eds., 2007).

24. *See* E. Sandvik et al., *Subjective Well-Being: The Convergence and Stability of Self-Report and Non-Self-Report Measures*, 61 J. PERSONALITY 317 (1993); Heidi Lepper, *Use of Other-Reports to Validate Subjective Well-Being Measures*, 44 SOC. INDICATORS RES. 367 (1998).

25. Tiffany A. Ito & John T. Cacioppo, *The Psychophysiology of Utility Appraisals, in* WELL-BEING: THE FOUNDATIONS OF HEDONIC PSYCHOLOGY 470, 479 (Daniel Kahneman et al. eds., 1999).

26. Ito and Cacioppo, *Utility Appraisals*, at 479; T.G. Dinan, *Glucocorticoids and the Genesis of Depressive Illness: A Psychobiological Model*, 164 BRIT. J. PSYCHIATRY 365 (1994).

27. Heli-Tuulie Koivumaa-Honkanen et al., *Self-Reported Happiness in Life*

and Suicide in Ensuing 20 Years, 38 Soc. Psychiatry & Psychiatric Epidemiology 244 (2003).

28. *See* Richard E. Lucas, *Personality and Subjective Well-Being, in* The Science of Subjective Well-Being 171, 185 (Michael Eid and Randy J. Larsen eds., 2007).

29. *See* Ed Diener & Richard E. Lucas, *Personality and Subjective Well-Being, in* Well-Being: The Foundations of Hedonic Psychology 213, 214 (Daniel Kahneman et al. eds., 1999).

30. *See* Sandvik, *Subjective Well-Being.*

31. *See* Lucas et al., *Reexamining Adaptation.*

32. Oswald & Powdthavee, *Compensatory Damages*, S217.

33. *See* Oswald & Powdthavee, *Compensatory Damages.* This is in contrast to findings that people's responses to contingent valuation surveys used in CBA display considerable scope neglect—e.g., they are willing to pay the same amount of money to save 2,000, 20,000, or 200,000 endangered birds.

34. This would be the case if no comparable ESM or DRM studies had yet been done for the relevant conditions.

35. *See* Betsey Stevenson & Justin Wolfers, *Bargaining in the Shadow of the Law: Divorce Laws and Family Distress*, 121 Q.J. Econ. 267 (2006).

36. Richard A. Easterlin, *Does Economic Growth Improve the Human Lot? Some Empirical Evidence, in* Nations and Households in Economic Growth 89, 118 (Paul A. David and Melvin W. Reder eds., 1974).

37. Philip Brickman et al., *Lottery Winners and Accident Victims: Is Happiness Relative?*, 36 J. Personality & Soc. Psychol. 917 (1978).

38. Betsey Stevenson & Justin Wolfers, *Economic Growth and Subjective Well-Being: Reassessing the Easterlin Paradox, in* Brookings Papers on Economic Activity (2008); Jonathan Gardner & Andrew J. Oswald, *Money and Mental Well-Being: A Longitudinal Study of Medium-Sized Lottery Wins*, 26 J. Health Econ. 49–60 (2006).

39. Ed Diener & Robert Biswas-Diener, *Will Money Increase Subjective Well-Being?*, 57 Soc. Indicators Res. 119 (2002).

40. Daniel Kahneman & Angus Deaton, *High Income Improves Evaluation of Life but Not Emotional Well-Being*, 107 Proc. Nat'l Acad. Sci. 16489 (2010).

41. Ed Diener et al., *The Relationship Between Income and Subjective Well-Being: Relative or Absolute?*, 28 Soc. Indicators Res. 195, 221 (1993).

42. Philip Brickman et al., *Lottery Winners and Accident Victims: Is Happiness Relative?*, 36 J. Personality & Soc. Psychol. 917 (1978).

43. Brickman et al., *Lottery Winners*, at 920–21.

44. *See* Brickman et al., *Lottery Winners*, at 918 (describing processes of "Contrast and Habituation" that tend to mitigate effects of extreme good or bad fortune). For a further explanation of the hedonic treadmill theory, *see* Daniel

Kahneman, *Objective Happiness*, *in* WELL-BEING: THE FOUNDATIONS OF HE-
DONIC PSYCHOLOGY 3, 13–15 (Daniel Kahneman et al. eds., 1999).

45. See Ed Diener et al., *Beyond the Hedonic Treadmill: Revising the Adaptation Theory of Well-Being*, 61 AM. PSYCHOLOGIST 305, 306–11 (2006) (suggesting modifications to the treadmill model); Richard E. Lucas, *Adaptation and the
Set-Point Model of Subjective Well-Being: Does Happiness Change After Major Life Events?*, 16 CURRENT DIRECTIONS IN PSYCHOL. SCI. 75, 76–78 (2007) (arguing that hedonic adaptation is not inevitable and may depend on individual
differences).

46. *See* Vida L. Tyc, *Psychosocial Adaptation of Children and Adolescents
with Limb Deficiencies: A Review*, 12 CLINICAL PSYCHOL. REV. 275, 276–77
(1992) (collecting studies).

47. C. Lundqvist et al., *Spinal Cord Injuries: Clinical, Functional, and Emotional Status*, 16 SPINE 78, 80 (1991).

48. David R. Patterson et al., *Psychological Effects of Severe Burn Injuries*,
113 PSYCHOL. BULL. 362, 370 (1993).

49. Norman F. Boyd et al., *Whose Utilities for Decision Analysis?*, 10 MED.
DECISION MAKING 58, 66 (1990).

50. Jason Riis et al., *Ignorance of Hedonic Adaptation to Hemodialysis: A
Study Using Ecological Momentary Assessment*, 134 J. EXPERIMENTAL PSYCHOL.
3, 6 (2005).

51. Riis, *Ignorance of Hedonic Adaptation*, at 7.

52. Andrew J. Oswald & Nattavudh Powdthavee, *Does Happiness Adapt? A
Longitudinal Study of Disability with Implications for Economists and Judges*,
92 J. PUB. ECON. 1061 (2008).

53. The survey contains over 10,000 adults who were interviewed between
September and December each year since 1991. Oswald & Powdthavee, *Does
Happiness Adapt?*, at 1065.

54. Oswald & Powdthavee, *Does Happiness Adapt?*, at 1065. There were 675
person-year observations in the "Moderately Disabled" category and 3,442 observations in the "Severely Disabled" category. *Id.*

55. Oswald & Powdthavee, *Does Happiness Adapt?*, at 1066.

56. Oswald & Powdthavee, *Does Happiness Adapt?*, at 1070. That is to say,
over the course of two years, moderately disabled people recover approximately
50 percent of their "lost" happiness, and even severely disabled people regain
more than 30 percent of the happiness they lost because of their injury. *Id.*

57. *But see* Richard E. Lucas, *Long-Term Disability Is Associated with Lasting Changes in Subjective Well-Being: Evidence from Two Nationally Representative Longitudinal Studies*, 92 J. PERSONALITY & SOC. PSYCHOL. 717, 722 (2007)
(finding no evidence of adaptation from the same data set). Oswald and Powdthavee note methodological differences between their paper and Lucas's, but

they write, "[W]e cannot be certain why we find much more adaptation than does Lucas." Oswald & Powdthavee, *Does Happiness Adapt?*, at 1065 n.10.

58. Shane Frederick & George Loewenstein, *Hedonic Adaptation, in* WELL-BEING: THE FOUNDATIONS OF HEDONIC PSYCHOLOGY 302, 311–12 (Daniel Kahneman et al. eds., 1999).

59. Neil D. Weinstein, *Individual Differences in Reaction to Noise: A Longitudinal Study in a College Dormitory*, 63 J. APPLIED PSYCHOL. 458, 460 (1978).

60. *See* Richard F. Antonak & Hanoch Livneh, *Psychosocial Adaption to Disability and Its Investigation Among Persons with Multiple Sclerosis*, 40 SOC. SCI. & MED. 1099, 1105 (1995) ("Regressions to earlier phases of the hypothesized adaptation process are predictable from the renewed life crises associated with unexpected exacerbations of physical symptoms and the resultant imposition of disability."); Craig A. Smith & Kenneth A. Wallston, *Adaptation in Patients with Chronic Rheumatoid Arthritis: Application of a General Model*, 11 HEALTH PSYCHOL. 151, 151 (1992) ("[Rheumatoid arthritis] and its associated pain have been linked to poor adjustment, including depressive symptoms and impaired quality of life." (citations omitted)). Frederick and Loewenstein note, however, that the degree of adaptation may be particularly difficult to measure with these progressive diseases. Frederick & Loewenstein, *Hedonic Adaptation*, at 312 ("Even maintaining a constant hedonic state in the face of these deteriorating conditions would be impressive evidence of hedonic adaptation.").

61. *See* Diener et al., *Beyond the Hedonic Treadmill*, at 310–11 ("[W]e have found individual differences in the rate and extent of adaptation that occurs even to the same event. In our longitudinal studies, the size and even the direction of the change in life satisfaction varied considerably across individuals.").

62. Michael Argyle, *Causes and Correlates of Happiness, in* WELL-BEING: THE FOUNDATIONS OF HEDONIC PSYCHOLOGY 361 (Daniel Kahneman et al. eds., 1999).

63. Lucas, *Adaptation and Set-Point*, at 77.

64. Lucas, *Adaptation and Set-Point*, at 77.

65. Andreas Knabe et al., *Dissatisfied with Life but Having a Good Day: Time-Use and Well-Being of the Unemployed*, 120 ECON. J. 867, 878 (2010).

66. Knabe, *Dissatisfied with Life*, at 876.

67. Knabe, *Dissatisfied with Life*, at 876.

68. *E.g.*, Knabe, *Dissatisfied with Life*, at 876.

69. David Lykken & Auke Tellegen, *Happiness Is a Stochastic Phenomenon*, 7 PSYCHOL. SCI. 186 (1996).

70. Daniel T. Gilbert et al., *Immune Neglect: A Source of Durability Bias in Affective Forecasting*, 75 J. PERSONALITY & SOC. PSYCHOL. 619 (1998).

71. Gilbert, *Immune Neglect*, 619.

72. *See, e.g.*, Timothy D. Wilson & Daniel T. Gilbert, *Affective Forecasting:*

Knowing What to Want, 14 CURRENT DIRECTIONS IN PSYCHOL. SCI. 131, 131 (2005) ("Research on *affective forecasting* has shown that people routinely mispredict how much pleasure or displeasure future events will bring and, as a result, sometimes work to bring about events that do not maximize their happiness.").

73. For an excellent recent review of research on misprediction of hedonic reactions, *see* Daniel T. Gilbert & Timothy D. Wilson, *Prospection: Experiencing the Future*, 317 SCI. 1351 (2007).

74. Wilson & Gilbert, *Affective Forecasting*, at 131.

75. *See* Boyd et al., *Whose Utilities*, at 63 (finding that healthy controls assigned lower utilities to colostomies than did patients who had recently undergone the procedure); David L. Sackett & George W. Torrance, *The Utility of Different Health States as Perceived by the General Public*, 31 J. CHRONIC DISEASES 697, 702 (1978) (finding that patients undergoing dialysis gave higher utilities to that treatment than did healthy controls); Peter A. Ubel et al., *Disability and Sunshine: Can Hedonic Predictions Be Improved by Drawing Attention to Focusing Illusions or Emotional Adaptation?*, 11 J. EXPERIMENTAL PSYCHOL.: APPLIED 111, 111 (2005) ("One of the most commonly replicated 'happiness gaps' is that observed between the self-rated quality of life of people with health conditions and healthy people's estimates of what their quality of life would be if they had those conditions. . . ." (citation omitted)); Peter A. Ubel et al., *Do Nonpatients Underestimate the Quality of Life Associated with Chronic Health Conditions Because of a Focusing Illusion?*, 21 MED. DECISION MAKING 190, 197 (2001) (finding that healthy people's underestimates of quality of life for paraplegics could not be altered by defocusing tasks); Peter A. Ubel et al., *Misimagining the Unimaginable: The Disability Paradox and Health Care Decision Making*, 24 HEALTH PSYCHOL. (SUPPL.) S57, S57 (2005) ("Across a wide range of health conditions, patients typically report greater happiness and [quality of life] than do healthy people under similar circumstances. . . .").

76. For an example of a focusing illusion, see David A. Schkade & Daniel Kahneman, *Does Living in California Make People Happy? A Focusing Illusion in Judgments of Life Satisfaction*, 9 PSYCHOL. SCI. 340, 344–45 (1998) (describing indications of focusing illusion when people asked how happy they are and then asked how happy they would be in another region). Ubel and his colleagues define a "focusing illusion" as "a failure to appreciate that not all life domains or life events will be equally affected by a given change in circumstances." Ubel et al., *Disability and Sunshine*, at 112.

77. Timothy D. Wilson et al., *Focalism: A Source of Durability Bias in Affective Forecasting*, 78 J. PERSONALITY & SOC. PSYCHOL. 821, 822 (2000).

78. Gilbert and Wilson discuss four reasons why affective forecasting errors occur—mental simulations of future events tend to be "unrepresentative" because they are based on faulty memories, "essentialized" because they include only central features, "abbreviated" because they are shorter than the ac-

tual event, and "decontextualized" because they do not take place in the same circumstances as the actual event. Gilbert & Wilson, *Prospection*, at 1352–54. Summarizing the research, they write: "[The mind's] simulations are deficient because they are based on a small number of memories, they omit large numbers of features, they do not sustain themselves over time, and they lack context. Compared to sensory perceptions, mental simulations are mere cardboard cutouts of reality." *Id.* at 1354.

79. Wilson et al., *Focalism*, at 822.

80. Ubel et al., *Disability and Sunshine*, at 113.

81. Gilbert et al., *Immune Neglect*, at 619. Ubel and his coauthors describe a similar phenomenon that they call "failure to consider adaptation." Ubel et al., *Disability and Sunshine*, at 113.

82. Ubel et al., *Disability and Sunshine*, at 113.

83. Gilbert & Wilson, *Prospection*, at 1353.

84. As noted, the research compares the predictions of healthy people to the actual ratings of disabled people. This research does not exactly match the situation that we are concerned with in settlement negotiations, where the person making the prediction is actually a recently injured victim. There is every reason to believe, however, that the same biases affecting healthy people will also affect the recently injured. The latter are as likely (if not more likely) to suffer from abbreviated, decontextualized, and essentialized simulations of future states because they will be currently experiencing the intense hedonic effects that tend to improperly color predictions.

85. Sackett & Torrance, *Utility of Different Health States*, at 702 tbl.4.

86. Boyd et al., *Whose Utilities*, at 60.

87. Schkade & Kahneman, *Living in California*, at 345.

88. Kahneman, *Objective Happiness*, at 15.

89. Dylan M. Smith et al., *Misremembering Colostomies? Former Patients Give Lower Utility Ratings than Do Current Patients*, 25 HEALTH PSYCHOL. 688, 691 (2006).

90. *See* RICHARD THALER & CASS SUNSTEIN, NUDGE (2006).

91. Neurobiology may also provide insights into people's experience of life in ways that law should take account of. *See, e.g.*, Adam J. Kolber, *The Experiential Future of the Law*, 60 EMORY L.J. 585 (2011).

92. Fred Feldman, *Two Questions About Pleasure, in* PHILOSOPHICAL ANALYSIS 59, 60–61 (D.F. Austin ed., 1988).

93. *See, e.g.*, Aaron Smuts, *The Feels Good Theory of Pleasure*, 155 PHILOS. STUD. 241 (2011).

94. Daniel Kahneman, *Experienced Utility and Objective Happiness: A Moment-Based Approach, in* CHOICES, VALUES, AND FRAMES 673, 683 (Daniel Kahneman & Amos Tversky eds., 2000); Daniel Kahneman, *Objective Happiness, in* WELL-BEING: THE FOUNDATIONS OF HEDONIC PSYCHOLOGY 3, 8 (Daniel

Kahneman et al. eds., 1999); see also JAY SCHULKIN, BODILY SENSIBILITY: INTEL-LIGENT ACTION 14 (2004).

95. ROGER CRISP, REASONS AND THE GOOD 109 (2006) ("Enjoyable experiences do differ from one another, . . . [b]ut there is a certain common quality—feeling good. . . .").

Chapter Two

1. The reason is that businesses may have to spend more money to produce their products in a way that avoids polluting. If so, then someone must bear that cost and have less buying power as a result. It may be consumers (via higher prices), employees (via lower wages or job cuts), or business owners (via lower profits); but it must be someone.

Economic analysis of the effect of price increases on welfare can be complicated, because the effect may depend upon how consumers are likely to react to an increase in a specific context. Whether income effects or substitution effects predominate will vary. For simplicity, we refer here to reductions in buying power as an example of a potential cost or negative consequence of regulation, without specifying the complications from possible substitution effects.

2. This question is typically the first step in analyzing a law, but other steps may follow. We use the terms "costs" and "benefits" to refer to a law's effects on people's quality of life, and such effects may not be the only consideration in evaluating a law. For example, there may be moral reasons to support a law even if it would decrease human welfare. Thus, this chapter concerns one step in the decision-making process, the step of assessing a law's effects on the quality of human life. It is an important step, but not necessarily the only one.

3. Cost-effectiveness analysis (CEA) is an alternative that has been used as well, albeit far less frequently than CBA by government agencies in the United States. We mention CEA in chapter 3 in the context of assessing quality-adjusted life years (QALYs), which are CEA's primary measure of outcomes. Other methods of systematic evaluation, such as multi-attribute analysis, exist as well, though they are even less commonly used by U.S. government regulators than is CEA.

4. Exec. Order No. 13,563, 3 C.F.R. 215 (2012).

5. Exec. Order No. 13,563, 3 C.F.R. 215 (2012). Exec. Order No. 12,866, 3 C.F.R. 638 (1994), *reprinted as amended in* 5 U.S.C. § 601 note at 745–49 (2006); Economic Analysis of Federal Regulations Under Executive Order 12,866 (1996), *available at* http://www.whitehouse.gov/omb/inforeg_riaguide.

6. Exec. Order No. 12,291, 3 C.F.R. 127 (1982), *reprinted in* 5 U.S.C. § 601 note at 431–34 (1982).

7. Exec. Order No. 12,866, 3 C.F.R. 638 (1994), *reprinted as amended in* 5 U.S.C. § 601 note at 745–49 (2006).

8. 3 C.F.R. 215 (2012).

9. *See, e.g.*, Steven Kelman, *Cost-Benefit Analysis: An Ethical Critique*, 5 REGULATION 33, 33 (1981) ("In areas of environmental, safety, and health regulation, there may be many instances where a certain decision might be right even though its benefits do not outweigh its costs.").

10. *See, e.g.*, Alexander Volokh, *Rationality or Rationalism? The Positive and Normative Flaws of Cost-Benefit Analysis*, 48 HOUS. L. REV. 79, 82 (2011).

11. *See, e.g.*, David M. Driesen, *The Societal Cost of Environmental Regulation: Beyond Administrative Cost-Benefit Analysis*, 24 ECOLOGY L.Q. 545 (1997); Robert H. Frank, *Why Is Cost-Benefit Analysis So Controversial?*, 29 J. LEGAL STUD. 913 (2000) (evaluating the various objections to cost-benefit analysis); Daniel Kahneman & Jack Knetsch, *Valuing Public Goods: The Purchase of Moral Satisfaction*, 22 J. ENVTL. ECON. & MGMT. 57 (1992); Duncan Kennedy, *Cost-Benefit Analysis of Entitlement Problems: A Critique*, 33 STAN. L. REV. 387 (1981); Thomas O. McGarity, *A Cost-Benefit State*, 50 ADMIN. L. REV. 7 (1998); Thomas O. McGarity, *Media-Quality, Technology, and Cost-Benefit Balancing Strategies for Health and Environmental Regulation*, 46 LAW & CONTEMP. PROBS. 159, 179–91 (1983); Richard L. Revesz, *Environmental Regulation, Cost-Benefit Analysis, and the Discounting of Human Lives*, 99 COLUM. L. REV. 941 (1999); Amy Sinden, *Cass Sunstein's Cost-Benefit Lite: Economics for Liberals*, 29 COLUM. J. ENVTL. L. 191 (2004).

12. *E.g.*, FRANK ACKERMAN & LISA HEINZERLING, PRICELESS: ON KNOWING THE PRICE OF EVERYTHING AND THE VALUE OF NOTHING 234 (2004) ("Cost-benefit analysis of health and environmental policies trivializes the very values that gave rise to those policies in the first place."); Kennedy, *Cost-Benefit Analysis*, at 388 ("[T]he program of generating a complete system of private law rules by application of the criterion of efficiency is incoherent.").

13. *See, e.g.*, WINSTON HARRINGTON ET AL., EDS., REFORMING REGULATORY IMPACT ANALYSIS (2009); RICHARD L. REVESZ & MICHAEL A. LIVERMORE, RETAKING RATIONALITY: HOW COST-BENEFIT ANALYSIS CAN BETTER PROTECT THE ENVIRONMENT AND OUR HEALTH (2008); MATTHEW D. ADLER & ERIC A. POSNER, NEW FOUNDATIONS OF COST-BENEFIT ANALYSIS (2006); RICHARD D. MORGENSTERN, ECONOMIC ANALYSES AT EPA: ASSESSING REGULATORY IMPACT (1997); Matthew D. Adler & Eric A. Posner, *Rethinking Cost-Benefit Analysis*, 109 YALE L.J. 165 (1999); Robert W. Hahn & Cass R. Sunstein, *A New Executive Order for Improving Federal Regulation? Deeper and Wider Cost-Benefit Analysis*, 150 U. PA. L. REV. 1489 (2002); Robert H. Frank & Cass R. Sunstein, *Cost-Benefit Analysis and Relative Position*, 68 U. CHI. L. REV. 323 (2001); Cass R. Sunstein, *Cognition and Cost-Benefit Analysis*, 29 J. LEGAL STUD. 1059 (2000).

14. This part of the book also advances our primary objective, which is to show the superiority of the alternative we propose. In contrasting the two methods, we consider not only CBA as it is now practiced but also the proposed improvements in it that have been advanced by CBA's defenders.

15. ADLER & POSNER, NEW FOUNDATIONS; REVESZ & LIVERMORE, RETAKING RATIONALITY. One of us has argued to this effect before. *See* Jonathan S. Masur & Eric A. Posner, *Against Feasibility Analysis*, 77 U. CHI. L. REV. 657, 710 (2010).

16. In ultimate policymaking, CBA is very often combined with non-monetized qualitative considerations—as authorized by the executive orders themselves. But it is the monetization that primarily differentiates CBA from mere intuitionistic decision analysis, because the monetization constitutes an attempt to directly and fully commensurate negative and positive consequences. This is the foundation of CBA's appeal, and it is the thing to which we offer an alternative here.

17. Again, we refer to "buying power" because it is a simple way to signify the economic cost. We mean the term to include, not to ignore, the potential complications introduced by considerations such as the extent to which consumers are able to substitute other goods for those whose prices will increase. See also the second paragraph of note 1 in this chapter.

18. *See* chapter 1.

19. G.A. Res. 65/309, U.N. Doc. A/RES/65/309 (July 19, 2011). The resolution contrasted such new measures with "the gross domestic product indicator," which "was not designed to and does not adequately reflect the happiness and well-being of people in a country." *Id.*

20. Roger Cohen, Op-Ed., *The Happynomics of Life*, N.Y. TIMES, Mar. 13, 2011, at 12.

21. Henry Samuel, *Nicolas Sarkozy Wants to Measure Economic Success in 'Happiness'*, THE TELEGRAPH, Sept. 14, 2009. http://www.telegraph.co.uk/news/worldnews/europe/france/6189530/Nicolas-Sarkozy-wants-to-measure-economic-success-in-happiness.html.

22. They are Joseph Stiglitz, Amartya Sen, and Daniel Kahneman. JOSEPH E. STIGLITZ, AMARTYA SEN & JEAN-PAUL FITOUSSI, REPORT BY THE COMMISSION ON THE MEASUREMENT OF ECONOMIC PERFORMANCE AND SOCIAL PROGRESS (2009); Daniel Kahneman & Robert Sugden, *Experienced Utility as a Standard of Policy Evaluation*, 32 ENVTL. & RESOURCE ECON. 161 (2005).

23. DEREK BOK, THE POLITICS OF HAPPINESS: WHAT GOVERNMENT CAN LEARN FROM THE NEW RESEARCH ON WELL-BEING 45 (2010). In legal scholarship, Adam Kolber has done pioneering work in elucidating the value that experiential measures can bring to the law. *E.g.*, Adam Kolber, *The Experiential Future of the Law*, 60 EMORY L.J. 585, 588 (2011) ("My central claim is that as new technologies emerge to better reveal people's experiences, the law ought to do more to take these experiences into account."). Kolber has focused more on neuroscientific measures than on those of hedonic psychology, and more on the civil and criminal justice systems than on administrative rule-making, but he places the

same emphasis on experiential measurement that we endorse here and throughout our work.

24. *See* John Bronsteen, Christopher Buccafusco & Jonathan S. Masur, *Welfare as Happiness*, 98 GEO. L.J. 1583, 1628–41 (2010); Anthony Vitarelli, Note, *Happiness Metrics in Federal Rulemaking*, 27 YALE J. ON REG. 115, 133 (2010) ("Despite the proliferation of these metrics, a core challenge remains—creating a useful translation between the happiness measures and traditional measures of economic cost."). Vitarelli suggests that hedonic metrics be used to supplement CBA. Although we take a somewhat more optimistic view of the hedonic measures and a somewhat more pessimistic view of CBA than he does, this book answers his call for a way to use the hedonic metrics to evaluate regulations.

25. This is due to the advantages of WBA, discussed in chapter 3, that stem from its use of a better proxy for welfare than CBA uses. Of course, the accuracy of any given CBA or WBA will depend in part on the quality of the methods used, which may vary according to the available data and other considerations.

26. Examples of such considerations would be pleasing their constituents and campaign donors, even in cases where doing so is at odds with the public good.

27. At a minimum, it is useful to know what the best policy would be before deciding how to weigh that consideration against others.

28. *E.g.*, Mark Seidenfeld, *A Civic Republican Justification for the Bureaucratic State*, 105 HARV. L. REV. 1511, 1514 (1992) (describing the civic republican model as one in which "government's primary responsibility is to enable the citizenry to deliberate about altering preferences and to reach consensus on the common good").

29. Adler & Posner, *Rethinking Cost-Benefit Analysis*, at 177.

30. We use the terms "welfare" and "well-being" interchangeably throughout this chapter and this book.

31. In limited circumstances, one's conception of welfare could affect whether one views CBA or WBA as a better proxy for it. For example, a person might want outcome A, but only because she mistakenly believes that it will bring her more pleasure than outcome B. An economist who takes the view that she would be better off getting what she wants, even when her preference is based on a mistake, may be more likely than others to deem CBA a closer proxy for welfare than WBA. We think most people reject this view.

32. Most theories of CBA do not equate this kind of Kaldor-Hicks efficiency with ultimate "rightness" because factors other than wealth maximization could affect such rightness. See Adler & Posner, *Rethinking Cost-Benefit Analysis*, at 195 ("[W]e conceive of CBA as a *decision procedure*, not as a criterion of moral rightness or goodness."). Still, learning whether a regulation would increase or decrease quality of life in the aggregate is widely viewed as an important part of assessing its desirability.

33. Again, increasing overall well-being need not be the only goal of policy-making. That goal may be weighed against considerations such as the distribution of well-being, as well as values independent of human well-being. ADLER & POSNER, NEW FOUNDATIONS, at 52–61; Bronsteen, Buccafusco & Masur, *Welfare as Happiness*, at 1589–90. Because overall well-being is one important consideration, however, both CBA and WBA are designed exclusively to measure it.

34. Those who perform CBA often object to characterizing a regulation as "saving lives" for two reasons. First, a life cannot be saved but merely prolonged; and second, a regulation simply reduces the risk to a population of people rather than prolonging the lives of specific, pre-identified individuals. We do not view either of these points as a reason to avoid the term "saving lives."

The first point is one we take very seriously and discuss in chapter 3 as an advantage of WBA, because WBA counts heavily the likely number of years by which lives are prolonged on average by given regulations, whereas the most common form of CBA does not. Moreover, everyone understands that people don't live forever, yet "saving lives" is a widely used term. When a firefighter pulls someone out of a burning building, it is typical and in no way misleading to say that he saved the person's life rather than that he merely prolonged it.

As for the second point, we believe that if a regulation will eliminate a death risk of 1-in-10,000 to a population of 1 million people, then it is best to characterize that as an estimated prospective benefit of saving 100 lives. To a significant degree, CBA effectively does this, regardless of the terminology it chooses. It is true that people are willing to pay more money to save identified individuals than they are to reduce statistical risks (whose reduction ends up saving as-yet-unspecified individuals), and the animating principles of CBA dictate that this matters. But as we explain in chapter 3, we consider that a flaw in CBA rather than a problem with the term "saving lives."

35. Choice experiments are another stated-preference method. They have been used far less frequently than contingent valuation surveys, but this may be starting to change. In any event, choice experiments are vulnerable to many of the same problems we discuss with contingent valuation surveys, and certainly to the same overarching disadvantages of CBA vis-à-vis WBA. To wit, they rely on predictions of welfare rather than in-the-moment measures of welfare.

36. Douglas A. Kysar, *Climate Change, Cultural Transformation, and Comprehensive Rationality*, 31 B.C. ENVTL. AFF. L. REV. 555, 586 (2004) ("[W]hatever preferences individuals seem to reveal through their market behavior are taken to be the best measure of true 'wants' or 'desires' and, therefore, also are taken exclusively to provide the valuation inputs that in critical part determine the policy outputs of CBA.").

37. Avoiding the *risk* is worth $600, but the regulators know that a certain number of people are likely to *actually* die without the regulation. Therefore, they need to know how much society is willing to pay to save those lives. If avoid-

ing a 1-in-10,000 risk is worth $600, then avoiding an actual death (that is, a 1-in-1 "risk") is worth $6 million ($600 × 10,000).

38. *E.g.*, W. Kip Viscusi, *How to Value a Life*, 32 J. Econ. & Fin. 311, 312–14 (2008); *see, e.g.*, Envtl. Prot. Agency, Arsenic in Drinking Water Rule: Economic Analysis 5–28 (2000) (estimating the value of a statistical life at $6.1 million).

39. *E.g.*, John B. Loomis & Douglas S. White, *Economic Benefits of Rare and Endangered Species: Summary and Meta-Analysis*, 18 Ecological Econ. 197, 203 (1996).

40. Daniel T. Gilbert & Timothy D. Wilson, *Prospection: Experiencing the Future*, 317 Science 1351 (2007); Timothy D. Wilson & Daniel T. Gilbert, *Affective Forecasting: Knowing What to Want*, 14 Current Directions in Psychol. Sci. 131 (2005).

41. Gilbert & Wilson, *Prospection*, at 1354 (emphasis added).

42. *See* Cass R. Sunstein, *Willingness to Pay vs. Welfare*, 1 Harv. L. & Pol'y Rev. 303, 305 (2007).

43. Even if feeling good is not identical to welfare, few would deny that it is at minimum a major part of welfare. Indeed, when CBA's proponents delineate which preferences count toward welfare, the result ends up looking remarkably like those preferences that result in feeling good. Bronsteen, Buccafusco & Masur, *Welfare as Happiness*, at 1622–27.

Moreover, even informed and accurate preferences are likely to be further removed from welfare than is happiness because many of those preferences are not self-interested. When someone expresses a preference by her willingness to pay for something, that preference is not necessarily aimed at increasing her own welfare (and thus should be excluded by CBA, which is a tool for welfare assessment).

44. *See, e.g.*, Adler & Posner, New Foundations.

45. Daniel Kahneman, Ed Diener & Norbert Schwarz, *Preface* to Well-Being: The Foundations of Hedonic Psychology ix, xii (Daniel Kahneman, Ed Diener & Norbert Schwarz eds., 1999).

46. In chapter 3 we describe the differences between QALYs and WBUs and the advantages of the latter.

47. Scales from 0 to 7 are also common.

48. Converting from one scale to another is also possible by using studies that pose the same questions to the same (or comparable) individuals on different scales.

49. This requires that the scale be *intra*personally cardinal.

50. This requires that the scale be *inter*personally cardinal. We discuss the issues raised by this cardinality requirement later in this chapter.

51. *See* Richard E. Lucas et al., *Unemployment Alters the Set Point for Life Satisfaction*, 15 Psychol. Sci. 8, 12 (2004).

52. For an excellent summary of the initial research on hedonic adaptation, see Shane Frederick & George Loewenstein, *Hedonic Adaptation, in* WELL-BEING: THE FOUNDATIONS OF HEDONIC PSYCHOLOGY 302, 311–18 (Daniel Kahneman, Ed Diener & Norbert Schwarz eds., 1999).

53. Frederick and Loewenstein, *Hedonic Adaptation*, at 312; Norun Hjertager et al., *The Association between Tinnitus and Mental Health in a General Population Sample: Results from the HUNT Study*, 69 J. PSYCHOSOMATIC RES. 289 (2010) (finding significantly lower subjective well-being in subjects with tinnitus but finding no evidence of differences in SWB over time); Neil D. Weinstein, *Community Noise Problems: Evidence Against Adaptation*, 2 J. ENVTL. PSYCH. 87 (1982); Berthold Langguth et al., *Tinnitus: Causes and Clinical Management*, 12 LANCET NEUROLOGY 920 (2013); Jing Chen et al., *Mental Health in Adults with Sudden Sensorineural Hearing Loss: An Assessment of Depressive Symptoms and Its Correlates*, 75 J. PSYCHOSOMATIC RES. 72 (2013).

54. Many studies show that people significantly overestimate the hedonic consequences of adaptable injuries. Peter A. Ubel, George Loewenstein & Christopher Jepson, *Disability and Sunshine: Can Hedonic Predictions Be Improved by Drawing Attention to Focusing Illusions or Emotional Adaptation?*, 11 J. EXPERIMENTAL PSYCHOL.: APPLIED 111, 111 (2005) ("One of the most commonly replicated 'happiness gaps' is that observed between the self-rated quality of life of people with health conditions and healthy people's estimates of what their quality of life would be if they had those conditions. . . ."); Peter A. Ubel et al., *Do Nonpatients Underestimate the Quality of Life Associated with Chronic Health Conditions Because of a Focusing Illusion?*, 21 MED. DECISION MAKING 190, 197 (2001). Because the difficulty of adapting to seemingly inconsequential disabilities like ringing in the ears is also surprising, there is reason to suspect that people will *under*estimate their effects.

55. Daniel Kahneman & Angus Deaton, *High Income Improves Evaluation of Life but Not Emotional Well-Being*, 107 PROC. NAT'L ACAD. SCI. 16489, 16492 (2010).

56. Consider Daniel Kahneman's famous colonoscopy study. In the study, patients *remembered* their colonoscopies as less bad if the procedures were extended longer so that the final moments involved less intense pain. The overall *experience* was more negative than the typical colonoscopy because of the increased length of the procedure, all of which was painful to varying degrees; but it was remembered as less negative. Some might ask why it is only the experience, rather than also (or instead) the memory, that matters. After all, if remembering the procedure less negatively causes people to be more likely to go back for future procedures, which in turn might extend their lives, then that might be more beneficial than merely giving those people less experiential negativity in the initial procedure.

Our response is that our approach to welfare—and the tool of well-being analysis (WBA) that seeks to make that approach implementable—would count *all* past, present, and future moments of experienced well-being in its calculus. Not only would this mean that memories count insofar as they constitute experiences while they are occurring in someone's mind, but it would also mean that the way people act on their memories gets factored in because those actions affect their welfare by affecting their ultimate sum of experienced happiness. So, suppose Jack and Jill each have a colonoscopy. Jack has an ordinary procedure, whereas Jill has a longer one with a less-painful ending. Suppose that Jack's procedure, while it was happening, caused Jack to experience negative-5 well-being units (WBUs), whereas Jill's procedure caused her to experience negative-7 WBUs. However, Jill remembers her procedure as though it caused only negative-3 WBUs. It is true that that memory is ignored by WBA (except insofar as it might improve the moments in which Jill experiences the memory), *but* actions taken based on the memory are counted. So if Jill goes back and gets another colonoscopy because she doesn't remember it as being so bad, and if that second colonoscopy ends up saving Jill's life, then that life-saving absolutely gets counted by WBA because it preserves a huge number of moments in which Jill is likely to experience net positivity (since most people are relatively happy most of the time). And that's as it should be, because the reason that the memory matters (other than as an experience in its own right) is that it can influence future action.

Thus, the colonoscopy issue would be analyzed by our theory as follows. We would calculate the extra experiential negativity of each extended procedure and multiply that by all the procedures that are done. This would give us the total harm of using the longer procedure. We would then use whatever evidence is available or could be generated to predict how many more people would return for future colonoscopies if they had the longer procedure (which is remembered more favorably) as opposed to the shorter procedure. And then we would use whatever data are available to predict how many people would be saved by having the future colonoscopies, and how much welfare would be gained by thereby prolonging those lives.

To be sure, this analysis would involve very difficult predictions about the future. But that problem is hardly unique to WBA. Any sort of policy analysis involves making extremely difficult guesses about the future. For most prospective policies, the majority of those guesses will be identical regardless of what tool of policy analysis is used—cost-benefit analysis (CBA), well-being analysis (WBA), or qualitative assessment. Consider the colonoscopy example. There, the crucial prediction is: what effect will a certain type of colonoscopy have on an individual's likelihood of undergoing that procedure in the future? Determining the likely answer to that question has nothing to do with WBA; any type of welfarist decision procedure will require an answer.

57. Adler & Posner, *Rethinking Cost-Benefit Analysis*, at 245 ("CBA does not capture, and is not meant to capture, nonwelfarist considerations.").

58. *See* Exec. Order 13,563 (2011).

59. ADLER & POSNER, NEW FOUNDATIONS, at 53 (noting the possible roles of "moral rights, the fair distribution of welfare, and even moral considerations wholly detached from welfare, such as intrinsic environmental values" that could be considered alongside the value of aggregate welfare when making public policy).

60. *See generally* Don Bradford Hardin, Jr., *Why Cost-Benefit Analysis? A Question (and Some Answers) About the Legal Academy*, 59 ALA. L. REV. 1135 (2008) (providing a general history of CBA).

61. EPA National Emission Standards for Hazardous Air Pollutants for Source Category: Pulp and Paper Industry 40 C.F.R. pt. 63, subpt. S (1998); EPA Identification and Listing of Hazardous Waste 40 C.F.R. pt. 261 (1998); EPA The Pulp, Paper, and Paperboard Point Source Category 40 C.F.R. 430 (1998). The regulation, 40 C.F.R. 430, was upheld by the D.C. Circuit. Nat'l Wildlife Fed'n v. EPA, 286 F.3d 554, 557 (D.C. Cir. 2002). One of us has written about this regulation before. Masur & Posner, *Against Feasibility Analysis*; Jonathan S. Masur & Eric A. Posner, *Regulation, Unemployment, and Cost-Benefit Analysis*, 98 VA. L. REV. 579 (2012). The EPA simultaneously regulated airborne emissions from pulp and paper mills under the Clean Air Act, but for ease of explication we limit our examination here to the Clean Water Act portion of the regulation.

62. National Emission Standards for Hazardous Air Pollutants for Source Category: Pulp and Paper Production; Effluent Limitations Guidelines, Pretreatment Standards, and New Source Performance Standards: Pulp, Paper, and Paperboard Category, 63 Fed. Reg. at 18,542 (noting that, in mills used to provide data for Option A, "kappa factors for softwood furnish averaged .17 and all were less than .2").

63. National Emission Standards for Hazardous Air Pollutants, at 18,541–42.

64. National Emission Standards for Hazardous Air Pollutants, at 18,542.

65. U.S. Envtl. Prot. Agency, EPA Contract No. 68-C3–0302, Economic Analysis for the National Emission Standards for Hazardous Air Pollutants for Source Category: Pulp and Paper Production; Effluent Limitations Guidelines, Pretreatment Standards, and New Source Performance Standards: Pulp, Paper, and Paperboard Category—Phase 1, (1997), *available at* http://water.epa .gov/scitech/wastetech/guide/pulppaper/upload/1997_11_13_guide_pulppaper _jd_pulp.pdf tbl.8-6 (calculating the annual monetized benefits from reduction in cancer cases). The EPA also stated that the regulations would reduce risk of noncancer illnesses but did not report monetary estimates because of inadequate data. *Id.* at 8–14. In addition, the EPA estimated that the regulation would reduce deaths among Native Americans who are subsistence anglers. *Id.* at 8–15 tbl.8-8. It declined, however, to include this benefit within the analysis because of uncertainty in the data. Although this decision is probably indefen-

sible, we adhere to it here in the interest of parallelism between our WBA and the EPA's CBA.

66. EPA, Economic Analysis for Pulp and Paper Production, at 8–12 tbl.8–6.

67. We will attempt to approximate this cost—more accurately described as a benefit, actually, because these are cancer cases avoided—in the WBA we perform below.

68. EPA, Economic Analysis for Pulp and Paper Production, at 8–23. The EPA also surmised that more anglers would elect to fish if toxic effluents were reduced, and it estimated the benefit of this increased fishing at $4.7 to $15.5 million per year. However, because of uncertainties in the data the EPA did not end up including these figures in its benefit estimate. *Id.* at 8–23, 8–24, 8–26 tbl.8–12. We adhere to the EPA's decision without endorsing it.

69. EPA, Economic Analysis for Pulp and Paper Production, at 8–24.

70. *See generally* EPA, Economic Analysis for Pulp and Paper Production, at ch. 5 (discussing costs of implementing the rule).

71. The EPA calculated that Option A coupled with regulation under the Clean Air Act would result in net benefits, and so the agency's eventual outcome is cost-benefit justified. EPA, Economic Analysis for Pulp and Paper Production, at 8–27 tbl.8–13. Of course, this does not explain why the EPA didn't simply regulate only under the Clean Air Act if doing so produced substantial net benefits whereas regulation under the Clean Water Act produced substantial net costs.

72. *See* EPA, Economic Analysis for Pulp and Paper Production, at 6–18 ("Although the mills stay open with a price increase, consumers pay the price increase.").

73. *See* EPA, Economic Analysis for Pulp and Paper Production, at 6–19 tbl.6–6 (summarizing impact on employment).

74. *See* Masur & Posner, *Regulation & Unemployment*, at 582.

75. Masur & Posner, *Regulation & Unemployment*, at 580–81.

76. *See* Masur & Posner, *Regulation & Unemployment*, at 618.

77. We do not apply a discount rate in this WBA because it is uncertain whether discounting is appropriate in WBA. As we explain in the next chapter, this is a potential strength of WBA, rather than a weakness. If further research reveals that discounting is appropriate, then it would be straightforward to discount costs and benefits accordingly.

78. Because the *total* dollar cost is a constant number, our analysis is largely unaffected by whether that total cost is spread across virtually everyone who consumes paper products (say, 200 million Americans) or a much smaller subset (say, 1 million). The only difference is that if the total is borne by a smaller subset rather than spread across everyone, then each person affected must pay a higher amount. That results in a larger effect of cost on well-being, given that money af-

fects welfare in a logarithmic rather than linear fashion. We anticipate that our analysis may be criticized for placing too little weight on the value of money, so we choose the smaller number of 1 million (as opposed to, say, 200 million or everyone) purely to make the most conservative possible assumption. That is, we accentuate the welfare effects of lost income, and it still has only a small effect. Our calculation on this point should thus be considered an upper bound on the welfare effect of monetary costs for a regulation of this type.

79. U.S. Census Bureau, Money Income in the United States (1998), at v, *available at* http://www2.census.gov/prod2/popscan/p60–206.pdf.

As does CBA, we calculate the expected welfare effects of monetary costs based on the median income. If a policy were likely to affect people at a different income, the welfare effects could easily be calculated using happiness data relevant to the specified income level. For instance, if this pulp and paper regulation were likely to increase the cost of paper for a great number of people living below the poverty line, WBA should take the (greater) welfare effects on those individuals into account.

80. Nattavudh Powdthavee & Bernard van den Berg, *Putting Different Price Tags on the Same Health Condition: Re-evaluating the Well-Being Valuation Approach*, 30 J. Health Econ. 1032, 1038 tbl.3 (2011).

81. Powdthavee & van den Berg, *Different Price Tags*, 1038 tbl.3.

82. Powdthavee & van den Berg, *Different Price Tags*, 1038 tbl.3.

83. Powdthavee & van den Berg, *Different Price Tags*, 1038 tbl.3.

84. To arrive at this number, we begin by noting that the average American life span is 78 years. U.S. Census Bureau, Statistical Abstract of the United States 77 (2012). If anglers were evenly distributed across age categories, then the average angler would be 39 years old, meaning that saving such a person from death would save her nearly 40 years of life. In recognition that our well-being numbers may be criticized for valuing life much more heavily than does CBA, we "round down" to make a more conservative estimate of 30 years.

85. *See* chapter 3.

86. *See* Ed Diener & Carol Diener, *Most People Are Happy*, 7 Psychol. Sci. 181, 182 tbl.1 (1996). Studies have shown that older individuals are typically happier than younger and middle-aged people. Yang Yang, *Social Inequalities in Happiness in the United States, 1972 to 2004: An Age-Period Cohort Analysis*, 73 Am. Soc. Rev. 204, 213 (2008). Individuals who do not become sick and die from cancer as a result of this regulation will be adding years to the end of their lives, when they are happiest. Accordingly, by using the average American life-satisfaction figure we will tend to underestimate slightly the benefits of avoiding cancer.

87. We do not include any benefits to the family or friends of individuals who do not develop cancer because CBA typically does not include these third-party

benefits. *See* Sean Williams, *Statistical Children*, 30 YALE J. REG. (forthcoming 2013), *available at* http://papers.ssrn.com/sol3/papers.cfm?abstract_id=2176463.

88. Richard E. Lucas, *Adaptation and the Set-Point Model of Subjective Well-Being: Does Happiness Change After Major Life Events?*, 16 CURRENT DIRECTIONS PSYCHOL. SCI. 75, 77 (2007); Lucas et al., *Unemployment Alters*, at 11.

89. *See* Lucas et al., *Unemployment Alters*, at 11.

90. *See* Lucas, *Adaptation*, at 77; Lucas et al., *Unemployment Alters*, at 11. Lucas and his coauthors do not have data past the seven-year mark, and we are reluctant to speculate as to what future studies might reveal. Four German scholars have also recently conducted an excellent study of the effect of current (but not past) unemployment on moment-by-moment happiness. Andreas Knabe, Steffen Rätzel, Ronni Schöb & Joachim Weimann, *Dissatisfied with Life, but Having a Good Day: Time-Use and Well-Being of the Unemployed* 2 (CESifo, Working Paper No. 2604, 2009), *available at* http://ideas.repec.org/p/ces/ceswps/_2604.html. This is precisely the sort of data that we hope policymakers will collect in the service of analyzing regulations via WBA. We do not incorporate this study in our analysis because all our other data come from life-satisfaction studies, and it would complicate the analysis substantially if we were to attempt to combine these different types of data. We emphasize that the purpose of our example is merely to show how WBA could be conducted.

91. *See* Bureau of Labor Statistics, *Unemployed Total and Full-Time Workers by Duration of Unemployment*, *available at* http://www.bls.gov/cps/cpsaat30.pdf.

92. EPA, Economic Analysis for Pulp and Paper Production, at 4–23.

93. For a review of the extensive literature, see Ed Diener & Robert Biswas-Diener, *Will Money Increase Subjective Well-Being? A Literature Review and Guide to Needed Research*, 57 SOC. INDICATORS RES. 119, 120–51 (2002). These findings are also congruent with the emphasis that advocates of feasibility analysis have long placed on job loss, as opposed to other types of monetary costs. *See, e.g.*, David Driesen, *Distributing the Costs of Environmental, Health, and Safety Protection: The Feasibility Principle, Cost-Benefit Analysis, and Regulatory Reform*, 32 B.C. ENVTL. AFF. L. REV. 1, 36–37 (2005).

94. Later in this chapter, we briefly discuss the extent to which non-numerical approaches constitute viable alternatives.

95. As chapter 3 explains, though, we believe that even this initial form of WBA improves upon CBA and thus would be beneficial to use in policy analysis.

96. *See* Matthew Adler & Eric A. Posner, *Happiness Research and Cost-Benefit Analysis*, 37 J. LEGAL STUD. S253, S280–81 ("The question is whether the numerical scales used in SWB surveys correspond to a true, interpersonally comparable scale of happiness."). In fact, concerns about the interpersonal cardinality of utility pushed economists toward monetization in the first place. *See*

William Nordhaus, *Measuring Real Income with Leisure and Household Production*, *in* MEASURING THE SUBJECTIVE WELL-BEING OF NATIONS: NATIONAL
ACCOUNTS OF TIME USE AND WELL-BEING 125, 125 (Alan B. Krueger ed., 2009).

97. *See, e.g.*, Ed Diener & Carol Diener, *The Wealth of Nations Revisited: Income and Quality of Life*, 36 SOC. INDICATORS RES. 275, 279–81 (1995) ("[F]or
lower levels of income, there is a rapid rise in meeting physical needs as income
increases, but for much of the income distribution there is a ceiling effect. . . .");
Robert H. Frank, *The Frame of Reference as a Public Good*, 107 ECON. J. 1832,
1834–35 (1997) (discussing variation in the significance of income's role in satisfaction across income levels).

98. *See* JAMES C. MCDAVID & LAURA R.L. HAWTHORN, PROGRAM EVALUATION
& PERFORMANCE MEASUREMENT: AN INTRODUCTION TO PRACTICE 265–66 (2006);
see also ADLER & POSNER, NEW FOUNDATIONS, at 142–46; Adler & Posner, *Rethinking Cost-Benefit Analysis*, at 177–81 (illustrating the difficulty of forward
looking CBA under income effects).

99. *See* PER-OLOV JOHANSSON, AN INTRODUCTION TO MODERN WELFARE ECO-
NOMICS 40 (1991); ROBERT L. NADEAU, THE WEALTH OF NATURE 115–16 (2003).

100. Uncertainty concerning individual welfare functions is especially problematic when attempting to make interpersonal comparisons of utility, which are
likely possible in only limited circumstances. *See, e.g.*, John C. Harsanyi, *Cardinal Welfare, Individualistic Ethics, and Interpersonal Comparisons of Utility*,
63 J. POL. ECON. 309, 315–19 (1955).

101. *See, e.g.*, Adler & Posner, *Rethinking Cost-Benefit Analysis*, at 193.

102. *See, e.g.*, Adler & Posner, *Rethinking Cost-Benefit Analysis*, at 181–87;
Rafael Di Tella & Robert MacCulloch, *Some Uses of Happiness Data in Economics*, 20 J. ECON. PERSP. 25, 29 (2006).

103. There is some reason to believe that citizens of different nations with
different cultures will treat happiness surveys systematically differently. *See* Ed
Diener & Eunkook M. Suh, *Measuring Subjective Well-Being to Compare Quality of Life of Cultures*, *in* CULTURE AND SUBJECTIVE WELL-BEING 1, 3 (Ed Diener
& Eunkook M. Suh eds., 2000) ("If societies have different sets of values, people
in them are likely to consider different criteria relevant when judging the success
of their society."). Empirical studies have found, however, that similarly situated individuals in different countries have similar levels of life satisfaction. Betsey Stevenson & Justin Wolfers, *Economic Growth and Happiness: Reassessing the Easterlin Paradox*, *in* BROOKINGS PAPERS ON ECONOMIC ACTIVITY 67, 69
(2008). This suggests that subjective well-being measures may even be comparable across countries. If that is the case, they will very likely be comparable across
regions or communities within a given country.

104. *See* Di Tella & MacCulloch, *Some Uses of Happiness Data*, at 29–32
(discussing the possibility of reducing systemic differential reporting biases by
comparing across larger groups). In addition, the U-Index proposed by Krue-

ger et al. is designed to mitigate differences in scale usage. *See* Alan B. Krueger et al., *National Time Accounting: The Currency of Life, in* Measuring the Subjective Well-Being of Nations 30, 18–20 (Alan B. Krueger ed., 2009).

105. Some might contend that circumstances such as disability and unemployment create the potential for some degree of scale re-norming. That is, they might argue that ideal happiness could mean something different to a person after she becomes seriously disabled or unemployed, and that the person might report a higher score for the same level of positive feeling than she would have reported before she was injured or unemployed. There is no reason to believe this is true, but even if it were, techniques like the U-index developed by Alan Krueger, Daniel Kahneman, and colleagues avoid the issue of different scale usage by comparing responses only within-subjects. *See* Krueger et al., *National Time Accounting*, at 20. The hedonic data are interpreted with respect to individuals and converted into externally comparable numbers. Although this approach does not encompass all relevant data, it nonetheless constitutes an interpersonally cardinal scale.

In addition, if scale re-norming were taking place, we would expect to see evidence of adaptation to all debilitating health conditions. All affected individuals would be altering the way that they report their happiness to take into account their changed circumstances. Yet this is not what hedonic psychologists have found. Instead, humans appear to exhibit almost complete adaptation to some conditions, partial adaptation to others, and zero adaptation to others still, including health problems like chronic pain and ringing in the ears. *See* Bronsteen, Buccafusco & Masur, *Hedonic Adaptation and the Settlement of Civil Lawsuits*, 108 Colum. L. Rev. 1516, 1540–42 (2008). This is a strong indication that scale re-norming is not taking place.

106. Twenty-five people have each gained 0.1, for a total gain of 2.5, and one person has lost 1.0, for a net of 1.5.

107. *See* Adler & Posner, *Happiness Research*, at S281.

108. As we note in chapter 6 and also discussed in Bronsteen, Buccafusco & Masur, *Welfare as Happiness*, we are weak welfarists in the following sense: we contend that increasing aggregate welfare is desirable, all else being equal, but we make no claims regarding the relative value of welfare vis-à-vis other possible values, such as the distribution of welfare or welfare-unrelated moral concerns.

109. This is true if Person A and Person B have different welfare functions, such that the project might diminish overall welfare, but it is also true even if they have identical welfare functions and aggregate welfare will increase.

110. Amy Sinden, *In Defense of Absolutes: Combating the Politics of Power in Environmental Law*, 90 Iowa L. Rev. 1405, 1415 (2005). Or, put another way, a project is Kaldor-Hicks efficient if it is possible to make a transfer of wealth that would leave all parties better off than before the project was implemented.

See, e.g., ANTHONY E. BOARDMAN, DAVID H. GREENBERG, AIDAN R. VINNING & DAVID L. WEIMER, COST-BENEFIT ANALYSIS: CONCEPTS AND PRACTICE 53 (1996).

111. *See* ADLER & POSNER, NEW FOUNDATIONS, at 22 ("Because Kaldor-Hicks is, taken as a moral principle, unsound, CBA cannot be justified by reference to Kaldor-Hicks."); Adler & Posner, *Rethinking Cost-Benefit Analysis*, at 195. *But see* Richard A. Posner, *The Ethical and Political Basis of the Efficiency Norm in Common Law Adjudication*, 8 HOFSTRA L. REV. 487, 491–97 (1980) (attempting to justify Kaldor-Hicks efficiency as a moral criterion); Richard A. Posner, *Utilitarianism, Economics, and Legal Theory*, 8 J. LEGAL STUD. 103, 103 (1979) (same).

112. As with many of the prior examples, we draw this hypothetical (and this objection) from Adler & Posner, *Happiness Research*, at S281.

113. *See* Laura L. Myers, *Same-Sex Couples Wed in Washington State for First Time*, REUTERS, Dec. 9, 2012, *available at* http://www.reuters.com/article/2012/12/09/us-usa-gaymarriage-idUSBRE8B801S20121209. We thank Lior Strahilevitz for raising this issue.

114. *See* Lior Jacob Strahilevitz, *"How's My Driving?" For Everyone (and Everything?)*, 81 N.Y.U. L. REV. 1699, 1732–37 (2006) (suggesting that similar algorithms could screen malicious feedback in "How's My Driving" programs).

115. Strahilevitz, *"How's My Driving?"*, at 1733.

116. Strahilevitz, *"How's My Driving?"*, at 1733.

117. Strahilevitz, *"How's My Driving?"*, at 1734 n.145 ("Collusive ratings are a problem for online feedback systems generally, though eBay has been able to keep this problem at tolerable (albeit nonzero) levels to date.").

118. Well-conducted contingent valuation studies attempt to control for these issues, but doing so is difficult. *See* John C. Whitehead & Glenn C. Blomquist, *The Use of Contingent Valuation in Benefit-Cost Analysis, in* HANDBOOK ON CONTINGENT VALUATION 92 (Anna Alberini & James R. Kahn eds., 2006); Richard T. Carson & W. Michael Hanemann, *Contingent Valuation, in* 2 HANDBOOK OF ENVIRONMENTAL ECONOMICS 821, 883 (Karl-Goran Maler and Jeffrey R. Vincent eds., 2005) ("[P]eople only try to tell the truth when it is in their economic interest to do so.").

119. *See* Carson and Hanemann, *Contingent Valuation* (explaining that respondents' incentives to prevaricate "make[] the design of CV survey questions and their analysis much more challenging").

120. In the United States, there is the General Social Survey. In Great Britain, happiness data come from the British Household Panel Survey, a nationally representative sample of 27,000 individuals collected since 1991. German data come from the German Socioeconomic Panel Study, which includes 40,000 individuals who have been tracked yearly for at least twenty-one years.

121. *See, e.g.*, Matthew A. Killingsworth & Daniel T. Gilbert, *A Wandering Mind Is an Unhappy Mind*, 330 SCIENCE 932 (2010); George MacKerron &

Susana Mourato, *Happiness Is Greater in Natural Environments*, 23 GLOBAL
ENVTL. CHANGE 992 (2013).

122. JEREMY BENTHAM, AN INTRODUCTION TO THE PRINCIPLES OF MORALS
AND LEGISLATION 12–13 (J.H. Burns & H.L.A. Hart eds., Clarendon Press 1996)
(1789) ("An action . . . may be said to be conformable to the principle of utility . . . (meaning with respect to the community at large) when the tendency it
has to augment the happiness of the community is greater than any it has to diminish it.").

123. *See generally* Adler & Posner, *Rethinking Cost-Benefit Analysis*, at 188.

124. *See* David G. Blanchflower & Andrew J. Oswald, *Well-Being over Time
in Britain and the USA*, 88 J. PUB. ECON. 1359, 1378 (2004); Richard A. Easterlin, *Will Raising the Incomes of All Increase the Happiness of All?*, 27 J. ECON.
BEHAV. & ORG. 35, 44 (1995).

125. *See, e.g.*, JOHN RAWLS, A THEORY OF JUSTICE 140 (1971) ("[T]he principle
of average utility directs society to maximize not the total but the average utility
(per capita). This seems to be a more modern view. . . .").

126. *See* JOHN BROOME, WEIGHING GOODS 192–200 (1991) (setting forth a theory of equality grounded in relational fairness, or the distribution of good according to individuals' claims for it); FRED FELDMAN, UTILITARIANISM, HE-
DONISM, AND DESERT 154–74 (1997) (proposing a form of utilitarian theory that
takes into account distributive justice).

127. For a review of research on how people value utilities at different times,
see Shane Frederick et al., *Time Discounting and Time Preference: A Critical
Review*, 40 J. ECON. LIT. 351 (2002).

128. Daniel Kahneman & Angus Deaton, *High Income Improves Evaluation
of Life but Not Emotional Well-Being*, 107 PROC. NAT'L ACAD. SCI. 16489 (2010).

129. ACKERMAN & HEINZERLING, PRICELESS.

130. ACKERMAN & HEINZERLING, PRICELESS, at 234.

131. Indeed, this is taken seriously in the context of CBA. In the very example we gave in this chapter, the results of the CBA were not strictly followed. Instead, they were merely factored in to the ultimate decision-making process. This
is precisely the role we envision for WBA. Like CBA, it will influence the conversation about what should be done, without being determinative. The difference is that it should approximate overall welfare better than does CBA, thereby
doing a better job of filling that role in the policymaking analysis.

Chapter Three

1. Amartya Sen, *The Discipline of Cost-Benefit Analysis*, 29 J. LEGAL STUD.
931, 945 (2000) ("In mainstream cost-benefit analysis, the primary work of valuation is done by the use of willingness to pay."). Some cost-benefit studies instead examine subjects' willingness to accept money in exchange for sacrificing

a benefit or bearing a cost. These willingness-to-accept (WTA) measures often yield different results than do WTP measures, but the methodologies used to determine them are effectively identical, and the problems that affect WTP similarly plague WTA. *See generally* John K. Horowitz & Kenneth E. McConnell, *A Review of WTA/WTP Studies*, 44 J. ENVTL. ECON. & MGMT. 426 (2002). Accordingly, we use WTP here as shorthand to mean WTP or WTA.

2. Richard H. Pildes & Cass R. Sunstein, *Reinventing the Regulatory State*, 62 U. CHI. L. REV. 1, 76 (1995) ("[P]eople reveal the values they attach to various goods through their actual behavior in market or market-like settings. If we attend to the choices people actually make, we will be able to infer from them the valuations assigned to various goods.").

3. *See, e.g.*, W. KIP VISCUSI, RATIONAL RISK POLICY 46–47 (1998) ("[R]isky jobs must be attractive in some other way, such as higher pay, for workers to be willing to bear the risk.").

4. Frank Ackerman & Lisa Heinzerling, *Pricing the Priceless: Cost-Benefit Analysis of Environmental Protection*, 150 U. PA. L. REV. 1553, 1557 (2002) ("Since there are no natural prices for a healthy environment, cost-benefit analysis requires the creation of artificial ones."); Miriam Montesinos, Comment, *It May Be Silly, but It's an Answer: The Need to Accept Contingent Valuation Methodology in Natural Resource Damage Assessments*, 26 ECOLOGY L.Q. 48, 49–50 (1999) ("The problem with placing values on natural resources is that natural resources are not market commodities and therefore do not have market prices.").

5. *See, e.g.*, Daniel Kahneman et al., *Stated Willingness to Pay for Public Goods: A Psychological Perspective*, 4 PSYCHOL. SCI. 310, 310 (1993) ("Hundreds of contingent valuations have been carried out in the last two decades. . . ."); Pildes & Sunstein, *Reinventing the Regulatory State*, at 80 ("Rather than looking at actual choices, these methods ask people hypothetical questions about how much they would be willing to pay to avoid certain harms or conditions.").

6. *See, e.g.*, Edna T. Loehman et al., *Willingness to Pay for Gains and Losses in Visibility and Health*, 70 LAND ECON. 476, 479–85 (1994) (examining how much people would pay for improved air quality).

7. *See* VISCUSI, RATIONAL RISK POLICY, at 312–13 (stating that the literature on wage-risk trade-offs has become the basis for government policy).

8. *See, e.g.*, VISCUSI, RATIONAL RISK POLICY, at 312–13 ("Estimates from the U.S. labor market indicate that a worker currently would require an annual wage premium of $700 to face a fatality risk of 1/10,000. . . ."); *see also, e.g.*, ENVTL. PROT. AGENCY, ARSENIC IN DRINKING WATER RULE: ECONOMIC ANALYSIS 5–28 (2000) (illustrating how the value of a statistical life increases as the cancer latency period decreases).

9. Richard Revesz, *Environmental Regulation, Cost-Benefit Analysis, and the Discounting of Human Lives*, 99 COLUM. L. REV. 941, 943 (1999) ("The primary

benefit of many important environmental statutes, as determined by the dollar value assigned by cost-benefit analysis, is the human lives that are saved.").

10. Revesz, *Environmental Regulation*, at 943–44 ("Thus, in determining whether a particular regulation can be justified on cost-benefit grounds, the central questions revolve around the value assigned to the lives that would be saved by the program.").

11. Frank B. Cross, *Natural Resource Damage Valuation*, 42 VAND. L. REV. 269, 315 (1989) ("Contingent valuation is controversial, however, because it is entirely hypothetical and because it assumes that people respond to the survey as they would to a marketplace transaction. . . . Economists are much more comfortable measuring revealed preferences in genuine market sales.").

12. *See* Jonathan S. Masur, *Probability Thresholds*, 92 IOWA L. REV. 1293, 1331–37 (2007) ("Study after study has demonstrated that individuals experience great difficulty, purely as a matter of estimation and intuition, when dealing with high-magnitude, low-probability threats.").

13. Young Sook Eom, *Pesticide Residue Risk and Food Safety Valuation: A Random Utility Approach*, 76 AM. J. AGRIC. ECON. 760, 769 (1994); M.W. Jones-Lee, M. Hammerton & P.R. Philips, *The Value of Safety: Results of a National Sample Survey*, 95 ECON. J. 49, 65–66 (1985); Michael W. Jones-Lee, Graham Loomes & P.R. Philips, *Valuing the Prevention of Non-Fatal Road Injuries: Contingent Valuation vs. Standard Gambles*, 47 OXFORD ECON. PAPERS 676, 688 (1995); C.T. Jordan Lin & J. Walter Milon, *Contingent Valuation of Health Risk Reductions for Shellfish Products*, *in* VALUING FOOD SAFETY AND NUTRITION 83–114 (J.A. Caswell ed., 1995); V. Kerry Smith & William H. Desvousges, *An Empirical Analysis of the Economic Value of Risk Changes*, 95 J. POL. ECON. 89, 100 tbl.2 (1987).

14. Masur, *Probability Thresholds*, at 1335.

15. Cass R. Sunstein, *Probability Neglect: Emotions, Worst Cases, and Law*, 112 YALE L.J. 61, 73–74 (2002) ("For most of us, most of the time, the relevant differences—between, say, 1/100,000 and 1/1,000,000—are not pertinent to our decisions, and by experience we are not well equipped to take those differences into account.").

16. *See* Maureen Cropper, James K. Hammitt & Lisa A. Robinson, *Valuing Mortality Risk Reductions: Progress and Challenges*, 3 ANN. REV. RESOUR. ECON. 313, 317 (2011) ("[E]stimates of VSL based on hedonic wage equations assume that the measure of job risk used by the researcher matches workers' risk perceptions.").

17. FRANK ACKERMAN & LISA HEINZERLING, PRICELESS: ON KNOWING THE PRICE OF EVERYTHING AND THE VALUE OF NOTHING 87 (2004) ("Average real wages for truck drivers declined 30 percent between 1977 and 1995, due to the combination of deregulation and the declining power of the Teamsters union. . . ."); MICHAEL H. BELZER, SWEATSHOPS ON WHEELS: WINNERS AND LOS-

ERS IN TRUCKING DEREGULATION 21–22 (2000) ("While unions . . . represented about 60% of all truck drivers twenty years ago, today they represent less than 25% of all drivers.").

18. *See, e.g.,* Janusz R. Mrozek & Laura O. Taylor, *What Determines the Value of Life? A Meta-Analysis,* 21 J. POL'Y ANALYSIS & MGMT. 253, 266–70 (2002) ("Restricting the sample of workers to 100 percent unionized workers resulted in larger VSL estimates. . . ."). Some studies attempt to control for unionization. *See* W. Kip Viscusi, *The Value of Life: Estimates with Risks by Occupation and Industry,* 42 J. ECON. INQUIRY 29 (2004).

19. Mrozek & Taylor, *Value of Life,* at 254; *see also* ENVTL. PROT. AGENCY, VALUING MORTALITY RISK REDUCTIONS FOR ENVIRONMENTAL POLICY: A WHITE PAPER 85–88 tbl.4 (2010) (compiling data from many hedonic wage studies into a table). Another indication of the spread of possible results from such studies is a compilation of thirty-seven hedonic wage studies that the EPA recently assembled. The standard deviation of the values of life among those thirty-seven studies was $14.1 million, or approximately *twice* the value that the EPA currently places on a statistical life. *See id.* (standard deviation calculated by author); *see also* W. Kip Viscusi & Joseph E. Aldy, *The Value of a Statistical Life: A Critical Review of Market Estimates Throughout the World,* 27 J. RISK & UNCERTAINTY 5, 19–21 (2003) (summarizing a series of hedonic wage studies performed over the last three decades that identify VSLs ranging from $0.5 million to $20.8 million).

20. *See generally* Andrew J. Oswald & Nattavudh Powdthavee, *Does Happiness Adapt? A Longitudinal Study of Disability with Implications for Economists and Judges,* 92 J. PUB. ECON. 1061 (2008) (using a longitudinal study to determine the hedonic cost of disability).

21. *See* Viscusi & Aldy, *The Value of a Statistical Life,* at 36–43 (finding an income elasticity between 0.5 and 0.6, such that a 10 percent rise in income would increase WTP by 5 to 6 percent); *see also* Thomas Kniesner, W. Kip Viscusi & James P. Ziliak, *Policy Relevant Heterogeneity in the Value of Statistical Life: New Evidence from Panel Data Quantile Regressions,* 40 J. RISK & UNCERTAINTY 14, 28 (2010) (finding an income elasticity approaching or exceeding 1.0, such that a 10 percent rise in income would increase WTP by more than 10 percent); W. Kip Viscusi, *The Heterogeneity of the Value of Statistical Life: Introduction and Overview,* 40 J. RISK & UNCERTAINTY 1, 7–11 (2010) (summarizing more recent research finding that WTP values are more sensitive to income than previously thought).

22. The reason is the declining marginal value of money. *See, e.g.,* Adam J. Kolber, *The Comparative Nature of Punishment,* 89 B.U. L. REV. 1565, 1599 n.88 (2009) ("Even rights denominated in dollars cannot meaningfully be compared to each other without considering how people value those dollars. Due to the declining marginal value of money, most people value the liberty to spend $100,000

less than 100 times the amount that they value the liberty to spend $1000."); Andrew P. Morriss & Roger E. Meiners, *Borders and the Environment*, 39 ENVTL. L. 141, 155 n.64 (2009) ("Of course, richer people lose more money when they miss a day of work due to illness than do poor people, but the declining marginal value of money means that what they lose may not be as valuable as the smaller in magnitude losses incurred by the poorer people.").

23. Anup Malani, *Valuing Laws as Local Amenities*, 121 HARV. L. REV. 1273, 1276–80 (2008) (describing such a methodology and using it to value certain legal changes).

24. In addition, if the agency chose the second-best solution and located the project in the wealthy area, residents of that neighborhood could conceivably bargain with residents of the poorer neighborhood to have the project moved in exchange for a side payment. This bargain is of course unlikely; transaction costs or legal barriers might prevent it. But it is at least possible. No such Coasean bargain is possible if the project is located in the poor neighborhood, because the poorer people do not have the funds to pay off the wealthier people.

25. *See* Matthew D. Adler, Equity by the Numbers: Measuring Poverty, Inequality, and Injustice (2013) (unpublished manuscript) (on file with authors), *available at* http://ssrn.com/abstract=2263433 (proposing a means of attempting to assign equity weights to costs and benefits experienced by populations at different levels of wealth).

26. *See* Marjorie E. Kornhauser, *Equality, Liberty, and a Fair Income Tax*, 23 FORDHAM URB. L.J. 607, 617 (1996) (explaining that there is no way to determine an individual's marginal utility of money).

27. As we have noted, some of these problems also implicate WBA, though not to the same degree.

28. Cass Sunstein, *Willingness to Pay vs. Welfare*, 1 HARV. L. & POL'Y REV. 303, 305 (2007).

29. *See* Jennifer Gerarda Brown, *The Role of Hope in Negotiation*, 44 UCLA L. REV. 1661, 1666 (1997) (analyzing a hypothetical "suggest[ing] . . . that a [homeowner]'s hopes or aspirations influence negotiation analysis and behavior").

30. *See* Paul Boudreaux, *An Individual Preference Approach to Suburban Racial Desegregation*, 27 FORDHAM URB. L.J. 533, 547 (1999) ("Housing prices are affected by buyers' desires for certain amenities, such as air conditioning, a large kitchen or a driveway. Housing prices will vary when certain features rise or fall in desirability. Housing prices are also affected by whether the location of housing is near desirable or undesirable metropolitan features.").

31. *See* Timothy D. Wilson & Daniel T. Gilbert, *Affective Forecasting: Knowing What to Want*, 14 CURRENT DIRECTIONS PSYCHOL. SCI. 131, 131 (2005) ("Research on affective forecasting has shown that people routinely mispredict how much pleasure or displeasure future events will bring and, as a result, some-

times work to bring about events that do not maximize their happiness." (emphasis omitted)); *see also* David A. Schkade & Daniel Kahneman, *Does Living in California Make People Happy? A Focusing Illusion in Judgments of Life Satisfaction*, 9 PSYCHOL. SCI. 340, 344–45 (1998) (discussing affective forecasting errors).

32. *See* Dylan M. Smith et al., *Misremembering Colostomies? Former Patients Give Lower Utility Ratings than Do Current Patients*, 25 HEALTH PSYCHOL. 688, 691 (2006) (describing difficulties with remembering affective states).

33. For Wilson & Gilbert's description of this phenomenon, see Wilson & Gilbert, *Affective Forecasting*.

34. *See, e.g.*, Matthew D. Adler, *Fear Assessment: Cost-Benefit Analysis and the Pricing of Fear and Anxiety*, 79 CHI.-KENT L. REV. 977, 1024 (2004) ("WTP/WTA for the risk of death can be inferred from the wage differential between more and less dangerous occupations."); Cass R. Sunstein, *The Arithmetic of Arsenic*, 90 GEO. L. REV. 2255, 2268–75 (2002) (explaining how the EPA developed its arsenic regulations under the Clinton administration). *But cf.* OFFICE OF INFO. & REGULATORY AFFAIRS, 2011 REPORT TO CONGRESS ON THE BENEFITS AND COSTS OF FEDERAL REGULATIONS AND UNFUNDED MANDATES ON STATE, LOCAL, AND TRIBAL ENTITIES 18 n.20 (2011) (stating that OSHA developed its rule on occupational exposure to hexavalent chromium using $7 million value of life).

35. We do not mean to imply that lack of experience is the only problem. Affective forecasting errors are common even when people do have experience with the thing in question.

36. *See* Jonathan S. Masur & Eric A. Posner, *Against Feasibility Analysis*, 77 U. CHI. L. REV. 657, 671 (2010) (describing a regulation in which the agency ignores certain health costs for lack of data); Occupational Exposure to Hexavalent Chromium, 71 Fed. Reg. 10,100, 10,307 (Feb. 28, 2006) (codified at 29 C.F.R. pts. 1910, 1915, 1917, 1918 & 1926) (ignoring these risks).

37. We explain other problems with value-of-life calculations below.

38. *See, e.g.*, Nattavudh Powdthavee & Bernard van den Berg, *Putting Different Price Tags on the Same Health Condition: Re-evaluating the Well-Being Valuation Approach* 30 J. HEALTH ECON. 1032, 1034 (2011) (providing self-assessment data related to a variety of ailments). The preferred method for collecting this data is to ask the same people for assessments of their own well-being before and after those people contract emphysema. Large-scale data collection efforts like the British Household Panel Survey make this approach feasible, and Powdthavee and van den Berg rely on those types of sources. *See id.*

39. *See* Cross, *Natural Resource Damage Valuation*.

40. Lisa Heinzerling, *Markets for Arsenic*, 90 GEO. L.J. 2311, 2315 (2002) ("The valuation is 'contingent' because the valuation produced is contingent upon the hypothetical market that was contrived. A famous example is the large-scale survey taken in the wake of the Exxon Valdez oil spill, which sought to

elicit the monetary value citizens around the country placed on avoiding another comparable spill.").

41. *See, e.g.*, Matthew D. Adler & Eric A. Posner, *Implementing Cost-Benefit Analysis When Preferences Are Distorted*, 29 J. LEGAL STUD. 1105, 1117 (2000) ("Textbook CBA, as generally understood, directs agencies to translate people's moral attitudes about the environment into CVs for the existence of environmental goods that they do not directly enjoy, usually called 'existence value' or 'nonuse value.'").

42. *See* Malani, *Valuing Laws*, at 1275 (discussing housing prices as a means of measuring "the welfare effect of a law," but noting that "[t]his is, of course, not the standard practice").

43. *See* John M. Heyde, Comment, *Is Contingent Valuation Worth the Trouble?*, 62 U. CHI. L. REV. 331, 343 (1995) (summarizing criticisms of contingent valuation); *see also* Ackerman & Heinzerling, *Pricing the Priceless*, at 1558 (same).

44. Cross, *Natural Resource Damage Valuation*, at 317 ("Because people have little experience placing monetary value on unpriced natural resources, survey results may be hypothetical and inaccurate.").

45. *See, e.g.*, John E. Calfee & Clifford Winston, *The Consumer Welfare Effects of Liability for Pain and Suffering: An Exploratory Analysis*, in 1 BROOKINGS PAPERS ON ECONOMIC ACTIVITY: MICROECONOMICS 142, 143 n.17 (1993) (stating that contingent valuation surveys rarely involve budget constraints).

46. *See* Thomas O. McGarity, *A Cost-Benefit State*, 50 ADMIN. L. REV. 7, 66 (1998) ("Another frequent criticism of contingent valuation techniques is that they allow value to be measured by the uninformed opinions of uneducated individuals who have had no experience in valuing the things that are the subject matter of the surveys."); Cross, *Natural Resource Damage Valuation*, at 316.

47. *See* Peter A. Diamond & Jerry A. Hausman, *Contingent Valuation: Is Some Number Better than No Number?*, 8 J. ECON. PERSP. 45, 49 (1994) (discussing the recurrent problems with contingent valuation surveys and providing an overview of alternative explanations for the responses given in willingness-to-pay questions).

48. ENVTL. PROT. AGENCY, MORTALITY RISK REDUCTIONS, at 82–83. The EPA also compiled forty contingent valuation surveys of the value of life. The standard deviation of the value of life among those forty surveys was over $3 million. *Id.* (standard deviation calculated by author).

49. *See* Cropper et al., *Valuing Mortality*, at 327.

50. *See* Cropper et al., *Valuing Mortality*, at 327 (surveying the literature).

51. Anna Alberini et al., *Does the Value of a Statistical Life Vary with Age and Health Status? Evidence from the US and Canada*, 48 J. ENVTL. ECON. & MGMT. 769, 782 tbl.6 (2004).

52. Cropper et al., *Valuing Mortality*, at 327–28 (citing ENVTL. PROT. AGENCY, MORTALITY RISK REDUCTIONS).

53. Cropper et al., *Valuing Mortality*, at 328.

54. ED DIENER ET AL., WELL-BEING FOR PUBLIC POLICY 71–73 (2009).

55. *See also* Andrew J. Oswald & Nattavudh Powdthavee, *Death, Happiness, and the Calculation of Compensatory Damages*, 37 J. LEGAL STUD. S232 (2008) (providing an example of sophisticated multivariate regression being used to isolate the effect of one factor on happiness).

56. As a matter of last recourse, WBA could also ask individuals to predict their well-being if they were to receive some benefit or suffer some harm. This would be the contingent valuation version of WBA, and as such it would be subject to all the problems with affective forecasting and hypothetical questions we describe here. But at least it would circumvent issues related to wealth and the translation of welfare into dollars, and thus even this approach might well be superior to standard contingent valuation studies.

57. Had the person lived, she would have experienced many moments that were, instead, extinguished by her death. WBA would aggregate the expected number and average level of positivity of those moments to determine how much positive life experience her early death deprived her of.

58. *Cf.* F.Y. EDGEWORTH, MATHEMATICAL PSYCHICS: AN ESSAY ON THE APPLICATION OF MATHEMATICS TO THE MORAL SCIENCES 98–102 (London, C. Kegan Paul & Co. 1881) (hypothesizing about a hedonimeter); David Colander, *Retrospectives: Edgeworth's Hedonimeter and the Quest to Measure Utility*, 21 J. ECON. PERSP. 215, 216–19 (2007) (reviewing psychophysic concepts that "dovetail[] with Edgeworth's description of the hypothesized hedonimeter").

59. Sunstein, *Willingness to Pay vs. Welfare*, at 304.

60. We thank David Weisbach for suggesting this point to us. This is contrary to many of the most sophisticated modern defenders of CBA, who describe it as a welfarist decision procedure. *See* MATTHEW D. ADLER & ERIC A. POSNER, NEW FOUNDATIONS OF COST-BENEFIT ANALYSIS 194 (2006).

61. *See, e.g.*, David Weisbach, *Toward a New Approach to Disability Law*, 1 U. CHI. LEGAL F. 47, 90 n.90 (2009) (stating the common assumption that welfare is quasi-linear in consumption).

62. *See generally* Louis Kaplow & Steven Shavell, *Why the Legal System Is Less Efficient than the Income Tax at Redistributing Income*, 23 J. LEGAL STUD. 667 (1994) (arguing that the tax system is more efficient at redistributing wealth than are legal rules such as agency regulations).

63. *See, e.g.*, ANTHONY E. BOARDMAN ET AL., COST-BENEFIT ANALYSIS: CONCEPTS AND PRACTICE 53 (1996); E.J. MISHAN, COST-BENEFIT ANALYSIS 390 (1976).

64. Amy Sinden, *In Defense of Absolutes: Combating the Politics of Power in Environmental Law*, 90 IOWA L. REV. 1405, 1415 (2005).

65. *See, e.g.*, BOARDMAN ET AL., COST-BENEFIT ANALYSIS, at 53.

66. Matthew D. Adler & Eric A. Posner, *Happiness Research and Cost-Benefit Analysis*, 37 J. LEGAL. STUD. S253, S265 (2008).

67. *See* Edward J. McCaffery, *Bifurcation Blues: The Perils of Leaving Redistribution Aside* 2–3 (working paper 2013), *available at* http://www.law.nyu.edu/ecm_dlv4/groups/public/@nyu_law_website__academics__colloquia__tax_policy/documents/documents/ecm_pro_074659.pdf (suggesting that "real-world tax policy is not up to the burdens that the bifurcation strategy places on it—it is not, that is, situated to redistribute in any meaningful way"); Lee Anne Fennell & Richard H. McAdams, *Introduction* to FAIRNESS IN LAW AND ECONOMICS (Lee Anne Fennell & Richard H. McAdams eds.) (forthcoming 2013, unpublished manuscript, on file with authors), at 5 ("Any proposed distributive change, whether accomplished through legal rules or through tax policy, elicits a certain amount of political resistance. This resistance may impede movement to a preferred distributive position, or cause great welfare losses in the process of achieving such movement."); *cf. Share of GDP for Bottom 99th, 95th, and 90th*, VISUALIZING ECONOMICS (Oct. 17, 2006), http://visualizingeconomics.com/blog/2006/10/17/share-of-gdp-99th-95th-90th (showing that the proportion of wealth held by the richest Americans has risen over the past thirty-five years and implying that wealth transfers from wealthy to poor have become less common over time); *see generally* MANCUR OLSON, THE LOGIC OF COLLECTIVE ACTION: PUBLIC GOODS AND THE THEORY OF GROUPS (1965) (setting forth an interest-group theory of politics).

68. This amounts to an argument that WBA may be path dependent. *Cf.* Masur & Posner, *Against Feasibility Analysis* (arguing that CBA is not similarly path dependent, with the exception of projects and regulations that cause substantial unemployment).

69. Of course, as we explained above, even CBA's ability to measure increases and decreases in wealth is compromised when the prices it relies on are distorted. Nonetheless, the results generated by CBA are almost certainly highly correlated with changes in wealth.

70. Of course, there can be non-welfarist grounds for promulgating regulations, but these are separate from what either CBA or WBA tries to measure.

71. Some may find it distasteful to place a value on saving a life, but when policy choices must be made and trade-offs are necessary, there is no alternative. Any decision will involve such a valuation, so it is a virtue that CBA and WBA make their valuations explicit rather than hidden.

72. Recent tweaks to CBA have, on occasion, made slight ameliorations to this problem. But as we discuss in this section of the chapter, these improvements are far less effective than is WBA at solving the problem.

73. Endless arguments could be made on each side about the moral validity of equating the deaths of the young with those of the old, but CBA cannot avail

itself of those arguments. Like WBA, CBA is simply a tool for measuring aggregate welfare. Its conclusions, like those of WBA, purport to tell us whether a regulation increases or decreases quality of life on the whole. Once that verdict is in, policymakers can decide what to do with it, and their decision may well involve making welfare-independent moral judgments. But when analyzing aggregate welfare alone, as CBA does, it is indefensible to equate preserving one year of life with preserving seventy years of life. The latter unquestionably increases welfare more than does the former, for precisely the reason that saving a life at all increases welfare: it grants more time to live.

74. ACKERMAN & HEINZERLING, PRICELESS, at 130.

75. *E.g.*, STEPHEN BREYER, BREAKING THE VICIOUS CIRCLE: TOWARD EFFECTIVE RISK REGULATION 61–63 (1993); John D. Graham, *Making Sense of Risk: An Agenda for Congress, in* RISKS, COSTS, AND LIVES SAVED 183 (Robert W. Hahn ed., 1996); Timur Kuran & Cass Sunstein, *Availability Cascades and Risk Regulation*, 51 STAN. L. REV. 683, 753 (1999); Neil D. Weinstein, *Optimistic Biases About Personal Risks*, 245 SCIENCE 1232, 1232 (1989).

76. *See generally* ACKERMAN & HEINZERLING, PRICELESS, at 123–52.

77. Robert W. Hahn, *The Cost of Antiterrorist Rhetoric*, 19 REGULATION 51, 54 (1996).

78. ACKERMAN & HEINZERLING, PRICELESS, at 123–24.

79. Hahn, *Antiterrorist Rhetoric*, at 54.

80. ACKERMAN & HEINZERLING, PRICELESS, at 123–24, 136–38.

81. Paul Slovic, *The Perception of Risk*, 236 SCIENCE 280, 282 (1987).

82. Slovic, *Perception of Risk*, at 282.

83. ACKERMAN & HEINZERLING, PRICELESS, at 130.

84. ACKERMAN & HEINZERLING, PRICELESS, at 130.

85. Slovic, *Perception of Risk*, at 285.

86. Lisa Heinzerling, *Environmental Law and the Present Future*, 87 GEO. L.J. 2025, 2036–37 (1999).

87. ACKERMAN & HEINZERLING, PRICELESS, at 131.

88. MICHAEL EDELSTEIN, CONTAMINATED COMMUNITIES: THE SOCIAL AND PSYCHOLOGICAL IMPACTS OF RESIDENTIAL TOXIC EXPOSURE 44–46 (1988).

89. EDELSTEIN, CONTAMINATED COMMUNITIES, at 93–95 (noting that, for example, "[s]pouses sometimes held their mates responsible for getting them into the situation or for their coping strategy," frequently resulting in substantial "marital strife").

90. EDELSTEIN, CONTAMINATED COMMUNITIES, at 98–105.

91. *See generally* KAI ERIKSON, A NEW SPECIES OF TROUBLE: EXPLORATIONS IN DISASTER, TRAUMA AND COMMUNITY 226–42 (1994).

92. Paul Slovic, *Perceived Risk, Trust, and Democracy*, 13 RISK ANALYSIS 675, 677–80 (1993).

93. Hahn, *Antiterrorist Rhetoric*, at 54.

94. Hahn, *Antiterrorist Rhetoric*, at 54.

95. ACKERMAN & HEINZERLING, PRICELESS, at 130.

96. ACKERMAN & HEINZERLING, PRICELESS, at 71 ("[T]he circumstances preceding death are important: sudden, painless death in pleasant circumstances is different from agonizing, slow deterioration surrounded by medical technology.").

97. If the time of death would actually differ, such that a slow death would increase the length of life, then of course this should be factored in as well. WBA does factor it in, whereas CBA does not, as we discuss in the next section.

98. ACKERMAN & HEINZERLING, PRICELESS, at 71.

99. Or, to use CBA's preferred terminology, it counts the cost of subjecting the members of a population to an increased risk of death. We believe this amounts to the same thing.

100. Oswald & Powdthavee, *Death and Happiness*.

101. Oswald & Powdthavee, *Death and Happiness*.

102. As we explain below, no regulation actually saves lives; it merely prolongs them. To the extent CBA focuses on saving lives, it is measuring the value of lives that presumably would have ended more or less immediately without the regulation.

103. *See* RICHARD L. REVESZ & MICHAEL A. LIVERMORE, RETAKING RATIONALITY: HOW COST-BENEFIT ANALYSIS CAN BETTER PROTECT THE ENVIRONMENT AND OUR HEALTH 47 (2008) (explaining that reduced mortality risk is one of the greatest justifications for the EPA's cost-benefit decisions).

104. REVESZ & LIVERMORE, RETAKING RATIONALITY, at 47–49.

105. We do not here discuss other, extra-welfarist goals of regulation.

106. Cass R. Sunstein, *Lives, Life-Years, and Willingness to Pay*, 104 COLUM. L. REV. 205, 208 (2004). *See also* James K. Hammitt, *Valuing Changes in Mortality Risk: Lives Saved Versus Life Years Saved*, 1 REV. ENVTL. . ECON. & POL'Y 228, 229–31 (2007) (discussing differences between VSL and VSLY measures).

107. Sunstein, *Lives and Life-Years*, at 206 ("[I]t is sensible to think that government should consider not simply the number of lives at stake, or the VSL; it should concern itself also or instead with the number of life-years at stake, or the value of statistical life-years (VSLY).").

108. REVESZ & LIVERMORE, RETAKING RATIONALITY, at 78.

109. *See* REVESZ & LIVERMORE, RETAKING RATIONALITY, at 78 (using $180,000 as an example VSLY value).

110. Sunstein, *Lives and Life-Years*, at 208 ("If the goal is to promote people's welfare by lengthening their lives, a regulation that saves five hundred life-years (and, let us say, twenty-five people) is, other things being equal, better than a regulation that saves fifty life-years (also, let us say, twenty-five people).").

111. We do not here discuss concerns about whether VSLYs enact illegal age discrimination. For discussion, see Sunstein, *Lives and Life-Years*, at 220.

112. REVESZ & LIVERMORE, RETAKING RATIONALITY, at 81 ("Relevant studies have found that the willingness to pay does not resemble the constant age-dependent discount postulated by proponents of the life-years method.").

113. *See* Anna Alberini, Maureen Cropper, Alan Krupnick & Nathalie B. Simon, *Does the Value of a Statistical Life Vary with Age and Health Status? Evidence from the US and Canada*, 48 J. ENVTL. ECON. & MGMT. 769, 771 (2004) (finding no significant difference between older and younger people); V. Kerry Smith, Mary F. Evans, Hyun Kim & Donald H. Taylor, Jr., *Do the Near-Elderly Value Mortality Risks Differently?*, 86 REV. ECON. & STATS. 423, 423 (2004) (finding that older people have higher WTP than younger people); Viscusi & Aldy, *The Value of a Statistical Life*, at 50 (finding that older people have lower WTP than younger people).

114. REVESZ & LIVERMORE, RETAKING RATIONALITY, at 80–81.

115. REVESZ & LIVERMORE, RETAKING RATIONALITY, at 80–81.

116. Sunstein, *Lives and Life-Years*, at 233.

117. William H. Desvousges et al., *Measuring Natural Resource Damages with Contingent Valuation: Tests of Validity and Reliability*, in CONTINGENT VALUATION: A CRITICAL ASSESSMENT 91, 113 (Jerry A. Hausman ed., 1993).

118. REVESZ & LIVERMORE, RETAKING RATIONALITY, at 79 (quotation marks omitted).

119. Sunstein, *Lives and Life-Years*, at 214–15 ("If people do not know how old they are, would they have the slightest difficulty concluding that it is better to eliminate a 1/50,000 risk faced by one million teenagers than a 1/50,000 risk faced by one million senior citizens?").

120. *See* Sunstein, *Lives and Life-Years*, at 246.

121. Milton C. Weinstein, George Torrance & Alistair McGuire, *QALYs: The Basics*, 12 VALUE HEALTH S5, S5 (2009).

122. Amiram Gafni, *Economic Evaluation of Health-Care Programmes: Is CEA Better than CBA?*, 34 ENVTL. & RESOURCE ECON. 407, 408 (2006).

123. Adler, *Fear Assessment*, at 1044.

124. Am. Trucking Ass'n v. E.P.A., 175 F.3d 1027, 1039 (D.C. Cir. 1999) (suggesting that QALYs may be used by agencies to develop tools for judging harm).

125. Medical Devices; Patient Examination and Surgeons' Gloves; Test Procedures and Acceptance Criteria, 68 Fed. Reg. 15,404, 15,411 (proposed Mar. 31, 2003) (codified at 21 C.F.R. pt. 800).

126. *See generally* John Broome, *Qalys*, 50 J. PUB. ECON. 149 (1993).

127. Thomas Klose, *A Utility-Theoretic Model for QALYs and Willingness to Pay*, 12 HEALTH ECON. 17, 20 (2003). A QALY is "a utility-based, cardinal, interpersonally comparable, and time-dependent measure of effectiveness based on preferences over health and time." *Id.* at 17.

128. Gafni, *Economic Evaluation*, at 412.

129. *How to Use EQ-5D*, EuroQuol Group, http://www.euroqol.org/about
-eq-5d/how-to-use-eq-5d.html (last visited Jan. 20, 2013).

130. Cam Donaldson, Stephen Birch & Amiram Gafni, *The Distributional
Problem in Economic Evaluation: Income and the Valuation of Costs and Consequences of Health Care Programmes*, 11 Health Econ. 55, 60–61 (2002).

131. Donaldson, Birch & Gafni, *Distributional Problem*, at 60.

132. *See* Richard A. Hirth et al., *Willingness to Pay for a Quality-Adjusted
Life Year: In Search of a Standard*, 20 Med. Decision Making 332, 333 (2000).

133. Gafni, *Economic Evaluation*, at 410.

134. Hirth et al., *Willingness to Pay*, at 332.

135. Hirth et al. find WTP/QALY figures ranging from $24,000 to $428,000
with an average of $265,000, but they failed to find "a strong central tendency."
Hirth et al., *Willingness to Pay*, at 338–39; *see also* Paul Dolan & Richard Edlin, *Is It Really Possible to Build a Bridge Between Cost-Benefit Analysis and
Cost-Effectiveness Analysis?*, 21 J. Health Econ. 827, 838 (2002) (concluding that reconciling CBA and CEA is impossible and recommending that the
debate focus on determining which approach is more appropriate for a given
situation).

136. Some commonly noted problems in the literature are framing effects,
prospect theory, and scarcity. *See* Daniel Kahneman, *A Different Approach to
Health State Valuation*, 12 Value in Health S16 (2009).

137. *See* Daniel M. Hausman, *Valuing Health*, 34 Phil. & Pub. Affairs 246,
256 (2006).

138. John Bronsteen, Christopher Buccafusco & Jonathan S. Masur, *Hedonic Adaptation and the Settlement of Civil Lawsuits*, 108 Colum. L. Rev. 1516,
1526–35 (2008).

139. For a review, see Paul Dolan & Daniel Kahneman, *Interpretations of
Utility and Their Implications for the Valuation of Health*, 118 Econ. J. 215,
221–22 (2008).

140. Dolan & Kahneman, *Interpretations of Utility*, at 223.

141. *See, e.g.*, David L. Sackett & George W. Torrance, *The Utility of Different Health States as Perceived by the General Public*, 31 J. Chronic Diseases
697, 702 (1978) (reporting QALYs for dialysis treatment of 0.39 and 0.56 for
healthy subjects and patients, respectively). Often, patients are willing to sacrifice no or very little life, resulting in QALY scores at or near 1.0 for a variety of
diseases. *See* Erik Nord, Norman Daniels & Mark Kamlet, *QALYs: Some Challenges*, 12 Value in Health S10, S10–11 (2009) ("A[n] [issue] is the existence of
unwillingness to trade lifetime in elicitations of experienced utility.").

142. It is worth noting that other relatively minor negative health states prove
surprisingly resistant to adaptation, such as ringing in the ears and chronic headaches. To the extent that the public does not predict the substantial hedonic

losses associated with these conditions, QALY scores will underestimate welfare losses. *See* Bronsteen, Buccafusco & Masur, *Hedonic Adapation*, at 1541.

143. Donald A. Redelmeier & Daniel Kahneman, *Patients' Memories of Painful Medical Treatments: Real-Time and Retrospective Evaluations of Two Minimally Invasive Procedures*, 116 PAIN 3, 7 (1996).

144. Dolan & Kahneman, *Interpretations of Utility*, at 225.

145. The converse is similarly true. Matthew Adler notes that CBA analyses "almost never enumerate and price the distressing mental states, such as fear, anxiety, worry, panic, or dread, that are causally connected to environmental, occupational, and consumer hazards and would (or at least might) be reduced by more stringent regulation." Adler, *Fear Assessment*, at 997.

146. *See, e.g.*, Oswald & Powdthavee, *Does Happiness Adapt?*, at 1071 (discussing the possibility of estimating monetary compensating variations for changes in well-being).

147. Adler & Posner, *Implementing Cost-Benefit Analysis*, at 1142 (showing that agency freedom to choose a different discount rate for every regulation has led to large disparities in measuring benefits).

148. Lisa Heinzerling, *Risking It All*, 57 ALA. L. REV. 103, 107–08 (2005) (explaining the concept of a discount rate).

149. Cass R. Sunstein & Arden Rowell, *On Discounting Regulatory Benefits: Risk, Money, and Intergenerational Equity*, 74 U. CHI. L. REV. 171, 180 (using arsenic as an example of regulations that would impose present costs but provide benefits in the form of reduced cancer rates decades in the future).

150. *See Chronic Obstructive Pulmonary Disease*, NAT'L CENTER FOR BIO-TECHNOLOGY INFO. (May 1, 2011), http://www.ncbi.nlm.nih.gov/pubmedhealth/PMH0001153/.

151. *See* Jonathan S. Masur & Eric A. Posner, *Climate Regulation and the Limits of Cost-Benefit Analysis*, 99 CAL. L. REV. 1557, 1561 (2011).

152. Masur & Posner, *Climate Regulation*, at 1577–79.

153. *See* Masur & Posner, *Climate Regulation*, at 1598–99 (arriving at the same conclusion); David Weisbach & Cass R. Sunstein, *Climate Change and Discounting the Future: A Guide for the Perplexed*, 27 YALE L. & POL'Y REV. 433, 440 (2009) ("[B]ecause of the potentially profound effect of discount rates, these figures are central to major disagreements over climate change policy.").

154. *See* U.S. DEP'T OF LABOR, BUREAU OF LABOR STATISTICS, *Overview of BLS Statistics on Inflation and Prices*, *available at* http://www.bls.gov/bls/inflation.htm.

155. See BUREAU OF LABOR STATISTICS, CPI DETAILED REPORT: DATA FOR DE-CEMBER 2012, at 78 tbl.24 (2013), *available at* http://www.bls.gov/cpi/cpid1212.pdf (average inflation rate between 2002 and 2012, calculated by author).

156. *See, e.g.*, Weisbach & Sunstein, *Climate Change*, at 435–36.

157. *See generally* Paul A. Samuelson, *An Exact Consumption-Loan Model*

of Interest With or Without the Social Contrivance of Money, 66 J. Pol. Econ. 467 (1958).

158. *See* Office of Mgmt. & Budget, Exec. Office of the President, Circular A-94 Revised, Guidelines and Discount Rates for Benefit-Cost Analysis of Federal Programs, at Sec. 8.b.1 (1992), *available at* http://www.whitehouse.gov/omb/circulars_a094 ("Constant-dollar benefit-cost analyses of proposed investments and regulations should report net present value and other outcomes determined using a real discount rate of 7 percent. This rate approximates the marginal pretax rate of return on an average investment in the private sector in recent years.").

159. Office of Mgmt. & Budget, Exec. Office of the President, Circular A-4 on Regulatory Analysis 33–34 (2003), *available at* http://www.whitehouse.gov/omb/circulars_a004_a-4.

160. *See, e.g.*, Masur & Posner, *Against Feasibility Analysis*, at 672 (describing OSHA's use of both 7 percent and 3 percent discount rates in a CBA of hexavalent chromium exposure standards).

161. *See, e.g.*, Masur & Posner, *Against Feasibility Analysis*, at 673 (reporting the divergent results for a CBA of an OSHA regulation conducted at 3 percent and 7 percent discount rates); Jonathan S. Masur & Eric A. Posner, *Regulation, Unemployment and Cost-Benefit Analysis*, 98 Va. L. Rev. 579, 629 (2012) (reporting the same for an EPA regulation).

162. The calculation is $15,000/(1.03)^{10} = $11,161.41.

163. Similarly, the calculation is $15,000/(1.07)^{10} = $7,625.24.

164. *See* Richard L. Revesz, *Environmental Regulation, Cost-Benefit Analysis, and the Discounting of Human Lives*, 99 Colum. L. Rev. 941, 997–1002 (1999) (describing the argument for pure time preferences); *see also* Irving Fisher, The Theory of Interest: As Determined by Impatience to Spend Income and Opportunity to Invest It 25–32 (1930) (same).

165. Revesz, *Environmental Regulation*, at 997–1002.

166. *See* Weisbach & Sunstein, *Climate Change*, at 445.

167. *See* Tyler Cowen & Derek Parfit, *Against the Social Discount Rate, in* Justice Between Age Groups and Generations 144, 155 (Peter Laslett & James S. Fishkin eds., 1992) (arguing that pure time preferences are irrational). We note as well that there is a significant literature regarding whether a zero discount rate (which is equivalent to a decision not to discount) would produce one or more paradoxes. *See, e.g.*, Cass R. Sunstein & Arden Rowell, *On Discounting Regulatory Benefits: Risk, Money, and Intergenerational Equity*, 74 U. Chi. L. Rev. 171, 175–77 (2007); W. Kip Viscusi, *Rational Discounting for Regulatory Analysis*, 74 U. Chi. L. Rev. 209, 216–17 (2007). Further research will be necessary to determine whether these paradoxes would apply with the same force—or with any force—to the welfare units of WBA.

168. Adler & Posner, New Foundations, at 52–61. We adopt the same

"weak welfarist" position that Adler and Posner favor, using WBA in addition to or in place of CBA to measure welfare.

169. ADLER & POSNER, NEW FOUNDATIONS, at 52–61.

Chapter Four

1. Other possibilities exist as well, such as the need to protect society from Alan himself by incapacitating him from harming innocent people. We discuss such possibilities later in the chapter. Incapacitation is unaffected by hedonic data, but as we explain, incapacitation alone cannot be a complete explanation of why the state punishes or of why such punishment is morally justified.

2. Whether Alan himself must actually dislike it is an interesting question that we do not tackle. Adam Kolber has addressed it in his article *The Subjective Experience of Punishment*, 109 COLUM. L. REV. 182 (2009). For our part, we point out only that punishment does not make sense or achieve its primary aims unless the *typical* person would dislike the punishment.

3. Although we focus on fines and imprisonment, our arguments are certainly relevant to debates about less traditional forms of punishment, including shaming. *See, e.g.*, Dan M. Kahan, *What Do Alternative Sanctions Mean?*, 63 U. CHI. L. REV. 591, 594 (1996). For brevity's sake, we also do not discuss certain punishments that are often viewed as less severe than fines, such as probation and community service. For a discussion, *see* NORVAL MORRIS & MICHAEL TONRY, BETWEEN PRISON AND PROBATION: INTERMEDIATE PUNISHMENTS IN A RATIONAL SENTENCING SYSTEM 6–7 (1990).

4. *See* Richard A. Easterlin, *Does Economic Growth Improve the Human Lot? Some Empirical Evidence*, *in* NATIONS AND HOUSEHOLDS IN ECONOMIC GROWTH 89, 118 (Paul A. David & Melvin W. Reder eds., 1974) (studying nineteen countries and concluding that while there is a correlation between citizens' income and happiness within a single country, no such correlation exists when the national happiness levels of rich and poor countries are compared). The Easterlin paradox has since been called into serious question, but evidence that income has only a very small effect on happiness now appears more robust than ever.

5. For a review of the extensive literature, *see generally* Ed Diener & Robert Biswas-Diener, *Will Money Increase Subjective Well-Being? A Literature Review and Guide to Needed Research*, 57 SOC. INDICATORS RES. 119 (2002).

6. *See* Richard A. Easterlin, *Explaining Happiness*, 100 PROCEEDINGS NATL. ACADEMY SCI. 11176, 11180 (2003) (explaining that "material aspirations increase commensurately with income"). *But see* Daniel Kahneman et al., *A Survey Method for Characterizing Daily Life Experience: The Day Reconstruction Method*, 306 SCI. 1776 (2004) (finding no support for the "aspiration treadmill" hypothesis).

7. *See* Diener & Biswas-Diener, *Subjective Well-Being*, at 147 (noting that "social comparison . . . had a direct effect on satisfaction").

8. *E.g.*, Betsey Stevenson & Justin Wolfers, *Subjective Well-Being and Income: Is There Any Evidence of Satiation?*, 103 AM. ECON. REV. PAPERS & PROCEEDINGS 598 (2013).

9. It is worth pointing out that hedonic adaptation to losses may not be identical to adaptation to gains. Research from the field of behavioral decision theory has repeatedly shown that losses loom larger psychologically than do gains. *See* Daniel Kahneman & Amos Tversky, *Prospect Theory: An Analysis of Decision Under Risk*, 47 ECONOMETRICA 263, 279 (1979) (indicating that the value function is "steeper for losses than for gains"). Indeed, losses trigger stronger neural activity than do gains. *See generally* Roy F. Baumeister et al., *Bad Is Stronger than Good*, 5 REV. GEN. PSYCH. 323 (2001) ("Bad emotions, bad parents, and bad feedback have more impact than good ones, and bad information is processed more thoroughly than good."); John T. Cacioppo & Gary G. Berntson, *Relationship Between Attitudes and Evaluative Space: A Critical Review, with Emphasis on the Separability of Positive and Negative Substrates*, 115 PSYCH. BULL. 401 (1994) (proposing that the evaluative processes by which humans discriminate positive from negative environments are not activated reciprocally).

10. Ed Diener et al., *The Relationship Between Income and Subjective Well-Being: Relative or Absolute?*, 28 SOC. INDICATORS RES. 195, 221 (1993).

11. *See* Deborah A. Kermer et al., *Loss Aversion Is an Affective Forecasting Error*, 17 PSYCH. SCI. 649, 651 (2006).

12. Francis T. Cullen, Bonnie S. Fisher & Brandon K. Applegate, *Public Opinion About Punishment and Corrections*, 27 CRIME & JUST. 1, 2, 8–9 (2000).

13. *See* DONALD CLEMMER, THE PRISON COMMUNITY 299–300 (1940).

14. *See* Shane Frederick & George Loewenstein, *Hedonic Adaptation, in* WELL-BEING: THE FOUNDATIONS OF HEDONIC PSYCHOLOGY 311 (Daniel Kahneman, Ed Diener & Norbert Schwarz eds., 1999) ("Although incarceration is designed to be unpleasant, most of the research on adjustment to prison life points to considerable adaptation following a difficult initial adjustment period."). For an early review of the literature, *see* Lee H. Bukstel & Peter R. Kilmann, *Psychological Effects of Imprisonment on Confined Individuals*, 88 PSYCH. BULL. 469, 487 (1980) (finding no support for "the popular notion that correctional confinement is harmful to most individuals").

15. *See* Edward Zamble, *Behavior and Adaptation in Long-Term Prison Inmates: Descriptive Longitudinal Results*, 19 CRIM. JUST. & BEHAV. 409, 420–21 (1992); Edward Zamble & Frank Porporino, *Coping, Imprisonment, and Rehabilitation: Some Data and Their Implications*, 17 CRIM. JUST. & BEHAV. 53, 67 (1990); EDWARD ZAMBLE & FRANK J. PORPORINO, COPING, BEHAVIOR, AND ADAPTATION IN PRISON INMATES 116–20 (1988); Doris Layton MacKenzie & Lynne Goodstein, *Long-Term Incarceration Impacts and Characteristics of Long-Term*

Offenders: An Empirical Analysis, 12 Crim. Just. & Behav. 395, 409 (1985); Timothy J. Flanagan, *The Pains of Long-Term Imprisonment: A Comparison of British and American Perspectives*, 20 Brit. J. Criminol. 148, 155 (1980). *Consider also* Mandeep K. Dhami, Peter Ayton & George Loewenstein, *Adaptation to Imprisonment: Indigenous or Imported?*, 34 Crim. Just. & Behav. 1085, 1096 (2007).

16. *See* MacKenzie & Goodstein, *Long-Term Incarceration*, at 405 ("On average, [the early long-term offenders] had served 1.3 years in prison and were serving sentences requiring 12.1 years in prison. The [late long-term offenders] had served an average of 10.3 years in prison and were serving sentences with an average length of 15.7 years.").

17. MacKenzie & Goodstein, *Long-Term Incarceration*, at 406–07.

18. MacKenzie & Goodstein, *Long-Term Incarceration*, at 409.

19. *See, e.g.*, Zamble, *Behavior and Adaptation*, at 420–21; Zamble & Porporino, Coping, Behavior, and Adaptation, at 19, 116–20. *See also* Dhami, Ayton & Loewenstein, *Adaptation to Imprisonment*, at 1097 ("Ideally, adaptations should be studied longitudinally, but this can be difficult in practice.").

20. *See* Zamble & Porporino, *Coping, Imprisonment, and Rehabilitation*, at 64.

21. *See* Zamble & Porporino, *Coping, Imprisonment, and Rehabilitation*, at 64 (finding that although a majority of subjects exhibited emotional distress at the beginning of the prison term, the number of prisoners who were depressed or highly anxious fell by nearly one-third just three months later); Zamble & Porporino, Coping, Behavior, and Adaptation, at 109.

22. *See* Zamble & Porporino, *Coping, Imprisonment, and Rehabilitation*, at 64.

23. We believe that subjective reports of positive and negative affect provide the best available proxy for measuring well-being. See chapters 2 and 8. Nonetheless, broader measures of an inmate's quality of life can be useful, and here are in accord with the psychological findings on affect. During the same six-year period, inmates' reports of their quality of life rose from 32.2 to 42.0 on a 100-point scale. Although these findings are not statistically significant at the 10 percent level, they offer some additional evidence of adaptation to imprisonment. Zamble & Porporino, Coping, Imprisonment, and Rehabilitation, at 64. In addition, it is worth mentioning that some of these cognitive improvements may have been related to equivalent improvements in the inmates' objective conditions. *Id.*

24. As early as the sixteenth century, Thomas More recognized prison's limited impact on his own well-being, writing, from his cell to his wife, "[I]s not this house as nigh heaven as mine own?" Anthony Kenny & Charles Kenny, Life, Liberty, and the Pursuit of Utility: Happiness in Philosophical and Economic Thought 59–60 (2006) (quoting a letter from Thomas More to his wife).

25. There is, however, some evidence that the final few weeks of the sentence

prove stressful and thus decrease well-being. *See* Bukstel & Kilmann, *Psycho-logical Effects*, at 488 ("The typical pattern among these individuals might in-volve an initial adjustment reaction to incarceration, followed by a period of suc-cessful adjustment with another mild psychological reaction (e.g., 'short-timer's syndrome') occurring just prior to release.").

26. *See* GRESHAM M. SYKES, THE SOCIETY OF CAPTIVES: A STUDY OF A MAXI-MUM SECURITY PRISON 63–83 (1958) (examining the prison system from the pris-oner's perspective with respect to loss of liberty, goods and services, heterosex-ual relationships, autonomy, and security).

27. *See* Jason Schnittker & Andrea John, *Enduring Stigma: The Long-Term Effects of Incarceration on Health*, 48 J. HEALTH & SOC. BEHAV. 115, 117 (2007).

28. Schnittker & John, *Enduring Stigma*, at 115, 117.

29. *See generally* Michael Massoglia, *Incarceration, Health, and Racial Dis-parities in Health*, 42 L. & SOCY. REV. 275 (2008); Michael Massoglia, *Incarcer-ation as Exposure: The Prison, Infectious Disease, and Other Stress-Related Illnesses*, 49 J. HEALTH & SOC. BEHAV. 56 (2008); Schnittker & John, *Enduring Stigma*, at 117; BRUCE WESTERN, PUNISHMENT AND INEQUALITY IN AMERICA (2006) (tracking employment prospects and wage growth of ex-inmates); Leon-ard M. Lopoo & Bruce Western, *Incarceration and the Formation and Stabil-ity of Marital Unions*, 67 J. MARRIAGE & FAM. 721 (2005) (finding that "the prev-alence of marriage would change little if incarceration dates were reduced"). In the descriptions of these studies, it should be assumed unless otherwise stated that the results control for a variety of variables including age, gender, education level, health, and so forth. For specific control variables, please consult the indi-vidual studies.

30. Massoglia, *Incarceration as Exposure*, at 57.

31. Massoglia, *Incarceration, Health, and Racial Disparities*, at 296 (positing increased exposure to infectious disease while in prison and lower social status after release as explanations for the health-incarceration relationship).

32. Massoglia, *Incarceration as Exposure*, at 57. It is worth noting, however, that imprisonment does not result in higher incidences of all health problems. *See id.*

33. See Tonisha R. Jones & Travis C. Pratt, *The Prevalence of Sexual Vio-lence in Prison: The State of the Knowledge Base and Implications for Evidence-Based Correctional Policy Making*, 52 INTL. J. OFFENDER THERAPY & COMP. CRIMINOL. 280, 289 (2008) ("[T]he research indicates that such studies typically report prison sexual victimization rates of around 20%, suggesting that prison sexual victimization is a significant problem to be addressed.").

34. Massoglia, *Incarceration as Exposure*, at 57 ("[T]he experience of incar-ceration likely acts as a primary stressor, while characteristics of life after re-lease—stigma, decreased earnings and employment prospects, and family prob-lems—are a series of secondary stressors.").

35. Massoglia, *Incarceration as Exposure*, at 61 ("[E]xposure to incarceration, rather than length of incarceration, appears to be more important to the relationship between incarceration and health problems."). *See also* Schnittker & John, Enduring Stigma, at 125.

36. *See* Massoglia, *Incarceration as Exposure*, at 60–61. The studies we rely on for this proposition all concerned medium- and maximum-security prisons where no prisoner was incarcerated for less than twelve months. It thus may be that a shorter term in jail or a minimum-security work camp will not result in the same level of post-prison harm, and we make no claims regarding the effects of those types and durations of incarceration.

37. *See* WESTERN, PUNISHMENT AND INEQUALITY IN AMERICA, at 116 (showing that men who had been incarcerated received lower wages, were employed for fewer weeks, and earned less than before they were incarcerated and less than men who were never incarcerated); Bruce Western, Jeffrey R. Kling & David F. Weiman, *The Labor Market Consequences of Incarceration*, 47 CRIME & DELIN-QUENCY 410, 412 (2001) (reviewing research suggesting negative effects of prison time on earnings and discussing causal mechanisms, such as stigmatization and erosion of human and social capital). *See also* DEVAH PAGER, MARKED: RACE, CRIME, AND FINDING WORK IN AN ERA OF MASS INCARCERATION 32–35 (2007). *But see* Jeffrey R. Kling, *Incarceration Length, Employment, and Earnings*, 96 AM. ECON. REV. 863, 864 (2006) (finding "no substantial evidence of a negative effect of incarceration length on employment or earnings").

38. *See* Western, Kling & Weiman, *Labor Market Consequences*, at 412–14:

> [I]ncarceration can interrupt young men's transition to stable career employment. The inaccessibility of career jobs to ex-inmates can be explained in several ways. The stigma of incarceration makes ex-inmates unattractive for entry-level or union jobs that may require high levels of trust. In addition, civil disabilities limit ex-felons' access to career employment in skilled trades or the public sector. Ex-offenders are then relegated to spot markets with little prospect for earnings growth.

(citations omitted).

39. WESTERN, PUNISHMENT AND INEQUALITY IN AMERICA, at 116.

40. WESTERN, PUNISHMENT AND INEQUALITY IN AMERICA, at 123 (finding that the effect of incarceration on job tenure was not statistically significant for white men but was statistically significant for black and Hispanic men).

41. WESTERN, PUNISHMENT AND INEQUALITY IN AMERICA, 121. Western compared hypothetical workers differing only regarding past imprisonment and found that a "thirty-year-old black high school dropout, for example, earns on average nearly $9,000 annually, with incarceration resulting in a reduction of about $3,300. The parallel white earnings average $14,400, and the reduction

about $5,200." *Id.* at 120. He continues, "Without incarceration, 4 percent of young blacks—one-fifth of all poor blacks—would be lifted out of poverty, and the poverty rate would fall to 14.5 percent." *Id.* at 127.

42. WESTERN, PUNISHMENT AND INEQUALITY IN AMERICA, at 146–47 (finding that among white men, separation was more than twice as likely after incarceration); Lopoo & Western, *Formation and Stability*, at 721; Beth M. Huebner, *The Effect of Incarceration on Marriage and Work over the Life Course*, 22 JUST. Q. 281, 296 (2005).

43. *See* Schnittker & John, *Enduring Stigma*, at 117 (noting that the "prison environment may foster psychological orientations that prevent integration and intimacy, including suspicion and aggression").

44. Schnittker & John, *Enduring Stigma*, at 117.

45. *See* WESTERN, PUNISHMENT AND INEQUALITY IN AMERICA, at 146–48 (finding an increased likelihood of divorce for white men, though only a negligible difference for black men).

46. *See* Andrew E. Clark et al., *Lags and Leads in Life Satisfaction: A Test of the Baseline Hypothesis*, 118 ECON. J. F222, F231 (2008) (noting that it is "well-known" that unemployment has a "large and significant" correlation with subjective well-being); Richard E. Lucas, *Adaptation and the Set-Point Model of Subjective Well-Being: Does Happiness Change After Major Life Events?*, 16 CURRENT DIRECTIONS PSYCH. SCI. 75, 77 (2007) (reporting that individuals who "experience unemployment . . . [experience] permanent changes in life satisfaction"); Michael Argyle, *Causes and Correlates of Happiness, in* WELL-BEING 353, 362–63 (describing how unemployment decreases well-being even after controlling for the effects of reduced income). Lucas et al. write,

> The experience of unemployment did, on average, alter people's set-point levels of life satisfaction. People were less satisfied in the years following unemployment than they were before unemployment, and this decline occurred even though individuals eventually regained employment. Furthermore, the changes from baseline were very stable from the reaction period to the adaptation period—individuals who experienced a large drop in satisfaction during unemployment were very likely to be far from baseline many years after becoming reemployed.

Richard E. Lucas et al., *Unemployment Alters the Set Point for Life Satisfaction*, 15 PSYCHOL. SCI. 8, 11 (2004). Or as Clark et al. put it, "[U]nemployment starts off bad and pretty much stays bad." Clark et al., *Lags and Leads*, at F231.

47. *See* Lucas et al., *Unemployment Alters*, at 10. Psychologists have found that unemployment has a significant negative effect on well-being even after controlling for income. *Id.*

48. *See* Richard E. Lucas, *Time Does Not Heal All Wounds: A Longitudinal*

Study of Reaction and Adaptation to Divorce, 16 PSYCHOL. SCI. 945, 948 (2005);
David R. Johnson & Jian Wu, *An Empirical Test of Crisis, Social Selection, and
Role Explanations of the Relationship Between Marital Disruption and Psycho-
logical Distress: A Pooled Time-Series Analysis of Four-Wave Panel Data*, 64 J.
MARRIAGE & FAM. 211, 218, 223 (2002).

49. *See, e.g.*, Argyle, *Causes and Correlates of Happiness*, at 363 (noting
that the negative "effects of unemployment are greater if there is little social
support").

50. *Consider* Frederick & Loewenstein, Hedonic Adaptation, at 314–15 (describing the difficulty of adapting to negative outcomes when social contacts give
inadequate or inappropriate support).

51. *See* Schnittker & John, Enduring Stigma, at 126–27:

> For example, relinquishing initiative and relying on external
> constraints may be rewarded in a prison setting, but these char-
> acteristics can be problematic in a home or workplace. By the
> same token, vigilance, mistrust, and blunted emotions might
> help prisoners to cope with an especially violent environment.
> These dispositions might also, however, elevate risk for cardio-
> vascular disease and other stress-related illnesses.

Stress is strongly correlated with diminished well-being and with increased risk
of heart disease. *See* ED DIENER & ROBERT BISWAS-DIENER, HAPPINESS: UN-
LOCKING THE MYSTERIES OF PSYCHOLOGICAL WEALTH 39–41 (2008) ("People who
experience stressful situations, especially intense ones, often have a difficult time
adapting back to normal: that is, they continue to experience physiological distress even after the stressful or traumatic event has happened."). Consider also
Zamble & Porporino, *Coping, Imprisonment, and Rehabilitation*, at 68 (suggesting the use of treatment programs to change behaviors adopted in prison and to
teach coping skills).

52. Jeremy Bentham, *An Introduction to the Principles of Morals and Legislation, in* THE UTILITARIANS 5, 162 (1961). *See also id.* at 166 (discussing the costs
of punishment).

53. *See* Jeremy Bentham, *Principles of Penal Law, in* 1 THE WORKS OF JEREMY
BENTHAM 365, 396 (John Bowring ed., 1843). *See also* Letter from O.W. Holmes
to Harold J. Laski (Dec. 17, 1925), *in* 1 HOLMES-LASKI LETTERS: THE CORRESPON-
DENCE OF MR. JUSTICE HOLMES AND HAROLD J. LASKI, 1916–1935, at 806 (Mark
DeWolfe Howe ed., 1953).

54. Rehabilitation and incapacitation have crept out of favor as prisons have
proven to be poor vehicles for reforming offenders; *see* Robert Martinson, *What
Works?— Questions and Answers About Prison Reform*, 36 PUB. INTEREST 22, 25
(1974); and incapacitation has had little noticeable effect on the rates of serious
crimes; *see* John J. DiIulio, Jr., *Two Million Prisoners Are Enough*, WALL ST. J.,

Mar. 12, 1999, at A14; FRANKLIN E. ZIMRING & GORDON HAWKINS, INCAPACITATION: PENAL CONFINEMENT AND THE RESTRAINT OF CRIME 100–27 (1995). Rehabilitation and incapacitation also have lost support as working theories of punishment because they could offer no response to the critique that they seemed to compel excessive and indefinite punishment of even minor crimes. *See* Herbert Morris, *Persons and Punishment*, 52 THE MONIST 475, 485–86 (1968). We focus here on deterrence, which remains the principal utilitarian goal of punishment. *See, e.g.*, MODEL PENAL CODE (MPC) § 1.02(2) (ALI 1980). We acknowledge that the hedonic data may have less to say about rehabilitation and incapacitation, other than the crucial value of recording their hedonic costs. For example, both rehabilitation and incapacitation may be possible at lower hedonic cost if criminals adapt to confinement.

55. *See* Richard S. Frase, *Punishment Purposes*, 58 STAN. L. REV. 67, 68 (2005).

56. *See generally* Steven D. Levitt, *The Effect of Prison Population Size on Crime Rates: Evidence from Prison Overcrowding Litigation*, 111 Q.J. ECON. 319 (1996).

57. *See* Gary S. Becker, *Crime and Punishment: An Economic Approach*, 76 J. POLIT. ECON. 169, 193 (1968) ("[I]n the United States in 1965, about $1 billion was spent on 'correction,' and this estimate excludes, of course, the value of the loss in offenders' time.").

58. Louis Michael Seidman, *Soldiers, Martyrs, and Criminals: Utilitarian Theory and the Problem of Crime Control*, 94 YALE L.J. 315, 320 (1984); Margery Fry, *Bentham and English Penal Reform*, in JEREMY BENTHAM AND THE LAW 20, 28 (George W. Keeton & Georg Schwarzenberger eds., 1948) ("[T]he suffering of a punished criminal goes duly down on the debit side, and must be balanced by some greater good in the credit column."). *See also* Carl Emigholz, Note, *Utilitarianism, Retributivism and the White Collar–Drug Crime Sentencing Disparity: Toward a Unified Theory of Enforcement*, 58 RUTGERS L. REV. 583, 599 (2006) ("In the utilitarian calculus, the criminal justice system implicates a negative social cost: the crime . . . and pain inflicted upon the criminal as a result of the meted punishment."); Levitt, *Effect of Prison Population*, at 347 (acknowledging that typical studies may underestimate the costs of incarceration because of the unacknowledged "pain and suffering of prisoners and their families"); R.B. Brandt, *Conscience (Rule) Utilitarianism and the Criminal Law*, 14 L. & PHIL. 65, 73 (1995).

59. *Compare* MPC § 1.02(2)(a) (listing "to prevent the commission of offenses" as the first purpose of the Code section governing punishment), *with* MPC § 1.02(2)(c) (stating that the third purpose of the same section is "to safeguard offenders against *excessive*, disproportionate or arbitrary punishment") (emphasis added). *See, for example*, 18 USC § 3553(a) ("The court shall impose a sentence sufficient, but not greater than necessary. . . .").

60. *See, for example,* Bentham, *Principles of Morals and Legislation,* at 178–79.

61. *See* Timothy D. Wilson & Daniel T. Gilbert, *Affective Forecasting: Knowing What to Want,* 14 CURRENT DIRECTIONS PSYCH. SCI. 131, 132 (2005) (explaining that people "do not recognize beforehand" the extent to which adaptation will occur); Peter A. Ubel, George Loewenstein & Christopher Jepson, *Disability and Sunshine: Can Hedonic Predictions Be Improved by Drawing Attention to Focusing Illusions or Emotional Adaptation?,* 11 J. EXP. PSYCH.: APPLIED 111, 121–22 (2005) (reporting experimental results supporting the theory that "people often underappreciate their own powers of adaptation"). *See also* Daniel T. Gilbert & Timothy D. Wilson, *Prospection: Experiencing the Future,* 317 SCIENCE 1351, 1354 (2007); Peter Ayton, Alice Pott & Najat Elwakili, *Affective Forecasting: Why Can't People Predict Their Emotions?,* 13 THINKING & REASONING 62, 78 (2007) (studying people who repeatedly failed a driving test and "showed no improvement in their ability to forecast their moderate levels of happiness" following failure).

62. Our account in this respect differs from that of Paul H. Robinson & John M. Darley, *Does Criminal Law Deter? A Behavioral Science Investigation,* 24 OXFORD J. LEGAL STUD. 173, 188–89 (2004). Robinson and Darley suggest in passing that adaptation to prison will inhibit deterrence, but they do not account for the fact that putative criminals will evaluate whether to commit a crime before they have been incarcerated, and thus before they learn that they will adapt. In addition, even potential recidivists will forget about their own adaptation once they have been released; without this learning, they will be subject to the full deterrence force of threatened punishment each subsequent time they contemplate a crime. *See also* notes 459–460 and accompanying text.

63. From a utilitarian perspective, the harm inflicted on the criminal is a cost to be minimized wherever possible. *See, for example,* 18 USC § 3553(a) ("The court shall impose a sentence sufficient, but not greater than necessary."); MPC § 1.02(2) (stating that one of the general purposes of the provisions governing the sentencing and treatment of offenders is "to safeguard offenders against excessive, disproportionate or arbitrary punishment"). *See also* note 453 and accompanying text.

64. *See* Ayton, Pott & Elwakili, *Affective Forecasting,* at 78. *See also* note 456 and accompanying text.

65. Daniel T. Gilbert, Jay Meyers & Timothy D. Wilson, *Lessons from the Past: Do People Learn from Experience That Emotional Reactions Are Short-Lived?,* 27 PERSONALITY & SOC. PSYCH. BULL. 1648, 1649 (2001).

66. Massoglia, *Incarceration, Health, and Racial Disparities in Health,* at 297; Massoglia, *Incarceration as Exposure,* at 57.

67. *See* Levitt, *Effect of Prison Population,* at 346–47 (cataloging a variety of prior studies that fail to incorporate the post hoc costs of imprisonment to the

prisoner); Becker, *Crime and Punishment*, at 179–80 (limiting discussion of the costs of punishment to those incurred while the punishment is ongoing).

68. *See* Anthony C. Thompson, *Navigating the Hidden Obstacles to Ex-offender Reentry*, 45 B.C. L. REV. 255, 260 (2004); WESTERN, PUNISHMENT AND INEQUALITY, 119, 149–52 (finding strong effects of prison on unemployment and future life prospects, including a 30 percent diminution in wages and an 11 percent decline in the probability of getting married for African-American men); JOHN IRWIN, THE FELON viii (1987) ("Most ex-convicts live menial or derelict lives and many die early of alcoholism or drug use, or by suicide."); Dermot Sullivan, *Employee Violence, Negligent Hiring, and Criminal Records Checks: New York's Need to Reevaluate Its Priorities to Promote Public Safety*, 72 ST. JOHN'S L. REV. 581, 596 (1998) (noting the connection between unemployment and recidivism).

69. *See, for example*, Thompson, *Navigating the Hidden Obstacles*, at 260; Second Chance Act of 2007, codified at 42 USC § 17501 et seq. (encouraging "the development and support of . . . comprehensive reentry services" for former prisoners").

70. For instance, the Second Chance Act provides only for limited grants to programs that provide technical training and drug treatment for felons while they are still imprisoned. Rates of post-prison unemployment and drug use belie the notion that these grants are having a substantial effect.

71. The lone counterexample may be the treatment of juvenile offenders, who have the opportunity to expunge convictions from their records in many states. *See* T. Markus Funk, *A Mere Youthful Indiscretion? Reexamining the Policy of Expunging Juvenile Delinquency Records*, 29 MICH. J.L. REFORM 885, 887 n.9 (1996) (collecting state statutes allowing for expungement of juvenile records). Of course, the simple fact that a criminal record has been expunged will by no means ameliorate all the negative after-effects of prison, which are due as much to the social separation imposed by prison as to the legal status of being a convicted felon. *See* notes 437–440 and accompanying text.

72. *See, for example*, 18 USC § 3553(a) (directing federal judges to consider a host of factors when imposing a sentence, none of which relates to the prisoner's postcorrectional experience).

73. *See generally, for example*, JAMES Q. WILSON & RICHARD J. HERRNSTEIN, CRIME AND HUMAN NATURE (1985).

74. These laws were inspired by a New Jersey statute known as "Megan's Law" (after the child victim who inspired its passage). N.J. REV. STAT. § 2C:7–1 et seq. (West). There is now a federal mandate requiring every state to pass similar legislation. *See* 42 USC § 14071(e)(2):

> The State . . . shall release relevant information that is necessary to protect the public concerning a specific person required to register under this section. . . . The release of information un-

der this paragraph shall include the maintenance of an Internet
site containing such information that is available to the public.

75. J.J. Prescott & Jonah E. Rockoff, *Do Sex Offender Registration and Notification Laws Affect Criminal Behavior?* 54 J.L. & ECON. 161 (2011) (finding that
offender notification laws reduced first-time commissions of crimes).

76. *See, e.g.,* 720 ILCS 5/19–1 (classifying burglary as a Class 2 felony); 730
ILCS 5/5–4.5–35 (setting the penalty for commission of a Class 2 felony at
three to seven years in prison); 720 ILCS 5/18–2 (classifying armed robbery as
a Class X felony); 730 ILCS 5/5–4.5–25 (setting the penalty for commission of a
Class X felony at six to thirty years in prison); 720 ILCS 5/9–1 (declaring first-
degree murder a separate class of felony); 730 ILCS 5/5–4.5–20 (setting the penalty for first-degree murder, without enhancement, at 20 to 60 years in prison).

77. *See, for example,* Bentham, *Principles of Morals and Legislation,* at 169
(outlining reasons to maintain proportionality between punishment and offenses); Eyal Zadir & Barak Medina, *Law, Morality, and Economics: Integrating Moral Constraints with Economic Analysis,* 96 CAL. L. REV. 323, 379 n.211
(2008).

78. For a small sampling of this extensive literature (here applied to sex offenders), *see* Prescott & Rockoff, *Sex Offender Registration,* at 161 (finding that
reduced opportunities after conviction lead to greater rates of recidivism); Wil-
liam Edwards & Christopher Hensley, *Contextualizing Sex Offender Manage-
ment Legislation and Policy: Evaluating the Problem of Latent Consequences in
Community Notification Laws,* 45 INTL. J. OFFENDER THERAPY & COMP. CRIM-
INOL. 83 (2001) (same); Lois Presser & Elaine Gunnison, *Strange Bedfellows:
Is Sex Offender Notification a Form of Community Justice?,* 45 CRIME & DE-
LINQUENCY 299 (1999) (same); Robert A. Prentky, *Community Notification and
Constructive Risk Reduction,* 11 J. INTERPERSONAL VIOLENCE 295 (1996) (same).

79. *See* Frase, *Punishment Purposes,* at 73 (discussing the theory of pure retribution and its purposes).

80. Frase, *Punishment Purposes,* at 83.

81. MICHAEL MOORE, PLACING BLAME: A GENERAL THEORY OF THE CRIMINAL
LAW 88 (1997).

82. *See* Jean Hampton, *Correcting Harms Versus Righting Wrongs: The Goal
of Retribution,* 39 UCLA L. REV. 1659, 1663 (1992) ("[R]etributive justice is concerned with wrongful actions from which such harms result. Although a punishment may sometimes involve the wrongdoer compensating her victim in some
way, the purpose of punishment is not to compensate the person for the harm
suffered, but 'to right the wrong.'").

83. John Bronsteen, Christopher Buccafusco & Jonathan S. Masur, *Retribution and the Experience of Punishment,* 98 CALIF. L. REV. 1463 (2010).

84. As explained below, the consequences of adaptation for the parsimony

principle are the other side of the same coin: adaptation allows the state to achieve its desired level of deterrence without inflicting as much harm.

85. Frase, *Punishment Purposes*, at 68.

86. *See* Norval Morris, Madness and the Criminal Law 179 (1982):

> [A] deserved punishment . . . does not mean the infliction on the criminal offender of a pain precisely equivalent to that which he has inflicted on his victim; it means rather a not undeserved punishment which bears a proportional relationship in a hierarchy of punishments to the harm for which the criminal has been convicted.

87. *See* Frase, *Punishment Purposes*, at 68 (describing the principles used to fine-tune sentences, including deterrence, incapacitation, rehabilitation, and parsimony); Lawrence Crocker, *The Upper Limit of Just Punishment*, 41 Emory L.J. 1059, 1062 & n.8 (1992); Norval Morris, The Future of Imprisonment 58–84 (1974) (describing parsimony, dangerousness, and desert as guiding principles of imprisonment). *See also* John Bronsteen, *Retribution's Role*, 84 Ind. L. J. 1129 (2009).

88. Frase, *Punishment Purposes*, at 68.

89. Later in this section, we address whether post-prison harms should count toward the retributive calculus of punishment.

90. For an expressive view, see, for example, Dan M. Kahan, *The Secret Ambition of Deterrence*, 113 Harv. L. Rev. 413, 419–35 (1999). For a communicative view, see, for example, Dan Markel, *Are Shaming Punishments Beautifully Retributive? Retributivism and the Implications for the Alternative Sanctions Debate*, 54 Vand. L. Rev. 2157 (2001). We will refer to the two types of theories collectively as "expressive" theories. Our response to both is the same.

91. Dan M. Kahan, *What Do Alternative Sanctions Mean?*, 63 U. Chi. L. Rev. 591, 593 (1996).

92. As Jean Hampton explains, "The way to communicate to [criminals] that there is a barrier of a very special sort against these kinds of actions would seem to be to link performance of the actions with what such people care about most—the pursuit of their own pleasure." Jean Hampton, *The Moral Education Theory of Punishment*, *in* Punishment: A Philosophy and Public Affairs Reader 130 (A. John Simmons et al. eds., 1995). According to Andrew von Hirsch, "The censure and the hard treatment are intertwined in the way punishment is structured. A penal measure provides that a specified type of conduct is punishable by certain onerous consequences. Those consequences both constitute the hard treatment and express the reprobation. Altering those consequences—by raising or lowering the penalty on the scale—will alter the degree of censure conveyed." Andrew von Hirsch, *Censure and Proportionality*, *in* A Reader on Punishment 128 (R.A. Duff & David Garland eds., 1994). Similarly, Fein-

berg writes, "Given our conventions, of course, condemnation is expressed by hard treatment, and the degree of harshness of the latter expresses the degree of reprobation of the former." JOEL FEINBERG, *The Expressive Function of Punishment, in* DOING AND DESERVING: ESSAYS IN THE THEORY OF RESPONSIBILITY 95, 118 (1970). Other retributivists are largely in accord. *See, e.g.,* NORVAL MORRIS & MICHAEL TONRY, BETWEEN PRISON AND PROBATION: INTERMEDIATE PUNISHMENTS IN A RATIONAL SENTENCING SYSTEM 93 (1991) ("[F]rom a moral perspective, the measure of punishment is not its objective appearance but its subjective impact."); H.L.A. HART, PUNISHMENT AND RESPONSIBILITY 4 (1968) (stating that punishment "must involve pain or other consequences normally considered unpleasant"); GEORGE FLETCHER, THE GRAMMAR OF THE CRIMINAL LAW 228 (2007) ("The question is always whether the sanction is typically or characteristically onerous."). *But see* Kenneth W. Simons, *Retributivists Need Not and Should Not Endorse the Subjectivist Account of Punishment,* 109 COLUM. L. REV. SIDEBAR 1, 2 (2009), *available at* http://www.columbialawreview.org/wp -content/uploads/2009/03/1_Simons.pdf. Douglas Husak equivocates somewhat between these two views. Douglas N. Husak, *Retribution in Criminal Theory,* 37 SAN DIEGO L. REV. 959, 973 (2000) ("My point is that the fit we intuit does not really obtain between crime and punishment, but rather between crime (as culpable wrongdoing) and suffering (or deprivation or hardship).").

93. Bronsteen, Buccafusco & Masur, *Experience of Punishment,* at 1463.

94. For example, the state could punish via imprisonment, fines, beatings, shaming, probation, community service, or talion, to name a few. On the practice of talion, *see* WILLIAM IAN MILLER, EYE FOR AN EYE 20–24 (2005).

95. Markel, *Punishments Beautifully Retributive?,* at 2157, 2163 n.28.

96. Bronsteen, Buccafusco & Masur, *Experience of Punishment,* at 1488–95.

97. *See* WESTERN, PUNISHMENT AND INEQUALITY IN AMERICA; Western, Kling & Weiman, *Labor Market Consequences,* at 412; PAGER, MARKED, at 32–35.

98. *See* Schnittker & John, *Enduring Stigma,* at 117 (noting that the "prison environment may foster psychological orientations that prevent integration and intimacy, including suspicion and aggression").

99. In a reply to Adam Kolber's argument that retributivists must accommodate subjective experiences into proportionality calculus, Kenneth Simons contends that the state need not adjust its punishments to individuals' sensitivities because it is not responsible for those sensitivities. Simons, *Retributivists Need Not and Should Not Endorse,* at 6. But unlike an inmate's claustrophobia, her post-prison psychological dysfunction is caused by the prison environment.

100. Two scholars have asked whether the state should also be responsible for the *positive* effects of prison on prisoners. For example, they ask whether our argument would recognize the benefits a prisoner received if, while in prison, he fell in love with his prison guard and married her upon his release. Dan Markel

& Chad Flanders, *Bentham on Stilts: The Bare Relevance of Subjectivity to Retributive Justice*, 98 CALIF. L. REV. 907, 970–71 (2010). Our response is that of course this would matter to punishment proportionality *if* the typical experience of inmates was to find romantic love during the period of their incarceration. It should be quite obvious that prison is generally understood as a negative experience in part because most prisoners *do not* have such an experience.

101. Craig Haney, *Mental Health Issues in Long-Term Solitary and "Supermax" Confinement*, 49 CRIME & DELINQUENCY 124 (2003).

Chapter Five

1. Daniel Kahneman writes: "The fundamental surprise of well-being research is the robust finding that life circumstances make only a small contribution to the variance of happiness. . . ." Daniel Kahneman, *Experienced Utility and Objective Happiness: A Moment-Based Approach, in* CHOICES, VALUES AND FRAMES 187, 199 (Daniel Kahneman & Amos Tversky eds., 2000).

2. *See* Daniel T. Gilbert et al., *Immune Neglect: A Source of Durability Bias in Affective Forecasting*, 75 J. PERSONALITY & SOC. PSYCHOL. 617, 634–35 (1998) (discussing reasons why people may not be attuned to their ability to emotionally adapt to undesired outcomes).

3. Marc Galanter, *The Vanishing Trial: An Examination of Trials and Related Matters in Federal and State Courts*, 1 J. EMPIRICAL LEGAL STUD. 459, 462–63 tbl.1 (2004) (depicting trial rates declining since 1962 to less than 2 percent in 2002).

4. CHARLES DICKENS, BLEAK HOUSE (Norman Page ed., Penguin Books 1971) (1853).

5. *E.g.*, Warren E. Burger, *Isn't There a Better Way?*, 68 A.B.A. J. 274, 274 (1982) (criticizing the "delay" and "time lapse" associated with litigation).

6. James C. Duff, Admin. Office of the U.S. Courts, 2006 Judicial Business of the United States Courts 192 tbl.C-5 (2006), *available at* http://www.uscourts.gov/uscourts/Statistics/JudicialBusiness/2006/appendices/c5.pdf (depicting "median time intervals from filing to disposition of civil cases" for U.S. district courts).

7. William M. Landes, *An Economic Analysis of the Courts*, 14 J.L. & ECON. 61 (1971); Richard A. Posner, *An Economic Approach to Legal Procedure and Judicial Administration*, 2 J. LEGAL STUD. 399 (1973); *see also* John P. Gould, *The Economics of Legal Conflicts*, 2 J. LEGAL STUD. 279 (1973) (seeking to show why a larger percentage of lawsuits are settled out of court and providing a hypothesis about what causes cases to go to trial). Building on their work, George Priest and Benjamin Klein later proposed a model of settlement—predicting that when cases fail to settle, they will be adjudicated in favor of the plaintiff 50 per-

cent of the time—that has come to be identified with the assumption of wealth maximizing behavior. George L. Priest & Benjamin Klein, *The Selection of Disputes for Litigation*, 13 J. LEGAL STUD. 1, 4–5 (1984).

8. Posner, *Economic Approach to Legal Procedure*, at 418.

9. *See* Samuel Issacharoff & George Loewenstein, *Second Thoughts About Summary Judgment*, 100 YALE L.J. 73, 101 (1990) ("[I]t is natural—as well as customary in the legal and economic literature—to assume that the likelihood of settlement is positively related to the width of the settlement zone."); D. Theodore Rave, Note, *Questioning the Efficiency of Summary Judgment*, 81 N.Y.U. L. REV. 875, 892 (2006) ("Generally, the wider the settlement zone, the more likely the case is to settle."). The existence and size of the bargaining (or "settlement") zone is, on this account, the primary condition on which settlement depends. *See* Russell B. Korobkin, *Aspirations and Settlement*, 80 CORNELL L. REV. 6 (noting disputes will settle in the bargaining zone or not at all if the zone does not exist).

10. *See* Posner, *Economic Approach to Legal Procedure*, at 419 ("[A]ny increase in the stakes must increase the likelihood of litigation by making the plaintiff's minimum settlement offer grow faster than the defendant's maximum settlement offer.").

11. We do not address here the important questions of whether courts will and should take adaptation into account when they assess the value of an injury. For some early ideas on that score, *see* Cass R. Sunstein, *Illusory Losses*, 37 J. LEGAL STUD. S157 (2008); Samuel Bagenstos & Margo Schlanger, *Hedonic Damages, Hedonic Adaptation, and Disability*, 60 VAND. L. REV. 745 (2007); Sean Williams, *Self-Altering Injury*, 96 CORNELL L. REV. 535 (2011); David Ennio DePianto, *Tort Damages and the (Misunderstood) Money-Happiness Connection*, 44 ARIZ. ST. L.J. 1385 (2012).

12. Fairness is not the only non-monetary consideration that can matter to litigants. Russell B. Korobkin & Chris Guthrie, *Psychology, Economics, and Settlement: A New Look at the Role of the Lawyer*, 76 TEX. L. REV. 77, 79–80 (1997) ("Litigants litigate not just for money, but to attain vindication; to establish precedent; 'to express their feelings'; to obtain a hearing; and to satisfy a sense of entitlement regarding use of the courts. . . ." (quoting Austin Sarat, *Alternatives in Dispute Processing: Litigation in a Small Claims Court*, 10 LAW & SOC'Y REV. 339, 346 (1976)) (footnotes omitted)).

13. *See, e.g.*, Owen M. Fiss, *Against Settlement*, 93 YALE L.J. 1073 (1984); George Loewenstein et al., *Self-Serving Assessments of Fairness and Pretrial Bargaining*, 22 J. LEGAL STUD. 135, 139 (1992) ("[S]ubject disputants seemed more concerned with achieving what they considered to be a fair settlement of the case than maximizing their own expected value."); *see also* John Bronsteen & Owen Fiss, *The Class Action Rule*, 78 NOTRE DAME L. REV. 1419, 1448–49

(2003) (distinguishing between actual justice and adequate settlements in the class action context).

14. *See* Ernst Fehr & Simon Gächter, *Fairness and Retaliation: The Economics of Reciprocity*, 14 J. Econ. Perspectives 159 (2000).

15. Fehr & Gächter, *Fairness and Retaliation*, at 161.

16. Neuroscientific research indicates that people receive pleasure from "punishing" others for providing unfair distributions. See Dominique J.-F. de Quervain et al., *The Neural Basis of Altruistic Punishment*, 305 Sci. 1254 (2004). Interestingly, though, another study indicates that taking revenge can reduce happiness. *See* Kevin M. Carlsmith, Timothy D. Wilson, & Daniel T. Gilbert, *The Paradoxical Consequences of Revenge*, 95 J. Personality & Soc. Psych. 1316 (2008).

17. Fehr & Gächter, *Fairness and Retaliation*, at 162.

18. Russell B. Korobkin & Chris Guthrie, *Psychological Barriers to Litigation Settlement: An Experimental Approach*, 93 Mich. L. Rev. 107, 110–11 (1994).

19. Korobkin & Guthrie, *Psychological Barriers*, at 132–33.

20. Another way to characterize the divergence is as a simple offshoot of the core idea of prospect theory, the well-established idea that people evaluate decisions in terms of losses and gains rather than with regard to overall value. Group B, unlike Group A, views the $21,000 settlement offer as a loss rather than a gain because it falls short of the injury Group B has suffered. Accordingly, Group B would be more likely to gamble on recovering the "full" amount of $28,000 at trial.

21. Daniel Kahneman & Amos Tversky, *Choices, Values, and Frames*, 39 Am. Psychologist 341, 344 (1984); *see also* Amos Tversky & Daniel Kahneman, *The Framing of Decisions and the Psychology of Choice*, 211 Science 453 (1981); Daniel Kahneman & Amos Tversky, *Prospect Theory: An Analysis of Decision Under Risk*, 47 Econometrica 263 (1979).

22. One might speculate that, at least under certain circumstances, plaintiffs would not view the money at stake as a gain and defendants would not view it as a loss. If, for example, a defendant had taken money from the plaintiff via the underlying tort or contract violation, then anything less than a full repayment of that baseline sum could be treated by the defendant as an overall gain and by the plaintiff as an overall loss. However, as we explain in the present paragraph in the main text, Rachlinski's experimental findings suggest otherwise, indicating that plaintiffs view settlements as gains, whereas defendants view them as losses.

23. Jeffrey J. Rachlinski, *Gains, Losses, and the Psychology of Litigation*, 70 S. Cal. L. Rev. 113 (1996). In one experiment, undergraduates were assigned the role of attorney for either a plaintiff or a defendant in a property lawsuit. They were told the amount the plaintiff stood to gain at trial and the percentage

chance of such a plaintiff victory. Then they were told that the opposing side had offered to settle for an amount that corresponded to the probability times the amount; e.g., if a trial victory would yield $100,000 and the plaintiff had a 70 percent chance to win, then the offer was $70,000. Far more plaintiff-attorney subjects than defendant-attorney subjects accepted the offer rather than take the all-or-nothing risk of a trial. *Id.* at 135–40.

24. We certainly do not mean to suggest that all types of tort damages are susceptible to adaptation. Tort damages typically comprise a variety of linked payments designed to compensate the plaintiff for various aspects of her injury. Plaintiffs can recover damages for medical expenses and economic costs (typically lost wages due to disability) incurred as a result of the injury. These expenses are not "adaptable" in the sense we describe here; a plaintiff's view of these costs is unlikely to change. But plaintiffs may also recover damages for present and future pain and suffering, and in many jurisdictions they are permitted to recoup so-called hedonic damages to compensate for lost enjoyment of their lives. *See* Sunstein, *Illusory Losses*, at S157. For specific examples of hedonic damage awards, *see* Allen v. Wal-Mart Stores, Inc., 241 F.3d 1293, 1297–98 (10th Cir. 2001) (upholding jury instructions entitling plaintiff to damages for loss of ability to ride horses); Day v. Ouachita Parish Sch. Bd., 823 So. 2d 1039, 1044 (La. Ct. App. 2002) (affirming damage award for loss of ability to play high school sports). Plaintiffs will adjust to the losses for which these latter types of damages are meant to compensate. Pain and suffering awards constitute approximately 50 percent of the total value of monetary damages in personal injury cases, *see* W. KIP VISCUSI, REFORMING PRODUCTS LIABILITY 102–07 (1991) (finding that pain and suffering damages account for "30 to 57 percent of all awards in which bodily injury payment has been received," and well over 50 percent of all awards in which there is a nonzero pain and suffering award); Neil Vidmar et al., *Jury Awards for Medical Malpractice and Post-Verdict Adjustments of Those Awards*, 48 DEPAUL L. REV. 265, 296 (1998) ("[I]t seems reasonable to conclude that the general damages portion of jury awards in malpractice cases is, on average, between 50 and 60%."), and so adaptation that reduces pain and suffering damages could have a substantial effect on the overall valuation of a personal injury case.

25. This is a reasonable approximation of a typical plaintiff's ability to adapt. As we noted previously, moderately disabled plaintiffs typically recover 50 percent of their "lost happiness" through adaptation over a period of two years. *See* Andrew J. Oswald & Nattavudh Powdthavee, *Does Happiness Adapt? A Longitudinal Study of Disability with Implications for Economists and Judges*, 92 J. PUB. ECON. 1070 (2008).

26. This dichotomy is discussed in Sunstein, *Illusory Losses*, at S157.

27. *See, e.g.*, C. Lundqvist et al., *Spinal Cord Injuries: Clinical, Functional, and Emotional Status*, 16 SPINE 80 (1991) (demonstrating that subjects who have

incurred spinal injuries are nearly as happy as the general population four years after their injuries).

28. *See* Posner, *An Economic Analysis*, at 422–26 (discussing this function performed by pretrial procedure).

29. *See* Robert E. Scott & George G. Triantis, *Anticipating Litigation in Contract Design*, 115 YALE L.J. 814, 829 n.34 (2006) (describing the Eastern District of Virginia's reputation for rapid resolution of litigation).

30. This trend, which is generally viewed unfavorably, is closely related to the less pejorative theory of "directive lawyering," in which lawyers make "moral" decisions irrespective of the bad intentions of their clients. Robert F. Cochran, Jr. et al., *Symposium: Client Counseling and Moral Responsibility*, 30 PEPP. L. REV. 591, 594–96 (2003).

31. Similarly, if the plaintiff has already recovered from her insurer, and the insurance company is the true plaintiff at suit, *see* June F. Entman, *More Reasons for Abolishing Federal Rule of Civil Procedure 17(a): The Problem of the Proper Plaintiff and Insurance Subrogation*, 68 N.C. L. REV. 893, 908–11 (1990) (describing the subrogation of claims by insurance companies), the plaintiff's adaptation will not affect the lawsuit. Of course, even insured tort victims are typically uninsured as to pain and suffering and are never insured for anything resembling a punitive damages claims. *See* Randall R. Bovbjerg et al., *Valuing Life and Limb in Tort: Scheduling "Pain and Suffering,"* 83 NW. U. L. REV. 908, 932 n.125 (1989) ("No health coverage, public or private, explicitly pays for noneconomic damages. . . ."); Catherine M. Sharkey, *Unintended Consequences of Medical Malpractice Damages Caps*, 80 N.Y.U. L. REV. 391, 401 (2005) ("[E]vidence confirms that patients do not purchase coverage for noneconomic damages as part of first-party health care insurance.").

32. *See* Model Code of Prof'l Responsibility EC 7–7 (2001) ("[I]t is for the client to decide whether he will accept a settlement offer. . . .").

33. Richard W. Painter, *Litigating on a Contingency: A Monopoly of Champions or a Market for Champerty?*, 71 CHI.-KENT L. REV. 625, 626 n.3 (1995).

34. *See* John Bronsteen, *Class Action Settlements: An Opt-In Proposal*, 2005 U. ILL. L. REV. 903, 911–12 ("The lawyer could settle many cases in the time it takes to litigate one, so it is rational for her to settle quickly even if doing so reduces her profit in the individual case."); Charles Silver, *Class Actions— Representative Proceedings*, *in* 5 ENCYCLOPEDIA OF LAW AND ECONOMICS 194, 213 (B. Bouckaert & G. De Geest eds., 2000) (suggesting that economic factors make plaintiffs' attorneys predisposed to settle).

35. This type of strategic behavior might eventually result in a type of cycling equilibrium, in which defendants first refused to settle early, followed by plaintiffs' credible threats to refuse settlement late in the litigation, followed by defendants' loosening their strategic stance and returning to early settlements, and so forth.

36. This would add a wrinkle to the typical picture of lawyers in these cases as merely imposing costs on their plaintiff-clients due to misaligned incentives. *See, e.g.*, FRANK A. SLOAN ET AL., SUING FOR MEDICAL MALPRACTICE 77–78 (1993) (noting even greater attorney-client agency costs when an injured plaintiff seeks to fulfill noneconomic goals, including disclosure of information, revenge, and specific deterrence, which are unavailing to her attorney); Leandra Lederman & Warren B. Hrung, *Do Attorneys Do Their Clients Justice? An Empirical Study of Lawyers' Effects on Tax Court Litigation Outcomes*, 41 WAKE FOREST L. REV. 1235, 1244 (2006) ("The presence of a lawyer as agent of a client-principal introduces costs that unrepresented litigants do not face, because, if lawyers are rational actors, they may tend to maximize interests that differ from those of their clients.").

37. See Oswald & Powdthavee, *Does Happiness Adapt?*, at 1068–69 tbl.1. Although family size and marital status—along with income—have statistically meaningful effects on the rate and extent of post-injury adaptation, these effects do not account for the entirety of adaptation. Oswald and Powdthavee's regressions demonstrate that the effects of time—which they interpret as the workings of the psychological immune system—are at minimum between five and ten times larger than the effects generated by marriage, family size, income, or any other potential confounding factor.

Part Three

1. There is widespread agreement both that happiness contributes to welfare and that welfare is valuable. For the point that happiness contributes to welfare, see, for example, Simon Keller, *Welfare as Success*, 43 NoÛs 656, 674 (2009) ("[N]obody doubts that pleasure contributes to welfare. . . ."); Dan Moller, *Wealth, Disability, and Happiness*, 39 PHIL. & PUB. AFF. 177, 179 (2011) ("[H]appiness is one component of welfare: we do not think people's lives are going well for them if they themselves are miserable."); RICHARD KRAUT, WHAT IS GOOD AND WHY: THE ETHICS OF WELL-BEING 126 n.48 (2007) ("[T]here is no doubt that pleasure and, more generally, positive affect . . . play an important role in a flourishing human life."); and MATTHEW D. ADLER, WELL-BEING AND FAIR DISTRIBUTION 297 (2012) ("No one doubts that mental states are *one* component of well-being.") (emphasis in original). For the point that welfare is valuable, see, for example, T.M. SCANLON, WHAT WE OWE TO EACH OTHER 141 (1998) ("It would be absurd to deny that well-being is important. . . ."); Mark Kelman, *Hedonic Psychology and the Ambiguities of "Welfare,"* 33 PHIL. & PUB. AFF. 391, 391 (2005) ("Philosophers have disagreed about the place of human welfare in judgments about public policies generally and their distributive outcomes in particular. But virtually all agree that welfare effects should play *some* role, at

least when welfare improvements can be achieved without violating 'side constraints.'") (emphasis in original).

2. DANIEL M. HAYBRON, THE PURSUIT OF UNHAPPINESS: THE ELUSIVE PSYCHOLOGY OF WELL-BEING 5 (2008). Haybron's conception of happiness is different from ours, but as others have noted, the two conceptions seem to yield very similar results in practice. *See id.* at 181, 300 n.10.

3. HAYBRON, PURSUIT OF UNHAPPINESS, at 4–5.

Chapter Six

1. *E.g.*, DEREK PARFIT, REASONS AND PERSONS 494 (1984).

2. *E.g.*, L.W. SUMNER, WELFARE, HAPPINESS, AND ETHICS 20 (1996) ("Welfare assessments concern what we may call the prudential value of a life, namely how well it is going *for the individual whose life it is.*") (emphasis in original); JAMES GRIFFIN, WELL-BEING: ITS MEANING, MEASUREMENT AND MORAL IMPORTANCE 21 (1986) ("The notion we are after is not the notion of value in general, but the narrower notion of a life's being valuable solely to the person who lives it."); Richard J. Arneson, *Human Flourishing Versus Desire Satisfaction, in* HUMAN FLOURISHING 113, 113 (Ellen Frankel Paul et al. eds., 1999) (describing well-being as "not the morally best life, but the life that is best for me"); J. David Velleman, *Well-Being and Time, in* THE POSSIBILITY OF PRACTICAL REASON 56, 56 n.3 (2000) (defining welfare as "how well [a life] goes for the person living it").

3. This claim is certainly open to dispute, though we believe it represents the current majority view in ethical philosophy.

4. JOHN RAWLS, A THEORY OF JUSTICE 41 (1971).

5. RAWLS, A THEORY OF JUSTICE, at 41.

6. RAWLS, A THEORY OF JUSTICE, at 41.

7. We refer to the theory we favor as the "hedonic" or "happiness" theory. In certain places we may instead call it the "Benthamite" theory to differentiate it from other theories—like Fred Feldman's—that could also be labeled "hedonic" or "happiness." Still, all references to the hedonic or happiness account are meant to refer to the theory we espouse, not to Feldman's view or to both views, unless the alternative is made specific. See FRED FELDMAN, WHAT IS THIS THING CALLED HAPPINESS? (2010).

8. These are often called "desire-fulfillment" theories. We use the terms interchangeably, and our critiques of the theories apply to both preferences and desires.

9. See ADLER, WELL-BEING AND FAIR DISTRIBUTION, at 180 ("Imagine the penitent wrongdoer who develops a moral preference that he suffer pain and anguish as punishment for the wrongdoing. Surely *that* preference is not self-interested. . . .") (emphasis in original).

10. ADLER, WELL-BEING AND FAIR DISTRIBUTION, at 180.

11. This example comes from Stephen Darwall's invocation of Jane's predicament in Edgar Rice Burroughs's story *The Return of Tarzan*. Stephen Darwall, *Self-Interest and Self-Concern*, 14 SOCIAL PHIL. & POLICY 158 (1997).

12. *See* Arneson, *Human Flourishing*, at 124 (calling preference theories "viciously circular" if they include only preferences for well-being); SUMNER, WELFARE, HAPPINESS, AND ETHICS, at 135 (calling such preference theories "patently circular"); *cf.* GRIFFIN, WELL-BEING, at 22 (endorsing a version of such a theory that is concededly "[in] a way . . . circular"). Griffin argues that any theory has this same sort of circularity, but Sumner is right to reject that claim. The hedonic theory, for example, points to a thing—feeling good—that it claims captures the concept of well-being. Feeling good can be understood without reference to well-being, so there is no circularity. Griffin's theory, unlike hedonism, is thus vulnerable to the criticisms of preference theories made in the main text.

13. *E.g.*, Mark Carl Overvold, *Self-Interest and the Concept of Self-Sacrifice*, 10 CANADIAN J. OF PHIL. 105 (1980); Darwall, *Self-Interest and Self-Concern*, at 175–76; SUMNER, WELFARE, HAPPINESS, AND ETHICS, at 134–35; ADLER, WELL-BEING AND FAIR DISTRIBUTION, at 177–78; Arneson, *Human Flourishing*, at 124.

14. RAWLS, A THEORY OF JUSTICE, at 407–46.

15. John C. Harsanyi, *Morality and the Theory of Rational Behavior*, *in* UTILITARIANISM AND BEYOND 39, 54–56 (Amartya Sen & Bernard Williams eds., 1982).

16. DEREK PARFIT, REASONS AND PERSONS 494 (1984).

17. *See* Overvold, *Self-Interest and the Concept of Self-Sacrifice*, 105, 117–18 n.10 ("On this account the only outcomes or features of acts which are logically relevant to the determination of an agent's self-interest are those in which the agent is an essential constituent.").

18. *Cf.* Shelly Kagan, *The Limits of Well-Being*, 9 SOC. PHIL. & POLICY 169, 186 (1992) ("Since a person is just a body and a mind, changes in well-being would have to involve changes in the person's body or mind.").

19. Matthew Adler has suggested that whether a preference counts for well-being may depend on whether it is based in an attitude of self-sympathy. ADLER, WELL-BEING AND FAIR DISTRIBUTION, at 180, 203. On its face, the term "self-sympathy" seems to disguise the theory's circularity rather than cure it. What it means for Jill to adopt an attitude of self-sympathy is for her to focus on what is good for her—that is, to focus on her well-being. Thus, instead of conceiving well-being circularly as "preferences for one's own well-being," Adler would seem to be conceiving well-being circularly as "preferences one has when focusing on one's own well-being." Adler denies this by saying that what he means by self-sympathy is what Stephen Darwall has used the term to refer to. *Id.* at 180. But Darwall provides no help on this score. For Darwall, sympathy is the feeling people have when, for example, they see a child about to fall into a well. STEPHEN

DARWALL, WELFARE AND RATIONAL CARE 51 (2002). Well-being, for Darwall, is what one hopes for someone when feeling sympathy toward her. But Darwall is not claiming to supply any *content* that could complete a theory of well-being— any explanation of what those hopes (and thus, well-being itself) actually are. Stephen Darwall, *Reply to Griffin, Raz, and Wolf*, 18 UTILITAS 434, 436 (2006). Darwall's contribution "operate[s] at [a] different level[]" from "a list theory" or a preference theory like Adler's, because unlike Darwall's contribution, Adler's theory requires "a substantive normative claim, a thesis concerning the kinds of experiences and activities that make a life good for someone rather than an account of the concept of welfare." *Id.* In other words, Adler—unlike Darwall— needs to provide some way to identify which preferences one would have when adopting an attitude of self-sympathy. Without doing so, Adler can make no "substantive normative claim"—that is, he can have no theory akin to an objective theory or hedonic theory—about well-being. *Id.*

The hedonic theory is not similarly opaque or devoid of content. Consider a theory that says well-being is height. Although disqualified by its substantive absurdity, such a theory scores very highly with regard to clarity and content even though height is *not* perfectly clear: measuring instruments are imperfect, so a person's "true" height can never be known. Yet the "height" theory still supplies clear content because someone's height is so much *more* clear and knowable than is well-being. Intuition conflicts about how tall someone is will be *markedly* less intractable than intuition conflicts about well-being itself. Thus, one does not need to know true height with exactitude in order to assess the theory that height is well-being. It can easily be assessed via reflective equilibrium because one knows (better than one does with the bare concept of well-being itself) the answer the theory yields in every case. Feeling good is not nearly as clear as height, but it is far clearer than well-being itself. So the theory that well-being is feeling good advances the ball a significant amount. Moreover, there will easily be enough agreement about whether people feel good in particular cases to judge the theory via reflective equilibrium. But the same is not true of Adler's theory, because one can have no idea what it says about any case. It does not specify which preferences count and which do not, or how to tell which ones count. And to the extent that self-sympathy is interpreted, contra Darwall, to supply such content, self-sympathy merely supplies circularity and reduces Adler's theory to the claim that well-being is the preference for well-being.

Finally, we note that as an alternative to self-sympathy, Adler suggests that preferences could be counted as self-interested if and only if Jill (when informed and rational) judges those preferences to be self-interested. ADLER, WELL-BEING AND FAIR DISTRIBUTION, at 180, 203. We think this cannot be right. Adler's narrow conception of rationality (*see id.* at 215–16) leaves the field wide open for Jill to judge that anything—including a small increase in the temperature on a far-off planet 2 million years after Jill's death—will increase her well-being. The fact that she believes it does not make it so, as virtually every other account of well-being acknowledges. *E.g.*, Richard J. Arneson, *Human Flourishing*, at 124 ("It will not do to stipulate that each agent determines for herself which of her basic desires bear on her well-being. Surely an agent could make a mistake in making this determination, and we need some way of deciding when a mistake occurs.").

20. For criticisms of restricted-preference theories on this score, see, for example, Connie S. Rosati, *Persons, Perspectives, and Full Information Accounts of the Good*, 105 ETHICS 296 (1995); and David Sobel, *Full Information Accounts of Well-Being*, 104 ETHICS 784 (1994). For a different criticism, see Arneson, *Human Flourishing*, at 133–35.

21. The primary way to test a theory of well-being is to compare its answers with people's intuitions. *See, e.g.*, RAWLS, A THEORY OF JUSTICE, at 20. Consider the most famous criticism of the happiness theory: that it deems a life on an experience machine to have as much welfare as a life off of one. (We will discuss the example later in this chapter.) For all anyone knows, a superhuman idealized preference theory would yield *the same answer* about the experience machine as does the happiness theory. This is not just a fanciful possibility because, as we will note later, many critics of the machine hypothetical have suggested that people's reactions to it are pumped by the difficulty in conceiving its hypothesized conditions. Idealizing preferences would cure that problem, if a problem it is.

Matthew Adler has acknowledged that his idealized preference theory "is consistent with the proposition that mental states are, as a matter of contingent fact, the sole source of well-being." ADLER, WELL-BEING AND FAIR DISTRIBUTION, at 297. In other words, Adler's theory might yield the *identical* answer to *every* question that our theory yields. To be sure, this would be merely a coincidence (although perhaps not much of one, given how closely people identify happiness with self-interest), but that is irrelevant to the point we are currently making. Our point is that Adler's theory cannot be tested because no one can know what his theory says. The same examples raised against the happiness theory, or against any other theory, might apply to Adler's theory as well.

Moreover, how can Adler mount any argument *in favor* of his theory? He cannot show that it accords better with intuitions than do rival theories, because no one can know what answer it yields to any question. Adler must seek other avenues to argue for his theory, but those seem unpromising. For one thing, testing a theory's answers via intuition has been the dominant philosophical approach for decades. And for another thing, idealized preferences do not seem to capture people's theory-level understanding of well-being. People might think it plausible to equate well-being with happiness, but we doubt they would see the same plausibility in equating well-being with the highly complicated set of idealized preferences Adler proposes.

22. It is thus surprising that Matthew Adler, a leading proponent of this sort of theory, connects it with implementation in real-world CBA. ADLER, WELL-BEING AND FAIR DISTRIBUTION. Whatever proxies could be used for Jill's super-human preferences are far less valid and reliable than the proxies that are used for determining earthly things like how good Jill feels. Matthew Adler proposes to use surveys as the proxies for idealized preferences because the surveys "allow the researcher to provide information to respondents, and to take steps to debias respondents." *Id.* at 300. But it is utterly unrealistic to believe that these steps will yield results that even remotely approximate people's perfectly idealized preferences or Adler's theory's version of those preferences. Significant evidence suggests that providing this sort of information actually makes people's choices worse than if they had not received the information. This is due to people's cognitive limitations and to the resulting errors in processing the information. *E.g.*, George Loewenstein, Cass R. Sunstein & Russell Golman, *Disclosure: Psychology Changes Everything*, ANNUAL REVIEW OF ECONOMICS (forthcoming).

Moreover, Adler conceives one's welfare as idealized preferences formed with "full information regarding the origins of his own preferences"—"for example that he prefers outcome x because of social or parental pressure imposed on him as a child, or because of his association between his attributes in x and something pleasant." ADLER, WELL-BEING AND FAIR DISTRIBUTION, at 214. How could surveys possibly provide such information, which by its nature is highly individualized and almost impossible to know? Furthermore, one can never acquire even a rough sense of how good a proxy is because idealized preferences, unlike feeling good, are so remote from the typical experience of life: they cannot be studied or even imagined, because omniscience is inconceivable. (Adler does not require omniscience, but his requirements for idealization are comparably inconceivable.) We think it obvious that happiness data are a more valid and reliable proxy for feeling good than these sorts of surveys are for idealized preferences. In fact, happiness surveys are almost surely a better proxy for *Adler's* conception of well-being than are survey data or revealed preferences (and Adler acknowledges that happiness surveys could be used in this way, *id.* at 297–99) given the strong (perhaps near-total) overlap between happiness and self-interested preferences. *See, e.g.*, BRAD HOOKER, IDEAL CODE, REAL WORLD 42 (2000) ("[W]hat gives people pleasure or enjoyment is normally also what satisfies their desires. . . .") (citing J.J.C. Smart, *Outline of a System of Utilitarian Ethics, in* UTILITARIANISM: FOR AND AGAINST 3, 26 (J.J.C. Smart & Bernard Williams eds., 1973)); RICHARD B. BRANDT, A THEORY OF THE GOOD AND THE RIGHT 247 (1998) (noting "the normally close relation between what a person wants and what will make him happy").

23. Consider the questions posed earlier: Is Jim better off if he doubles his salary by working twice as much? Is Jane better off if she becomes famous but

falls out of touch with her friends? Is Sam better off if he extends his life an extra year by making healthy choices that sacrifice some of his enjoyment of life? Is Beth better off if her novel becomes popular after her death?

The fully informed preference theory yields no answers to any of these questions, or indeed to any real- or hypothetical-case questions at all. It says that the answers depend on something no one can ever know or even remotely approximate. The happiness theory, by contrast, says that the answers depend on what makes each person feel better. Although this too might be theoretically unknowable in the same way that an *actual* (not idealized) preference is unknowable, the proxies for feeling good are testable by ordinary social-science methods. We have described those proxies, and the way they are tested, in chapter 1. Moreover, common sense dictates that feeling good is a far more accessible thing than is that which we would want under conditions where we know everything. Everyone has experienced feeling good, whereas no one has or could experience preference idealization or anything remotely like it.

24. *E.g.*, SUMNER, WELFARE, HAPPINESS, AND ETHICS, at 45–80; PARFIT, REASONS AND PERSONS, at 493.

25. *E.g.*, HAYBRON, PURSUIT OF UNHAPPINESS, at 35–36.

26. Martha C. Nussbaum, *Capabilities as Fundamental Entitlements: Sen and Social Justice*, 9 FEMINIST ECON. 33, 41–42 (2003). Although it is not clear whether Nussbaum considers these sorts of lists to constitute her own theory of well-being, they are regularly viewed as constituting theories thereof. *E.g.*, ADLER, WELL-BEING AND FAIR DISTRIBUTION, at 167 n.24; HAYBRON, PURSUIT OF UNHAPPINESS, at 35–36. In any event, our purpose here is not to discuss Nussbaum's view of well-being but rather to give examples of typical list items. For collections of other list theories, see ADLER, WELL-BEING AND FAIR DISTRIBUTION, at 167 n.24; and HAYBRON, PURSUIT OF UNHAPPINESS, at 287 n.23.

27. If the toxin had killed Jack at age seventy, then it would have decreased his well-being on our view by depriving him of the happiness he would have had in the years between age seventy and his ultimate (toxin-unrelated) death.

28. If one objects that health should be understood to refer only to things that affect one's felt experience, then one is either collapsing health into happiness or else connecting the two in a way that makes it impossible for health to have happiness-independent value as a constituent of well-being.

Alternatively, if one believes that the toxin *does* decrease Jill's well-being if Jill would prefer not to have it, then we think one is trading on the impossibility of the following: Jill must know of the toxin in order to form the preference, but she must not know of the toxin in order for her to be totally unaffected by it. If Jill knows about the toxin, then her preference will be based on a completely understandable unwillingness to believe that the toxin will definitely not affect her felt experience of life in any way.

29. This makes it effectively impossible to solve the problem via the type of

lexical ordering that Rawls uses to resolve conflicts between the two components of his theory of justice. See RAWLS, A THEORY OF JUSTICE, at 42–43. For example, is Jane's life better if she has 100 percent of whatever constitutes complete satisfaction of the affiliation requirement and none of the control-over-life requirement, or vice versa, than if she has some of each? Presumably she is better off with some of each, which makes a lexical ordering impossible. This question could be asked with virtually any two list items.

30. RAWLS, A THEORY OF JUSTICE, at 41. Rawls was of course referring to a conception of justice rather than well-being, but the point applies identically in each context.

31. SUMNER, WELFARE, HAPPINESS, AND ETHICS, at 45 & n.1 ("Although it is easy to find philosophers who count themselves as objectivists about welfare, it is surprising how few of them have anything like a genuine theory to offer. . . . [A] list of human goods is not a theory of welfare."); SCANLON, WHAT WE OWE TO EACH OTHER, at 125 ("[T]his list of fixed points does not amount to a *theory* of well-being.") (emphasis in original).

32. SCANLON, WHAT WE OWE TO EACH OTHER, at 125.

33. BERNARD GERT, MORALITY: ITS NATURE AND JUSTIFICATION 84 (rev. ed. 2005).

34. Martha Nussbaum, *Non-relative Virtues: An Aristotelian Approach*, *in* THE QUALITY OF LIFE 242, 243 (Martha C. Nussbaum & Amartya Sen eds., 1993).

35. Simon Keller, *Welfare as Success*, 43 Noûs 656, 664–65 (2009).

36. Keller, *Welfare as Success*, at 665.

37. Keller, *Welfare as Success*, at 665.

38. We also note that even if intuitions were better than theories, that does not undermine the value of happiness or the data about it. We think that happiness tracks people's intuitions about well-being in the mass of cases. *See* Joseph Mendola, *Intuitive Hedonism*, 128 PHILOS. STUD. 441 (2006). And even if we were wrong about this, too, the data would still be valuable because people surely care a lot about happiness (feeling good) whether or not they see it as the only component of welfare. Consider, just as one example, how important it is for people to avoid or mitigate physical pain.

39. GRIFFIN, WELL-BEING, at 21.

40. SUMNER, WELFARE, HAPPINESS, AND ETHICS, at 20.

41. HAYBRON, PURSUIT OF UNHAPPINESS, at 29.

42. 579 Arneson, *Human Flourishing*, at 113.

43. SCANLON, WHAT WE OWE TO EACH OTHER, at 109.

44. Velleman, *Well-Being and Time*, at 56 n.3.

45. Joseph Raz, *Darwall on Rational Care*, 18 UTILITAS 400, 401 n.5 (2006).

46. SUMNER, WELFARE, HAPPINESS, AND ETHICS, at 20–25, 45–80.

47. SUMNER, WELFARE, HAPPINESS, AND ETHICS, at 45 ("By their very nature,

objective theories of welfare share a common problem: without recourse to the subjective point of view they must somehow account for the perspectival character of prudential value.").

48. *See* SUMNER, WELFARE, HAPPINESS, AND ETHICS, at 46–53.

49. SUMNER, WELFARE, HAPPINESS, AND ETHICS, at 51–53.

50. If one wants the question to be filled out with more detail, we may do so as follows. Suppose Bob is independently wealthy and spends most of his time socializing with friends and family. He has decided to fill two or three hours per day with either philosophy or TV and is trying to choose between them. To isolate the relevant question, let us stipulate that whichever he chooses will affect only those hours in which he engages in that activity: the rest of his life will be identical either way.

51. *E.g.*, Dale Dorsey, *Three Arguments for Perfectionism*, 44 NoÛs 59, 61 (2010) ("What is the structure of perfectionism as an account of welfare or well-being? Perfectionism is objective rather than subjective—on a perfectionist view, certain activities, achievements, etc., are intrinsically valuable in a way that does not depend on an agent's responses (desires, etc.).").

52. HAYBRON, PURSUIT OF UNHAPPINESS, at 32–33.

53. HAYBRON, PURSUIT OF UNHAPPINESS, at 287 n.19 ("The Aristotelian literature has yet to integrate fully with the contemporary literature on well-being, so it is often difficult to tell where an author stands on well-being.").

54. HAYBRON, PURSUIT OF UNHAPPINESS, at 35 ("If there was an important feature that eudaimonistic accounts of well-being shared in common, it was the teleological idea that well-being consists in *nature-fulfillment*.") (emphasis in original).

55. HAYBRON, PURSUIT OF UNHAPPINESS, at 35 (stressing that "moral virtue is essential to well-being as Aristotelians see it").

56. *E.g.*, Antti Kauppinen, *Working Hard and Kicking Back: The Case for Diachronic Perfectionism*, 3 J. ETHICS & SOC. PHIL. 1, 1 (2009) ("Let us loosely define welfare perfectionism as the view that well-being consists in the (enjoyable) exercise of the capacities that are characteristic of one's biological species.").

57. Lawrence B. Solum, *The Virtues and Vices of a Judge: An Aristotelian Guide to Judicial Selection*, 61 S. CAL. L. REV. 1735, 1739 (1988).

58. *E.g.*, PHILIPPA FOOT, NATURAL GOODNESS (2001). Within Foot's voluminous body of work, in which she refined her views over time, *Natural Goodness* was one of the latest examples of her take on well-being.

59. ROSALIND HURSTHOUSE, ON VIRTUE ETHICS (1999).

60. RICHARD KRAUT, WHAT IS GOOD AND WHY: THE ETHICS OF WELL-BEING (2007).

61. *E.g.*, Susan Wolf, *Happiness and Meaning: Two Aspects of the Good Life*, 14 SOC. PHIL. & POL'Y 207, 211 (2009).

62. Richard Arneson casts a similar point as a major objection to perfectionist theories:

> Among the goods that intrinsically enhance the quality of someone's life, some may have nothing whatsoever to do with fashioning oneself as a more perfect specimen of the human species or as a more perfect specimen of the type of individual one is. Consider what are sometimes called "cheap thrills," activities that provide pleasure and excitement without any significant effort or sacrifice on the part of the agent and also without the exercise or development of any of the agent's significant talents. Cheap thrills are pleasures with no redeeming social value beyond their pleasantness. The world being as it is, and human nature being what it is, such pleasures seem to me to be important sources of enjoyment that significantly enhance many people's lives in ways for which there is no practical substitute. I take it that the pleasures of cheap thrills will not register at all on a perfectionist measure of the prudential value of people's lives, but I would think that if these pleasures were to disappear without replacement, the world would be immensely worse and most human lives would be significantly blighted. At least, the issue will surely be open for discussion on an objective view, whereas according to the more narrow doctrine of perfectionism, the insignificance of cheap thrills to the prudential value of lives is a simple closed issue.

Arneson, *Human Flourishing*, at 120. To the extent a perfectionist concedes that cheap thrills do sometimes or often increase well-being, her theory becomes more difficult to distinguish from the happiness theory.

63. Indeed, the problem may be worse than that. Not only are the answers opaque, but eudaimonists themselves acknowledge that those answers may be nonexistent: "Once one has accepted a conception of self-interest that recognizes meaningfulness as an independent aspect of one's personal good, one may have to admit that in such cases there may be no answer to the question of what is most in one's self-interest." Wolf, *Happiness and Meaning*, at 224.

64. SUMNER, WELFARE, HAPPINESS, AND ETHICS, at 79–80.

65. HAYBRON, PURSUIT OF UNHAPPINESS, at 159–60.

66. HAYBRON, PURSUIT OF UNHAPPINESS, at 155–75.

67. *E.g.*, Amartya Sen, *Capability and Well-Being, in* THE QUALITY OF LIFE 30 (Martha C. Nussbaum & Amartya Sen eds., 1993).

68. HAYBRON, PURSUIT OF UNHAPPINESS, at 173 (Aristotelian theories); *see also* SUMNER, WELFARE, HAPPINESS, AND ETHICS, at 68 (capabilities).

69. HAYBRON, PURSUIT OF UNHAPPINESS, at 172.

70. Wolf, *Happiness and Meaning*, at 222. In her next sentence, Wolf seems not to be using "happiness" to refer to Benthamite feeling good because she says that the "feelings of fulfillment" from meaningful activities are "worth more, on qualitative grounds alone, than many other sorts of pleasure, and worth the cost of putting up with considerable quantities of pain." *Id.* But in the next sentence after that, Wolf returns to focusing on the benefits of meaningfulness in terms of its Benthamite qualities: "Moreover, the awareness, even dim and inarticulate, of a lack of anything that can constitute a source of pride or a source of connection to anything valuable outside of oneself can be awful, making one irritable, restless, and contemptuous of oneself." *Id.* We think that the intuitive plausibility of Wolf's view owes itself entirely to the sorts of things she says in the first and third quoted sentences—the ones making her view virtually indistinguishable from the happiness theory—and that such plausibility would be radically undermined by taking seriously what the second sentence seems to suggest. If Mike's meaningful activities bring him "considerable quantities of pain" that are not offset by even greater quantities of pleasure, then we doubt many people would think those activities increase Mike's well-being.

71. Adler, Well-Being and Fair Distribution, at 224.

Chapter Seven

1. Let us note one more preliminary before moving forward. Nothing in the theory we favor depends on our use of the term "happiness." One could quite legitimately argue, as Haybron does (Daniel M. Haybron, The Pursuit of Unhappiness: The Elusive Psychology of Well-Being 61–77 (2008)), that happiness should not be equated with feeling good. The possible truth of that claim does not affect, though, any of our points in this chapter, because we are discussing not the concept of happiness but rather the concept of well-being. We use "happiness" as a term of art that plays no substantive role in the discussion. Our view of well-being is thus best labeled a "feeling good" theory, but we use the term "happiness" instead because it is more familiar and easier to incorporate into typical sentences.

2. This does not mean, of course, that people enjoy every moment—just that they have more happiness than sadness on the whole. This is certainly borne out empirically by the psychological data on happiness. It is in those rare and tragic cases where a person's long-term sadness exceeds her long-term happiness that people understandably tend to seriously ponder suicide.

3. Fred Feldman, What is This Thing Called Happiness? (2010); L.W. Sumner, Welfare, Happiness, and Ethics 20 (1996).

4. Roger Crisp, Reasons and the Good 98–125 (2006).

5. Joseph Mendola, *Intuitive Hedonism*, 128 Philos. Stud. 441 (2006).

6. Adam Kolber, *The Experiential Future of the Law*, 60 EMORY L.J. 585, 591–94 (2011).

7. RICHARD LAYARD, HAPPINESS: LESSONS FROM A NEW SCIENCE 114–15 (2005).

8. Torbjörn Tännsjö, *Narrow Hedonism*, 8 J. HAPP. STUD. 79, 92–95 (2007).

9. Elinor Mason, *The Nature of Pleasure: A Critique of Feldman*, 19 UTILITAS 379 (2007).

10. Famous examples from times past include Jeremy Bentham and Henry Sidgwick. JEREMY BENTHAM, AN INTRODUCTION TO THE PRINCIPLES OF MORALS AND LEGISLATION (J.H. Burns & H.L.A. Hart eds., Clarendon Press 1996) (1789); HENRY SIDGWICK, THE METHODS OF ETHICS (7th ed., Hackett 1981) (1874). Famous examples from present times include Peter Singer. PETER SINGER, PRACTICAL ETHICS (2d ed. 1993). And of course there are many others as well. *E.g.*, T.L.S. Sprigge, *The Greatest Happiness Principle*, 3 UTILITAS 37 (1991).

11. Our approach to these issues is derived from our commitment to materialist or naturalist explanations of human behavior. *See* OWEN FLANAGAN, THE REALLY HARD PROBLEM: MEANING IN THE MATERIAL WORLD (2007). For a discussion of naturalism in legal philosophy, see BRIAN LEITER, NATURALIZING JURISPRUDENCE: ESSAYS ON AMERICAN LEGAL REALISM AND NATURALISM IN LEGAL PHILOSOPHY (2007). At many points, we refer to "feelings" without mentioning thoughts and sensory perceptions more generally. We mean that only as shorthand; each time we discuss "feelings," we mean to incorporate the full range of human thoughts and sensations.

12. *See* James A. Russell, *Core Affect and the Psychological Construction of Emotion*, 110 PSYCHOL. REV. 145 (2003); *see also* Lisa Feldman Barret & Eliza Bliss-Moreau, *Affect as a Psychological Primitive*, 41 ADVANCES IN EXPERIMENTAL SOC. PSYCHOL. 167 (2009). Studies of core affect conclude that the construct in fact combines two separate dimensions—valence and arousal. The valence dimension measures the goodness or badness of an experience, while the arousal dimension measures the degree of emotional excitement that a person is feeling (e.g., agitated, calm, etc.). This matrix creates four quadrants of core affect, each of which is possible. On our theory of well-being, variations in arousal are not relevant to how much welfare a person has: a person is just as well off if she is experiencing 7 out of 10 positive affect (that is, a 7 in valence) while in an excited state as she would be while experiencing that same level of positive affect (again, a valence of 7) in a calm state. Accordingly, we do not discuss arousal in the text.

13. According to psychologists, core affect also includes a dimension of "arousal" in addition to the dimension of "valence" that we discuss in the text. Because differing degrees of arousal are irrelevant for the purposes of computing someone's welfare, we refer only to the valence dimension of affect.

14. VICTOR S. JOHNSTON, WHY WE FEEL: THE SCIENCE OF HUMAN EMOTIONS (1999) (outlining the evolutionary origins of pleasure and displeasure).

15. *See* Daniel Kahneman, *Objective Happiness, in* WELL-BEING: THE FOUNDATIONS OF HEDONIC PSYCHOLOGY (Daniel Kahneman et al. eds., 1999).

16. Russell, *Core Affect,* at 148.

17. *See* Robert B. Zajonc, *Feeling and Thinking: Preferences Need No Inferences,* 35 AM. PSYCHOL. 151 (1980).

18. This analogy comes from Russell, *Core Affect,* at 148.

19. One can certainly feel pride in other people, as well. In that case, there would be other cognitive and reflective differences in addition to the objects toward which the positive affect is felt that would distinguish gratitude and pride.

20. *See* Kahneman, *Objective Happiness,* at 7–8; ROGER CRISP, REASONS AND THE GOOD 109 (2006); *cf.* Aaron Smuts, *The Feels Good Theory of Pleasure,* 155 PHILOS. STUD. 241 (2011).

21. For a review, see Russell, *Core Affect,* at 148–49.

22. Russell, *Core Affect,* at 153; ANNA WIERZBICKA, EMOTIONS ACROSS LANGUAGES AND CULTURES: DIVERSITY AND UNIVERSALS (1999).

23. Russell, *Core Affect,* at 153.

24. Russell, *Core Affect,* at 153.

25. *E.g.,* Kahneman, *Objective Happiness,* at 7–8.

26. Kahneman, *Objective Happiness,* at 7 (emphasis in original) (citing J.A. Bargh et al., *The Automatic Evaluation Effect,* 32 J. EXPERIMENTAL SOC. PSYCH. 104 (1996)).

27. Kahneman, *Objective Happiness,* at 8.

28. Kahneman, *Objective Happiness,* at 8.

29. Kahneman, *Objective Happiness,* at 8.

30. Daniel Kahneman, *Experienced Utility and Objective Happiness: A Moment-Based Approach, in* CHOICES, VALUES, AND FRAMES (Daniel Kahneman & Amos Tversky eds., 2000); Kahneman, *Objective Happiness.*

31. Bentham and Singer argue for maximizing utility, whereas we make no claims about the moral significance of welfare relative to that of other possible values. Therefore, most of the traditional arguments leveled against utilitarianism are inapplicable to our claims. *See* JEREMY BENTHAM, AN INTRODUCTION TO THE PRINCIPLES OF MORALS AND LEGISLATION 12–13 (J.H. Burns & H.L.A. Hart eds., Clarendon Press 1996) (1789) ("An action then may be said to be conformable to the principle of utility . . . (meaning with respect to the community at large) when the tendency it has to augment the happiness of the community is greater than any it has to diminish it."); PETER SINGER, PRACTICAL ETHICS 14 (2d ed. 1993) (articulating an interest-based theory of utility).

32. *E.g.,* J. David Velleman, *Well-Being and Time, in* THE POSSIBILITY OF PRACTICAL REASON 56 (2000). Velleman argues against aggregating moments primarily on the ground that the order of events matters: a life is better if it goes

from worse to better than from better to worse, even if the aggregated moments are equally positive. We think this example relies on two things that should be ruled out. First, it pumps the intuition that the aggregated moments are not in fact equal. People will understandably think that bad moments will feel even worse if they are contrasted with good moments that have gone before them, and that good moments will feel even better if contrasted with bad moments that have gone before them. So it will not seem intuitively like the two lives are equal on the dimension of aggregated feelings of positivity. Second, it is revealing that Velleman characterizes the life that moves from worse to better as the *story* of a better life. *Id.* at 59. Although he differentiates that from saying it makes for a better story, we think that is precisely what many readers will have in mind. Like objective theories, Velleman's example smuggles in means of valuing lives other than how well they go for the people living them.

33. We recognize that at the most basic level, it might be difficult to decide whether to characterize positivity itself as either a feeling or instead as some sort of instantaneous judgment. We think of it more as a feeling, but in any event, that deep question is beyond our scope. And the self-reports from the hedonic data are of course not feelings themselves, but rather *proxies* for the level of positivity of those feelings.

34. Mihaly Csikszentmihalyi, Flow: The Psychology of Optimal Experience 96–100, 223–27 (1991).

35. If the marathoner in fact meant that her welfare was increased notwithstanding an overall worsening of her aggregated moments of happiness, then we would say she was mistaken. We explain that point below.

36. Csikszentmihalyi, Flow, at 94–116.

37. This was not, we realize, the second condition from the previous paragraph. The condition was that she *anticipated* that her overall lifetime happiness would be increased when she made the statement, not that it actually was. In the next paragraph in the main text, we address the issue of what she meant by her statement.

38. *See* Christopher Peterson, *Personal Control and Well-Being, in* Well-Being: The Foundations of Hedonic Psychology 288 (Daniel Kahneman et al. eds., 1999) (citing various studies suggesting that maintaining an optimistic attitude in the face of adversity benefits one's welfare in measurable ways).

39. In fact, in many cases individuals' judgments about their own lives track their moment-by-moment experiences. Measures of "life satisfaction," which are associated to some degree with judgments about life quality, are correlated with moment-by-moment measures of affect, as we describe in chapter 1.

40. Feldman, What is This Thing, at 109–18.

41. Feldman, What is This Thing, at 145–46.

42. Feldman, What is This Thing, at 143 nn.10–11.

43. Feldman also uses three other examples to differentiate his theory from a

theory like ours. FELDMAN, WHAT IS THIS THING, at 124–26. We think those examples are revealing because in each example it is *not* an attitude, as Feldman
claims, but rather a feeling that reveals the person's level of well-being. We will
discuss one of the examples here, as an illustration. Feldman offers the example of Dolores, who is in great pain but takes a drug that relieves almost all that
pain. When she takes the drug and feels a precipitous and dramatic reduction in
pain, she is clearly happy—even though she still feels some pain and thus is experiencing more pain than pleasure on the whole. For Feldman, sensory hedonism
would call her unhappy, but attitudinal hedonism would reflect the fact that she
takes a positive attitude toward the change in her condition.

We think this example is insufficiently attentive to the psychological realities embodied by Benthamite hedonism. Our theory does not take the narrow
view of experience that the example attributes to it. Sensory hedonism, as we
conceive it, is broad enough to encompass the full spectrum of people's feelings
rather than just the sort of physical pain of an aching back. The *feeling* of relief
at having a reduction in back pain registers on our scale. Thus, if Dolores's dominant feeling is relief, then Feldman's stipulation that she feels some pain and
no pleasure will simply be untrue. And if we accept his stipulation that she feels
some pain and no pleasure, then that will necessarily mean that "relief" (or any
other positive feeling) is not registering at all as part of her felt experience of life.
Dolores will say that she is "surprised, delighted, and in general fairly happy"
only if she *feels* surprised, delighted, and in general fairly happy. And if she feels
those things, then sensory hedonism (properly understood) will count them toward her welfare level and weigh them against the remaining muscle pain she
feels. Presumably, the positives outweigh the negatives, which accounts for her
description. Indeed, hedonic studies show that changes in circumstances can exert a large influence on how people feel. It seems very likely that the change
makes Dolores happy enough that, at least in the short term, she feels happy on
the whole (even factoring in the small amount of pain that remains).

And the same is true in Feldman's other examples. In one of them, the revealing features about a man's well-being are his pained look and his expressions
of disappointment and anger. And in the other example, those features are a
woman's feelings of thrill and relief. All those things are best described in terms
of feelings. Feldman calls them attitudes, but in each case, the thing that contributes to well-being is the feeling itself rather than the preference or background
story that led to the feeling. Indeed, even Feldman counts only those attitudes
one is consciously experiencing at a particular time. The reason that only current thoughts are intuitively capable of affecting welfare is, we submit, that only
those are the ones that give rise to current feelings: those are the thoughts one
experiences at the relevant time, and it is the experience of them—in particular,
the way they make one feel—that affects one's well-being.

44. *See* MATTHEW D. ADLER & ERIC A. POSNER, NEW FOUNDATIONS OF COST-BENEFIT ANALYSIS 52–61 (2006).

45. ADLER & POSNER, NEW FOUNDATIONS OF COST-BENEFIT ANALYSIS, at 53. Accordingly, our approach differs also from that proposed by Kaplow and Shavell, who contend that welfare should trump considerations unrelated to welfare. *See* LOUIS KAPLOW & STEVEN SHAVELL, FAIRNESS VERSUS WELFARE (2002).

Chapter Eight

1. *E.g.*, JAMES GRIFFIN, WELL-BEING: ITS MEANING, MEASUREMENT AND MORAL IMPORTANCE 8 (1986); L.W. SUMNER, WELFARE, HAPPINESS, AND ETHICS 92–93 (1996); Martha C. Nussbaum, *Who Is the Happy Warrior? Philosophy Poses Questions to Psychology*, 37 J. LEGAL STUD. S82–86 (2008). *See generally* Stuart Rachels, *Is Unpleasantness Intrinsic to Unpleasant Experiences?*, 99 PHIL. STUD. 187, 207 & nn.29–31 (2000) (citing many philosophers who believe that pleasure has a common quality across experiences, but even more who believe it does not).

2. GRIFFIN, WELL-BEING, at 8.

3. *E.g.*, ROGER CRISP, REASONS AND THE GOOD 108–11 (2006); JAY SCHULKIN, BODILY SENSIBILITY: INTELLIGENT ACTION 14 (2004); Aaron Smuts, *The Feels Good Theory of Pleasure*, 155 PHILOS. STUD. 241 (2011); Elinor Mason, *The Nature of Pleasure: A Critique of Feldman*, 19 UTILITAS 379 (2007); Torbjörn Tännsjö, *Narrow Hedonism*, 8 J. HAPP. STUD. 79 (2007); Daniel Kahneman, *Objective Happiness, in* WELL-BEING: THE FOUNDATIONS OF HEDONIC PSYCHOLOGY 3, 8 (Daniel Kahneman et al. eds., 1999). Crisp cites many additional sources, as well as another text collecting yet more of them, that support this view. CRISP, REASONS AND THE GOOD, at 109 n.42.

4. *See* James A. Russell, *Core Affect and the Psychological Construction of Emotion*, 110 PSYCHOL. REV. 148–53 (2003); Kahneman, *Objective Happiness*, at 8–12.

5. Russell, *Core Affect*, at 153.

6. Nussbaum, *Happy Warrior*, at S86.

7. *See* Robert C. Mitchell & Richard T. Carson, *Evaluating the Validity of Contingent Valuation Studies, in* AMENITY RESOURCE VALUATION: INTEGRATING ECONOMICS WITH OTHER DISCIPLINES 187, 195 (George L. Peterson et al. eds., 1988) (noting that response rates for willingness-to-pay questions often do not exceed 70–80 percent, especially when the object respondents are valuing is one people are not accustomed to valuing in dollars).

8. Response rates for happiness questions on social surveys often exceed 95 percent, substantially higher than (for example) those for reported income. *See, e.g.*, Bernard M.S. van Praag & Barbara E. Baarsma, *Using Happiness Sur-*

veys to Value Intangibles, 115 ECON. J. 224, 230 (2005) (reporting a 96.1 percent response rate for a general quality-of-life question among respondents to a survey where responses to other questions were substantially lower).

9. SUMNER, WELFARE, HAPPINESS, AND ETHICS, at 93.

10. This view is clearly plausible. It is shared by hedonists like us, as well as objective-list theorists and even (to a degree) restricted-preference theorists.

11. *E.g.*, JONATHAN HAIDT, THE HAPPINESS HYPOTHESIS (2006).

12. This is even clearer when one thinks of specific examples. Suppose Jane doesn't care about her own happiness at all (i.e., she no preference for it) and cares only about things like helping the needy. But when she helps the needy, it makes her happy. We think it is very plausible to say, as our theory does, that her happiness makes her better off even though she doesn't pursue it or care about it. By contrast, suppose Jane does virtuous deeds and perfects her talents, but none of this makes her happy because she'd really enjoy lying on the beach instead. We think such an example brings out the force of the critique that a theory focusing on good acts rather than pleasure would not distinguish enough between "the best life" and "the best life for Jane," whereas the example of helping the needy does not bring out that objection with any particular force against the hedonic theory.

13. As we begin our discussion of these examples, we would like to note that utilitarianism is widely considered an important and respectable theory of ethics despite facing counterexamples that resemble the experience machine in many ways. Hedonism about well-being should be treated similarly. We also believe that the intuition conflicts generated by utilitarian ethical theory are stronger and more difficult to explain away than are the ones generated by the hedonic theory of well-being. *Cf.* Joseph Mendola, *Intuitive Hedonism*, 128 PHILOS. STUD. 441 (2006).

14. *See* Matthew D. Adler & Eric A. Posner, *Happiness Research and Cost-Benefit Analysis*, 37 J. LEGAL STUD. S253, S257–59 (2008); *see also* ADLER & POSNER, NEW FOUNDATIONS OF COST-BENEFIT ANALYSIS, at 30 (providing a related example); RICHARD B. BRANDT, A THEORY OF THE GOOD AND THE RIGHT 253 n.4 (1998).

15. This possibility also applies to the "Nepal" version of the example. Suppose someone intuits that Jack's well-being is decreased if Jill cheats on him in Nepal, either moments before or moments after Jack unrelatedly dies in the United States. What drives that intuition? One possibility is that people assume that the version of Jill who cheated must have treated Jack differently throughout their marriage than the version of Jill who remained faithful.

16. It is understandable that philosophers would be motivated to reject the sort of argument we employ here, since using examples to elicit intuitions is the stock-in-trade of ethical philosophy.

17. See Nussbaum, *Happy Warrior*, at S99–100.

18. *E.g.*, Andrew E. Clark et al., *Poverty and Well-Being: Panel Evidence from Germany*, 291 ECINE (March 2013); Eric A. Posner, *Human Welfare, Not Human Rights*, 108 COLUM. L. REV. 1758, 1785 (2008).

19. ROBERT NOZICK, ANARCHY, STATE, AND UTOPIA 42–45 (1974).

20. NOZICK, ANARCHY, STATE, AND UTOPIA, at 42.

21. NOZICK, ANARCHY, STATE, AND UTOPIA, at 43.

22. *E.g.*, CRISP, REASONS AND THE GOOD, at 117–25; Adam Kolber, *The Experiential Future of the Law*, 60 EMORY L.J. 585, 591–94 (2011); Tännsjö, *Narrow Hedonism*, at 92–95; Mendola, *Intuitive Hedonism*; Mark Bernstein, *Well-Being*, 35 AM. PHIL. QUART. 39 (1998).

23. RICHARD LAYARD, HAPPINESS: LESSONS FROM A NEW SCIENCE 115 (2005).

24. Mendola, *Intuitive Hedonism*, at 450 (internal citations omitted).

25. For example, it might be the case that positive feelings are more intense if a person has some negative feelings to contrast them with.

26. *Cf.* Nussbaum, *Happy Warrior*, at S107 ("Public policy should also focus on the mitigation of the sort of pain that is not an enrichment of the soul or a deepening of self-knowledge, and there is a lot of pain that is not conducive to anything good.").

27. *See* RICHARD LAYARD, HAPPINESS: LESSONS FROM A NEW SCIENCE 115 (2005) ("They would not trust the machine to deliver what it promised. . . . Or they might have obligations to others that they could not perform if they were inert. And so on."); CRISP, REASONS AND THE GOOD, at 118 ("[T]he question whether we as individuals would plug into such a machine . . . is likely to elicit answers influenced by contingent and differing attitudes each of us might have to risk."); SUMNER, WELFARE, HAPPINESS, AND ETHICS, at 95 ("We immediately begin to imagine the many ways in which things could go horribly wrong. How do we keep our bodies from atrophying from disuse? How do we know that the technology is foolproof? What happens if there is a power failure? . . . For the thought experiment to yield any results at all we must therefore imagine ourselves in a world quite alien to or own—and who knows what we would choose in a world like that?").

28. We thank Benjamin Callard for this point.

29. Susan Wolf, *Deconstructing Welfare: Reflections on Stephen Darwall's Welfare and Rational Care*, 18 UTILITAS 415, 425 (2006).

30. Indeed, as we (and others) noted about the experience machine, someone might well not believe that the dopamine drip would work.

31. *See* RICHARD KRAUT, WHAT IS GOOD AND WHY: THE ETHICS OF WELL-BEING 125 (2007).

32. *See* Russell, *Core Affect*, at 145.

33. KRAUT, WHAT IS GOOD AND WHY, at 125.

34. GRIFFIN, WELL-BEING, at 8; *see also* SUMNER, WELFARE, HAPPINESS, AND ETHICS, at 92–94.

35. *See* Mendola, *Intuitive Hedonism.*

36. For a discussion of self-alteration, hedonics, and law, see Sean Williams, *Self-Altering Injury,* 96 CORNELL L. REV. 535 (2011).

37. *See* STEPHEN DARWALL, WELFARE AND RATIONAL CARE (2002).

38. *E.g.,* DANIEL KAHNEMAN, THINKING, FAST AND SLOW 382–85 (2011).

39. *E.g.,* DANIEL M. HAYBRON, THE PURSUIT OF UNHAPPINESS: THE ELUSIVE PSYCHOLOGY OF WELL-BEING 61–77 (2008). We of course do not intend this paragraph as a response to Haybron, whose book lays out one of the most thorough accounts of happiness that we have encountered. Responding to even one of his points in a paragraph would be inadequate. We mean only to give the most cursory explanation of why a different, crude objection to our approach may be unwarranted.

Conclusion

1. Even if happiness were only a part of the quality of life, WBA would still be needed to assess the effect of laws on that part of life's quality.

2. We refer here to diary studies whose results correlate highly with those of beeper studies, and to smartphone studies that may costlessly collect oceans of data on true moment-by-moment affect.

Bibliography

BOOKS AND ARTICLES

Ackerman, Frank & Lisa Heinzerling, *Pricing the Priceless: Cost-Benefit Analysis of Environmental Protection*, 150 U. PA. L. REV. 1553 (2002).

ACKERMAN, FRANK & LISA HEINZERLING, PRICELESS: ON KNOWING THE PRICE OF EVERYTHING AND THE VALUE OF NOTHING (2004).

Adler, Matthew D., *Fear Assessment: Cost-Benefit Analysis and the Pricing of Fear and Anxiety*, 79 CHI.-KENT L. REV. 977 (2004).

ADLER, MATTHEW D., WELL-BEING AND FAIR DISTRIBUTION (2012).

Adler, Matthew D., Equity by the Numbers: Measuring Poverty, Inequality, and Injustice (2013) (unpublished manuscript) (on file with authors), *available at* http://ssrn.com/abstract=2263433.

Adler, Matthew D. & Eric A. Posner, *Rethinking Cost-Benefit Analysis*, 109 YALE L.J. 165 (1999).

Adler, Matthew D. & Eric A. Posner, *Implementing Cost-Benefit Analysis When Preferences Are Distorted*, 29 J. LEGAL STUD. 1105 (2000).

ADLER, MATTHEW D. & ERIC A. POSNER, NEW FOUNDATIONS OF COST-BENEFIT ANALYSIS (2006).

Adler, Matthew & Eric A. Posner, *Happiness Research and Cost-Benefit Analysis*, 37 J. LEGAL STUD. S253 (2008).

Alberini, Anna et al., *Does the'Value of a Statistical Life Vary with Age and Health Status? Evidence from the US and Canada*, 48 J. ENVTL. ECON. & MGMT. 769 (2004).

Antonak, Richard F. & Hanoch Livneh, *Psychosocial Adaption to Disability and Its Investigation Among Persons with Multiple Sclerosis*, 40 SOC. SCI. & MED. 1099 (1995).

Arneson, Richard J., *Human Flourishing Versus Desire Satisfaction, in* HUMAN FLOURISHING 113 (Ellen Frankel Paul et al. eds., 1999).

Argyle, Michael, *Causes and Correlates of Happiness, in* WELL-BEING: THE

FOUNDATIONS OF HEDONIC PSYCHOLOGY 352 (Daniel Kahneman et al. eds., 1999).

Ayton, Peter, Alice Pott & Najat Elwakili, *Affective Forecasting: Why Can't People Predict Their Emotions?*, 13 THINKING & REASONING 62 (2007).

Bagenstos, Samuel & Margo Schlanger, *Hedonic Damages, Hedonic Adaptation, and Disability*, 60 VAND. L. REV. 745 (2007).

Bargh, J.A. et al., *The Automatic Evaluation Effect*, 32 J. EXPERIMENTAL SOC. PSYCH. 104 (1996).

Baumeister, Roy F. et al., *Bad Is Stronger than Good*, 5 REV. GEN. PSYCH. 323 (2001).

Becker, Gary S., *Crime and Punishment: An Economic Approach*, 76 J. POLIT. ECON. 169 (1968).

BELZER, MICHAEL H., SWEATSHOPS ON WHEELS: WINNERS AND LOSERS IN TRUCKING DEREGULATION (2000).

Bentham, Jeremy, *Principles of Penal Law*, in 1 THE WORKS OF JEREMY BENTHAM 365 (John Bowring ed., 1843).

Bentham, Jeremy, *An Introduction to the Principles of Morals and Legislation*, in THE UTILITARIANS 5 (1961).

BENTHAM, JEREMY, AN INTRODUCTION TO THE PRINCIPLES OF MORALS AND LEGISLATION (J.H. Burns & H.L.A. Hart eds., Clarendon Press 1996) (1789).

Blanchflower, David G. & Andrew J. Oswald, *Well-Being over Time in Britain and the USA*, 88 J. PUB. ECON. 1359 (2004).

BOARDMAN, ANTHONY E., DAVID H. GREENBERG, AIDAN R. VINNING & DAVID L. WEIMER, COST-BENEFIT ANALYSIS: CONCEPTS AND PRACTICE (1996).

BOK, DEREK, THE POLITICS OF HAPPINESS: WHAT GOVERNMENT CAN LEARN FROM THE NEW RESEARCH ON WELL-BEING (2010).

Boudreaux, Paul, *An Individual Preference Approach to Suburban Racial Desegregation*, 27 FORDHAM URB. L.J. 533 (1999).

Bovbjerg, Randall R. et al., *Valuing Life and Limb in Tort: Scheduling "Pain and Suffering,"* 83 Nw. U. L. REV. 908 (1989).

Boyd, Norman F. et al., *Whose Utilities for Decision Analysis?*, 10 MED. DECISION MAKING 58 (1990).

Brandt, R.B., *Conscience (Rule) Utilitarianism and the Criminal Law*, 14 L. & PHIL. 65 (1995).

BRANDT, RICHARD B., A THEORY OF THE GOOD AND THE RIGHT (1998).

BREYER, STEPHEN, BREAKING THE VICIOUS CIRCLE: TOWARD EFFECTIVE RISK REGULATION (1993).

Brickman, Philip et al., *Lottery Winners and Accident Victims: Is Happiness Relative?*, 36 J. PERSONALITY & SOC. PSYCHOL. 917 (1978).

BROOME, JOHN, WEIGHING GOODS (1991).

Bronsteen, John, *Class Action Settlements: An Opt-In Proposal*, 2005 U. ILL. L. REV. 903.

Bronsteen, John, *Retribution's Role*, 84 IND. L. J. 1129 (2009).

Bronsteen, John, Christopher Buccafusco & Jonathan S. Masur, *Hedonic Adaptation and the Settlement of Civil Lawsuits*, 108 COLUM. L. REV. 1516 (2008).

Bronsteen, John, Christopher Buccafusco & Jonathan S. Masur, *Happiness and Punishment*, 76 U. CHI. L. REV 1037 (2009)

Bronsteen, John, Christopher Buccafusco & Jonathan S. Masur, *Retribution and the Experience of Punishment*, 98 CALIF. L. REV. 1463 (2010).

Bronsteen, John, Christopher Buccafusco & Jonathan S. Masur, *Welfare as Happiness*, 98 GEO. L.J. 1583 (2010).

Bronsteen, John, Christopher Buccafusco & Jonathan S. Masur, *Well-Being Analysis vs. Cost-Benefit Analysis*, 62 DUKE L.J. 1603 (2013)

Bronsteen, John & Owen Fiss, *The Class Action Rule*, 78 NOTRE DAME L. REV. 1419 (2003).

Bukstel, Lee H. & Peter R. Kilmann, *Psychological Effects of Imprisonment on Confined Individuals*, 88 PSYCH. BULL. 469 (1980).

Burger, Warren E., *Isn't There a Better Way?*, 68 A.B.A. J. 274 (1982).

Cacioppo, John T. & Gary G. Berntson, *Relationship Between Attitudes and Evaluative Space: A Critical Review, with Emphasis on the Separability of Positive and Negative Substrates*, 115 PSYCH. BULL. 401 (1994).

Calfee, John E. & Clifford Winston, *The Consumer Welfare Effects of Liability for Pain and Suffering: An Exploratory Analysis, in* 1 BROOKINGS PAPERS ON ECONOMIC ACTIVITY: MICROECONOMICS 142 (1993).

Carlsmith, Kevin M., Timothy D. Wilson, & Daniel T. Gilbert, *The Paradoxical Consequences of Revenge*, 95 J. PERSONALITY & SOC. PSYCH. 1316 (2008).

Carson, Richard T. & W. Michael Hanemann, *Contingent Valuation, in* 2 HANDBOOK OF ENVIRONMENTAL ECONOMICS 821 (Karl-Goran Maler and Jeffrey R. Vincent eds., 2005).

Chen, Jing et al., *Mental Health in Adults with Sudden Sensorineural Hearing Loss: An Assessment of Depressive Symptoms and Its Correlates*, 75 J. PSYCHOSOMATIC RES. 72 (2013).

Chronic Obstructive Pulmonary Disease, NAT'L CENTER FOR BIOTECHNOLOGY INFO. (May 1, 2011), http://www.ncbi.nlm.nih.gov/pubmedhealth/PMH000 1153/.

Clark, Andrew E. et al., *Lags and Leads in Life Satisfaction: A Test of the Baseline Hypothesis*, 118 ECON. J. F222 (2008).

Clark, Andrew E. et al., *Poverty and Well-Being: Panel Evidence from Germany*, 291 ECINE (March 2013).

CLEMMER, DONALD, THE PRISON COMMUNITY (1940).

Cochran, Robert F., Jr. et al., *Symposium: Client Counseling and Moral Responsibility*, 30 PEPP. L. REV. 591 (2003).

Cohen, Roger, Op-Ed., *The Happynomics of Life*, N.Y. TIMES, Mar. 13, 2011, at 12.

Colander, David, *Edgeworth's Hedonimeter and the Quest to Measure Utility*, 21 J. ECON. PERSPECTIVES 215 (2007).

Cowen, Tyler & Derek Parfit, *Against the Social Discount Rate, in* JUSTICE BETWEEN AGE GROUPS AND GENERATIONS 144 (Peter Laslett & James S. Fishkin eds., 1992).

CRISP, ROGER, REASONS AND THE GOOD (2006).

Crocker, Lawrence, *The Upper Limit of Just Punishment*, 41 EMORY L.J. 1059 (1992).

Cropper, Maureen, James K. Hammitt & Lisa A. Robinson, *Valuing Mortality Risk Reductions: Progress and Challenges*, 3 ANN. REV. RESOUR. ECON. 313 (2011).

Cross, Frank B., *Natural Resource Damage Valuation*, 42 VAND. L. REV. 269 (1989).

CSIKSZENTMIHALYI, MIHALY, FLOW: THE PSYCHOLOGY OF OPTIMAL EXPERIENCE (1991).

Cullen, Francis T., Bonnie S. Fisher & Brandon K. Applegate, *Public Opinion About Punishment and Corrections*, 27 CRIME & JUST. 1 (2000).

Darwall, Stephen, *Self-Interest and Self-Concern*, 14 SOCIAL PHIL. & POLICY 158 (1997).

DARWALL, STEPHEN, WELFARE AND RATIONAL CARE (2002).

Darwall, Stephen, *Reply to Griffin, Raz, and Wolf*, 18 UTILITAS 434 (2006).

de Quervain, Dominique J.-F. et al., *The Neural Basis of Altruistic Punishment*, 305 SCI. 1254 (2004).

DePianto, David Ennio, *Tort Damages and the (Misunderstood) Money-Happiness Connection*, 44 ARIZ. ST. L.J. 1385 (2012).

Desvousges, William H. et al., *Measuring Natural Resource Damages with Contingent Valuation: Tests of Validity and Reliability, in* CONTINGENT VALUATION: A CRITICAL ASSESSMENT 91 (Jerry A. Hausman ed., 1993).

Dhami, Mandeep K., Peter Ayton & George Loewenstein, *Adaptation to Imprisonment: Indigenous or Imported?*, 34 CRIM. JUST. & BEHAV. 1085 (2007).

Di Tella, Rafael & Robert MacCulloch, *Some Uses of Happiness Data in Economics*, 20 J. ECON. PERSP. 25 (2006).

Diamond, Peter A. & Jerry A. Hausman, *Contingent Valuation: Is Some Number Better than No Number?*, 8 J. ECON. PERSP. 45 (1994).

DICKENS, CHARLES, BLEAK HOUSE (Norman Page ed., Penguin Books 1971) (1853).

Diener, Ed & Robert Biswas-Diener, *Will Money Increase Subjective Well-Being?*, 57 SOC. INDICATORS RES. 119 (2002).

DIENER, ED & ROBERT BISWAS-DIENER, HAPPINESS: UNLOCKING THE MYSTERIES OF PSYCHOLOGICAL WEALTH (2008).

Diener, Ed & Carol Diener, *The Wealth of Nations Revisited: Income and Quality of Life*, 36 SOC. INDICATORS RES. 275 (1995).

Diener, Ed & Carol Diener, *Most People Are Happy*, 7 PSYCHOL. SCI. 181 (1996).

Diener, Ed & Richard E. Lucas, *Personality and Subjective Well-Being, in* WELL-BEING: THE FOUNDATIONS OF HEDONIC PSYCHOLOGY 213 (Daniel Kahneman et al. eds., 1999).

Diener, Ed & Eunkook M. Suh, *Measuring Subjective Well-Being to Compare Quality of Life of Cultures, in* CULTURE AND SUBJECTIVE WELL-BEING 1 (Ed Diener & Eunkook M. Suh eds., 2000).

Diener, Ed et al., *The Relationship Between Income and Subjective Well-Being: Relative or Absolute?*, 28 SOC. INDICATORS RES. 195 (1993).

Diener, Ed et al., *Beyond the Hedonic Treadmill: Revising the Adaptation Theory of Well-Being*, 61 AM. PSYCHOLOGIST 305 (2006).

DIENER, ED ET AL., WELL-BEING FOR PUBLIC POLICY (2009).

DiIulio, Jr., John J., *Two Million Prisoners Are Enough*, WALL ST. J., Mar. 12, 1999, at A14.

Dinan, T.G., *Glucocorticoids and the Genesis of Depressive Illness: A Psychobiological Model*, 164 BRIT. J. PSYCHIATRY 365 (1994).

Dolan, Paul & Richard Edlin, *Is It Really Possible to Build a Bridge Between Cost-Benefit Analysis and Cost-Effectiveness Analysis?*, 21 J. HEALTH ECON. 827 (2002).

Donaldson, Cam, Stephen Birch & Amiram Gafni, *The Distributional Problem in Economic Evaluation: Income and the Valuation of Costs and Consequences of Health Care Programmes*, 11 HEALTH ECON. 55 (2002).

Dorsey, Dale, *Three Arguments for Perfectionism*, 44 NOÛS 59 (2010).

Driesen, David M., *The Societal Cost of Environmental Regulation: Beyond Administrative Cost-Benefit Analysis*, 24 ECOLOGY L.Q. 545 (1997).

Driesen, David, *Distributing the Costs of Environmental, Health, and Safety Protection: The Feasibility Principle, Cost-Benefit Analysis, and Regulatory Reform*, 32 B.C. ENVTL. AFF. L. REV. 1 (2005).

Duff, James C., Admin. Office of the U.S. Courts, 2006 Judicial Business of the United States Courts 192 (2006), *available at* http://www.uscourts.gov/uscourts/Statistics/JudicialBusiness/2006/appendices/c5.pdf

Easterlin, Richard A., *Does Economic Growth Improve the Human Lot? Some Empirical Evidence, in* NATIONS AND HOUSEHOLDS IN ECONOMIC GROWTH 89 (Paul A. David and Melvin W. Reder eds., 1974).

Easterlin, Richard A., *Will Raising the Incomes of All Increase the Happiness of All?*, 27 J. ECON. BEHAV. & ORG. 35 (1995).

Easterlin, Richard A., *Explaining Happiness*, 100 PROCEEDINGS NATL. ACADEMY SCI. 11176 (2003).

EDELSTEIN, MICHAEL, CONTAMINATED COMMUNITIES: THE SOCIAL AND PSYCHOLOGICAL IMPACTS OF RESIDENTIAL TOXIC EXPOSURE (1988).

EDGEWORTH, F.Y., MATHEMATICAL PSYCHICS: AN ESSAY ON THE APPLICATION OF MATHEMATICS TO THE MORAL SCIENCES (London, C. Kegan Paul & Co. 1881).

Edwards, William & Christopher Hensley, *Contextualizing Sex Offender Management Legislation and Policy: Evaluating the Problem of Latent Consequences in Community Notification Laws*, 45 INTL. J. OFFENDER THERAPY & COMP. CRIMINOL. 83 (2001).

Eid, Michael & Ed Diener, *Global Judgments of Subjective Well-Being: Situational Variability and Long-Term Stability*, 65 SOC. INDICATORS RES. 245 (2004).

Emigholz, Carl, Note, *Utilitarianism, Retributivism and the White Collar–Drug Crime Sentencing Disparity: Toward a Unified Theory of Enforcement*, 58 RUTGERS L. REV. 583 (2006).

Entman, June F., *More Reasons for Abolishing Federal Rule of Civil Procedure 17(a): The Problem of the Proper Plaintiff and Insurance Subrogation*, 68 N.C. L. REV. 893 (1990).

Eom, Young Sook, *Pesticide Residue Risk and Food Safety Valuation: A Random Utility Approach*, 76 AM. J. AGRIC. ECON. 760 (1994).

ERIKSON, KAI, A NEW SPECIES OF TROUBLE: EXPLORATIONS IN DISASTER, TRAUMA AND COMMUNITY (1994).

Feinberg, Joel, *The Expressive Function of Punishment, in* DOING AND DESERVING: ESSAYS IN THE THEORY OF RESPONSIBILITY 95 (1970).

Fehr, Ernst & Simon Gächter, *Fairness and Retaliation: The Economics of Reciprocity*, 14 J. ECON. PERSPECTIVES 159 (2000).

Feldman, Fred, *Two Questions About Pleasure, in* PHILOSOPHICAL ANALYSIS 59 (D.F. Austin ed., 1988).

FELDMAN, FRED, UTILITARIANISM, HEDONISM, AND DESERT (1997).

FELDMAN, FRED, WHAT IS THIS THING CALLED HAPPINESS? (2010).

Feldman Barret, Lisa & Eliza Bliss-Moreau, *Affect as a Psychological Primitive*, 41 ADVANCES IN EXPERIMENTAL SOC. PSYCHOL. 167 (2009).

Fennell, Lee Anne & Richard H. McAdams, *Introduction* to FAIRNESS IN LAW AND ECONOMICS (Lee Anne Fennell & Richard H. McAdams eds.) (forthcoming 2013, unpublished manuscript, on file with authors).

Fiss, Owen M., *Against Settlement*, 93 YALE L.J. 1073 (1984).

FISHER, IRVING, THE THEORY OF INTEREST: AS DETERMINED BY IMPATIENCE TO SPEND INCOME AND OPPORTUNITY TO INVEST IT (1930).

FLANAGAN, OWEN, THE REALLY HARD PROBLEM: MEANING IN THE MATERIAL WORLD (2007).

Flanagan, Timothy J., *The Pains of Long-Term Imprisonment: A Comparison of British and American Perspectives*, 20 BRIT. J. CRIMINOL. 148 (1980).

FLETCHER, GEORGE, THE GRAMMAR OF THE CRIMINAL LAW (2007).

FOOT, PHILIPPA, NATURAL GOODNESS (2001).

Frank, Robert H., *The Frame of Reference as a Public Good*, 107 ECON. J. 1832 (1997).

Frank, Robert H., *Why Is Cost-Benefit Analysis So Controversial?*, 29 J. LEGAL STUD. 913 (2000)

Frank, Robert H. & Cass R. Sunstein, *Cost-Benefit Analysis and Relative Position*, 68 U. CHI. L. REV. 323 (2001).

Frase, Richard S., *Punishment Purposes*, 58 STAN. L. REV. 67 (2005).

Frederick, Shane & George Loewenstein, *Hedonic Adaptation, in* WELL-BEING: THE FOUNDATIONS OF HEDONIC PSYCHOLOGY 302 (Daniel Kahneman et al. eds., 1999).

Fry, Margery, *Bentham and English Penal Reform, in* JEREMY BENTHAM AND THE LAW 20 (George W. Keeton & Georg Schwarzenberger eds., 1948).

Funk, T. Markus, *A Mere Youthful Indiscretion? Reexamining the Policy of Expunging Juvenile Delinquency Records*, 29 MICH. J.L. REFORM 885 (1996).

Gafni, Amiram, *Economic Evaluation of Health-Care Programmes: Is CEA Better than CBA?*, 34 ENVTL. & RESOURCE ECON. 407 (2006).

Galanter, Marc, *The Vanishing Trial: An Examination of Trials and Related Matters in Federal and State Courts*, 1 J. EMPIRICAL LEGAL STUD. 459 (2004).

Gardner, Jonathan & Andrew J. Oswald, *Money and Mental Well-Being: A Longitudinal Study of Medium-Sized Lottery Wins*, 26 J. HEALTH ECON. 49 (2006).

Gerarda Brown, Jennifer, *The Role of Hope in Negotiation*, 44 UCLA L. REV. 1661 (1997).

GERT, BERNARD, MORALITY: ITS NATURE AND JUSTIFICATION (rev. ed. 2005).

Gilbert, Daniel T., Jay Meyers & Timothy D. Wilson, *Lessons from the Past: Do People Learn from Experience That Emotional Reactions Are Short-Lived?*, 27 PERSONALITY & SOC. PSYCH. BULL. 1648 (2001).

Gilbert, Daniel T. & Timothy D. Wilson, *Prospection: Experiencing the Future*, 317 SCI. 1351 (2007).

Gilbert, Daniel T. et al., *Immune Neglect: A Source of Durability Bias in Affective Forecasting*, 75 J. PERSONALITY & SOC. PSYCHOL. 619 (1998).

Gould, John P., *The Economics of Legal Conflicts*, 2 J. LEGAL STUD. 279 (1973).

Graham, John D., *Making Sense of Risk: An Agenda for Congress, in* RISKS, COSTS, AND LIVES SAVED 183 (Robert W. Hahn ed., 1996).

GRIFFIN, JAMES, WELL-BEING: ITS MEANING, MEASUREMENT AND MORAL IMPORTANCE (1986).

HAIDT, JONATHAN, THE HAPPINESS HYPOTHESIS (2006).

Hahn, Robert W., *The Cost of Antiterrorist Rhetoric*, 19 REGULATION 51 (1996).

Hahn, Robert W. & Cass R. Sunstein, *A New Executive Order for Improving Federal Regulation? Deeper and Wider Cost-Benefit Analysis*, 150 U. PA. L. REV. 1489 (2002).

Haney, Craig, *Mental Health Issues in Long-Term Solitary and "Supermax" Confinement*, 49 CRIME & DELINQUENCY 124 (2003).

Hammitt, James K., *Valuing Changes in Mortality Risk: Lives Saved Versus Life Years Saved*, 1 Rev. Envtl. . Econ. & Pol'y 228 (2007).

Hampton, Jean, *Correcting Harms Versus Righting Wrongs: The Goal of Retribution*, 39 UCLA L. Rev. 1659 (1992).

Hampton, Jean, *The Moral Education Theory of Punishment, in* Punishment: A Philosophy and Public Affairs Reader 130 (A. John Simmons et al. eds., 1995).

Hardin, Jr., Don Bradford, *Why Cost-Benefit Analysis? A Question (and Some Answers) About the Legal Academy*, 59 Ala. L. Rev. 1135 (2008).

Harrington, Winston et al., eds., Reforming Regulatory Impact Analysis (2009).

Harsanyi, John C., *Cardinal Welfare, Individualistic Ethics, and Interpersonal Comparisons of Utility*, 63 J. Pol. Econ. 309 (1955).

Harsanyi, John C., *Morality and the Theory of Rational Behavior, in* Utilitarianism and Beyond 39 (Amartya Sen & Bernard Williams eds., 1982).

Hart, H.L.A., Punishment and Responsibility (1968).

Hausman, Daniel M., *Valuing Health*, 34 Phil. & Pub. Affairs 246 (2006).

Haybron, Daniel M., The Pursuit of Unhappiness: The Elusive Psychology of Well-Being (2008).

Heinzerling, Lisa, *Environmental Law and the Present Future*, 87 Geo. L.J. 2025 (1999).

Heinzerling, Lisa, *Markets for Arsenic*, 90 Geo. L.J. 2311 (2002).

Heinzerling, Lisa, *Risking It All*, 57 Ala. L. Rev. 103 (2005).

Heyde, John M., Comment, *Is Contingent Valuation Worth the Trouble?*, 62 U. Chi. L. Rev. 331, 343 (1995)

Hirth, Richard A. et al., *Willingness to Pay for a Quality-Adjusted Life Year: In Search of a Standard*, 20 Med. Decision Making 332 (2000).

Hjertager, Norun et al., *The Association between Tinnitus and Mental Health in a General Population Sample: Results from the HUNT Study*, 69 J. Psychosomatic Res. 289 (2010).

Hooker, Brad, Ideal Code, Real World (2000).

Horowitz, John K. & Kenneth E. McConnell, *A Review of WTA/WTP Studies*, 44 J. Envtl. Econ. & Mgmt. 426 (2002).

How to Use EQ-5D, EuroQuol Group, http://www.euroqol.org/about-eq-5d/how-to-use-eq-5d.html (last visited Jan. 20, 2013).

Huebner, Beth M., *The Effect of Incarceration on Marriage and Work over the Life Course*, 22 Just. Q. 281 (2005).

Hursthouse, Rosalind, On Virtue Ethics (1999).

Husak, Douglas N., *Retribution in Criminal Theory*, 37 San Diego L. Rev. 959 (2000).

Irwin, John, The Felon (1987).

Issacharoff, Samuel & George Loewenstein, *Second Thoughts About Summary Judgment*, 100 YALE L.J. 73 (1990).

Ito, Tiffany A. & John T. Cacioppo, *The Psychophysiology of Utility Appraisals, in* WELL-BEING: THE FOUNDATIONS OF HEDONIC PSYCHOLOGY 470 (Daniel Kahneman et al. eds., 1999).

JOHANSSON, PER-OLOV, AN INTRODUCTION TO MODERN WELFARE ECONOMICS (1991).

Johnson, David R. & Jian Wu, *An Empirical Test of Crisis, Social Selection, and Role Explanations of the Relationship Between Marital Disruption and Psychological Distress: A Pooled Time-Series Analysis of Four-Wave Panel Data,* 64 J. MARRIAGE & FAM. 211 (2002).

JOHNSTON, VICTOR S., WHY WE FEEL: THE SCIENCE OF HUMAN EMOTIONS (1999).

Jones, Tonisha R. & Travis C. Pratt, *The Prevalence of Sexual Violence in Prison: The State of the Knowledge Base and Implications for Evidence-Based Correctional Policy Making,* 52 INTL. J. OFFENDER THERAPY & COMP. CRIMINOL. 280 (2008).

Jones-Lee, M.W., M. Hammerton & P.R. Philips, *The Value of Safety: Results of a National Sample Survey,* 95 ECON. J. 49 (1985).

Jones-Lee, Michael W., Graham Loomes & P.R. Philips, *Valuing the Prevention of Non-Fatal Road Injuries: Contingent Valuation vs. Standard Gambles,* 47 OXFORD ECON. PAPERS 676 (1995).

Kagan, Shelly, *The Limits of Well-Being,* 9 SOC. PHIL. & POLICY 169 (1992).

Kahan, Dan M., *What Do Alternative Sanctions Mean?,* 63 U. CHI. L. REV. 591 (1996).

Kahan, Dan M., *The Secret Ambition of Deterrence,* 113 HARV. L. REV. 413 (1999).

Kahneman, Daniel, *Objective Happiness, in* WELL-BEING: THE FOUNDATIONS OF HEDONIC PSYCHOLOGY 3 (Daniel Kahneman et al. eds., 1999).

Kahneman, Daniel, *Experienced Utility and Objective Happiness: A Moment-Based Approach, in* CHOICES, VALUES, AND FRAMES 673 (Daniel Kahneman & Amos Tversky eds., 2000).

Kahneman, Daniel, *A Different Approach to Health State Valuation,* 12 VALUE IN HEALTH S16 (2009).

KAHNEMAN, DANIEL, THINKING, FAST AND SLOW (2011).

Kahneman, Daniel & Angus Deaton, *High Income Improves Evaluation of Life but Not Emotional Well-Being,* 107 PROC. NAT'L ACAD. SCI. 16489 (2010).

Kahneman, Daniel, Ed Diener & Norbert Schwarz, *Preface* to WELL-BEING: THE FOUNDATIONS OF HEDONIC PSYCHOLOGY ix (Daniel Kahneman, Ed Diener & Norbert Schwarz eds., 1999).

Kahneman, Daniel & Jack Knetsch, *Valuing Public Goods: The Purchase of Moral Satisfaction,* 22 J. ENVTL. ECON. & MGMT. 57 (1992).

Kahneman, Daniel & Robert Sugden, *Experienced Utility as a Standard of Policy Evaluation*, 32 ENVTL. & RESOURCE ECON. 161 (2005).

Kahneman, Daniel & Amos Tversky, *Prospect Theory: An Analysis of Decision Under Risk*, 47 ECONOMETRICA 263 (1979).

Kahneman, Daniel & Amos Tversky, *Choices, Values, and Frames*, 39 AM. PSYCHOLOGIST 341 (1984).

Kahneman, Daniel et al., *Stated Willingness to Pay for Public Goods: A Psychological Perspective*, 4 PSYCHOL. SCI. 310 (1993).

Kahneman, Daniel et al., *Back to Bentham: Explorations of Experienced Utility*, 112 Q.J. ECON. 375 (1997).

Kahneman, Daniel et al., *A Survey Method for Characterizing Daily Life Experience: The Day Reconstruction Method*, 306 SCIENCE 1776 (2004).

Kaplow, Louis & Steven Shavell, *Why the Legal System Is Less Efficient than the Income Tax at Redistributing Income*, 23 J. LEGAL STUD. 667 (1994).

KAPLOW, LOUIS & STEVEN SHAVELL, FAIRNESS VERSUS WELFARE (2002).

Kauppinen, Antti, *Working Hard and Kicking Back: The Case for Diachronic Perfectionism*, 3 J. ETHICS & SOC. PHIL. 1 (2009).

Keller, Simon, *Welfare as Success*, 43 NoÛs 656 (2009).

Kelman, Steven, *Cost-Benefit Analysis: An Ethical Critique*, 5 REGULATION 33 (1981).

Kennedy, Duncan, *Cost-Benefit Analysis of Entitlement Problems: A Critique*, 33 STAN. L. REV. 387 (1981).

KENNY, ANTHONY & CHARLES KENNY, LIFE, LIBERTY, AND THE PURSUIT OF UTILITY: HAPPINESS IN PHILOSOPHICAL AND ECONOMIC THOUGHT (2006).

Kermer, Deborah A. et al., *Loss Aversion Is an Affective Forecasting Error*, 17 PSYCH. SCI. 649 (2006).

Killingsworth, Matthew A. & Daniel T. Gilbert, *A Wandering Mind Is an Unhappy Mind*, 330 SCIENCE 932 (2010).

Kling, Jeffrey R., *Incarceration Length, Employment, and Earnings*, 96 AM. ECON. REV. 863 (2006).

Klose, Thomas, *A Utility-Theoretic Model for QALYs and Willingness to Pay*, 12 HEALTH ECON. 17 (2003).

Knabe, Andreas et al., *Dissatisfied with Life but Having a Good Day: Time-Use and Well-Being of the Unemployed*, 120 ECON. J. 867 (2010).

Kniesner, Thomas, W. Kip Viscusi & James P. Ziliak, *Policy Relevant Heterogeneity in the Value of Statistical Life: New Evidence from Panel Data Quantile Regressions*, 40 J. RISK & UNCERTAINTY 14 (2010).

Koivumaa-Honkanen, Heli-Tuulie et al., *Self-Reported Happiness in Life and Suicide in Ensuing 20 Years*, 38 SOC. PSYCHIATRY & PSYCHIATRIC EPIDEMIOLOGY 244 (2003).

Kolber, Adam J., *The Comparative Nature of Punishment*, 89 B.U. L. REV. 1565 (2009).

Kolber, Adam J., *The Subjective Experience of Punishment*, 109 COLUM. L. REV. 182 (2009).

Kolber, Adam J., *The Experiential Future of the Law*, 60 EMORY L.J. 585 (2011).

Kornhauser, Marjorie E., *Equality, Liberty, and a Fair Income Tax*, 23 FORDHAM URB. L.J. 607 (1996).

Korobkin, Russell B., *Aspirations and Settlement*, 88 CORNELL L. REV. 1 (2002–2003).

Korobkin, Russell B. & Chris Guthrie, *Psychological Barriers to Litigation Settlement: An Experimental Approach*, 93 MICH. L. REV. 107 (1994).

Korobkin, Russell B. & Chris Guthrie, *Psychology, Economics, and Settlement: A New Look at the Role of the Lawyer*, 76 TEX. L. REV. 77 (1997).

KRAUT, RICHARD, WHAT IS GOOD AND WHY: THE ETHICS OF WELL-BEING (2007).

Krueger, Alan B. et al., *National Time Accounting: The Currency of Life*, *in* MEASURING THE SUBJECTIVE WELL-BEING OF NATIONS 30 (Alan B. Krueger ed., 2009).

Kuran, Timur & Cass Sunstein, *Availability Cascades and Risk Regulation*, 51 STAN. L. REV. 683 (1999).

Kysar, Douglas A., *Climate Change, Cultural Transformation, and Comprehensive Rationality*, 31 B.C. ENVTL. AFF. L. REV. 555 (2004).

Landes, William M., *An Economic Analysis of the Courts*, 14 J.L. & ECON. 61 (1971).

Langguth, Berthold et al., *Tinnitus: Causes and Clinical Management*, 12 LANCET NEUROLOGY 920 (2013).

LAYARD, RICHARD, HAPPINESS: LESSONS FROM A NEW SCIENCE (2005).

Lederman, Leandra & Warren B. Hrung, *Do Attorneys Do Their Clients Justice? An Empirical Study of Lawyers' Effects on Tax Court Litigation Outcomes*, 41 WAKE FOREST L. REV. 1235 (2006).

LEITER, BRIAN, NATURALIZING JURISPRUDENCE: ESSAYS ON AMERICAN LEGAL REALISM AND NATURALISM IN LEGAL PHILOSOPHY (2007).

Lepper, Heidi, *Use of Other-Reports to Validate Subjective Well-Being Measures*, 44 SOC. INDICATORS RES. 367 (1998).

Letter from O.W. Holmes to Harold J. Laski (Dec. 17, 1925), *in* 1 HOLMES-LASKI LETTERS: THE CORRESPONDENCE OF MR. JUSTICE HOLMES AND HAROLD J. LASKI, 1916–1935 (Mark DeWolfe Howe ed., 1953).

Levitt, Steven D., *The Effect of Prison Population Size on Crime Rates: Evidence from Prison Overcrowding Litigation*, 111 Q.J. ECON. 319 (1996).

Lin, C.T. Jordan & J. Walter Milon, *Contingent Valuation of Health Risk Reductions for Shellfish Products*, *in* VALUING FOOD SAFETY AND NUTRITION 83 (J.A. Caswell ed., 1995).

Loehman, Edna T. et al., *Willingness to Pay for Gains and Losses in Visibility and Health*, 70 LAND ECON. 476 (1994).

Loewenstein, George, Cass R. Sunstein & Russell Golman, *Disclosure: Psychology Changes Everything*, ANNUAL REVIEW OF ECONOMICS (forthcoming).

Loewenstein, George et al., *Self-Serving Assessments of Fairness and Pretrial Bargaining*, 22 J. LEGAL STUD. 135 (1992).

Loomis, John B. & Douglas S. White, *Economic Benefits of Rare and Endangered Species: Summary and Meta-Analysis*, 18 ECOLOGICAL ECON. 197 (1996).

Lopoo, Leonard M. & Bruce Western, *Incarceration and the Formation and Stability of Marital Unions*, 67 J. MARRIAGE & FAM. 721 (2005).

Lucas, Richard E., *Time Does Not Heal All Wounds: A Longitudinal Study of Reaction and Adaptation to Divorce*, 16 PSYCHOL. SCI. 945 (2005).

Lucas, Richard E., *Adaptation and the Set-Point Model of Subjective Well-Being: Does Happiness Change After Major Life Events?*, 16 CURRENT DIRECTIONS IN PSYCHOL. SCI. 75 (2007).

Lucas, Richard E., *Long-Term Disability Is Associated with Lasting Changes in Subjective Well-Being: Evidence from Two Nationally Representative Longitudinal Studies*, 92 J. PERSONALITY & SOC. PSYCHOL. 717 (2007).

Lucas, Richard E., *Personality and Subjective Well-Being, in* THE SCIENCE OF SUBJECTIVE WELL-BEING 171 (Michael Eid and Randy J. Larsen eds., 2007).

Lucas, Richard E. et al., *Reexamining Adaptation and the Set Point Model of Happiness: Reactions to Changes in Marital Status*, 84 J. PERSONALITY & SOC. PSYCHOL. 527 (2003).

Lucas, Richard E. et al., *Unemployment Alters the Set Point for Life Satisfaction*, 15 PSYCHOL. SCI. 8, 12 (2004).

Lundqvist, C. et al., *Spinal Cord Injuries: Clinical, Functional, and Emotional Status*, 16 SPINE 78 (1991).

Lykken, David & Auke Tellegen, *Happiness Is a Stochastic Phenomenon*, 7 PSYCHOL. SCI. 186 (1996).

MacKenzie, Doris Layton & Lynne Goodstein, *Long-Term Incarceration Impacts and Characteristics of Long-Term Offenders: An Empirical Analysis*, 12 CRIM. JUST. & BEHAV. 395 (1985).

MacKerron, George & Susana Mourato, *Happiness Is Greater in Natural Environments*, 23 GLOBAL ENVTL. CHANGE 992 (2013).

Malani, Anup, *Valuing Laws as Local Amenities*, 121 HARV. L. REV. 1273 (2008).

Markel, Dan, *Are Shaming Punishments Beautifully Retributive? Retributivism and the Implications for the Alternative Sanctions Debate*, 54 VAND. L. REV. 2157 (2001).

Markel, Dan & Chad Flanders, *Bentham on Stilts: The Bare Relevance of Subjectivity to Retributive Justice*, 98 CALIF. L. REV. 907 (2010).

Martinson, Robert, *What Works?—Questions and Answers About Prison Reform*, 36 PUB. INTEREST 22 (1974).

Mason, Elinor, *The Nature of Pleasure: A Critique of Feldman*, 19 UTILITAS 379 (2007).

Massoglia, Michael, *Incarceration as Exposure: The Prison, Infectious Disease, and Other Stress-Related Illnesses*, 49 J. HEALTH & SOC. BEHAV. 56 (2008)

Massoglia, Michael, *Incarceration, Health, and Racial Disparities in Health*, 42 L. & SOCY. REV. 275 (2008).

Masur, Jonathan S. & Eric A. Posner, *Against Feasibility Analysis*, 77 U. CHI. L. REV. 657 (2010).

Masur, Jonathan S. & Eric A. Posner, *Climate Regulation and the Limits of Cost-Benefit Analysis*, 99 CAL. L. REV. 1557 (2011).

Masur, Jonathan S. & Eric A. Posner, *Regulation, Unemployment, and Cost-Benefit Analysis*, 98 VA. L. REV. 579 (2012).

McCaffery, Edward J., *Bifurcation Blues: The Perils of Leaving Redistribution Aside* (working paper 2013), *available at* http://www.law.nyu.edu/ecm_dlv4/groups/public/@nyu_law_website__academics__colloquia__tax_policy/documents/documents/ecm_pro_074659.pdf

MCDAVID, JAMES C. & LAURA R.L. HAWTHORN, PROGRAM EVALUATION & PERFORMANCE MEASUREMENT: AN INTRODUCTION TO PRACTICE (2006).

McGarity, Thomas O., *Media-Quality, Technology, and Cost-Benefit Balancing Strategies for Health and Environmental Regulation*, 46 LAW & CONTEMP. PROBS. 159 (1983).

McGarity, Thomas O., *A Cost-Benefit State*, 50 ADMIN. L. REV. 7 (1998).

Mendola, Joseph, *Intuitive Hedonism*, 128 PHILOS. STUD. 441 (2006).

Messick, Samuel, *Validity of Psychological Assessment: Validation of Inferences from Persons' Responses and Performances as Scientific Inquiry into Score Meaning*, 50 AM. PSYCHOLOGIST 741 (1995).

MILLER, WILLIAM IAN, EYE FOR AN EYE (2005).

MISHAN, E.J., COST-BENEFIT ANALYSIS (1976).

Mitchell, Robert C. & Richard T. Carson, *Evaluating the Validity of Contingent Valuation Studies, in* AMENITY RESOURCE VALUATION: INTEGRATING ECONOMICS WITH OTHER DISCIPLINES 187 (George L. Peterson et al. eds., 1988).

Moller, Dan, *Wealth, Disability, and Happiness*, 39 PHIL. & PUB. AFF. 177 (2011).

MOORE, MICHAEL, PLACING BLAME: A GENERAL THEORY OF THE CRIMINAL LAW (1997).

MORGENSTERN, RICHARD D., ECONOMIC ANALYSES AT EPA: ASSESSING REGULATORY IMPACT (1997).

Morris, Herbert, *Persons and Punishment*, 52 THE MONIST 475 (1968).

MORRIS, NORVAL, THE FUTURE OF IMPRISONMENT (1974).

MORRIS, NORVAL, MADNESS AND THE CRIMINAL LAW (1982).

MORRIS, NORVAL & MICHAEL TONRY, BETWEEN PRISON AND PROBATION: INTERMEDIATE PUNISHMENTS IN A RATIONAL SENTENCING SYSTEM (1990).

Morriss, Andrew P. & Roger E. Meiners, *Borders and the Environment*, 39
   ENVTL. L. 141 (2009).
Mrozek, Janusz R. & Laura O. Taylor, *What Determines the Value of Life? A
   Meta-Analysis*, 21 J. POL'Y ANALYSIS & MGMT. 253 (2002).
Myers, Laura L., *Same-Sex Couples Wed in Washington State for First Time*,
   REUTERS, Dec. 9, 2012, *available at* http://www.reuters.com/article/2012/12/
   09/us-usa-gaymarriage-idUSBRE8B801S20121209.
NADEAU, ROBERT L., THE WEALTH OF NATURE (2003).
Nord, Erik, Norman Daniels & Mark Kamlet, *QALYs: Some Challenges*, 12
   VALUE IN HEALTH S10 (2009).
Nordhaus, William, *Measuring Real Income with Leisure and Household
   Production*, *in* MEASURING THE SUBJECTIVE WELL-BEING OF NATIONS: NA-
   TIONAL ACCOUNTS OF TIME USE AND WELL-BEING 125 (Alan B. Krueger ed.,
   2009).
NOZICK, ROBERT, ANARCHY, STATE, AND UTOPIA (1974).
Nussbaum, Martha, *Non-relative Virtues: An Aristotelian Approach*, *in* THE
   QUALITY OF LIFE 242 (Martha C. Nussbaum & Amartya Sen eds., 1993).
Nussbaum, Martha C., *Capabilities as Fundamental Entitlements: Sen and So-
   cial Justice*, 9 FEMINIST ECON. 33 (2003).
Nussbaum Martha C., *Who Is the Happy Warrior? Philosophy Poses Questions
   to Psychology*, 37 J. LEGAL STUD. S81 (2008).
OLSON, MANCUR, THE LOGIC OF COLLECTIVE ACTION: PUBLIC GOODS AND THE
   THEORY OF GROUPS (1965).
Oswald, Andrew J. & Nattavudh Powdthavee, *Death, Happiness, and the Calcu-
   lation of Compensatory Damages*, 37 J. LEGAL STUD. S217 (2008).
Oswald, Andrew J. & Nattavudh Powdthavee, *Does Happiness Adapt? A Longi-
   tudinal Study of Disability with Implications for Economists and Judges*, 92
   J. PUB. ECON. 1061 (2008).
Overvold, Mark Carl, *Self-Interest and the Concept of Self-Sacrifice*, 10 CANA-
   DIAN J. OF PHIL. 105 (1980).
PAGER, DEVAH, MARKED: RACE, CRIME, AND FINDING WORK IN AN ERA OF MASS
   INCARCERATION (2007).
Painter, Richard W., *Litigating on a Contingency: A Monopoly of Champions or
   a Market for Champerty?*, 71 CHI.-KENT L. REV. 625 (1995).
PARFIT, DEREK, REASONS AND PERSONS (1984).
Patterson, David R. et al., *Psychological Effects of Severe Burn Injuries*, 113
   PSYCHOL. BULL. 362 (1993).
Pavot, William & Ed Diener, *Review of the Satisfaction with Life Scale*, 5 PSY-
   CHOL. ASSESSMENT 164 (1993).
Peterson, Christopher, *Personal Control and Well-Being*, *in* WELL-BEING: THE
   FOUNDATIONS OF HEDONIC PSYCHOLOGY 288 (Daniel Kahneman et al. eds.,
   1999).

Pildes, Richard H. & Cass R. Sunstein, *Reinventing the Regulatory State*, 62 U. CHI. L. REV. 1 (1995).

Posner, Eric A., *Human Welfare, Not Human Rights*, 108 COLUM. L. REV. 1758 (2008).

Posner, Richard A., *An Economic Approach to Legal Procedure and Judicial Administration*, 2 J. LEGAL STUD. 399 (1973).

Posner, Richard A., *Utilitarianism, Economics, and Legal Theory*, 8 J. LEGAL STUD. 103 (1979).

Posner, Richard A., *The Ethical and Political Basis of the Efficiency Norm in Common Law Adjudication*, 8 HOFSTRA L. REV. 487 (1980).

Powdthavee, Nattavudh & Bernard van den Berg, *Putting Different Price Tags on the Same Health Condition: Re-evaluating the Well-Being Valuation Approach*, 30 J. HEALTH ECON. 1032 (2011).

Prentky, Robert A., *Community Notification and Constructive Risk Reduction*, 11 J. INTERPERSONAL VIOLENCE 295 (1996).

Prescott, J.J. & Jonah E. Rockoff, *Do Sex Offender Registration and Notification Laws Affect Criminal Behavior?*, 54 J.L. & ECON. 161 (2011).

Presser, Lois & Elaine Gunnison, *Strange Bedfellows: Is Sex Offender Notification a Form of Community Justice?*, 45 CRIME & DELINQUENCY 299 (1999).

Priest, George L. & Benjamin Klein, *The Selection of Disputes for Litigation*, 13 J. LEGAL STUD. 1 (1984).

Rachels, Stuart, *Is Unpleasantness Intrinsic to Unpleasant Experiences?*, 99 PHIL. STUD. 187 (2000).

Rachlinski, Jeffrey J., *Gains, Losses, and the Psychology of Litigation*, 70 S. CAL. L. REV. 113 (1996).

RAWLS, JOHN, A THEORY OF JUSTICE (1971).

Raz, Joseph, *Darwall on Rational Care*, 18 UTILITAS 400 (2006).

Redelmeier, Donald A. & Daniel Kahneman, *Patients' Memories of Painful Medical Treatments: Real-Time and Retrospective Evaluations of Two Minimally Invasive Procedures*, 116 PAIN 3 (1996).

Revesz, Richard L., *Environmental Regulation, Cost-Benefit Analysis, and the Discounting of Human Lives*, 99 COLUM. L. REV. 941 (1999).

REVESZ, RICHARD L. & MICHAEL A. LIVERMORE, RETAKING RATIONALITY: HOW COST-BENEFIT ANALYSIS CAN BETTER PROTECT THE ENVIRONMENT AND OUR HEALTH (2008).

Riis, Jason et al., *Ignorance of Hedonic Adaptation to Hemodialysis: A Study Using Ecological Momentary Assessment*, 134 J. EXPERIMENTAL PSYCHOL. 3 (2005).

Robinson, Paul H. & John M. Darley, *Does Criminal Law Deter? A Behavioral Science Investigation*, 24 OXFORD J. LEGAL STUD. 173 (2004).

Rosati, Connie S., *Persons, Perspectives, and Full Information Accounts of the Good*, 105 ETHICS 296 (1995).

Russell, James A., *Core Affect and the Psychological Construction of Emotion*, 110 PSYCHOL. REV. 145 (2003).

Sackett, David L. & George W. Torrance, *The Utility of Different Health States as Perceived by the General Public*, 31 J. CHRONIC DISEASES 697 (1978).

Samuel, Henry, *Nicolas Sarkozy Wants to Measure Economic Success in 'Happiness'*, THE TELEGRAPH, Sept. 14, 2009, http://www.telegraph.co.uk/news/worldnews/europe/france/6189530/Nicolas-Sarkozy-wants-to-measure-economic-success-in-happiness.html.

Samuelson, Paul A., *An Exact Consumption-Loan Model of Interest With or Without the Social Contrivance of Money*, 66 J. POL. ECON. 467 (1958).

Sandvik, E. et al., *Subjective Well-Being: The Convergence and Stability of Self-Report and Non-Self-Report Measures*, 61 J. PERSONALITY 317 (1993)

Sarat, Austin, *Alternatives in Dispute Processing: Litigation in a Small Claims Court*, 10 LAW & SOC'Y REV. 339 (1976).

SCANLON, T.M., WHAT WE OWE TO EACH OTHER (1998).

Schimmack, Ulrich, *The Structure of Subjective Well-Being, in* THE SCIENCE OF SUBJECTIVE WELL-BEING 115 (Michael Eid & Randy J. Larsen eds., 2007).

Schkade, David A. & Daniel Kahneman, *Does Living in California Make People Happy? A Focusing Illusion in Judgments of Life Satisfaction*, 9 PSYCHOL. SCI. 340 (1998).

Schnittker, Jason & Andrea John, *Enduring Stigma: The Long-Term Effects of Incarceration on Health*, 48 J. HEALTH & SOC. BEHAV. 115 (2007).

SCHULKIN, JAY, BODILY SENSIBILITY: INTELLIGENT ACTION (2004).

Scott, Robert E. & George G. Triantis, *Anticipating Litigation in Contract Design*, 115 YALE L.J. 814 (2006).

Seidenfeld, Mark, *A Civic Republican Justification for the Bureaucratic State*, 105 HARV. L. REV. 1511 (1992).

Seidman, Louis Michael, *Soldiers, Martyrs, and Criminals: Utilitarian Theory and the Problem of Crime Control*, 94 YALE L.J. 315 (1984).

Sen, Amartya, *Capability and Well-Being, in* THE QUALITY OF LIFE 30 (Martha C. Nussbaum & Amartya Sen eds., 1993).

Sen, Amartya, *The Discipline of Cost-Benefit Analysis*, 29 J. LEGAL STUD. 931 (2000).

Share of GDP for Bottom 99th, 95th, and 90th, VISUALIZING ECONOMICS (Oct. 17, 2006), http://visualizingeconomics.com/blog/2006/10/17/share-of-gdp-99th-95th-90th.

Sharkey, Catherine M., *Unintended Consequences of Medical Malpractice Damages Caps*, 80 N.Y.U. L. REV. 391 (2005).

SIDGWICK, HENRY, THE METHODS OF ETHICS (7th ed., Hackett 1981) (1874).

Silver, Charles, *Class Actions—Representative Proceedings, in* 5 ENCYCLOPEDIA OF LAW AND ECONOMICS 194 (B. Bouckaert & G. De Geest eds., 2000).

Simons, Kenneth W., *Retributivists Need Not and Should Not Endorse the Subjectivist Account of Punishment*, 109 COLUM. L. REV. SIDEBAR 1 (2009), *available at* http://www.columbialawreview.org/wp-content/uploads/2009/03/1_Simons.pdf.

Sinden, Amy, *Cass Sunstein's Cost-Benefit Lite: Economics for Liberals*, 29 COLUM. J. ENVTL. L. 191 (2004).

Sinden, Amy, *In Defense of Absolutes: Combating the Politics of Power in Environmental Law*, 90 IOWA L. REV. 1405 (2005).

SINGER, PETER, PRACTICAL ETHICS (2d ed. 1993).

SLOAN, FRANK A. ET AL., SUING FOR MEDICAL MALPRACTICE (1993).

Slovic, Paul, *The Perception of Risk*, 236 SCIENCE 280 (1987).

Smart, J.J.C., *Outline of a System of Utilitarian Ethics, in* UTILITARIANISM: FOR AND AGAINST 3 (J.J.C. Smart & Bernard Williams eds., 1973).

Smith, Craig A. & Kenneth A. Wallston, *Adaptation in Patients with Chronic Rheumatoid Arthritis: Application of a General Model*, 11 HEALTH PSYCHOL. 151 (1992).

Smith, Dylan M. et al., *Misremembering Colostomies? Former Patients Give Lower Utility Ratings than Do Current Patients*, 25 HEALTH PSYCHOL. 688 (2006).

Smith, V. Kerry & William H. Desvousges, *An Empirical Analysis of the Economic Value of Risk Changes*, 95 J. POL. ECON. 89 (1987).

Smith, V. Kerry, Mary F. Evans, Hyun Kim & Donald H. Taylor, Jr., *Do the Near-Elderly Value Mortality Risks Differently?*, 86 REV. ECON. & STATS. 423 (2004).

Smuts, Aaron, *The Feels Good Theory of Pleasure*, 155 PHILOS. STUD. 241 (2011).

Sobel, David, *Full Information Accounts of Well-Being*, 104 ETHICS 784 (1994).

Solum, Lawrence B., *The Virtues and Vices of a Judge: An Aristotelian Guide to Judicial Selection*, 61 S. CAL. L. REV. 1735 (1988).

Sprigge, T.L.S., *The Greatest Happiness Principle*, 3 UTILITAS 37 (1991).

Stevenson, Betsey & Justin Wolfers, *Bargaining in the Shadow of the Law: Divorce Laws and Family Distress*, 121 Q.J. ECON. 267 (2006).

Stevenson, Betsey & Justin Wolfers, *Economic Growth and Happiness: Reassessing the Easterlin Paradox, in* BROOKINGS PAPERS ON ECONOMIC ACTIVITY 67 (2008).

Stevenson, Betsey & Justin Wolfers, *Economic Growth and Subjective Well-Being: Reassessing the Easterlin Paradox, in* BROOKINGS PAPERS ON ECONOMIC ACTIVITY (2008).

Stevenson, Betsey & Justin Wolfers, *Subjective Well-Being and Income: Is There Any Evidence of Satiation?*, 103 AM. ECON. REV. PAPERS & PROCEEDINGS 598 (2013).

STIGLITZ, JOSEPH E., AMARTYA SEN & JEAN-PAUL FITOUSSI, REPORT BY THE COMMISSION ON THE MEASUREMENT OF ECONOMIC PERFORMANCE AND SOCIAL PROGRESS (2009).

Strahilevitz, Lior Jacob, *"How's My Driving?" For Everyone (and Everything?)*, 81 N.Y.U. L. REV. 1699 (2006).

STREINER, DAVID L. & GEOFFREY R. NORMAN, HEALTH MEASUREMENT SCALES: A PRACTICAL GUIDE TO THEIR DEVELOPMENT AND USE (4th ed. 2008).

Sullivan, Dermot, *Employee Violence, Negligent Hiring, and Criminal Records Checks: New York's Need to Reevaluate Its Priorities to Promote Public Safety*, 72 ST. JOHN'S L. REV. 581 (1998).

SUMNER, L.W., WELFARE, HAPPINESS, AND ETHICS (1996).

Sunstein, Cass R., *Cognition and Cost-Benefit Analysis*, 29 J. LEGAL STUD. 1059 (2000).

Sunstein, Cass R., *The Arithmetic of Arsenic*, 90 GEO. L. REV. 2255 (2002).

Sunstein, Cass R., *Probability Neglect: Emotions, Worst Cases, and Law*, 112 YALE L.J. 61 (2002).

Sunstein, Cass R., *Lives, Life-Years, and Willingness to Pay*, 104 COLUM. L. REV. 205 (2004).

Sunstein, Cass R., *Willingness to Pay vs. Welfare*, 1 HARV. L. & POL'Y REV. 303 (2007).

Sunstein, Cass R., *Illusory Losses*, 37 J. LEGAL STUD. S157 (2008).

Sunstein, Cass R. & Arden Rowell, *On Discounting Regulatory Benefits: Risk, Money, and Intergenerational Equity*, 74 U. CHI. L. REV. 171 (2007).

SYKES, GRESHAM M., THE SOCIETY OF CAPTIVES: A STUDY OF A MAXIMUM SECURITY PRISON (1958).

Tännsjö, Torbjörn, *Narrow Hedonism*, 8 J. HAPP. STUD. 79 (2007).

THALER, RICHARD & CASS SUNSTEIN, NUDGE (2006).

Thompson, Anthony C., *Navigating the Hidden Obstacles to Ex-offender Reentry*, 45 B.C. L. REV. 255 (2004).

Tversky, Amos & Daniel Kahneman, *The Framing of Decisions and the Psychology of Choice*, 211 SCIENCE 453 (1981).

Tyc, Vida L., *Psychosocial Adaptation of Children and Adolescents with Limb Deficiencies: A Review*, 12 CLINICAL PSYCHOL. REV. 275 (1992) (collecting studies).

Ubel, Peter A. et al., *Disability and Sunshine: Can Hedonic Predictions Be Improved by Drawing Attention to Focusing Illusions or Emotional Adaptation?*, 11 J. EXPERIMENTAL PSYCHOL.: APPLIED 111 (2005).

Ubel, Peter A. et al., *Do Nonpatients Underestimate the Quality of Life Associated with Chronic Health Conditions Because of a Focusing Illusion?*, 21 MED. DECISION MAKING 190 (2001).

Ubel, Peter A. et al., *Misimagining the Unimaginable: The Disability Paradox and Health Care Decision Making*, 24 HEALTH PSYCHOL. (SUPPL.) S57 (2005).

van Praag, Bernard M.S. & Barbara E. Baarsma, *Using Happiness Surveys to Value Intangibles*, 115 ECON. J. 224 (2005).

Velleman, J. David, *Well-Being and Time, in* THE POSSIBILITY OF PRACTICAL REASON 56 (2000).

Vidmar, Neil et al., *Jury Awards for Medical Malpractice and Post-Verdict Adjustments of Those Awards*, 48 DEPAUL L. REV. 265 (1998).

VISCUSI, W. KIP, REFORMING PRODUCTS LIABILITY (1991).

VISCUSI, W. KIP, RATIONAL RISK POLICY (1998).

Viscusi, W. Kip, *The Value of Life: Estimates with Risks by Occupation and Industry*, 42 J. ECON. INQUIRY 29 (2004).

Viscusi, W. Kip, *Rational Discounting for Regulatory Analysis*, 74 U. CHI. L. REV. 209 (2007).

Viscusi, W. Kip, *How to Value a Life*, 32 J. ECON. & FIN. 311 (2008).

Viscusi, W. Kip, *The Heterogeneity of the Value of Statistical Life: Introduction and Overview*, 40 J. RISK & UNCERTAINTY 1 (2010).

Viscusi, W. Kip & Joseph E. Aldy, *The Value of a Statistical Life: A Critical Review of Market Estimates Throughout the World*, 27 J. RISK & UNCERTAINTY 5 (2003).

Vitarelli, Anthony, Note, *Happiness Metrics in Federal Rulemaking*, 27 YALE J. ON REG. 115 (2010).

Volokh, Alexander, *Rationality or Rationalism? The Positive and Normative Flaws of Cost-Benefit Analysis*, 48 HOUS. L. REV. 79 (2011).

von Hirsch, Andrew, *Censure and Proportionality, in* A READER ON PUNISHMENT 128 (R.A. Duff & David Garland eds., 1994).

Weinstein, Milton C., George Torrance & Alistair McGuire, *QALYs: The Basics*, 12 VALUE HEALTH S5 (2009).

Weinstein, Neil D., *Individual Differences in Reaction to Noise: A Longitudinal Study in a College Dormitory*, 63 J. APPLIED PSYCHOL. 458 (1978).

Weinstein, Neil D., *Community Noise Problems: Evidence Against Adaptation*, 2 J. ENVTL. PSYCH. 87 (1982).

Weinstein, Neil D., *Optimistic Biases About Personal Risks*, 245 SCIENCE 1232 (1989).

Weisbach, David, *Toward a New Approach to Disability Law*, 1 U. CHI. LEGAL F. 47 (2009).

Weisbach, David & Cass R. Sunstein, *Climate Change and Discounting the Future: A Guide for the Perplexed*, 27 YALE L. & POL'Y REV. 433 (2009).

WESTERN, BRUCE, PUNISHMENT AND INEQUALITY IN AMERICA (2006).

Western, Bruce, Jeffrey R. Kling & David F. Weiman, *The Labor Market Consequences of Incarceration*, 47 CRIME & DELINQUENCY 410 (2001).

Whitehead, John C. & Glenn C. Blomquist, *The Use of Contingent Valuation in Benefit-Cost Analysis, in* HANDBOOK ON CONTINGENT VALUATION 92 (Anna Alberini & James R. Kahn eds., 2006).

WIERZBICKA, ANNA, EMOTIONS ACROSS LANGUAGES AND CULTURES: DIVERSITY AND UNIVERSALS (1999).

Williams Sean, *Self-Altering Injury*, 96 CORNELL L. REV. 535 (2011)

Williams, Sean, *Statistical Children*, 30 YALE J. REG. (forthcoming 2013), *available at* http://papers.ssrn.com/sol3/papers.cfm?abstract_id=2176463.

WILSON, JAMES Q. & RICHARD J. HERRNSTEIN, CRIME AND HUMAN NATURE (1985).

Wilson, Timothy D. & Daniel T. Gilbert, *Affective Forecasting: Knowing What to Want*, 14 CURRENT DIRECTIONS IN PSYCHOL. SCI. 131 (2005).

Wilson, Timothy D. et al., *Focalism: A Source of Durability Bias in Affective Forecasting*, 78 J. PERSONALITY & SOC. PSYCHOL. 821 (2000).

Wolf, Susan, *Deconstructing Welfare: Reflections on Stephen Darwall's Welfare and Rational Care*, 18 UTILITAS 415 (2006).

Wolf, Susan, *Happiness and Meaning: Two Aspects of the Good Life*, 14 SOC. PHIL. & POL'Y 207 (2009).

Yang, Yang, *Social Inequalities in Happiness in the United States, 1972 to 2004: An Age-Period Cohort Analysis*, 73 AM. SOC. REV. 204 (2008).

Zadir, Eyal & Barak Medina, *Law, Morality, and Economics: Integrating Moral Constraints with Economic Analysis*, 96 CAL. L. REV. 323 (2008).

Zajonc, Robert B., *Feeling and Thinking: Preferences Need No Inferences*, 35 AM. PSYCHOL. 151 (1980).

Zamble, Edward, *Behavior and Adaptation in Long-Term Prison Inmates: Descriptive Longitudinal Results*, 19 CRIM. JUST. & BEHAV. 409 (1992).

ZAMBLE, EDWARD & FRANK J. PORPORINO, COPING, BEHAVIOR, AND ADAPTATION IN PRISON INMATES (1988).

Zamble, Edward & Frank Porporino, *Coping, Imprisonment, and Rehabilitation: Some Data and Their Implications*, 17 CRIM. JUST. & BEHAV. 53 (1990).

ZIMRING, FRANKLIN E. & GORDON HAWKINS, INCAPACITATION: PENAL CONFINEMENT AND THE RESTRAINT OF CRIME (1995).

CASES, STATUTES, OTHER

3 C.F.R. 215 (2012).

18 USC § 3553(a)

42 USC § 14071(e)(2)

720 ILCS 5/18-2

720 ILCS 5/9-1

720 ILCS 5/19-1

730 ILCS 5/5-4.5-20

730 ILCS 5/5-4.5-25

730 ILCS 5/5-4.5-35

Allen v. Wal-Mart Stores, Inc., 241 F.3d 1293 (10th Cir. 2001).

Am. Trucking Ass'n v. E.P.A., 175 F.3d 1027 (D.C. Cir. 1999).

BUREAU OF LABOR STATISTICS, CPI DETAILED REPORT: DATA FOR DECEMBER 2012 (2013), *available at* http://www.bls.gov/cpi/cpid1212.pdf

Day v. Ouachita Parish Sch. Bd., 823 So. 2d 1039 (La. Ct. App. 2002).

ENVTL. PROT. AGENCY, ARSENIC IN DRINKING WATER RULE: ECONOMIC ANALYSIS (2000).

ENVTL. PROT. AGENCY, VALUING MORTALITY RISK REDUCTIONS FOR ENVIRONMENTAL POLICY: A WHITE PAPER (2010).

EPA Identification and Listing of Hazardous Waste 40 C.F.R. pt. 261 (1998).

EPA National Emission Standards for Hazardous Air Pollutants for Source Category: Pulp and Paper Industry 40 C.F.R. pt. 63 (1998).

EPA The Pulp, Paper, and Paperboard Point Source Category 40 C.F.R. 430 (1998).

Exec. Order No. 12,291, 3 C.F.R. 127 (1982), *reprinted in* 5 U.S.C. § 601 note (1982).

Exec. Order No. 12,866, 3 C.F.R. 638 (1994), *reprinted as amended in* 5 U.S.C. § 601 note (2006).

G.A. Res. 65/309, U.N. Doc. A/RES/65/309 (July 19, 2011).

Medical Devices; Patient Examination and Surgeons' Gloves; Test Procedures and Acceptance Criteria, 68 Fed. Reg. 15,404 (proposed Mar. 31, 2003) (codified at 21 C.F.R. pt. 800).

Model Code of Prof'l Responsibility EC 7-7 (2001).

MPC § 1.02(2)

MPC § 1.02(2)(a)

MPC § 1.02(2)(c)

National Emission Standards for Hazardous Air Pollutants for Source Category: Pulp and Paper Production; Effluent Limitations Guidelines, Pretreatment Standards, and New Source Performance Standards: Pulp, Paper, and Paperboard Category, 63 Fed. Reg. 18,542 (1998).

Nat'l Wildlife Fed'n v. EPA, 286 F.3d 554 (D.C. Cir. 2002).

N.J. REV. STAT. § 2C:7-1 *et seq.* (West).

Occupational Exposure to Hexavalent Chromium, 71 Fed. Reg. 10,100 (Feb. 28, 2006) (codified at 29 C.F.R. pts. 1910, 1915, 1917, 1918 & 1926).

OFFICE OF INFO. & REGULATORY AFFAIRS, 2011 REPORT TO CONGRESS ON THE BENEFITS AND COSTS OF FEDERAL REGULATIONS AND UNFUNDED MANDATES ON STATE, LOCAL, AND TRIBAL ENTITIES (2011).

OFFICE OF MGMT. & BUDGET, EXEC. OFFICE OF THE PRESIDENT, CIRCULAR A-94 REVISED, GUIDELINES AND DISCOUNT RATES FOR BENEFIT-COST ANALYSIS OF FEDERAL PROGRAMS (1992), *available at* http://www.whitehouse.gov/omb/circulars_a094

Office of Mgmt. & Budget, Exec. Office of the President, Circular A-4 on
   Regulatory Analysis (2003), *available at* http://www.whitehouse.gov/omb/
   circulars_a004_a-4.

Second Chance Act of 2007, codified at 42 USC § 17501 *et seq.*

U.S. Census Bureau, Money Income in the United States (1998), *available at*
   http://www2.census.gov/prod2/popscan/p60-206.pdf.

U.S. Census Bureau, Statistical Abstract of the United States (2012).

U.S. Dep't of Labor, Bureau of Labor Statistics (2013), *Overview of BLS
   Statistics on Inflation and Prices, available at* http://www.bls.gov/bls/inflation
   .htm.

U.S. Envtl. Prot. Agency, EPA Contract No. 68-C3-0302, Economic Analysis
   for the National Emission Standards for Hazardous Air Pollutants for Source
   Category: Pulp and Paper Production; Effluent Limitations Guidelines, Pretreatment Standards, and New Source Performance Standards: Pulp, Paper,
   and Paperboard Category—Phase 1, (1997), *available at* http://water.epa.gov/
   scitech/wastetech/guide/pulppaper/upload/1997_11_13_guide_pulppaper_jd
   _pulp.pdf

Index

Ackerman, Frank, 79
adaptation, 119, 184; and change, 4–5, 10,
    15; happiness data, 105; imprisonment,
    98–99, 101–3, 225n14, 227n34, 232n62;
    negative stimuli, adaptive responses to,
    106; post-prison life, 241n35; punish-
    ment, 104, 108, 112, 116; settlement be-
    havior, 125–29, 131
Adler, Matthew, 138, 152, 162, 244–46n19,
    246n21, 247n22
affective forecasting, 68, 70, 72, 88, 184,
    213–14n31; cost-benefit analysis (CBA),
    67; errors of, 10, 22, 106, 192–93n78; fo-
    cusing illusion, 21–22; hedonic adap-
    tation, 20–21; immune neglect, 21–22;
    misremembering, 20–23
aggregate welfare, 53, 57; aggregating mo-
    ments, 254–55n32; cost-benefit analysis
    (CBA), 52, 217–18n73; and government,
    52; well-being analysis (WBA), 217–
    18n73; well-being units (WBUs), 52
Aristotle, 147, 150
Arneson, Richard, 146, 251n62

bankruptcy, 184
beeper studies, 260
behavorial economics, 10, 55, 57, 155
behavorial game theory, 122; ultimatum
    game, 123
Bentham, Jeremy, 104, 134, 157, 254n31
Brickman, Philip, 16
British Household Panel Survey, 17,
    208n120, 214n38

Cameron, David, 29
Challenger (space shuttle), 3
civil lawsuits, 6, 184; bargaining, 121–
    22; classic economic model, 122; con-
    tracts, and hedonic effects, 184; fair-
    ness, 122; happiness data, 130; hedonic
    adaptation, 119, 124, 127; monetary
    gain, 123; motivations for, 120, 123; risk
    averse, 124; risk seeking, 124. *See also*
    settlement
civil rights, 184
Clean Air Act, 203n71
clean-air laws, 27–28
Clean Water Act (1998), 37
clean-water regulation, 29, 31
Clemmer, Donald, 98
Clinton, Bill, 27
cognitive limitations, 4–5
contingent valuation studies, 60, 214–
    15n40; cost-benefit analysis (CBA),
    32, 50, 60, 68–73, 92; flaws of, 69–70,
    215n46; well-being analysis (WBA), 88.
    See also willingness to pay (WTP)
copyright law, 184
core affect: approach and avoidance, 155;
    arousal, 253n12, 253n13; happiness, 155;
    as pervasive, 155; valence, 253nn12–13
cost-benefit analysis (CBA), 5, 7, 29,
    37, 38–39, 45–49, 53–55, 183, 194n3,
    196n16, 197n25, 198n34, 209n131, 209–
    10n1, 217n69, 219n102, 247n22; affec-
    tive forecasting, reliance on, 67; aggre-
    gate welfare, 52, 217–18n73; contingent

cost-benefit analysis (CBA) (*continued*)
valuation studies, 32, 50, 60, 68–73,
92; costs, monetizing of, 34–35, 60;
criticism of, 27–28, 79; death, equating types of, 78–79, 81–82; defenders
of, 33, 74; discounting in, 88–91; Environmental Protection Agency (EPA),
42–44; hedonic metrics, 197n24; as
Kaldor-Hicks efficient, 74–76, 197n32;
longitudinal studies, 64; methodology
of, 30–31; methodology, limitations
of, 28; nonmonetary goods, pricing of,
73; problems of, 59; prominence of, 27;
quality-adjusted life years (QALYs),
85–86; revealed preferences of, 31–32,
35, 59 60, 63 68, 71, 73; revealed preferences of, errors in, 61–62; and risk,
79–83; scope neglect, 189n33; stated
preferences, 31, 59–60; value of a statistical life (VSL), 82–83, 87; value of future money, discounting of, 59; value of
life, 78–79; value of life, limitations in,
59; wage premium studies, 61–63, 92;
wealth effects, 64, 72; welfare, 84–85,
197n31, 199n43; welfare-diminishing
results, 77; well-being, gauging of, 36;
well-being analysis (WBA), 32–33, 35–
36, 51, 60, 63, 68, 73, 76, 87–88, 92; well-
being analysis (WBA), as complement
to, 77–78
creativity, innovation and, 185
criminal justice system, 93, 96–98, 103,
183; sentencing, 109, 226n16. *See also*
punishment
Crisp, Roger, 155
cycling equilibrium, 241n35

Darwall, Stephen, 244–46n19
day reconstruction method (DRM), 11, 87;
of unemployment, 19
deterrence: criminal well-being, 105; hedonic adaptation, 105; and pain, 105;
punishment, 95–96, 104–8, 110–11
diary studies, 260n2
Dickens, Charles, 120
Diener, Ed, 98
discounting: in cost-benefit analysis
(CBA), 88–91; estimates of harm, effect on, 89; time value of money, 90; in
well-being analysis (WBA), 59, 88, 91

Easterlin, Richard, 16, 97; Easterlin paradox, 224n4
Eastern District of Virginia, 128
eBay, 50
ecological momentary assessment, 87
economics, 141
emotions: and negativity, 25; and positivity, 25
Environmental Protection Agency (EPA),
52, 76–77, 90, 203n68; cancer cases, 42,
44; compliance costs, 40–41, 44; cost-
benefit analysis (CBA), 42–44; fishing
advisories, 40–41; hedonic wage studies by, 212n19; Native Americans, 202–
3n65; Option A, 37–40, 43, 203n71; Option B, 37, 39; Option TCF, 37, 39–40;
regulatory options of, 37; sludge re-
moval, 40–41; unemployment, 42–43;
well-being analysis (WBA), 36–44;
well-being units (WBUs), 40–42
ethics, 169
eudaimonistic theories, 147–51, 176,
251n63; hedonic theory of well-being,
as consistent with, 148; human capabilities, perfecting of, 148; morality, 148; as
nature-fulfillment, 147–48
experience machine, 172–75, 246n21,
258n13
experience sampling method (ESM) studies, 11–12, 15
expressive theories, 110, 113–14
Exxon Valdez oil spill, 3, 214–15n40

Feldman, Fred, 154–55, 161–62, 243n7,
255–56n43
focusing illusion, 192n76
Foot, Philippa, 148
Freud, Sigmund, 179–80

Germany, 51; German Socioeconomic
Panel Study in, 208n120
Gert, Bernard, 143
Gilbert, Daniel, 19, 22, 32, 184
global warming, 89
government: aggregate welfare, 52; interpersonal distribution, 53; intrapersonal distribution, 53; per capita welfare, 52–53
Great Britain, 51; British Household Panel
Survey in, 17, 208n120, 214n38

Griffin, James, 146, 244n12
Guthrie, Chris, 123

Hahn, Robert, 79–80
Hampton, Jean, 235–26n92
Hand, Learned, 93
happiness, 46, 133, 252n2, 260n1; aggre-
    gation, 181–82; changes, effects on,
    10; core affect, 155; experience sam-
    pling methods, 11–12; feeling good,
    154, 181–82, 252n70, 252n1; flow, sense
    of, 159–60; good-bad dimension, 155–
    56; good health, 141–43, 152, 154; im-
    prisonment, 107; intuitions, 154,
    249n38; legal analysis, 23–26; life cir-
    cumstances, 237n1; life satisfaction,
    12–13, 16–17, 19, 22, 42, 51, 255n39; lov-
    ing relationships, 142, 152; "meaning-
    ful life," 152, 252n70; as moment-by-
    moment, 6, 12–14, 19, 51, 156–58, 184,
    205n90, 255n39, 260n2; money, 4, 142,
    152, 154; policymaking, and welfare
    effects, 46; predicting of, as difficult,
    4–5; preferences, 166; public policy, 3,
    133, 179, 259n26; punishment, 95–96,
    104, 110; quality of life (QoL), 24; re-
    gression analyses, 11; self-alteration,
    180; self-reporting, 10, 32; settlement,
    130; U-index, 207n105; unemploy-
    ment, 205n90; virtue, 148, 150; wel-
    fare, 242–43n1; well-being, 24, 29, 52,
    134–35, 150, 152–55, 176. See also he-
    donic adaptation; hedonic psychology;
    well-being
happiness data, 3–6, 10; adaptation, 105;
    civil lawsuits, 130; discount rates, 109;
    happiness surveys, 206n103, 247n22;
    hedonic experiences, as poorly re-
    membered, 12–13; income, and well-
    being, 15–16; income, changes in, 97–
    98; moment-by-moment basis, 14;
    on punishment, 110–11, 113–14, 117;
    randomness, 47; reliability of, 13;
    self-reporting, 14, 45; set points, 15;
    smartphone studies, 260n2; on un-
    employment, 42–43; valence, 20–21;
    well-being data, 13–15, 46, 49–51
happiness studies, 4–5, 16–17, 23, 28, 82,
    92, 148; criticism of, 46; intellectual
    property law, 184; punishment, 96, 104;

trustworthiness of, 45–46; well-being
    analysis (WBA), 76
happiness theory, 148–50, 155, 161, 243n7;
    counterintuitive results, 168, 176; crit-
    ics of, 170–71; experience machine,
    246n21, 258n13; feeling good, 164–66,
    244n12, 244–46n19; good-bad affec-
    tive core, 165; happiness treadmill, 15;
    "higher-order" experiences, 165; in-
    tuitions, 166–67, 169, 175–76; "lower-
    order" experiences, 165; objections to,
    164–75, 246n21; renaissance of, 154; as
    subjective, 166; well-being, 152, 175. See
    also welfare; well-being
Harsanyi, John, 139
Haybron, Daniel, 133, 146, 150, 252n1,
    260n39
hedonic adaptation, 16, 191n60, 200n54,
    225n9; affective forecasting, 20–21;
    chronic stimuli, 18; civil lawsuits, 119,
    124, 127; deterrence, 105; disabili-
    ties, 16–17, 19–20; empirical testing,
    128; family relations, 18; happiness set
    points, and genetic factors, 19; lottery
    winners, 17; negative effects, and atten-
    tion, 19–20; paraplegia/quadriplegia,
    17; progressive deterioration, 18; psy-
    chological and physiological processes
    of, 19; settlement, 124–30; as "unadapt-
    able," 18; unemployment, 18, 42. See
    also happiness; hedonic psychology
hedonic data. See happiness data
hedonic psychology, 9, 28–29, 75, 118,
    183–85; affective forecasting errors, 10;
    affective forecasting errors, and mis-
    remembering, 20–23; data of, as trust-
    worthy, 13; governmental policy, 28;
    happiness, predicting of, 10, 16, 32, 54;
    hedonic adaptation, 15–20, 118–19; he-
    donic positivity, 180; hedonism, and
    well-being, 258n13; human happiness,
    measuring of, 5; imprisonment, 6; key
    findings of, 15–23; law, 23–24, 26, 93;
    monetary fines, 6; negativity or posi-
    tivity, 25; personal injury lawsuits, 120;
    and policymaking, 7; punishment, 103;
    well-being analysis (WBA), 57. See also
    happiness; hedonic adaptation
hedonic studies. See happiness studies
hedonic theory. See happiness theory

Heinzerling, Lisa, 79
Hursthouse, Rosalind, 148

imprisonment: adaptation to, 98–99,
101–3, 225n14, 232n62; after-effects of,
106–10; employment, 100–101; and happiness, 107; health problems, 100–101;
hedonic effects of, 101; hedonic psychology, 6; hedonic response to, 99;
job skills, erosion of, 100; and marriage, 227n29; post-prison harm, coping mechanisms of, as maladaptive,
115–16; post-prison life, 107, 227n34; as
primary stressor, 227n34; prisoners, re-
integration into society, 116; prisonization, 98; rehabilitation, 230–31n54;
sentencing, 226n16; social stigma,
100. See also criminal justice system;
punishment
income: happiness, lack of correlation between, 97; hedonic data, 97–98; life satisfaction, 41, 97; reasons for, 97; subjective well-being (SWB), 16; well-being,
15–16
intellectual property laws, 184–85

Jarndyce and Jarndyce, 120
justice, 137
juvenile offenders, 233n71

Kahan, Dan, 113
Kahneman, Daniel, 22, 25, 124, 164,
207n105, 237n1; colonoscopy study
of, 200–201n56; day reconstruction
method (DRM) technique of, 11; decision utility, 87; "experienced utility,"
11; objective happiness, 156–57
Kaldor-Hicks efficiency, 207n110; cost-
benefit analysis (CBA), 74–76,
197n32; well-being analysis (WBA),
48, 74–75
Keller, Simon, 143–45
Klein, Benjamin, 237–38n7
Kolber, Adam, 155, 236n99
Korobkin, Russell, 123
Kraut, Richard, 148
Krueger, Alan, 207n105

Landes, William, 121
law, 4, 27, 54, 141, 185; behavioral approach

to, 5; decision utility, 11; hedonic psychology, 23–24, 26, 93; policy work, 4;
positive and negative consequences
of, 28; psychology, 184; quality of life
(QoL), 3, 7, 24–25; well-being analysis
(WBA), 183
Layard, Richard, 155, 172
life satisfaction data: happiness, 12–13,
16–17, 19, 22, 42, 51, 255n39; and income, 41, 97; positive and negative affect, 13; subjective well-being (SWB),
12; surveys of, 12–13, 87–88, 165; unemployment, 19, 229n46. See also happiness data
linguistics, 155–56
list theories of welfare, 141–42, 144,
146–47, 150; algorithm, 143; as opaque,
145
Livermore, Michael, 84
Los Angeles (California), 72
lottery winners, 16–17
Lucas, Richard E., 18, 229n46

Mason, Elinor, 155
Massoglia, Michael, 100
Medicare, 53
Mendola, Joseph, 155, 172
morality: self-interest, 151; well-being, 173,
177–78
More, Thomas, 226n24

National Longitudinal Survey of Youth,
100
neuroscience, 155, 164, 193n91
neuroticism, positive affect and, 14
Nozick, Robert, 172
Nudge (Thaler and Sunstein), 4
Nussbaum, Martha, 143, 165

Obama, Barack, 27, 89
objective theories of well-being, 134, 166;
eudaemonist theories, 141, 147–51; list
theories, 141–47; nature-fulfillment
theories, 171–72
Occupational Safety and Health Administration (OSHA), 34, 90
Office of Management and Budget (OMB),
90
Oswald, Andrew, 17–18, 242n37
Overvold, Mark, 139

Pareto principle, 52
Parfit, Derek, 139
patent law, 184
per capita welfare, 52–53
perfectionist welfare theories, 250n51,
    251n62
philosophy, 141, 164
policy analysis, 29–30, 36; binary choices,
    56; moment-by-moment data, 51;
    moment-by-moment happiness, 184;
    well-being data, 50
positive affect, extraversion, 14
positivity, 164
Posner, Eric, 162
Posner, Richard, 121
Powdthavee, Nattavudh, 17–18, 242n37
preference-satisfaction theories of well-
    being, 134, 137–41, 151, 244n12, 246n21,
    247–48n23
Priceless (Ackerman and Heinzerling),
    56–57
Priest, George, 237–38n7
Princeton Affect and Time Survey
    (PATS), 12
prison. *See* imprisonment
prospect theory, 239n20
psychology, 155, 164
punishment: adaptation, 108, 112, 116; bal-
    ancing, 105; deterrence, 95–96, 104–8,
    110–11; economic loss, adaptation to,
    97–98; happiness, 104, 110; happiness
    data, 110–11, 113–14, 117; happiness re-
    duction, 95–96, 104; happiness stud-
    ies, 96, 104; hedonic consequences of,
    97–102; hedonic data on, 110–11, 117;
    hedonic psychology, implications of
    on, 103; imprisonment, adaptation to,
    98–99; limiting retributivism, 112–13;
    mixed categories, 6; mixed theories,
    112–13; monetary fines, 116; as moral
    condemnation, 113; post-prison ef-
    fects, 114–15; prison, long-term effects,
    on well-being, 100–102; rehabilitation,
    230–31n54; retribution, 6, 95–96, 110–
    11; retribution, expressive theories of,
    113–14; retributive justice, 234n82; re-
    tributivism, 112, 114, 116–17; sentence
    lengths, 95, 108–10, 116; and simple re-
    tributivism, 111–12; theories of, 6; un-
    adaptable conditions, 116–17; unhap-

piness, 96; utilitarian calculus, 106–8,
    231n58, 232n63; utilitarianism, 6, 104,
    112, 155, 157, 162, 184, 254n31, 258n13;
    utilitarian punishment theory, 103–8,
    112–13, 116–17. *See also* criminal jus-
    tice system; imprisonment; utilitarian-
    ism; utilitarian punishment theory

quality-adjusted life years (QALYs), 34, 82,
    88; cost-benefit analysis (CBA), 85–86;
    cost-effectiveness analysis (CEA), 85;
    as problematic, 86; standard gamble
    time studies, 86–87; survey techniques
    of, 86; trade-off studies, 86–87; well-
    benefit analysis (WBA), 87–88; as well-
    being units (WBUs), 87; WTP-per-
    QALY figure, calculation of, 86
quality of life (QoL), 30, 135–36, 154,
    260n1; disabilities, 22; happiness, 24;
    law, 3, 7, 24–25. *See also* happiness; wel-
    fare; well-being

Rachlinski, Jeffrey, 124, 239n22
Rawls, John, 137, 139, 143, 145, 248–49n29,
    249n30
Raz, Joseph, 146
Reagan, Ronald, 27
reflective equilibrium, 150
regression analysis, 71
retribution, 110; expressive theories,
    113–14; limiting retributivism, 112–13;
    penal policy, 112; retributive justice,
    234n82; retributivism, 114, 116–17; sim-
    ple retributivism, 111–12
revealed preferences: cost-benefit analy-
    sis (CBA), 31–32, 35, 59–68, 71, 73;
    revealed-preferences studies, 60–61,
    64, 67–69, 71, 81, 83, 87–88; and wealth,
    64, 88; well-being analysis (WBA), 61,
    67–69, 88; willingness to pay (WTP),
    60, 69
Revesz, Richard, 84
Russell, James, 164

Sarkozy, Nicolas, 29
Scanlon, T. M., 143, 146
Schkade, David A., 22
Second Chance Act, 233n70
Sen, Amartya, 134
September 11 attacks, 79–80

settlement: adaptation, 125–29; attorney-centered litigation model, 128; bargaining, 122; contingent fee basis, 128; fair compensation, 120, 124–25; happiness, 130; hard bargaining, 130; hard bargaining, and delays, 128–29; hedonic adaptation, 124, 127–30; negotiations, 121; principal objections, 128–30; testable predictions, 126–28; tort victims, 130. *See also* civil lawsuits

Simons, Kenneth, 236n99
Singer, Peter, 157, 254n31
social science, 3; social science research, 122
Social Security, 53
stated preferences: choice experiments, 198n35; cost-benefit analysis (CBA), 31, 59–60
subjective well-being (SWB), 15, 20; as counterintuitive, 9–10; family relationships, 18; and income, 16; life satisfaction survey, 12; longitudinal studies of, 17; measuring of, 12; studying of, 10–11; well-benefit analysis (WBA), 33. *See also* happiness; welfare
Sumner, Wayne, 146–47, 150–51, 154–55, 166, 244n12
Sunstein, Cass, 4, 67, 74, 85

Tännsjö, Torbjörn, 155
Thaler, Richard, 4
tort law, 93, 183, 241n31; damages, 240n24
Tversky, Amos, 124

unemployment: day reconstruction method (DRM), 19; happiness, 205n90; happiness data, 42–43; hedonic adaptation, 18, 42; hedonic data on, 42–43; hedonic effects of, 19; life satisfaction data on, 19, 229n46; well-being, 19, 229n46; well-benefit analysis (WBA), 35
United Nations General Assembly, 28–29
United States, 42, 51, 54, 97, 175, 194n3; copyright and patent law in, 184; cost-effectiveness analysis (CEA) in, 194n3; General Social Survey in, 208n120; greenhouse gas emissions, 89–90; imprisonment in, 98; income and subjective well-being (SWB), correlation of in, 16; penal policy in, 112

U.S. General Social Survey, life satisfaction surveys, 12
utilitarianism, 104, 155, 157, 162, 184, 254n31, 258n13; penal policy, influence on, 112
utilitarian punishment theory, 103, 112–13, 116–17; deterrence, 104–5, 107–8; post-prison harm, 107; utilitarian calculus, 106–8, 231n58, 232n63

validity, 13, 188n19
value of a statistical life (VSL), 75, 88, 219n107; cost-benefit analysis (CBA), 82–83, 87; limitations of, 82–83
value of a statistical life year (VSLY), 88, 219n107; cost-benefit analysis (CBA), 82–83, 87; criticism of, 84; quality of years, 85; senior death discount, 84; value of a statistical life (VSL), improvement over, 85; well-being analysis (WBA), 87
Velleman, J. David, 146, 254–55n32
virtue: happiness, 148; welfare, 150; well-being, 150–51
von Hirsch, Andrew, 235–26n92

Washington State, 49
weak welfarism, 162
Weisbach, David, 216n60
welfare, 25, 56, 157, 166, 194n1, 207n108, 247n22; consumption, 74; cost-benefit analysis (CBA), 84–85, 197n31, 199n43; happiness, 242–43n1; moral considerations, 84–85, 202n59; positive-negative valence, 26; preference satisfaction of, 30; relative value, 46; virtue, 150; wealth, as weak proxy for, 52; well-being analysis (WBA), 58, 74, 76, 84–85, 197n31, 205n90. *See also* happiness; quality of life (QoL); well-being
welfare perfectionism, 250n56
well-being, 20, 133, 151, 160, 184–85; aggregate well-being, and wealth, redistributing of, 76; alternative views of, 6; children, 180–81; cost-benefit analysis (CBA), 36; definitions of, 146; disabled v. nondisabled, 17–18; drugs, 176–80; ex-inmates, effects on, 101–2; family relationships, 18; feeling good, 176, 181, 244n12; fitness, 144; "for you"

requirement of, 145–47; good health, 141–42; happiness, 24, 29, 52, 134–35, 150, 153–55, 176; happiness theory, 152, 175; hedonic theory, 152, 175; hedonism, 258n13; idealization, 140; imprisonment, long-term effects on, 100–103; income, 15–16; intuitions, 136, 140, 145, 150; loving relationships, 142; measuring of, 13, 80; money, as weak proxy for, 16; morality, 173, 177–78; as net affect, 135, 152, 163–64; objections to, 6; objective measures of, 14; objective theories of, 145–48; objective value of, 146–47; policymakers, 50; as positive attitudes, 161; preferences, 138–40; preference satisfaction, 134; and prison, 100–102; proposed laws, effect on, 7; reason, 144; self-sacrifice, 138–39; self-sympathy, 244–46n19; "sense of meaning," 180–81; stress, 230n51; subjective reports of, 14; success, 148; "Success Theory," 139; suffering, 138; superhuman preference theory, 140–41; theories of, 134–40; unemployment, effect on, 19, 229n46; virtue, 149–51; well-being analysis (WBA), 36. *See also* happiness

well-being analysis (WBA), 5, 7, 28–29, 55–56, 59, 83, 160, 183, 197n25, 209n131, 216n56, 216n57, 260n1; accuracy of, 35, 44; aggregated happiness, 176–77; aggregate welfare, 217–18n73; aggregating interpersonal welfare states, 47–48; as alternative, 92; argument for, 75; basic framework of, 33–36; contingent-valuation, 88; cost-benefit analysis (CBA), advantage of over, 32–33, 63–68, 73, 76, 87–88, 92; cost-benefit analysis (CBA), differences between, 35–36, 51, 60; costs, hedonizing of, 60; criticism of, 46–51, 74–75; current well-being, concern with, 67–68, 70; death, different types of, 81–82; demand effects, 88; discounting in, 88, 91; distributional effects, 74; Environmental Protection Agency (EPA), 36–44; framing effects, 88; global concerns about, 53; governmental policy, 51; hedonic compensations, 48; hedonic psychology, as emerging from, 57; hedonic studies, use of, 76; Kaldor-Hicks efficiency, 48, 74–75; and law, 183; longitudinal studies, 63; mapping of, 34; as moment-by-moment net affect, 156–58; moral considerations, 57; national wealth; 16; net welfare, 44; Pareto principle, 52; positive feelings, 162; project-based approach, 161; quality-adjusted life years (QALYs), 87–88; regression analysis, 71; regulation, effects of, 80–81; regulation, "hedonizing" of, 33; relative value of, 51; reliability of, 13; revealed preferences, 61, 67–69, 88; risk, 80; self-reports, as proxies, 73; strengths of, 70; as subjective, 160; subjective well-being (SWB), 33; unemployment, quantifying of, 35; value of a statistical life year (VSLY), 87; value of life, 87; wealth, 77; wealth effects, 65–66, 72, 88; welfare, 58, 84–85, 197n31, 205n90; well-being, gauging of, 36; welfare, measuring of, 74, 76; well-being units (WBUs), 34; willingness-to-pay (WTP) measures, 73

well-being data. *See* happiness data

well-being units (WBUs), 87, 91; aggregate welfare, 52; Environmental Protection Agency (EPA), 40–42; as quality-adjusted life years (QALYs), 87; well-being analysis (WBA), 34

Western, Bruce, 101

Williams, Bernard, 150–51

willingness to pay (WTP): cost-benefit analysis (CBA), 60, 69–70, 73; cost-effectiveness analysis (CEA), 27, 85, 194n3; revealed preferences, 60, 69; scope neglect, 84; well-being analysis (WBA), 73. *See also* contingent valuation studies

Wilson, Timothy, 21–22

Wolf, Susan, 152, 252n70

Zagat, 50